Yuto Tsukuda

This is a picture of the *Food Wars!* pin that was made for a *Weekly Shonen Jump* special promotion. Taking a second look at Soma's super-deformed expression... well, it's a pretty darn good face. (*laughs*) No matter which way you look at it, it really screams "Soma Yukihira!"

Shun Saeki

Recently, I've been losing the battle of dominance over my work chair. Every time this little guy claims it, he flops over and stares at me with that smug little face. It's so utterly adorable I can't help but post pictures for all to see.

About the authors

Yuto Tsukuda won the 34th Jump Juniketsu Newcomers' Manga Award for his one-shot story *Kiba ni Naru*. He made his *Weekly Shonen Jump* debut in 2010 with the series *Shonen Shikku*. His follow-up series, *Food Wars!: Shokugeki no Soma*, is his first English-language release.

Shun Saeki made his *Jump NEXT!* debut in 2011 with the one-shot story *Kimi to Watashi no Renai Soudan*. *Food Wars!: Shokugeki no Soma* is his first *Shonen Jump* series.

Food Wars!
SHOKUGEKI NO SOMA

Volume 13
Shonen Jump Advanced Manga Edition
Story by Yuto Tsukuda, Art by Shun Saeki
Contributor Yuki Morisaki

Translation: Adrienne Beck
Touch-Up Art & Lettering: Mara Coman
Design: Izumi Evers
Editor: Jennifer LeBlanc

First published in Japan in 2012 by SHUEISHA Inc., Tokyo.
English translation rights arranged by SHUEISHA Inc.

Printed in the U.S.A.

Published by VIZ Media, LLC
P.O. Box 77010
San Francisco, CA 94107

10 9 8 7 6 5 4 3 2 1
First printing, August 2016

www.viz.com

THE WORLD'S MOST CUTTING-EDGE MANGA
SHONEN JUMP ADVANCED
www.shonenjump.com

RATED T+ FOR OLDER TEEN

PARENTAL ADVISORY
FOOD WARS! is rated T+ for Older Teen and is recommended for ages 16 and up. This volume contains sexual situations/humor.

ratings.viz.com

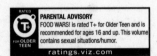

Food Wars!
Shokugeki no Soma

*STAGIAIRE

**

ORIGINAL CREATOR:
YUTO TSUKUDA
ARTIST:
SHUN SAEKI
CONTRIBUTOR:
YUKI MORISAKI

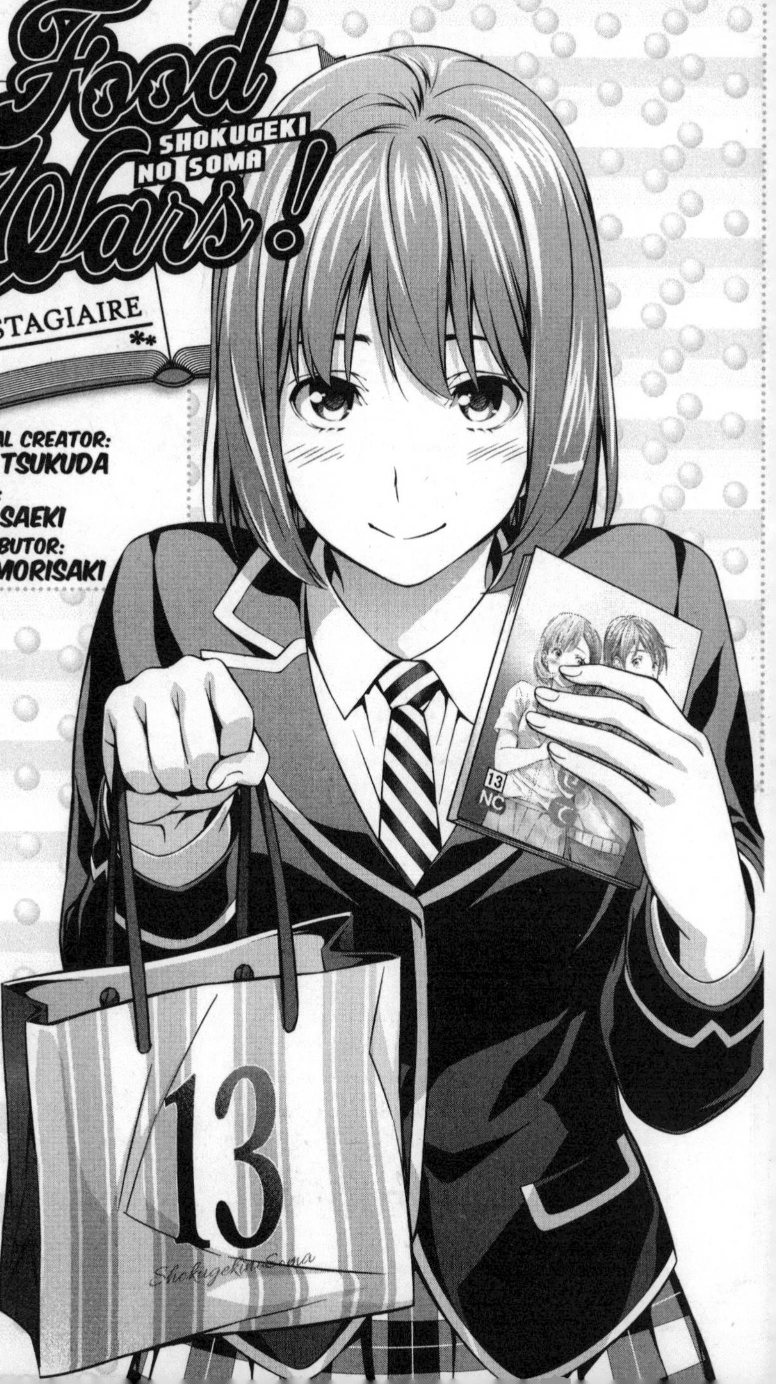

13
13
NC

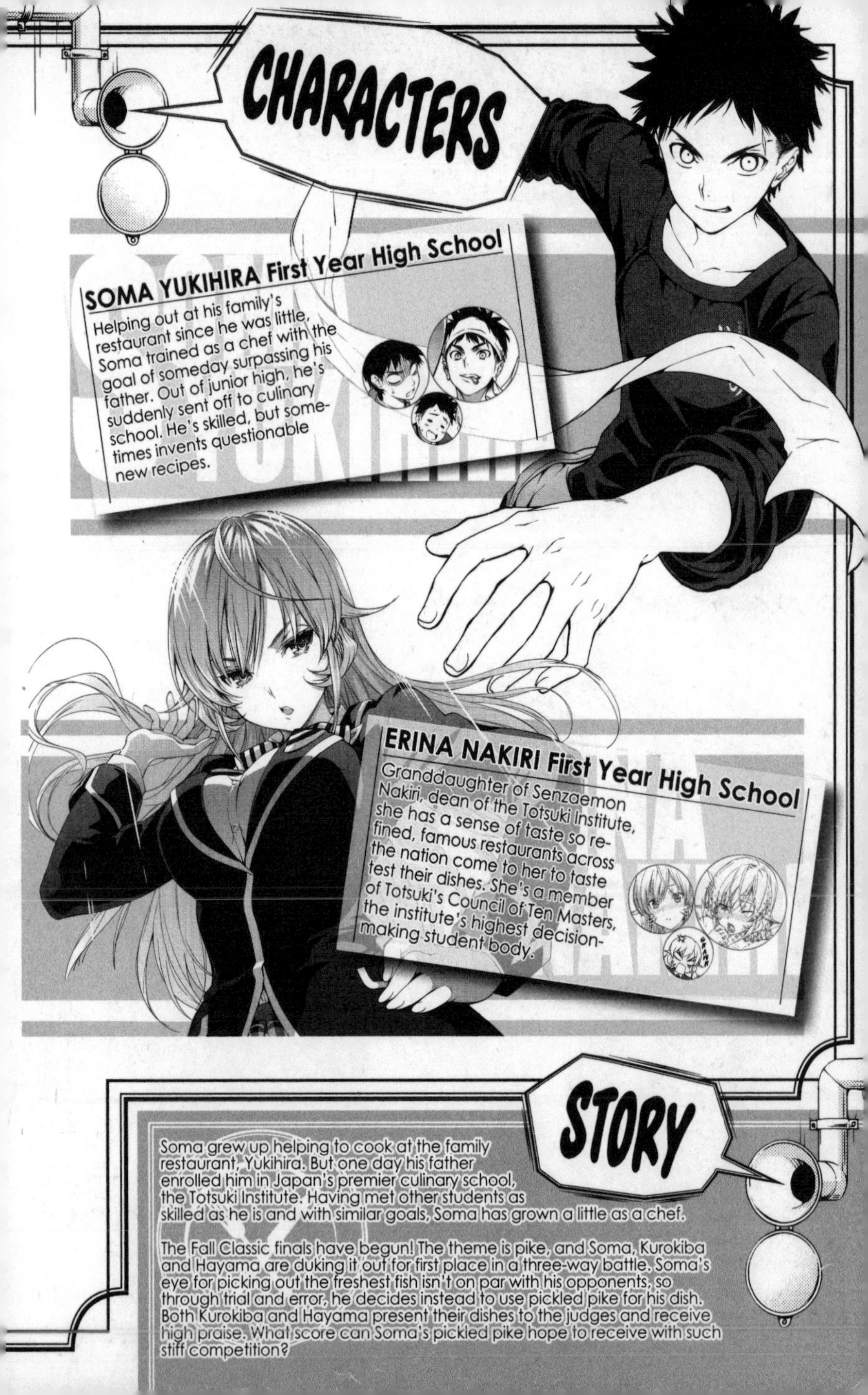

CHARACTERS

SOMA YUKIHIRA First Year High School

Helping out at his family's restaurant since he was little, Soma trained as a chef with the goal of someday surpassing his father. Out of junior high, he's suddenly sent off to culinary school. He's skilled, but sometimes invents questionable new recipes.

ERINA NAKIRI First Year High School

Granddaughter of Senzaemon Nakiri, dean of the Totsuki Institute, she has a sense of taste so refined, famous restaurants across the nation come to her to taste test their dishes. She's a member of Totsuki's Council of Ten Masters, the institute's highest decision-making student body.

STORY

Soma grew up helping to cook at the family restaurant, Yukihira. But one day his father enrolled him in Japan's premier culinary school, the Totsuki Institute. Having met other students as skilled as he is and with similar goals, Soma has grown a little as a chef.

The Fall Classic finals have begun! The theme is pike, and Soma, Kurokiba and Hayama are duking it out for first place in a three-way battle. Soma's eye for picking out the freshest fish isn't on par with his opponents, so through trial and error, he decides instead to use pickled pike for his dish. Both Kurokiba and Hayama present their dishes to the judges and receive high praise. What score can Soma's pickled pike hope to receive with such stiff competition?

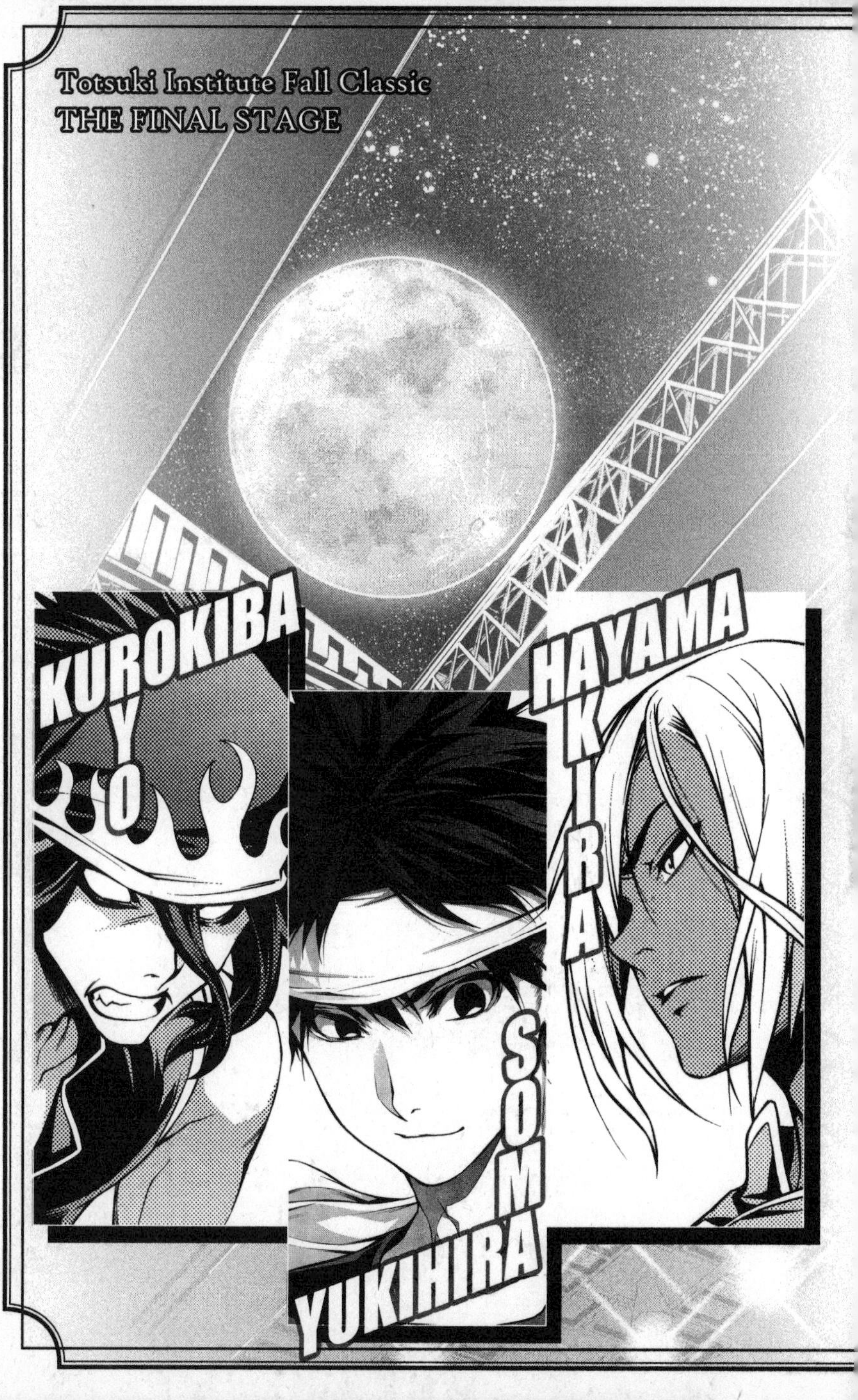
Totsuki Institute Fall Classic
THE FINAL STAGE
HAYAMA AKIRA
SOMA YUKIHIRA
KUROKIBA RYO

Food Wars! Shokugeki no Soma 13

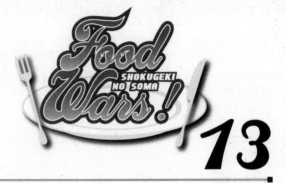

Table of Contents

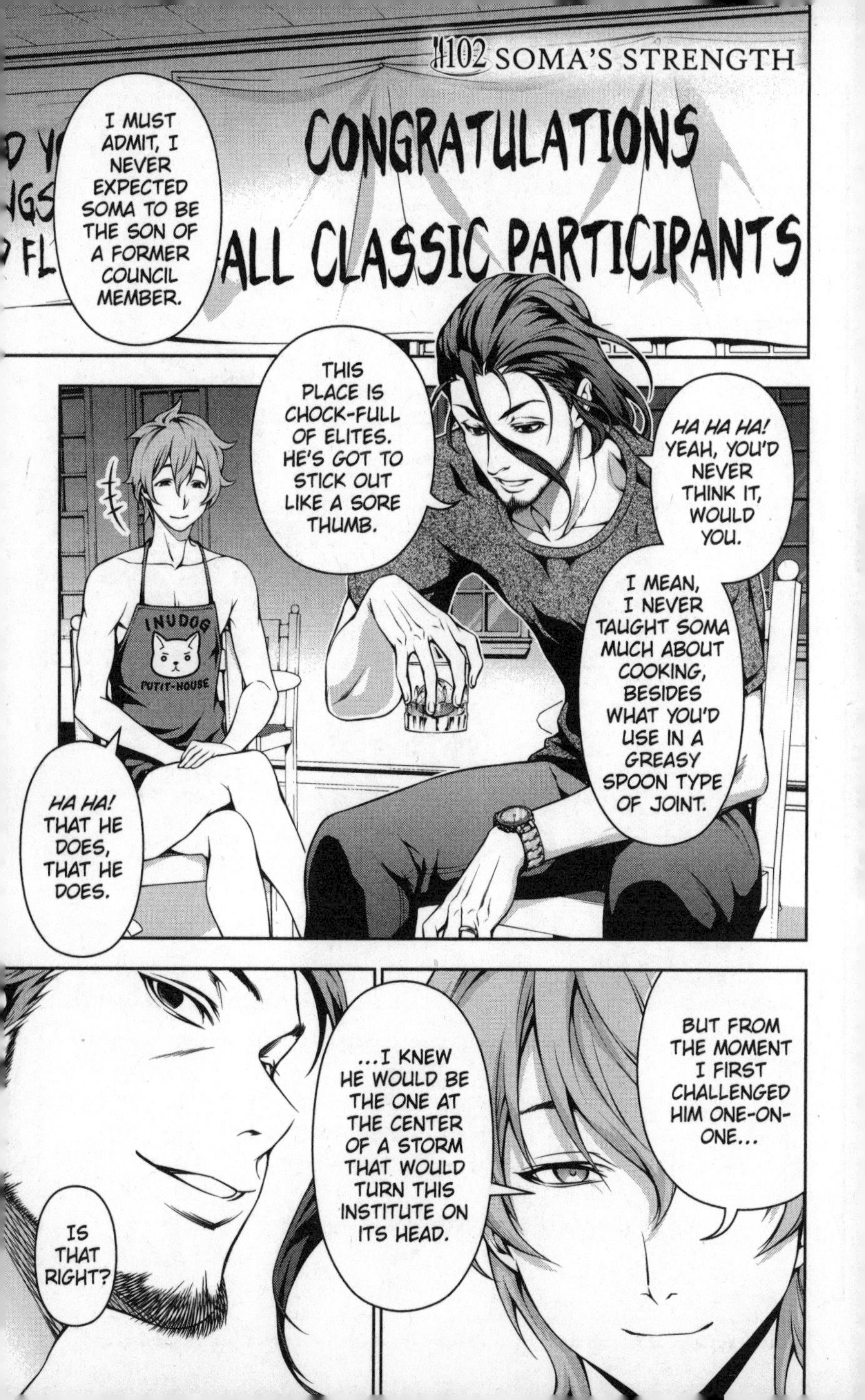
#102 SOMA'S STRENGTH
CONGRATULATIONS ALL CLASSIC PARTICIPANTS
I MUST ADMIT, I NEVER EXPECTED SOMA TO BE THE SON OF A FORMER COUNCIL MEMBER.
HA HA HA! YEAH, YOU'D NEVER THINK IT, WOULD YOU.
I MEAN, I NEVER TAUGHT SOMA MUCH ABOUT COOKING, BESIDES WHAT YOU'D USE IN A GREASY SPOON TYPE OF JOINT.
THIS PLACE IS CHOCK-FULL OF ELITES. HE'S GOT TO STICK OUT LIKE A SORE THUMB.
HA HA! THAT HE DOES, THAT HE DOES.
INUDOG
PUTIT-HOUSE
BUT FROM THE MOMENT I FIRST CHALLENGED HIM ONE-ON-ONE...
...I KNEW HE WOULD BE THE ONE AT THE CENTER OF A STORM THAT WOULD TURN THIS INSTITUTE ON ITS HEAD.
IS THAT RIGHT?

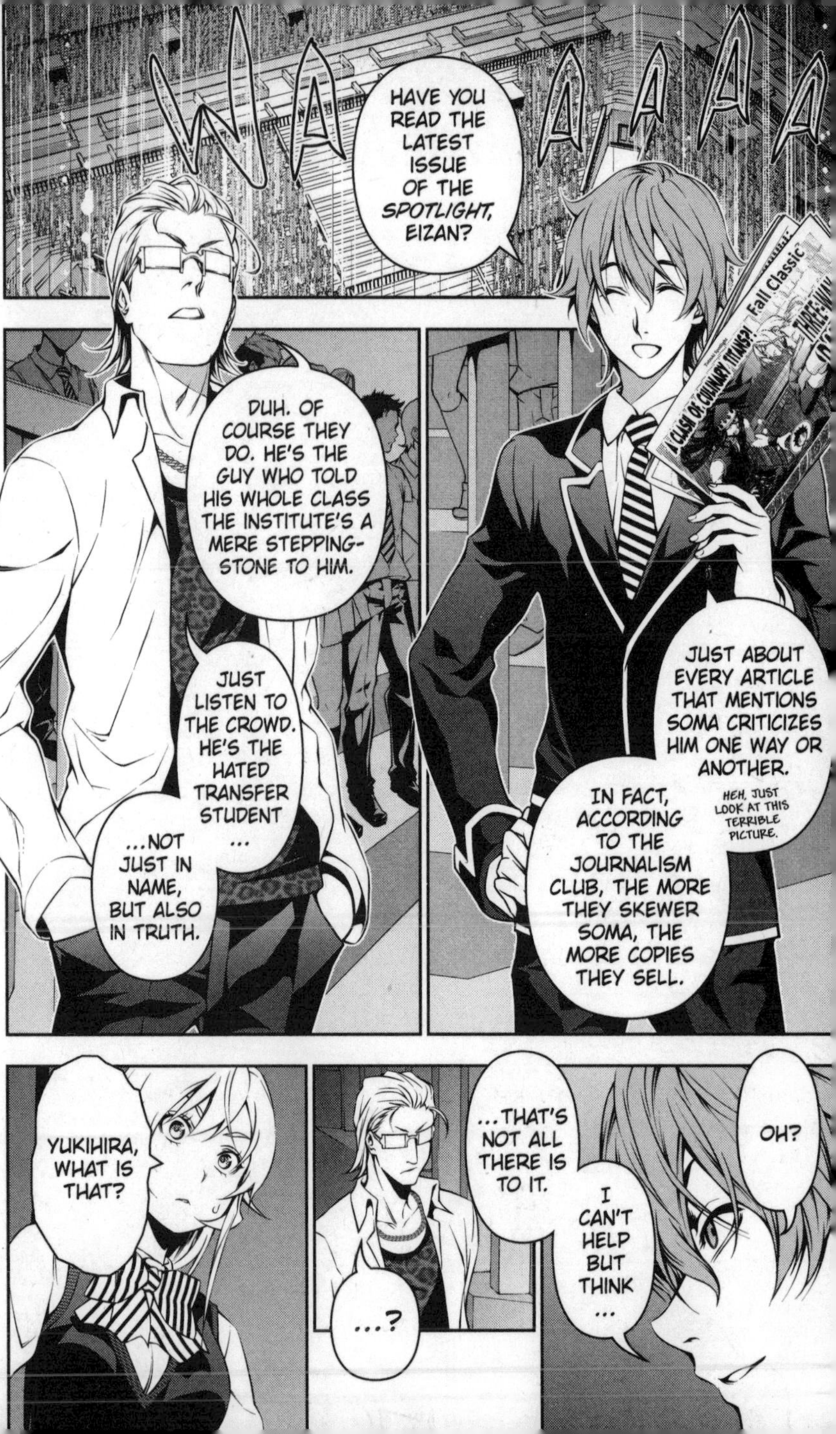
WAAAAA
HAVE YOU READ THE LATEST ISSUE OF THE SPOTLIGHT, EIZAN?
Fall Classic
A CLASH OF CULINARY TITANS?!
JUST ABOUT EVERY ARTICLE THAT MENTIONS SOMA CRITICIZES HIM ONE WAY OR ANOTHER.
HEH, JUST LOOK AT THIS TERRIBLE PICTURE.
IN FACT, ACCORDING TO THE JOURNALISM CLUB, THE MORE THEY SKEWER SOMA, THE MORE COPIES THEY SELL.
DUH. OF COURSE THEY DO. HE'S THE GUY WHO TOLD HIS WHOLE CLASS THE INSTITUTE'S A MERE STEPPING-STONE TO HIM.
JUST LISTEN TO THE CROWD. HE'S THE HATED TRANSFER STUDENT...
...NOT JUST IN NAME, BUT ALSO IN TRUTH.
OH?
...THAT'S NOT ALL THERE IS TO IT.
I CAN'T HELP BUT THINK...
...?
YUKIHIRA, WHAT IS THAT?

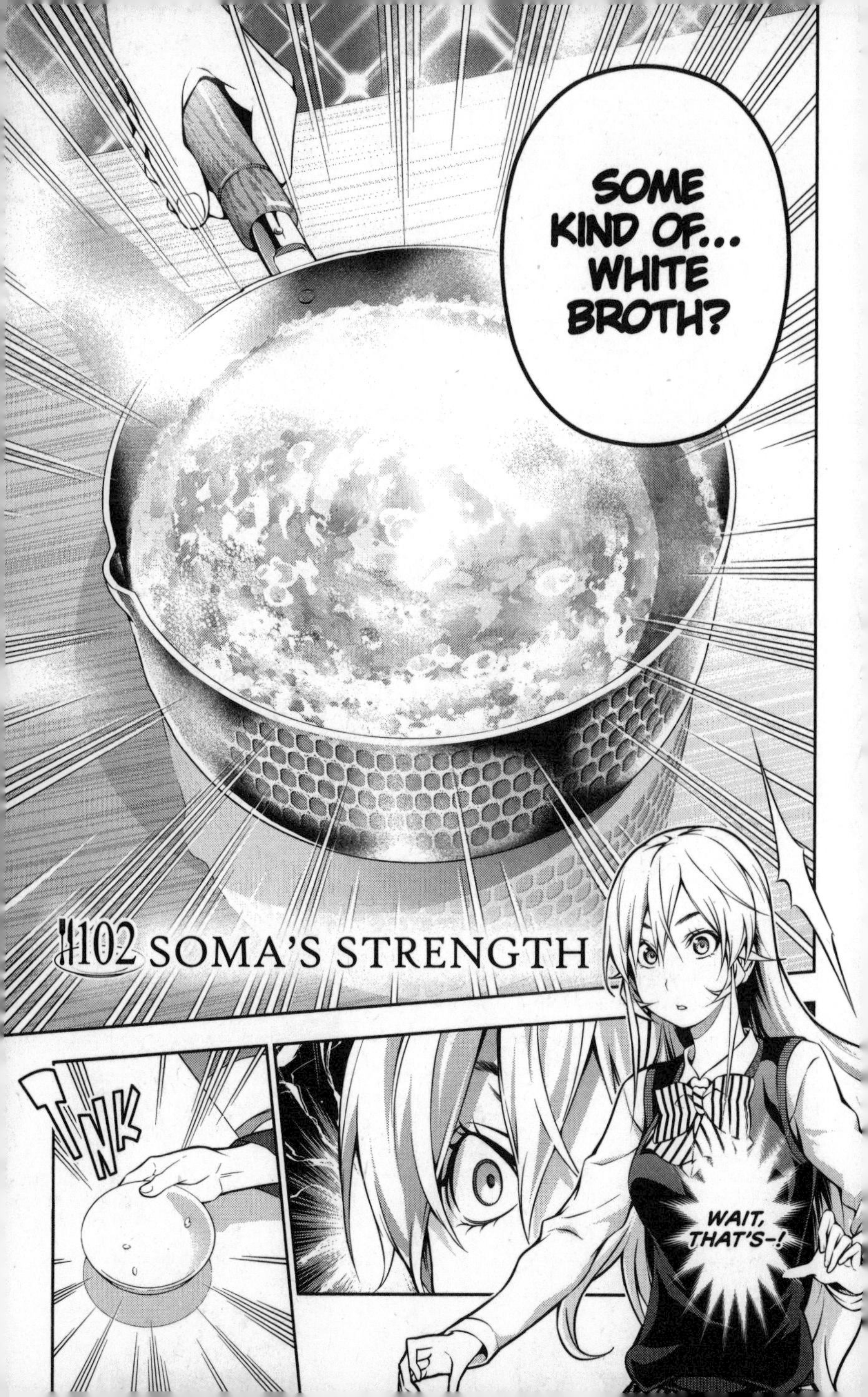
SOME KIND OF... WHITE BROTH?
102 SOMA'S STRENGTH
WAIT, THAT'S-!
TINK

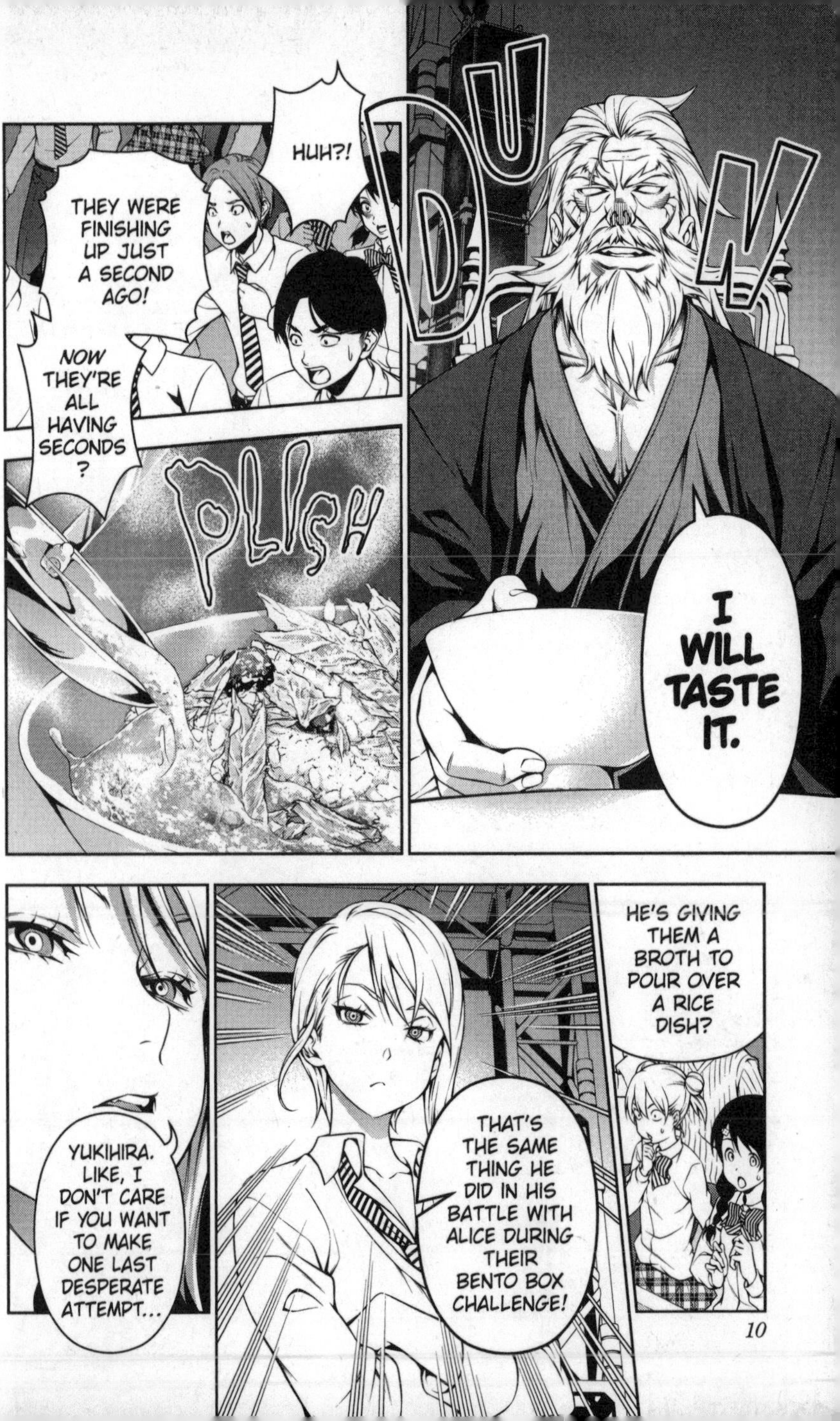
I WILL TASTE IT.
HUH?!
THEY WERE FINISHING UP JUST A SECOND AGO!
NOW THEY'RE ALL HAVING SECONDS?
PLISH
HE'S GIVING THEM A BROTH TO POUR OVER A RICE DISH?
THAT'S THE SAME THING HE DID IN HIS BATTLE WITH ALICE DURING THEIR BENTO BOX CHALLENGE!
YUKIHIRA. LIKE, I DON'T CARE IF YOU WANT TO MAKE ONE LAST DESPERATE ATTEMPT...

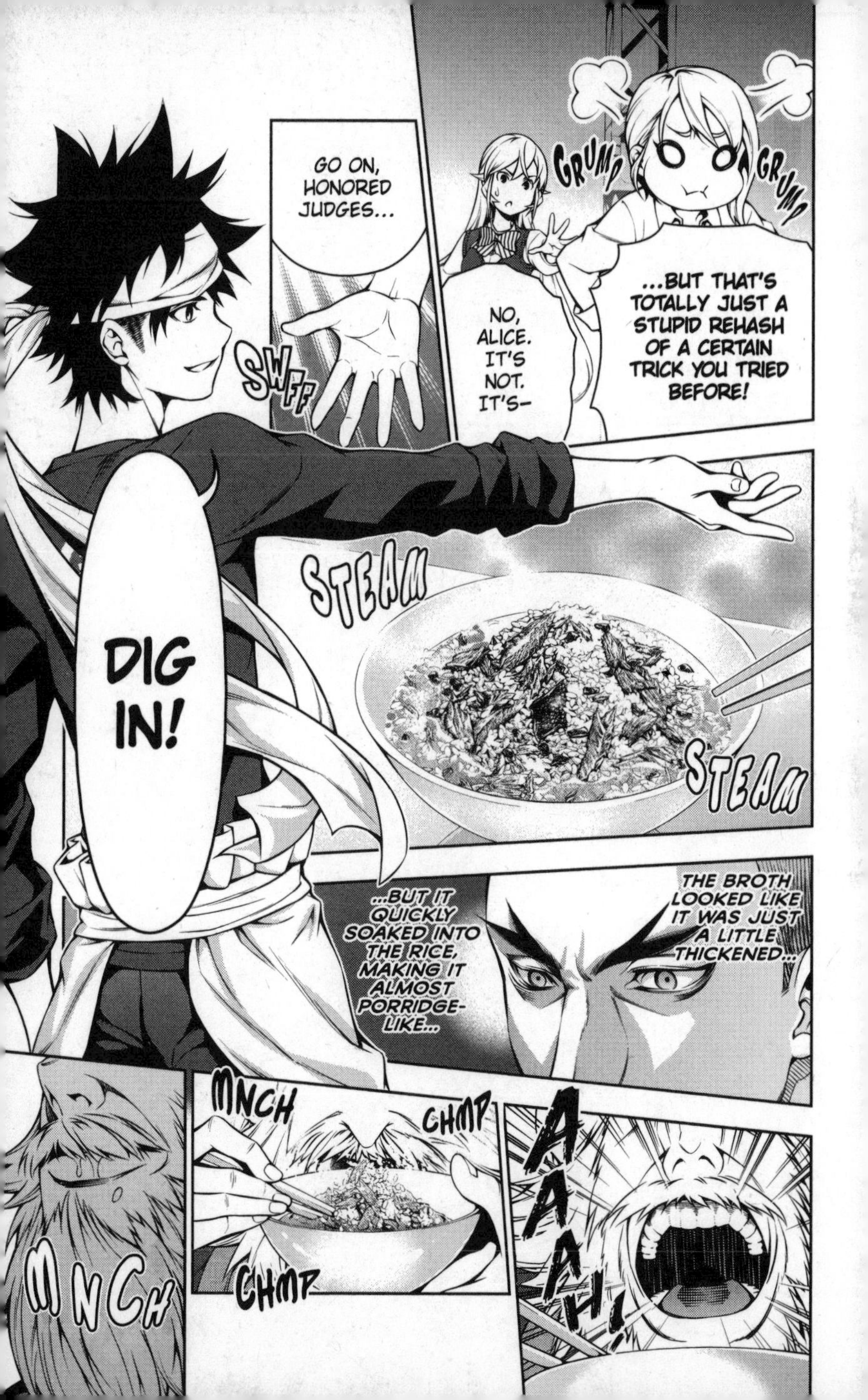
GRUMP
GRUMP
...BUT THAT'S TOTALLY JUST A STUPID REHASH OF A CERTAIN TRICK YOU TRIED BEFORE!
NO, ALICE. IT'S NOT. IT'S-
GO ON, HONORED JUDGES...
SWFF
DIG IN!
STEAM
STEAM
THE BROTH LOOKED LIKE IT WAS JUST A LITTLE THICKENED...
...BUT IT QUICKLY SOAKED INTO THE RICE, MAKING IT ALMOST PORRIDGE-LIKE...
AAAH!
CHMP
MNCH
CHMP
MNCH

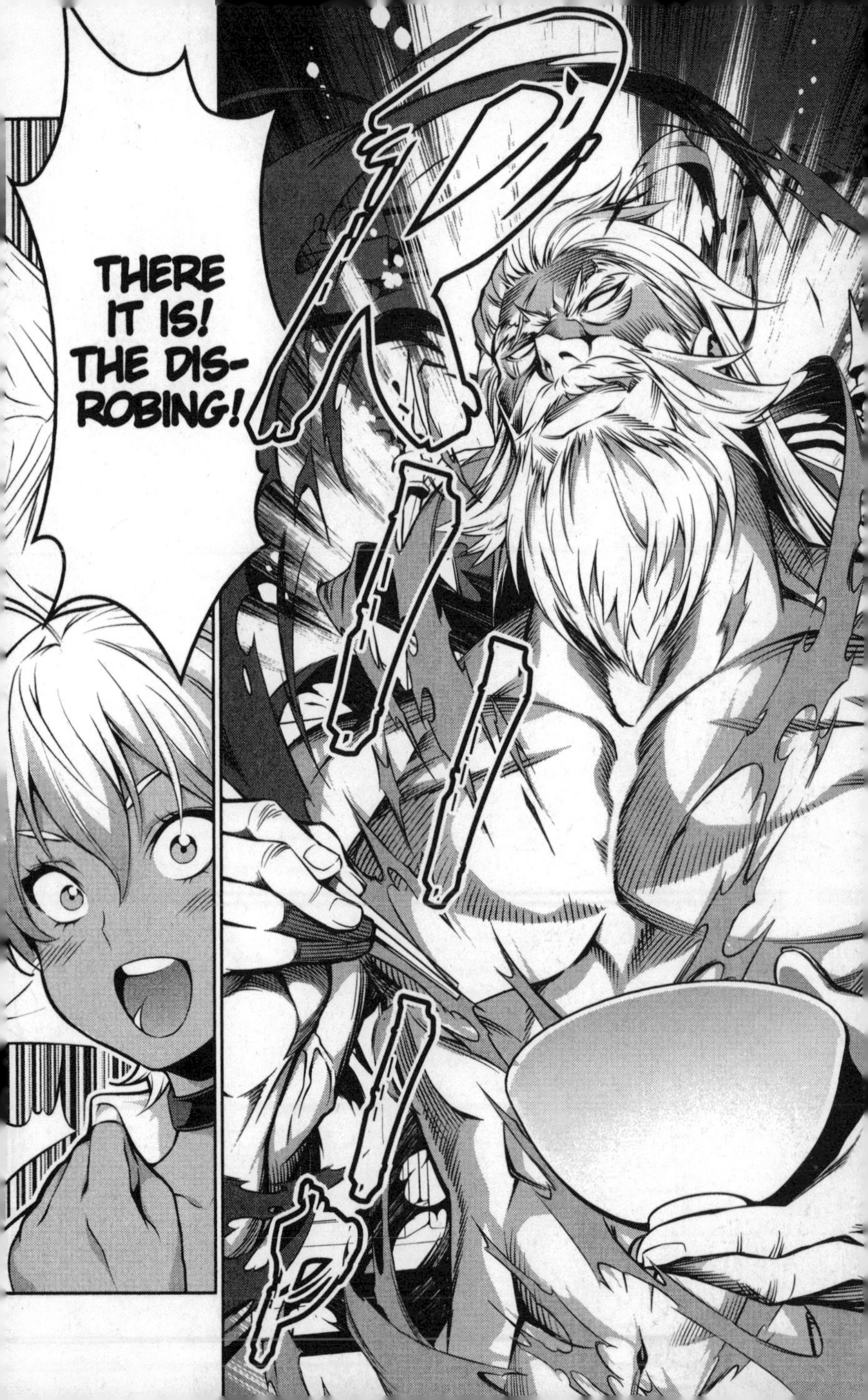
THERE IT IS! THE DIS-ROBING!

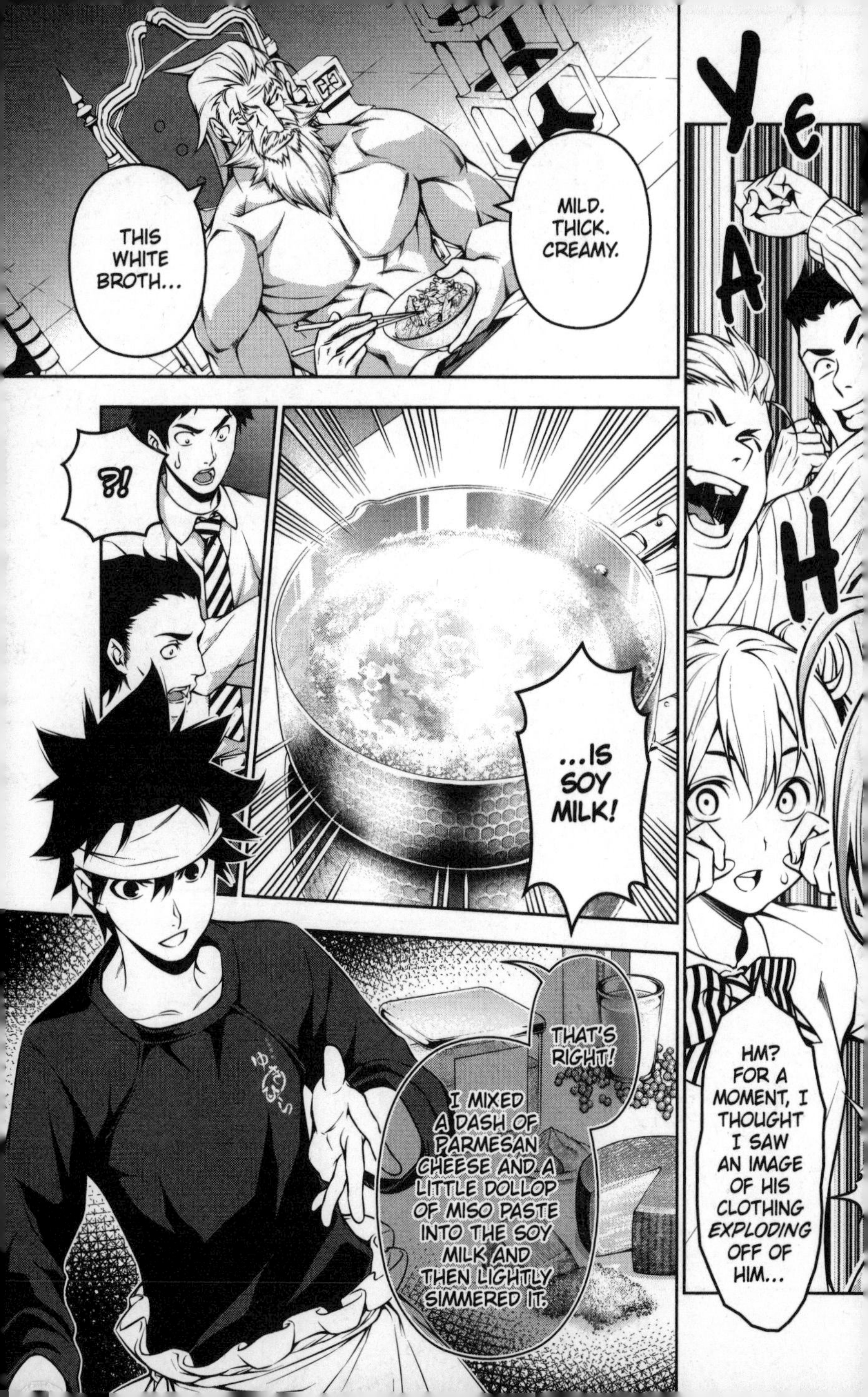
YEAH
HM? FOR A MOMENT, I THOUGHT I SAW AN IMAGE OF HIS CLOTHING *EXPLODING* OFF OF HIM...
MILD. THICK. CREAMY.
THIS WHITE BROTH...
...IS SOY MILK!
?!
THAT'S RIGHT!
I MIXED A DASH OF PARMESAN CHEESE AND A LITTLE DOLLOP OF MISO PASTE INTO THE SOY MILK AND THEN LIGHTLY SIMMERED IT.

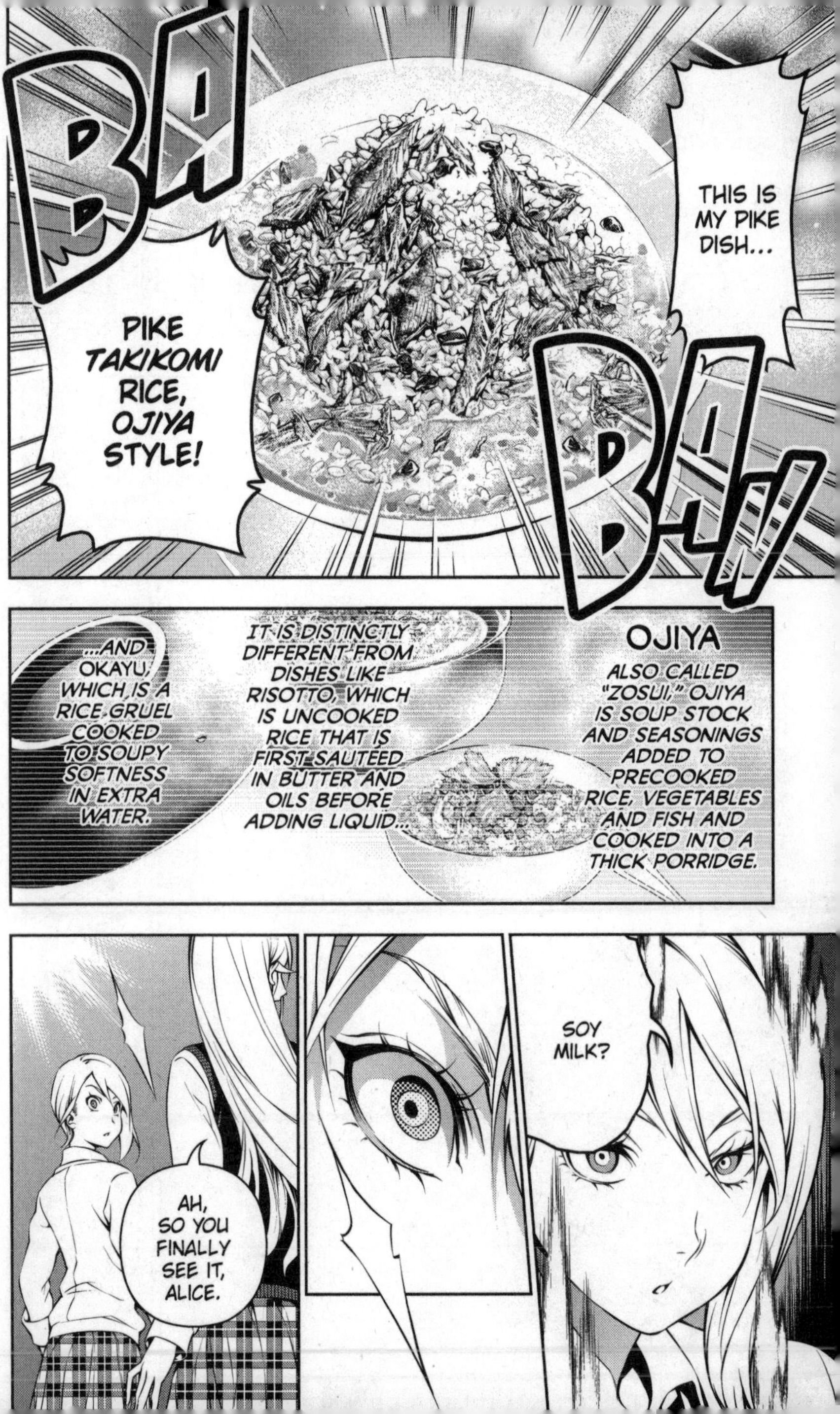
THIS IS MY PIKE DISH...
BA
PIKE TAKIKOMI RICE, OJIYA STYLE!
BA
OJIYA
ALSO CALLED "ZOSUI," OJIYA IS SOUP STOCK AND SEASONINGS ADDED TO PRECOOKED RICE, VEGETABLES AND FISH AND COOKED INTO A THICK PORRIDGE.
IT IS DISTINCTLY DIFFERENT FROM DISHES LIKE RISOTTO, WHICH IS UNCOOKED RICE THAT IS FIRST SAUTEED IN BUTTER AND OILS BEFORE ADDING LIQUID...
...AND OKAYU, WHICH IS A RICE GRUEL COOKED TO SOUPY SOFTNESS IN EXTRA WATER.
SOY MILK?
AH, SO YOU FINALLY SEE IT, ALICE.

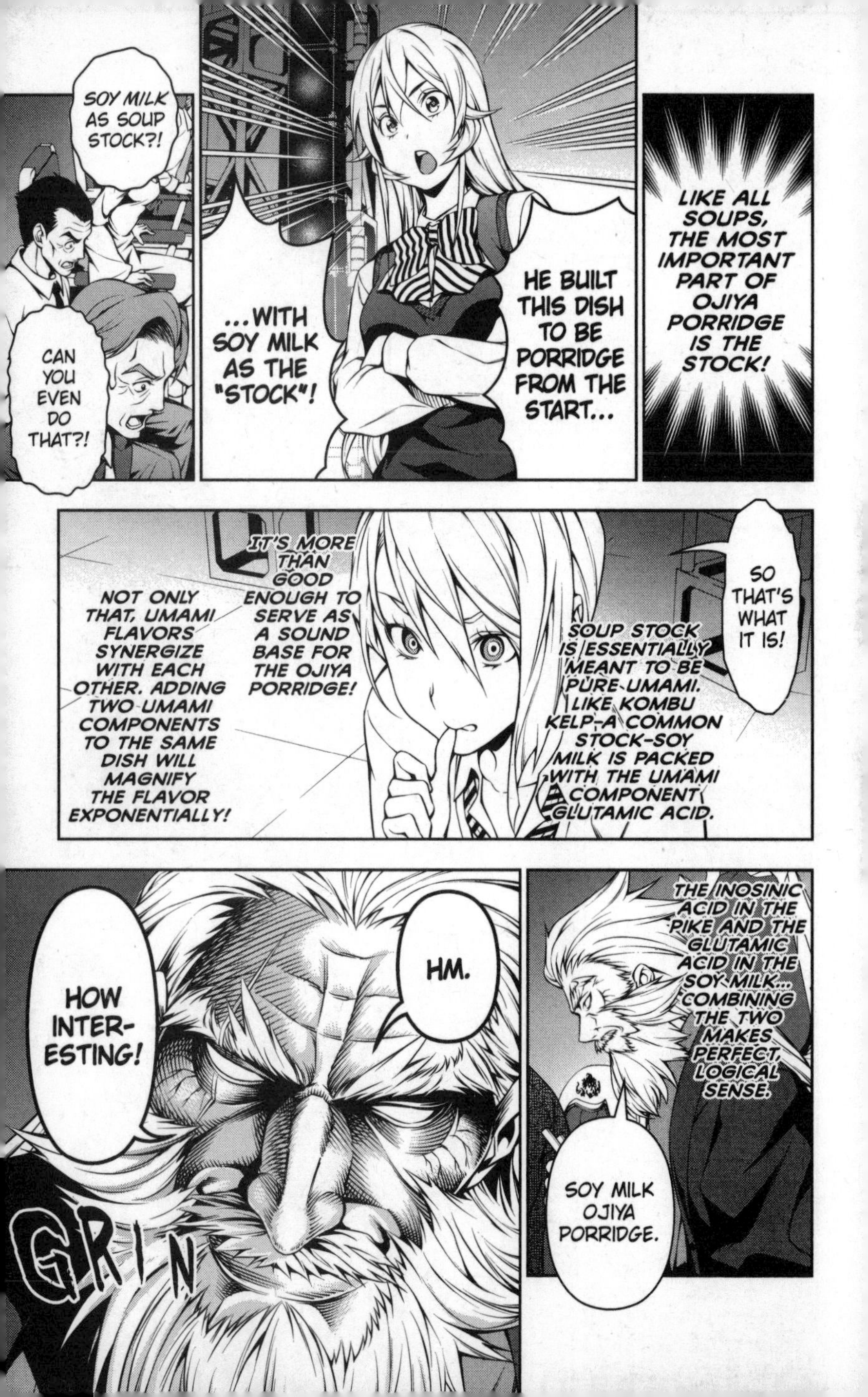
LIKE ALL SOUPS, THE MOST IMPORTANT PART OF OJIYA PORRIDGE IS THE STOCK!
HE BUILT THIS DISH TO BE PORRIDGE FROM THE START...
...WITH SOY MILK AS THE "STOCK"!
SOY MILK AS SOUP STOCK?!
CAN YOU EVEN DO THAT?!
SO THAT'S WHAT IT IS!
SOUP STOCK IS ESSENTIALLY MEANT TO BE PURE UMAMI. LIKE KOMBU KELP—A COMMON STOCK—SOY MILK IS PACKED WITH THE UMAMI COMPONENT GLUTAMIC ACID.
IT'S MORE THAN GOOD ENOUGH TO SERVE AS A SOUND BASE FOR THE OJIYA PORRIDGE!
NOT ONLY THAT, UMAMI FLAVORS SYNERGIZE WITH EACH OTHER. ADDING TWO UMAMI COMPONENTS TO THE SAME DISH WILL MAGNIFY THE FLAVOR EXPONENTIALLY!
THE INOSINIC ACID IN THE PIKE AND THE GLUTAMIC ACID IN THE SOY MILK... COMBINING THE TWO MAKES PERFECT, LOGICAL SENSE.
SOY MILK OJIYA PORRIDGE.
HM.
HOW INTER-ESTING!
GRIN

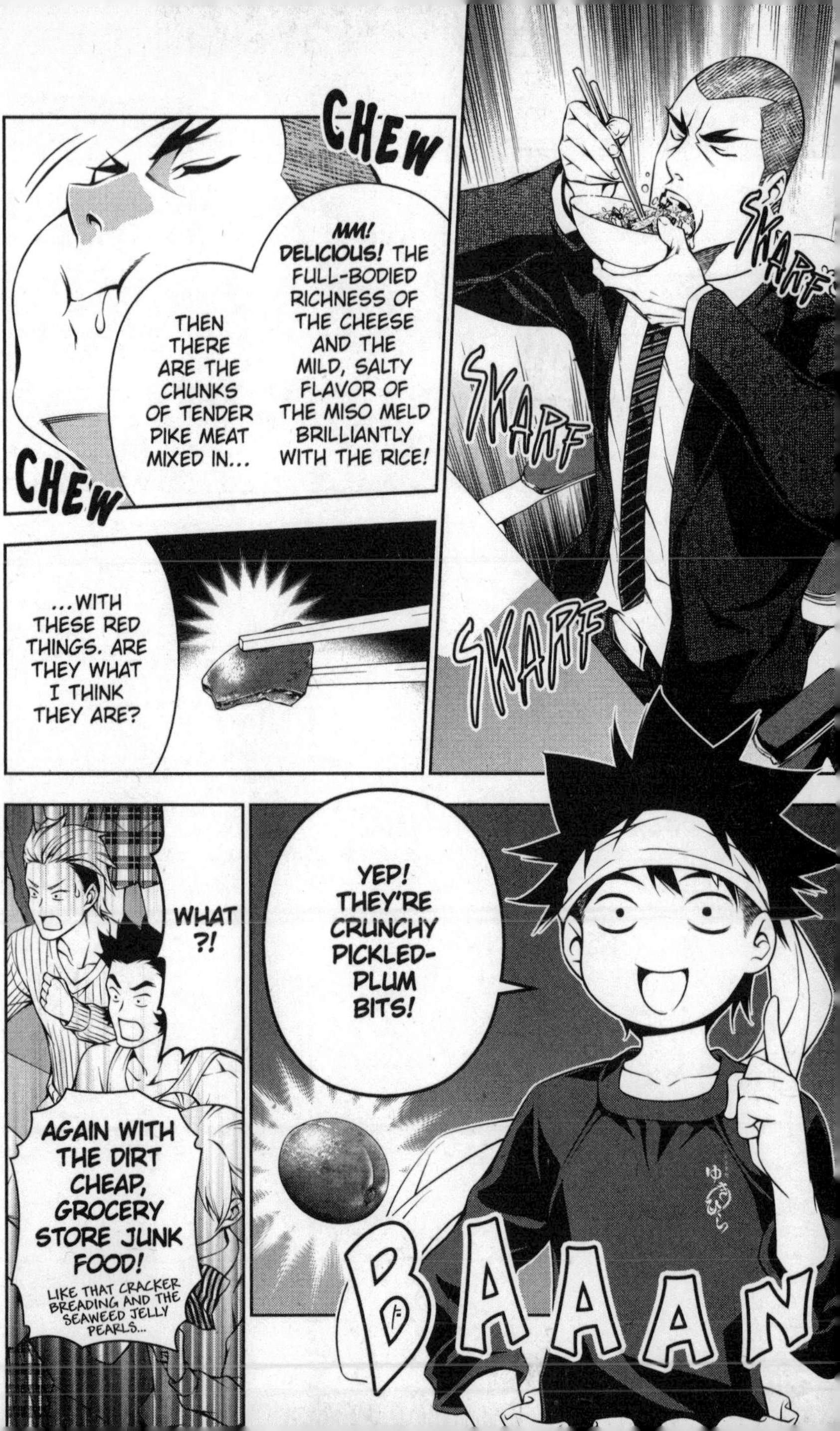
SKARF
SKARF
SKARF
CHEW
CHEW
MM! DELICIOUS! THE FULL-BODIED RICHNESS OF THE CHEESE AND THE MILD, SALTY FLAVOR OF THE MISO MELD BRILLIANTLY WITH THE RICE!
THEN THERE ARE THE CHUNKS OF TENDER PIKE MEAT MIXED IN...
...WITH THESE RED THINGS. ARE THEY WHAT I THINK THEY ARE?
YEP! THEY'RE CRUNCHY PICKLED-PLUM BITS!
BAAAN
WHAT?!
AGAIN WITH THE DIRT CHEAP, GROCERY STORE JUNK FOOD!
LIKE THAT CRACKER BREADING AND THE SEAWEED JELLY PEARLS...

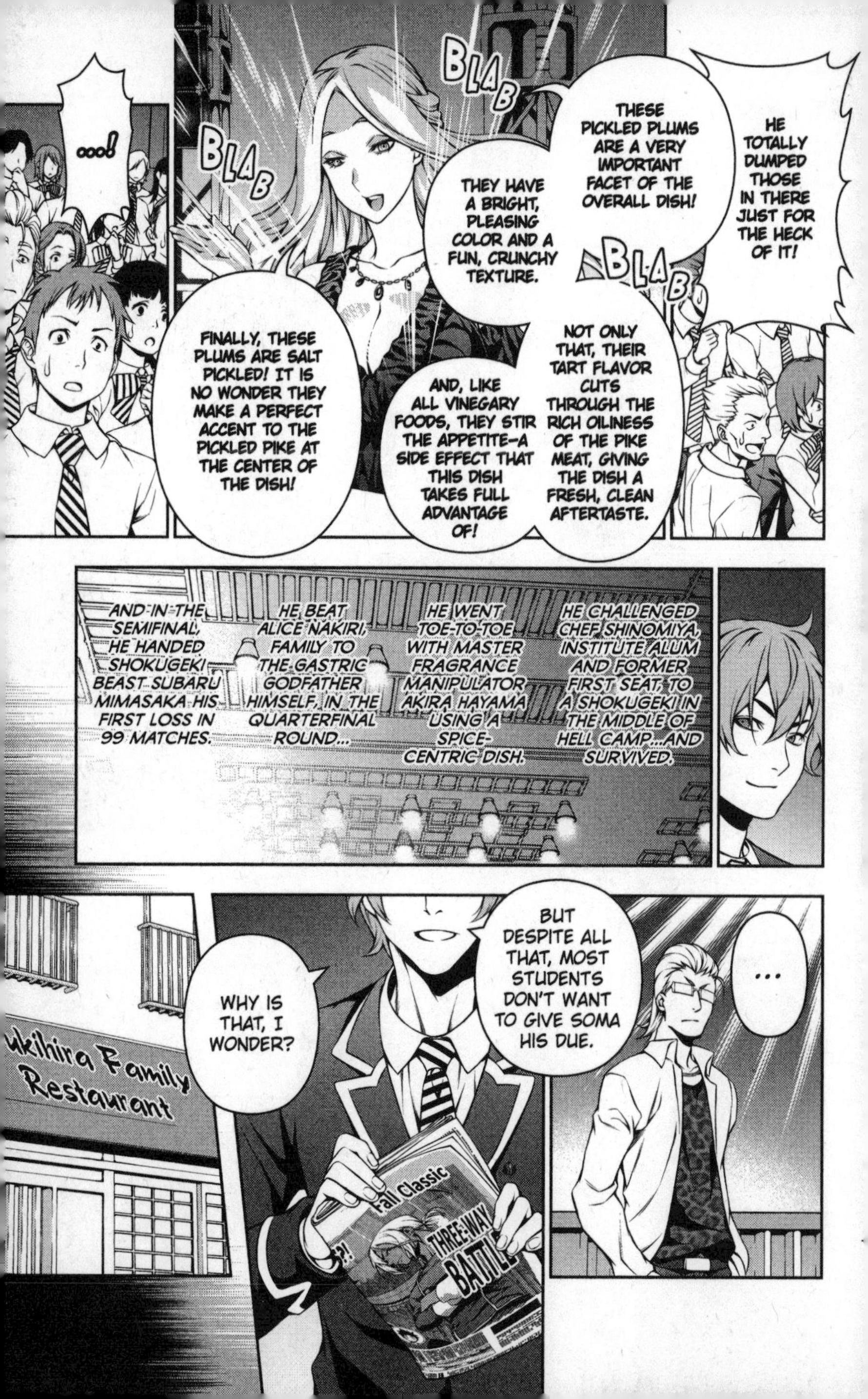
HE TOTALLY DUMPED THOSE IN THERE JUST FOR THE HECK OF IT!
BLAB
THESE PICKLED PLUMS ARE A VERY IMPORTANT FACET OF THE OVERALL DISH!
BLAB
THEY HAVE A BRIGHT, PLEASING COLOR AND A FUN, CRUNCHY TEXTURE.
BLAB
NOT ONLY THAT, THEIR TART FLAVOR CUTS THROUGH THE RICH OILINESS OF THE PIKE MEAT, GIVING THE DISH A FRESH, CLEAN AFTERTASTE.
AND, LIKE ALL VINEGARY FOODS, THEY STIR THE APPETITE—A SIDE EFFECT THAT THIS DISH TAKES FULL ADVANTAGE OF!
FINALLY, THESE PLUMS ARE SALT PICKLED! IT IS NO WONDER THEY MAKE A PERFECT ACCENT TO THE PICKLED PIKE AT THE CENTER OF THE DISH!
ooo!
HE CHALLENGED CHEF SHINOMIYA, INSTITUTE ALUM AND FORMER FIRST SEAT, TO A SHOKUGEKI IN THE MIDDLE OF HELL CAMP...AND SURVIVED.
HE WENT TOE-TO-TOE WITH MASTER FRAGRANCE MANIPULATOR AKIRA HAYAMA USING A SPICE-CENTRIC DISH.
HE BEAT ALICE NAKIRI, FAMILY TO THE GASTRIC GODFATHER HIMSELF, IN THE QUARTERFINAL ROUND...
AND IN THE SEMIFINAL, HE HANDED SHOKUGEKI BEAST SUBARU MIMASAKA HIS FIRST LOSS IN 99 MATCHES.
...
BUT DESPITE ALL THAT, MOST STUDENTS DON'T WANT TO GIVE SOMA HIS DUE.
WHY IS THAT, I WONDER?
Fall Classic
THREE-WAY BATTLE
ukihira Family Restaurant

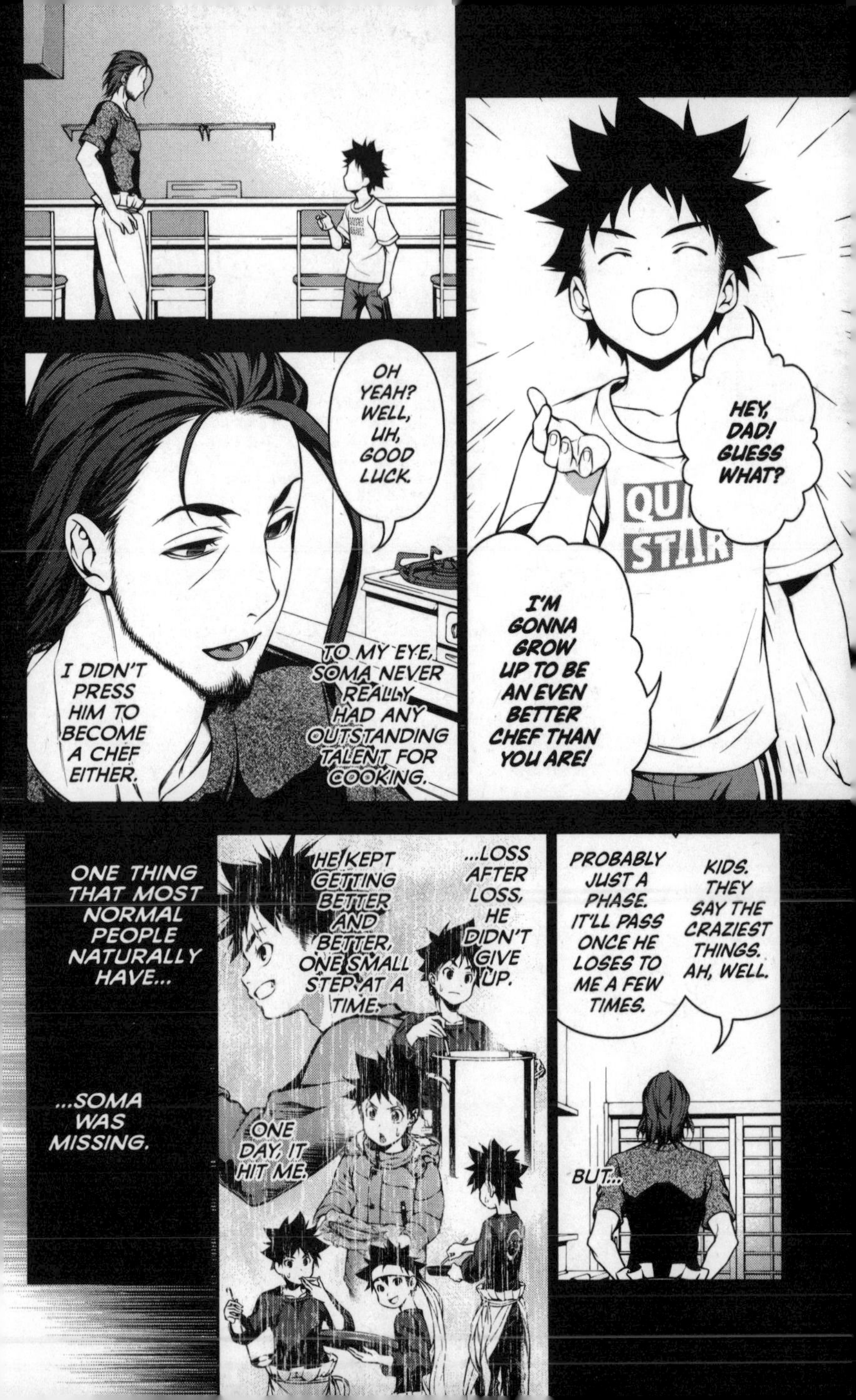
HEY, DAD! GUESS WHAT?
I'M GONNA GROW UP TO BE AN EVEN BETTER CHEF THAN YOU ARE!
OH YEAH? WELL, UH, GOOD LUCK.
TO MY EYE, SOMA NEVER REALLY HAD ANY OUTSTANDING TALENT FOR COOKING.
I DIDN'T PRESS HIM TO BECOME A CHEF EITHER.
KIDS. THEY SAY THE CRAZIEST THINGS. AH, WELL.
PROBABLY JUST A PHASE. IT'LL PASS ONCE HE LOSES TO ME A FEW TIMES.
BUT...
...LOSS AFTER LOSS, HE DIDN'T GIVE UP.
HE KEPT GETTING BETTER AND BETTER, ONE SMALL STEP AT A TIME.
ONE DAY, IT HIT ME.
ONE THING THAT MOST NORMAL PEOPLE NATURALLY HAVE...
...SOMA WAS MISSING.

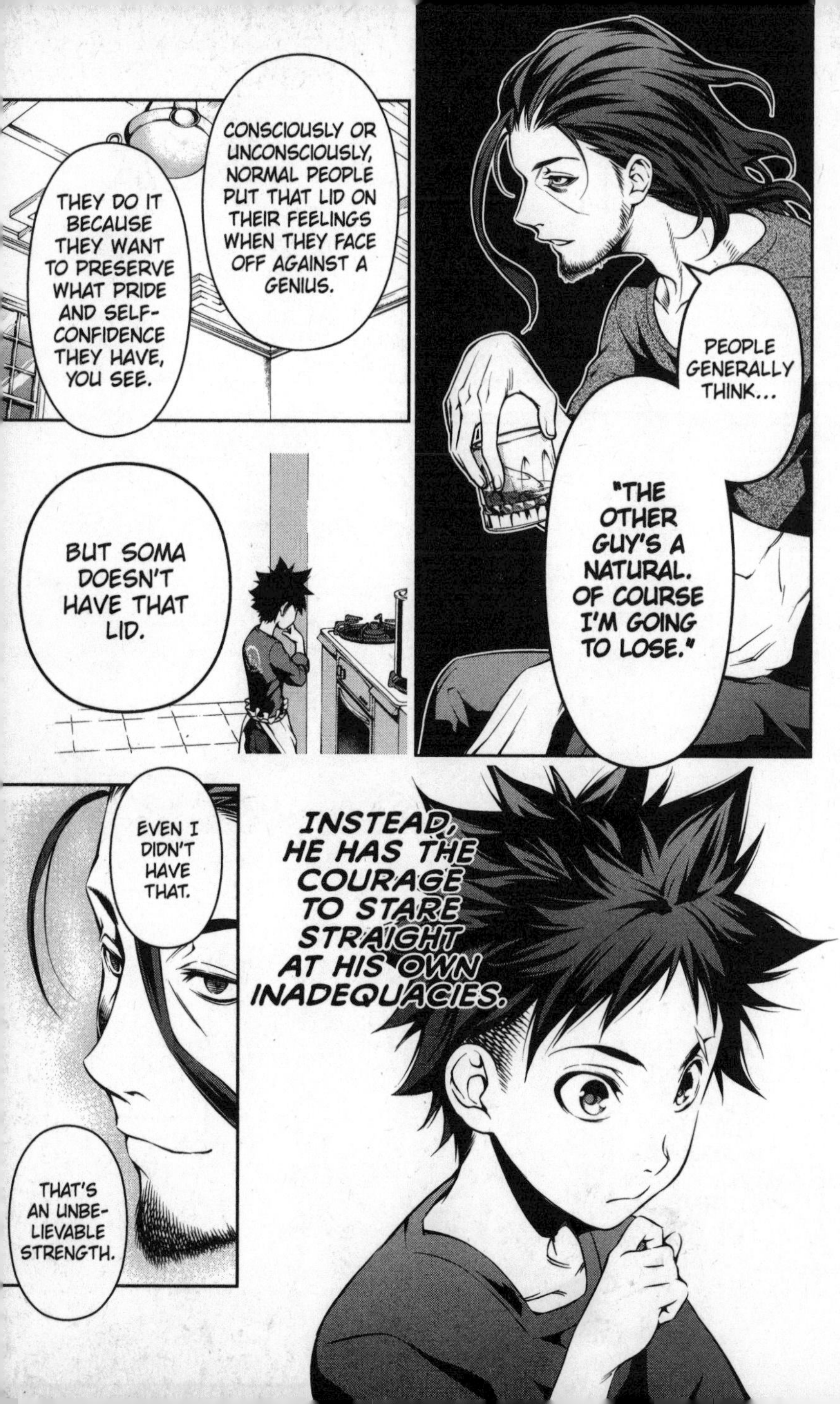
PEOPLE GENERALLY THINK...
"THE OTHER GUY'S A NATURAL. OF COURSE I'M GOING TO LOSE."
CONSCIOUSLY OR UNCONSCIOUSLY, NORMAL PEOPLE PUT THAT LID ON THEIR FEELINGS WHEN THEY FACE OFF AGAINST A GENIUS.
THEY DO IT BECAUSE THEY WANT TO PRESERVE WHAT PRIDE AND SELF-CONFIDENCE THEY HAVE, YOU SEE.
BUT SOMA DOESN'T HAVE THAT LID.
INSTEAD, HE HAS THE COURAGE TO STARE STRAIGHT AT HIS OWN INADEQUACIES.
EVEN I DIDN'T HAVE THAT.
THAT'S AN UNBE-LIEVABLE STRENGTH.

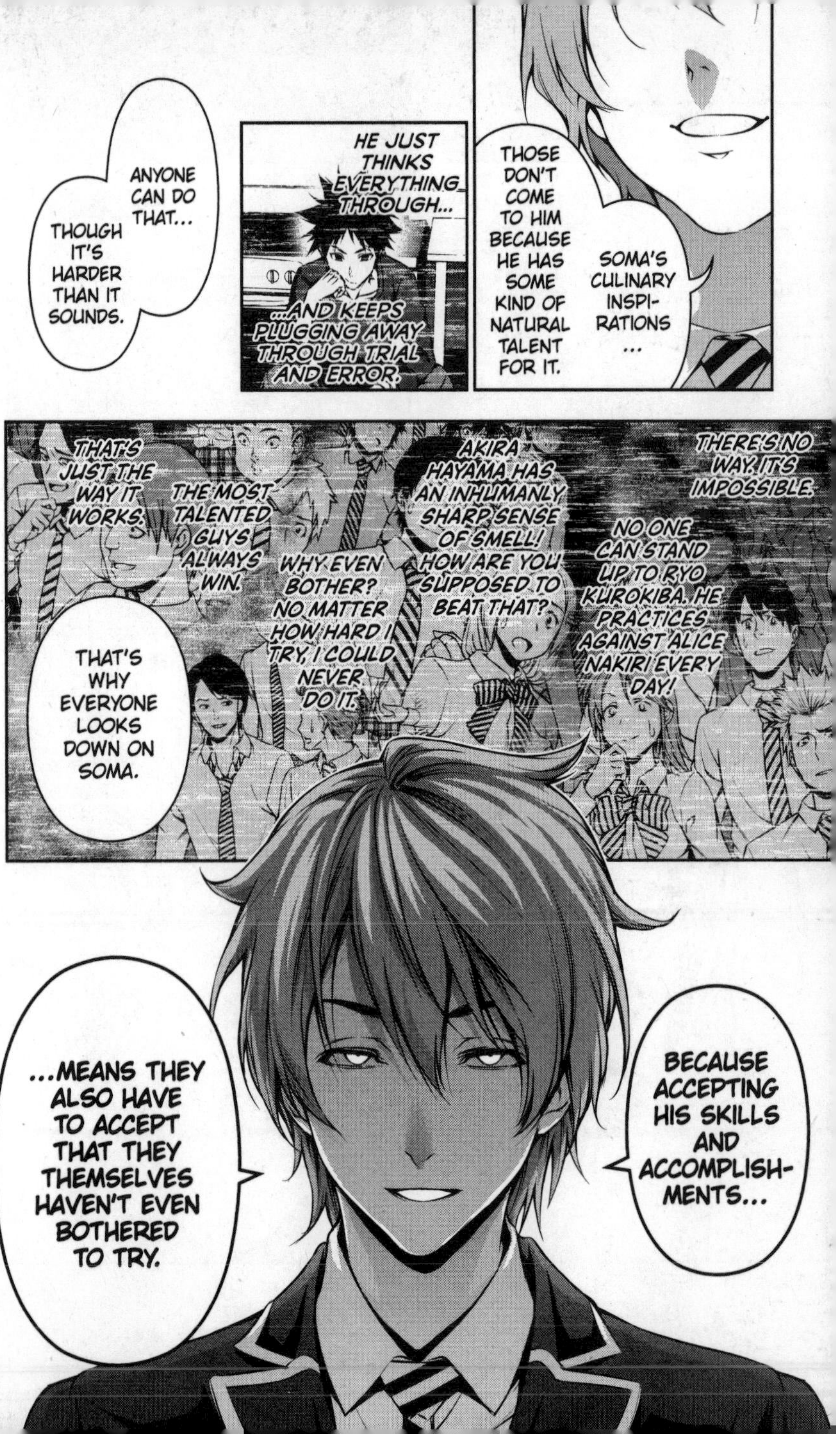
SOMA'S CULINARY INSPIRATIONS...
THOSE DON'T COME TO HIM BECAUSE HE HAS SOME KIND OF NATURAL TALENT FOR IT.
HE JUST THINKS EVERYTHING THROUGH...
...AND KEEPS PLUGGING AWAY THROUGH TRIAL AND ERROR.
ANYONE CAN DO THAT...
THOUGH IT'S HARDER THAN IT SOUNDS.
THERE'S NO WAY. IT'S IMPOSSIBLE.
NO ONE CAN STAND UP TO RYO KUROKIBA. HE PRACTICES AGAINST ALICE NAKIRI EVERY DAY!
AKIRA HAYAMA HAS AN INHUMANLY SHARP SENSE OF SMELL! HOW ARE YOU SUPPOSED TO BEAT THAT?
WHY EVEN BOTHER? NO MATTER HOW HARD I TRY, I COULD NEVER DO IT.
THE MOST TALENTED GUYS ALWAYS WIN.
THAT'S JUST THE WAY IT WORKS.
THAT'S WHY EVERYONE LOOKS DOWN ON SOMA.
BECAUSE ACCEPTING HIS SKILLS AND ACCOMPLISHMENTS...
...MEANS THEY ALSO HAVE TO ACCEPT THAT THEY THEMSELVES HAVEN'T EVEN BOTHERED TO TRY.

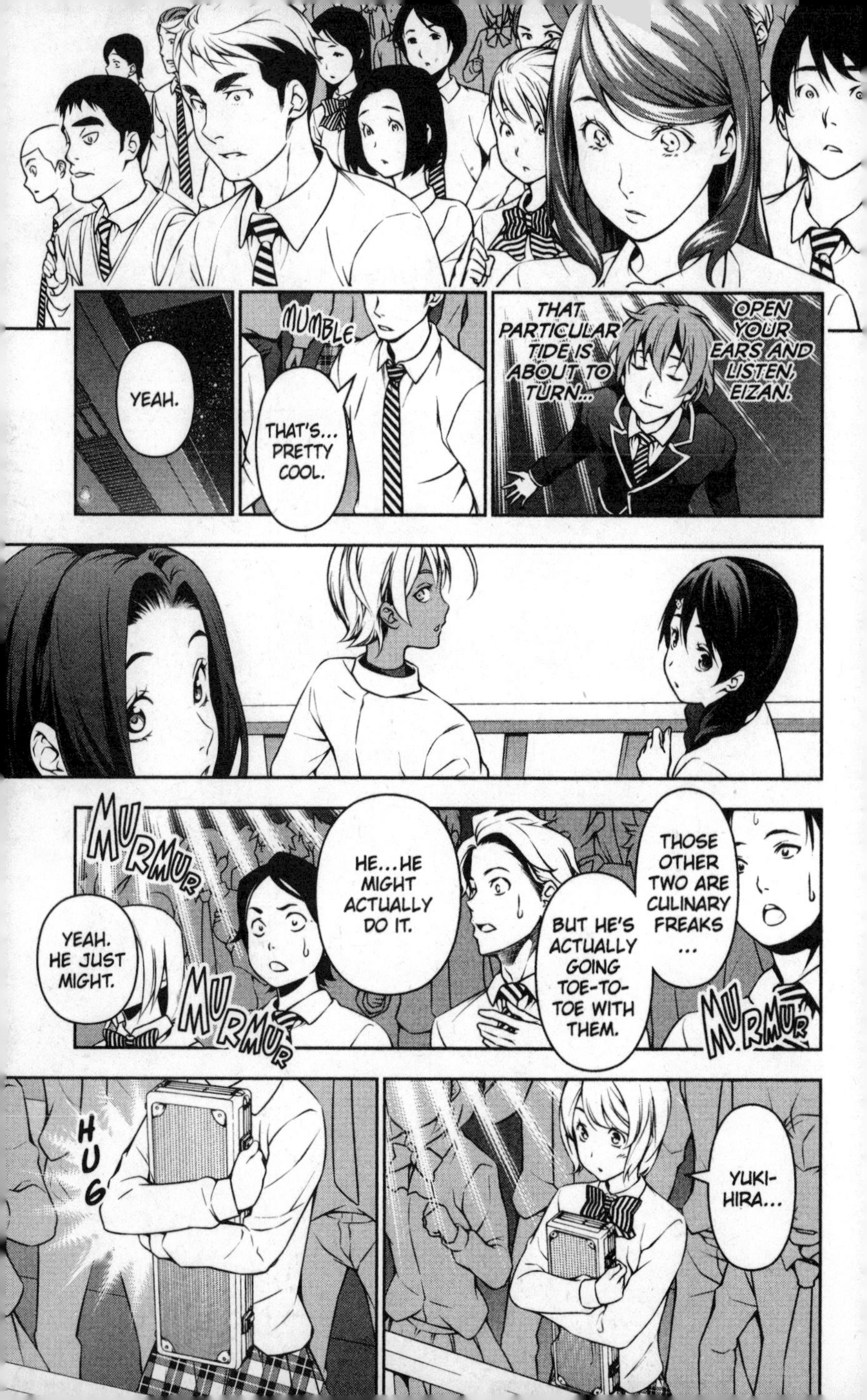
OPEN YOUR EARS AND LISTEN, EIZAN.
THAT PARTICULAR TIDE IS ABOUT TO TURN...
MUMBLE
THAT'S... PRETTY COOL.
YEAH.
MURMUR
THOSE OTHER TWO ARE CULINARY FREAKS...
BUT HE'S ACTUALLY GOING TOE-TO-TOE WITH THEM.
HE...HE MIGHT ACTUALLY DO IT.
MURMUR
YEAH. HE JUST MIGHT.
MURMUR
YUKI-HIRA...
HUG

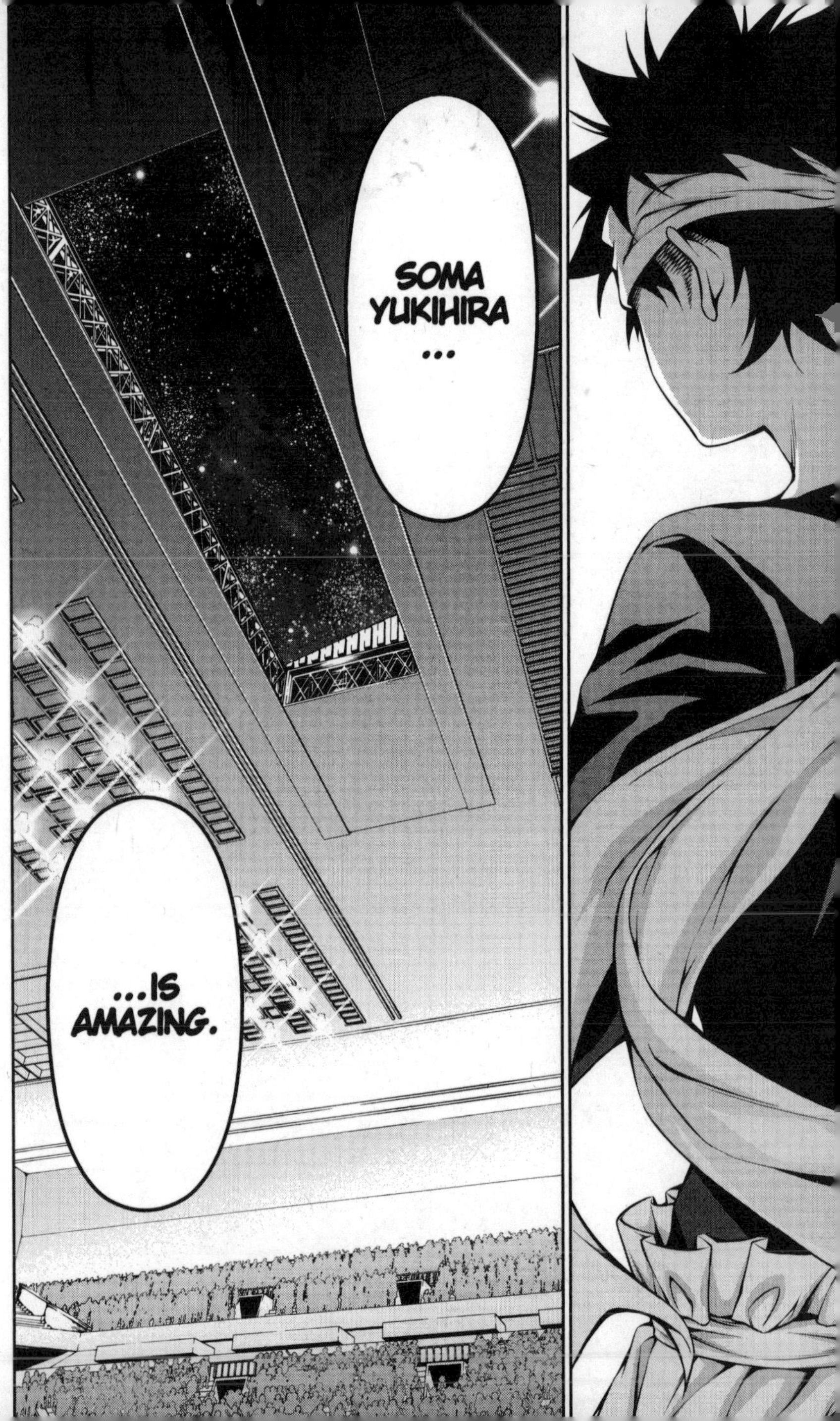
SOMA YUKIHIRA ...
...IS AMAZING.

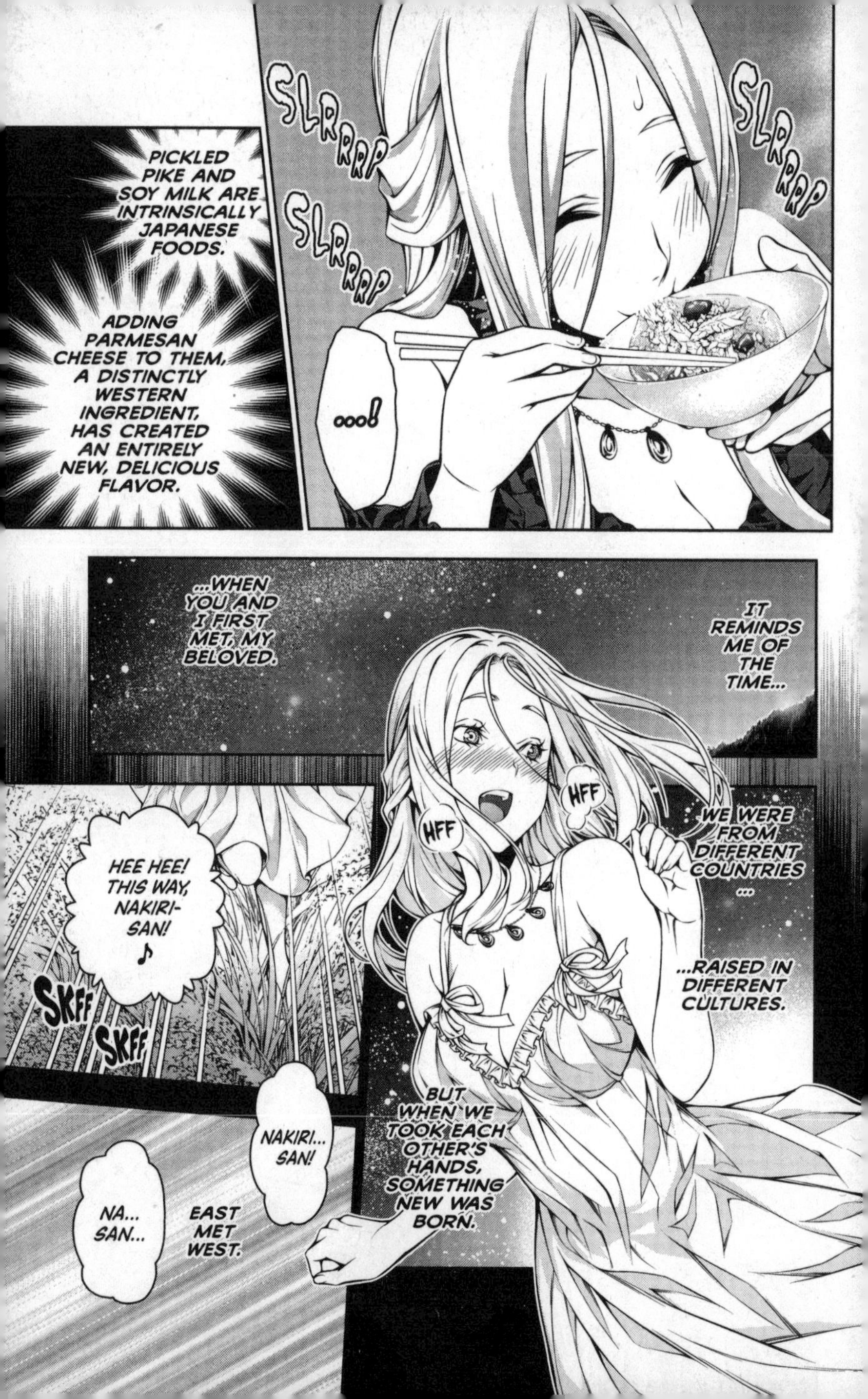
SLRRRP
SLRRRP
SLRRRP
...!
PICKLED PIKE AND SOY MILK ARE INTRINSICALLY JAPANESE FOODS.
ADDING PARMESAN CHEESE TO THEM, A DISTINCTLY WESTERN INGREDIENT, HAS CREATED AN ENTIRELY NEW, DELICIOUS FLAVOR.
IT REMINDS ME OF THE TIME...
...WHEN YOU AND I FIRST MET, MY BELOVED.
HFF
HFF
WE WERE FROM DIFFERENT COUNTRIES...
...RAISED IN DIFFERENT CULTURES.
BUT WHEN WE TOOK EACH OTHER'S HANDS, SOMETHING NEW WAS BORN.
HEE HEE! THIS WAY, NAKIRI-SAN! ♪
SKFF
SKFF
NAKIRI... SAN!
EAST MET WEST.
NA... SAN...

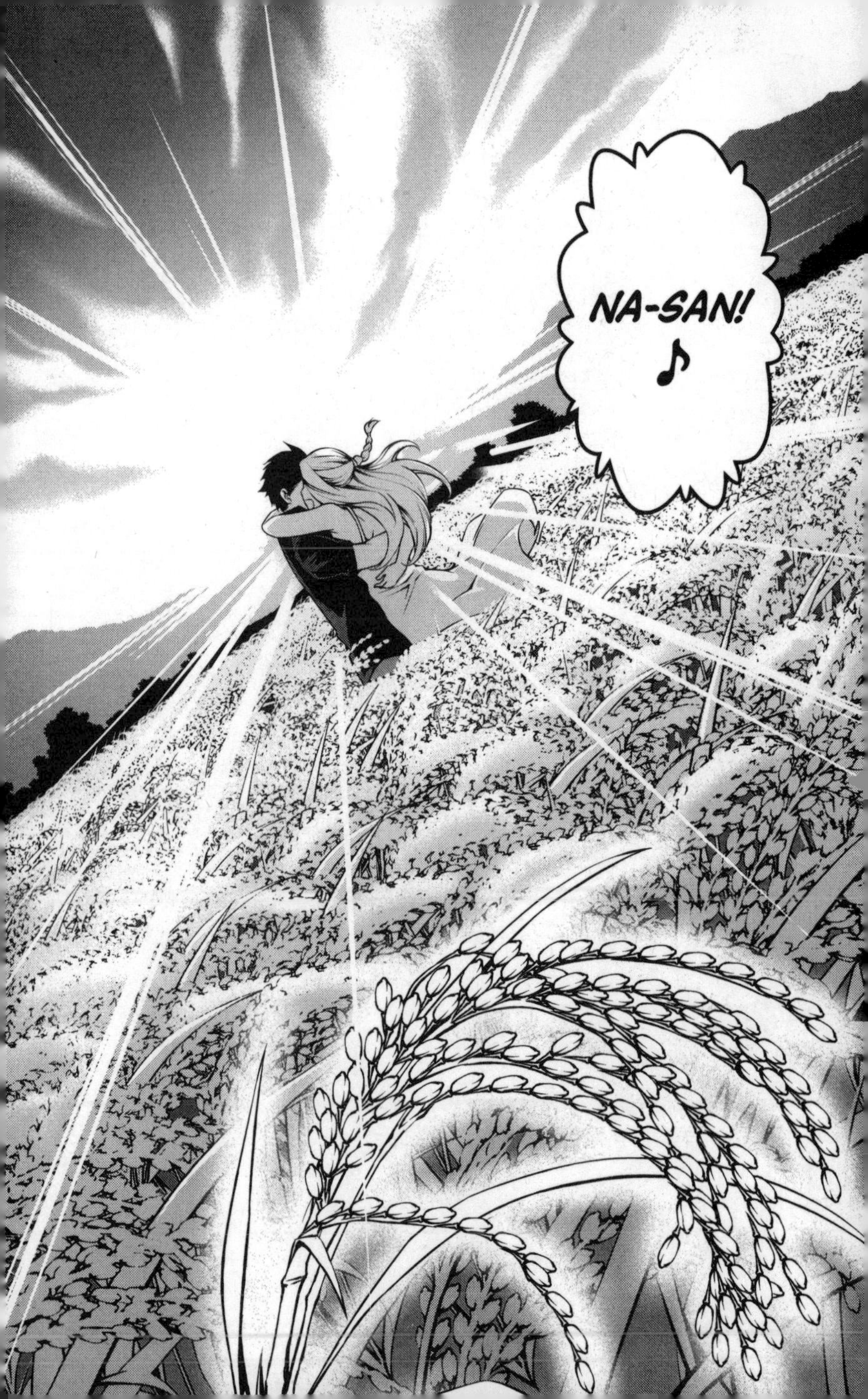
NA-SAN! ♪

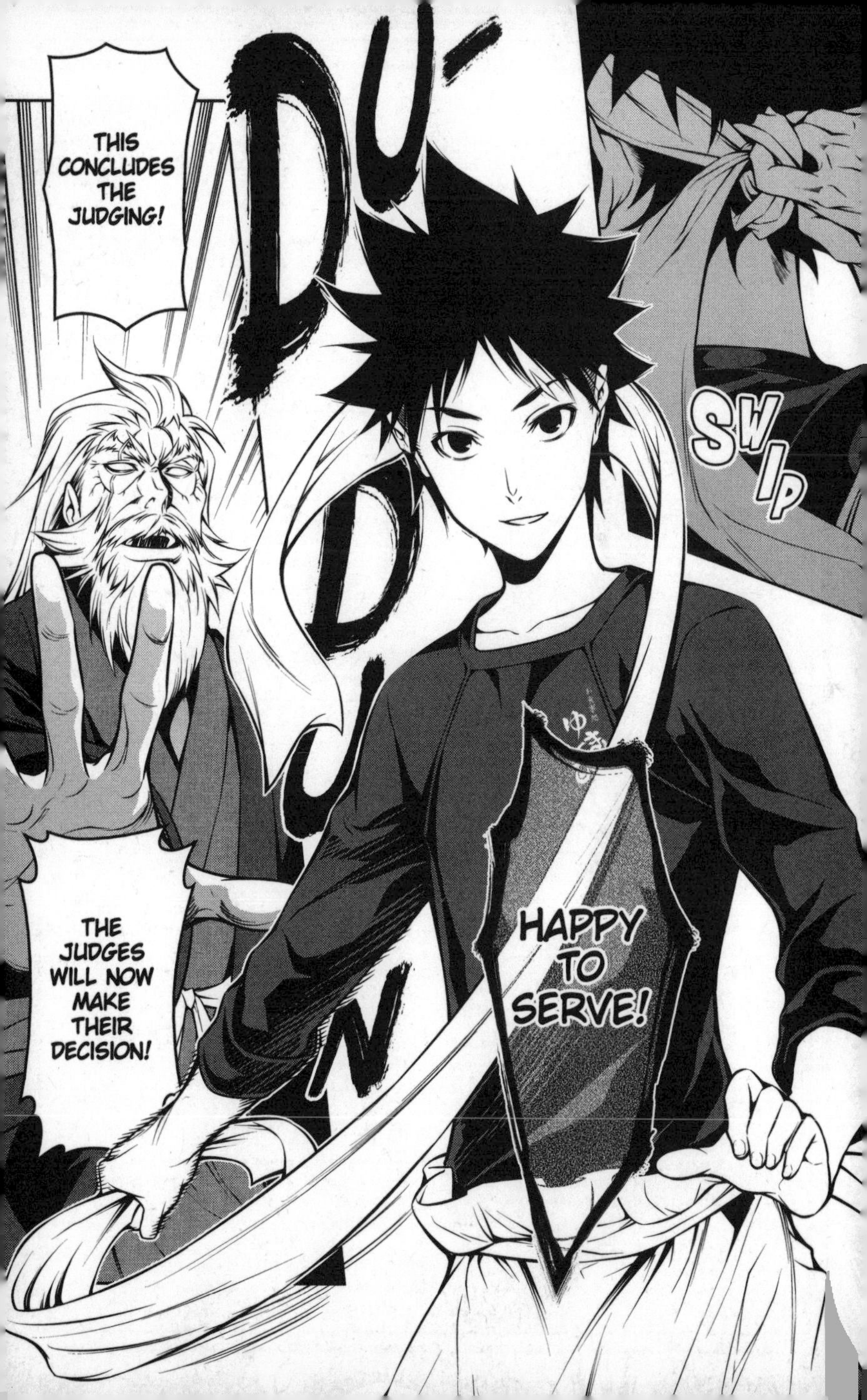
SWIP
THIS CONCLUDES THE JUDGING!
DU-D-N
HAPPY TO SERVE!
THE JUDGES WILL NOW MAKE THEIR DECISION!

ARTIST: YUTO TSUKUDA RECIPE BY: YUKI MORISAKI

PRACTICAL RECIPE #1

VOLUME 13 SPECIAL SUPPLEMENT!

COOK IN A DONABE POT!

PIKE TAKIKOMI RICE, OJIYA-STYLE

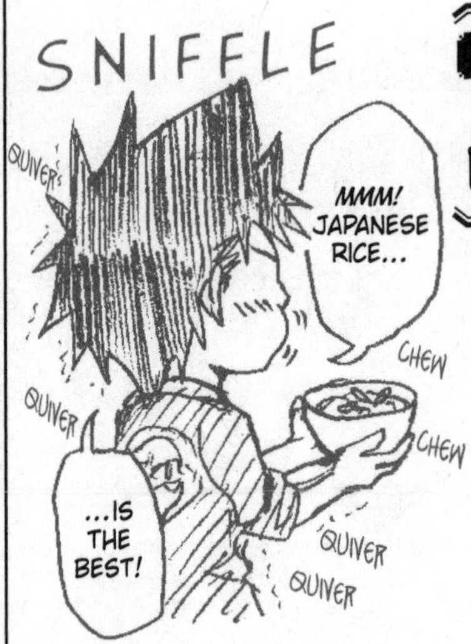
SNIFFLE
QUIVER
MMM! JAPANESE RICE...
CHEW
CHEW
QUIVER
...IS THE BEST!
QUIVER
QUIVER

INGREDIENTS (SERVES 4)

2 CUPS UNCOOKED RICE
400 CC WATER
2 PIKE
1 PACKAGE SHIMEJI MUSHROOMS
1 THUMB GINGER
4 CRUNCHY PICKLED PLUMS
1 10 CM^2 SHEET OF KOMBU SEAWEED

A [1 TABLESPOON EACH COOKING SAKE, LIGHT SOY SAUCE
½ TABLESPOON MIRIN

SHISO LEAVES, ROASTED SESAME SEEDS, SOY MILK

1. SOAK THE UNCOOKED RICE IN WATER FOR AT LEAST 30 MINUTES AND THEN DRAIN.

2. SLICE THE PIKE IN HALF LENGTHWISE. SALT THOROUGHLY, LET SIT FOR 10 MINUTES AND THEN USE A PAPER TOWEL TO DRY OFF ANY EXCESS MOISTURE. GRILL UNTIL FRAGRANT, ABOUT 7 MINUTES.

3. SLICE THE GINGER AND SHISO LEAVES INTO STRIPS. REMOVE THE BASE OF THE SHIMEJI MUSHROOMS AND SEPARATE. CHOP THE PICKLED PLUMS INTO SMALL CHUNKS.

4. IN A DONABE POT, ADD THE KOMBU SHEET, THE RICE FROM (1) AND THE WATER. SPRINKLE THE GINGER SLICES, SHIMEJI MUSHROOMS, PICKLED PLUMS, AND PIKE FROM (2) ON TOP. PUT THE LID ON THE POT AND TURN THE HEAT ON HIGH.

5. ONCE BOILING, TURN THE HEAT TO LOW FOR 15 MINUTES. THEN TURN THE HEAT OFF AND LET STEAM FOR ANOTHER 15 MINUTES.

6. TOP WITH SHISO LEAVES AND ROASTED SESAME SEEDS. ENJOY THE FIRST BOWL AS IS, AND TRY A SECOND BOWL WITH SOY MILK POURED OVER IT.

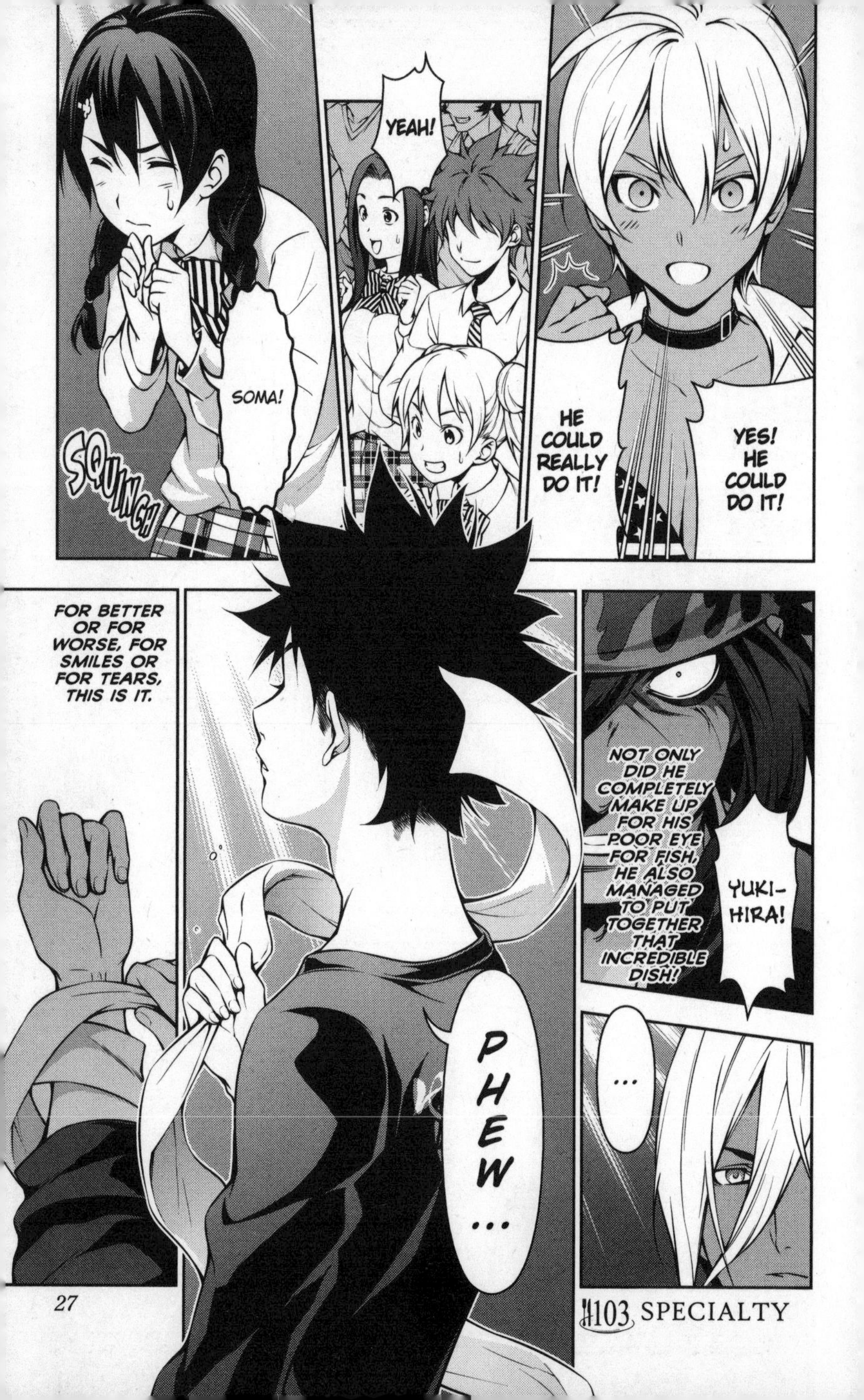
YES! HE COULD DO IT!
HE COULD REALLY DO IT!
YEAH!
SOMA!
SQUINCH
YUKI-HIRA!
NOT ONLY DID HE COMPLETELY MAKE UP FOR HIS POOR EYE FOR FISH, HE ALSO MANAGED TO PUT TOGETHER THAT INCREDIBLE DISH!
...
PHEW...
FOR BETTER OR FOR WORSE, FOR SMILES OR FOR TEARS, THIS IS IT.

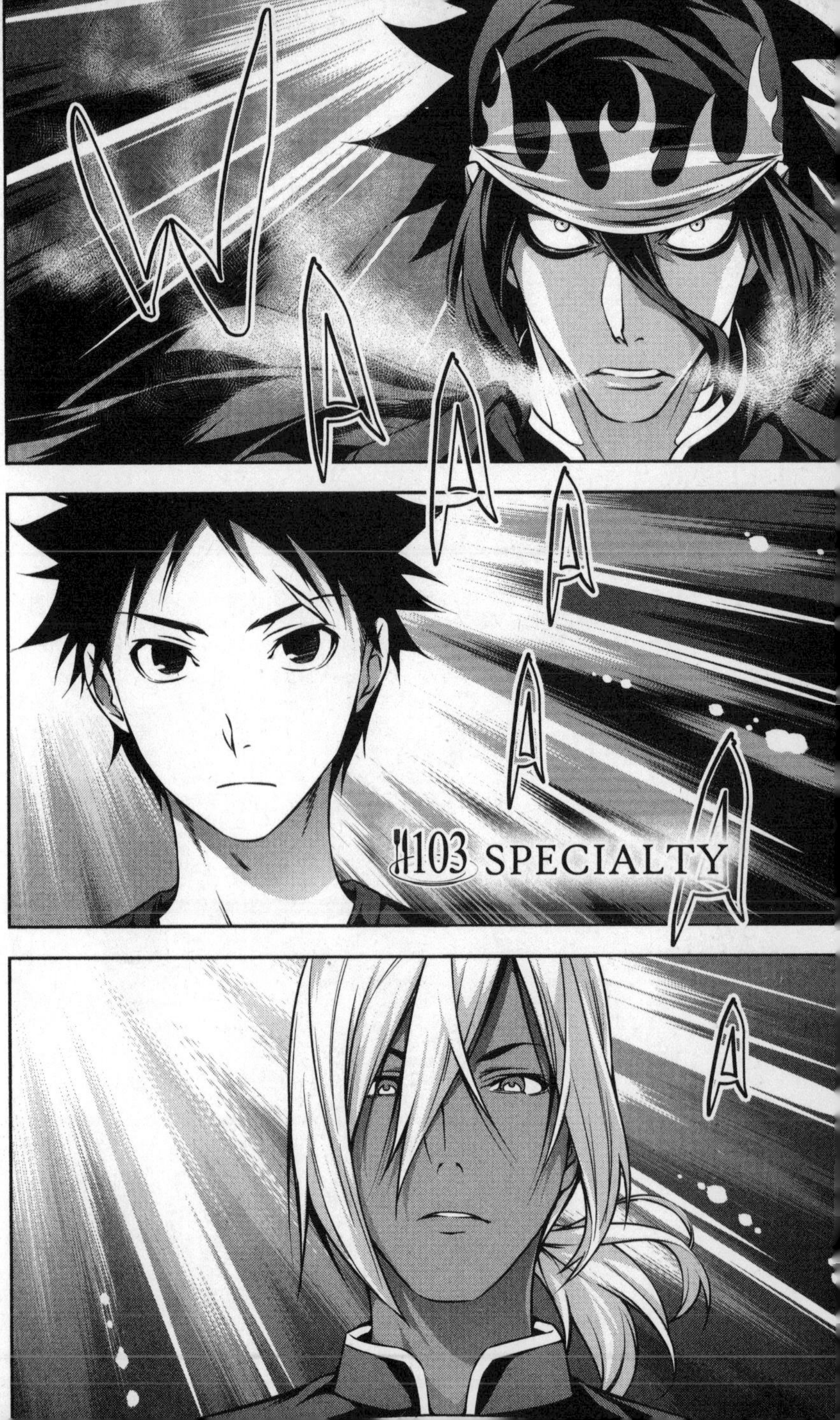
WAAAAAAAAA
103 SPECIALTY

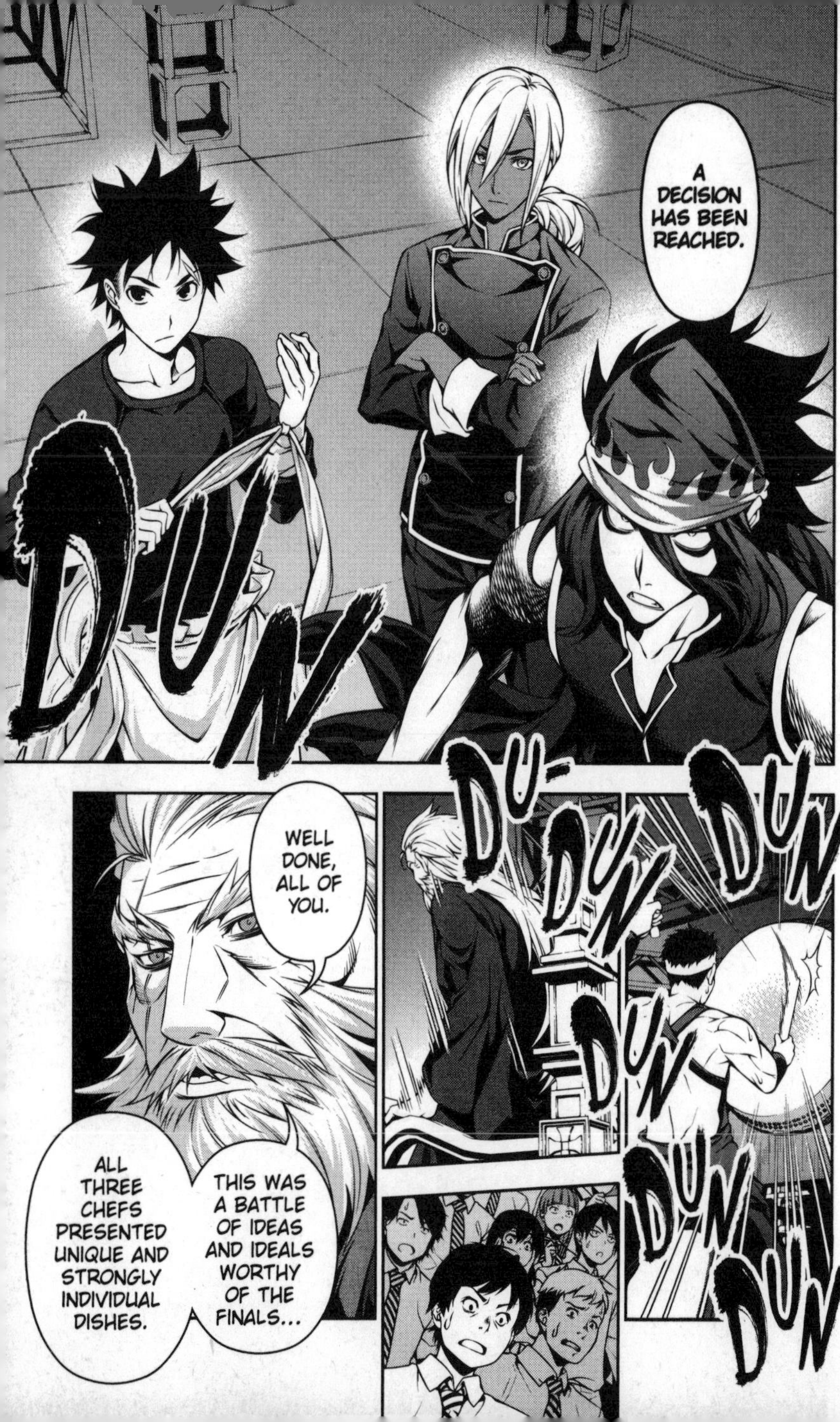
A DECISION HAS BEEN REACHED.
DUN
DU-DUN
DUN
DUN
DUN
DUN
WELL DONE, ALL OF YOU.
THIS WAS A BATTLE OF IDEAS AND IDEALS WORTHY OF THE FINALS...
ALL THREE CHEFS PRESENTED UNIQUE AND STRONGLY INDIVIDUAL DISHES.

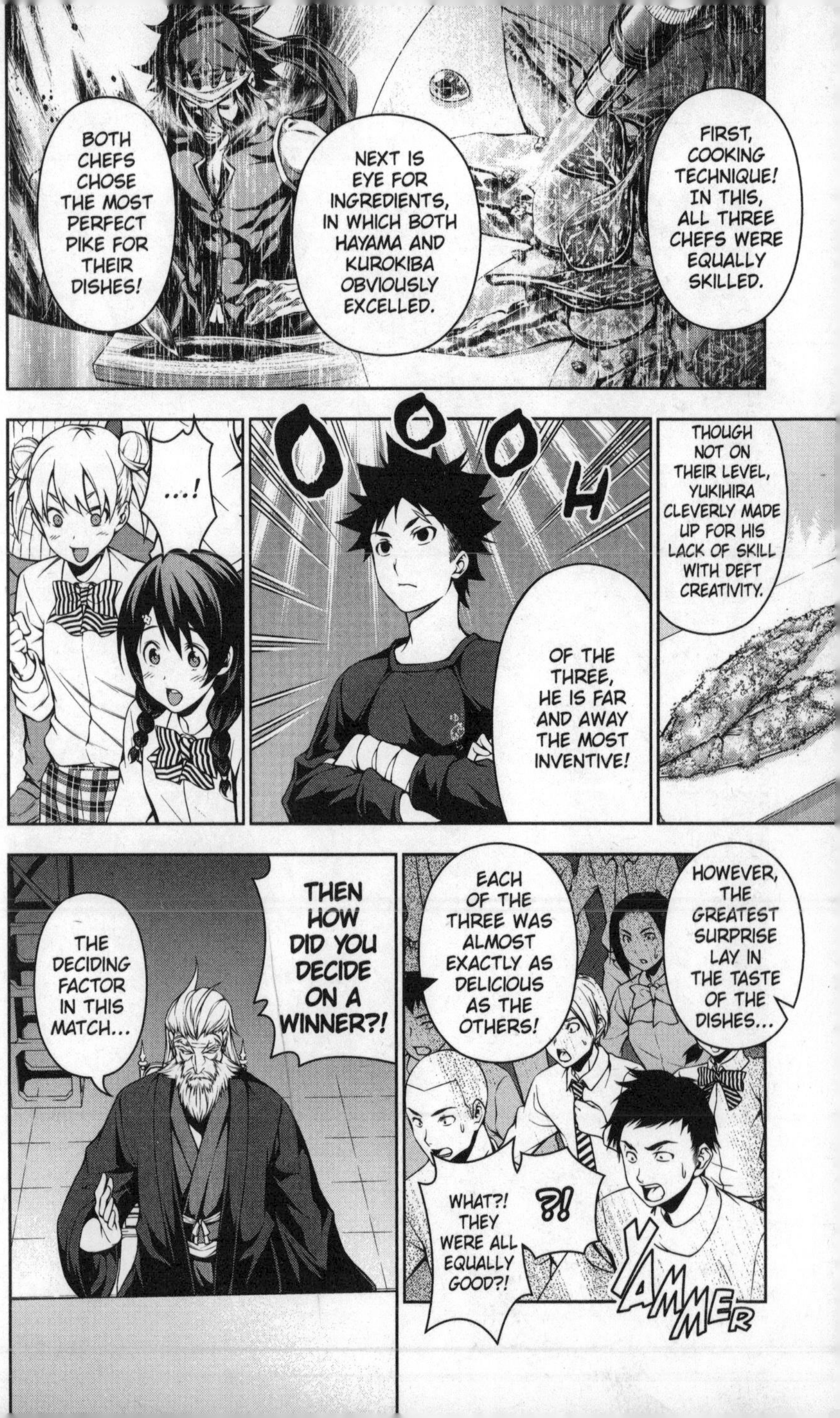
FIRST, COOKING TECHNIQUE! IN THIS, ALL THREE CHEFS WERE EQUALLY SKILLED.
NEXT IS EYE FOR INGREDIENTS, IN WHICH BOTH HAYAMA AND KUROKIBA OBVIOUSLY EXCELLED.
BOTH CHEFS CHOSE THE MOST PERFECT PIKE FOR THEIR DISHES!
THOUGH NOT ON THEIR LEVEL, YUKIHIRA CLEVERLY MADE UP FOR HIS LACK OF SKILL WITH DEFT CREATIVITY.
OOOOH
OF THE THREE, HE IS FAR AND AWAY THE MOST INVENTIVE!
...!
HOWEVER, THE GREATEST SURPRISE LAY IN THE TASTE OF THE DISHES...
EACH OF THE THREE WAS ALMOST EXACTLY AS DELICIOUS AS THE OTHERS!
?!
WHAT?! THEY WERE ALL EQUALLY GOOD?!
YAMMER
THEN HOW DID YOU DECIDE ON A WINNER?!
THE DECIDING FACTOR IN THIS MATCH...

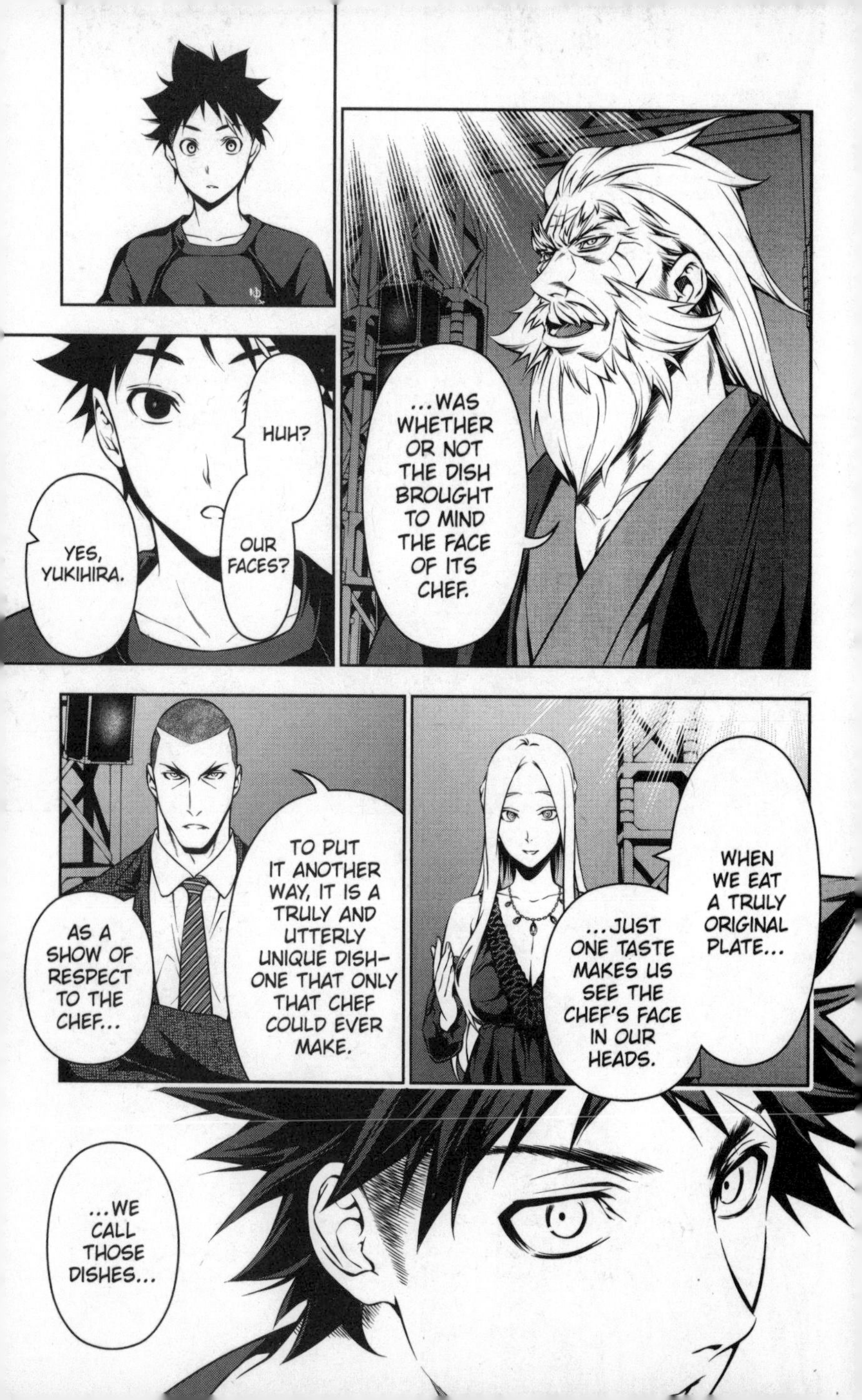
...WAS WHETHER OR NOT THE DISH BROUGHT TO MIND THE FACE OF ITS CHEF.
HUH?
OUR FACES?
YES, YUKIHIRA.
WHEN WE EAT A TRULY ORIGINAL PLATE...
...JUST ONE TASTE MAKES US SEE THE CHEF'S FACE IN OUR HEADS.
TO PUT IT ANOTHER WAY, IT IS A TRULY AND UTTERLY UNIQUE DISH—ONE THAT ONLY THAT CHEF COULD EVER MAKE.
AS A SHOW OF RESPECT TO THE CHEF...
...WE CALL THOSE DISHES...

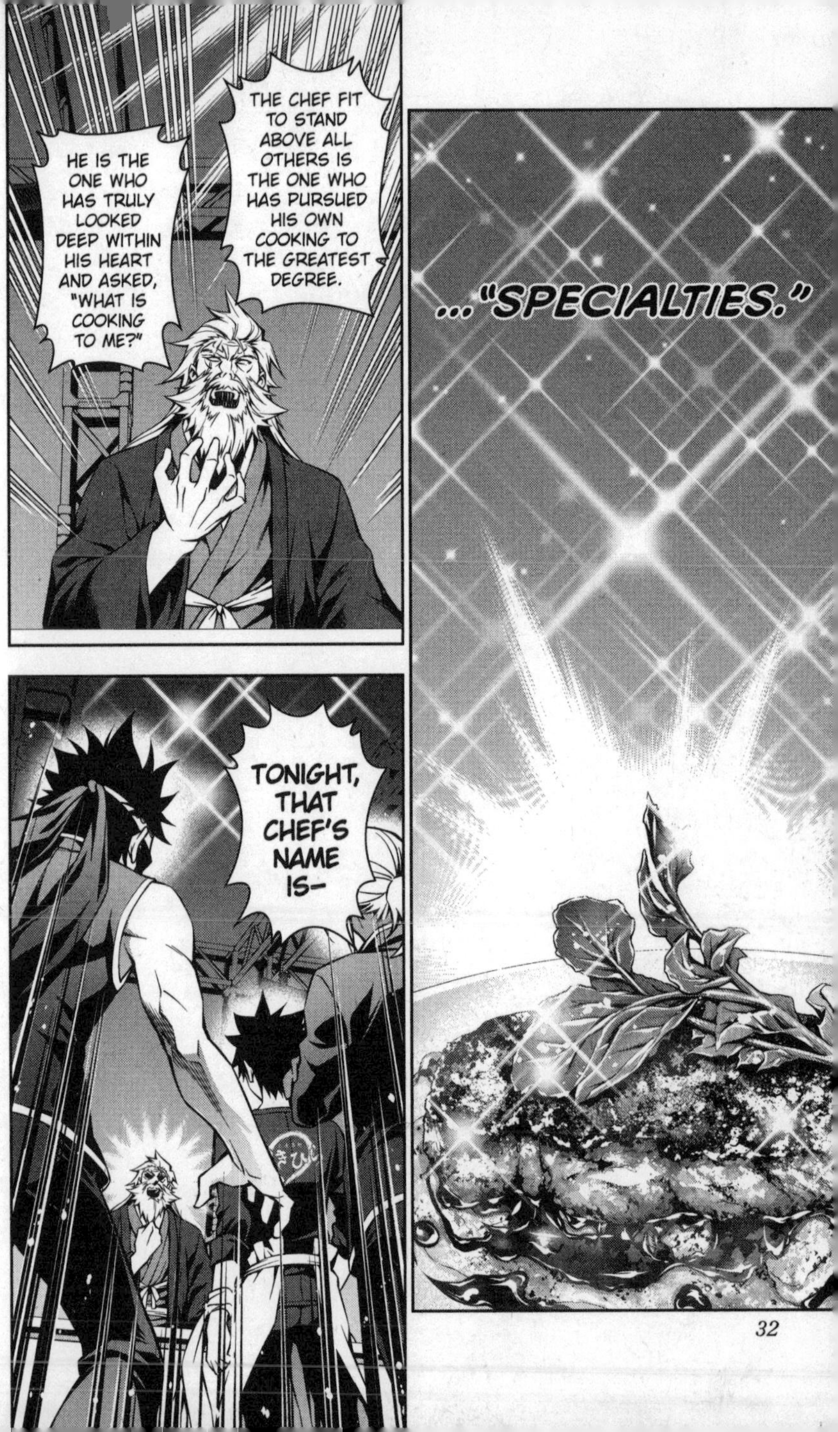
THE CHEF FIT TO STAND ABOVE ALL OTHERS IS THE ONE WHO HAS PURSUED HIS OWN COOKING TO THE GREATEST DEGREE.
HE IS THE ONE WHO HAS TRULY LOOKED DEEP WITHIN HIS HEART AND ASKED, "WHAT IS COOKING TO ME?"
TONIGHT, THAT CHEF'S NAME IS–
..."SPECIALTIES."

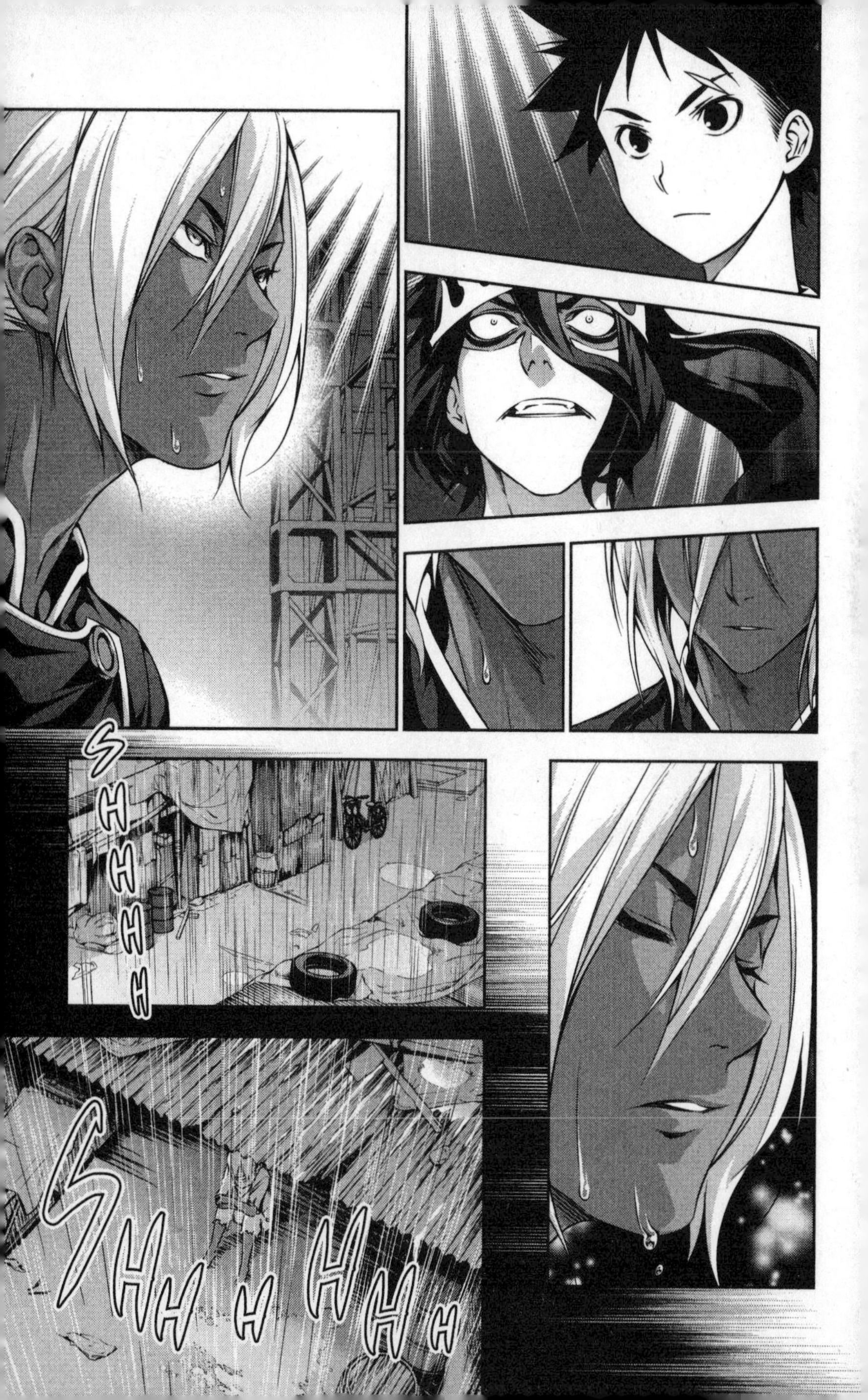
SHHHHH
SHHHHHHH

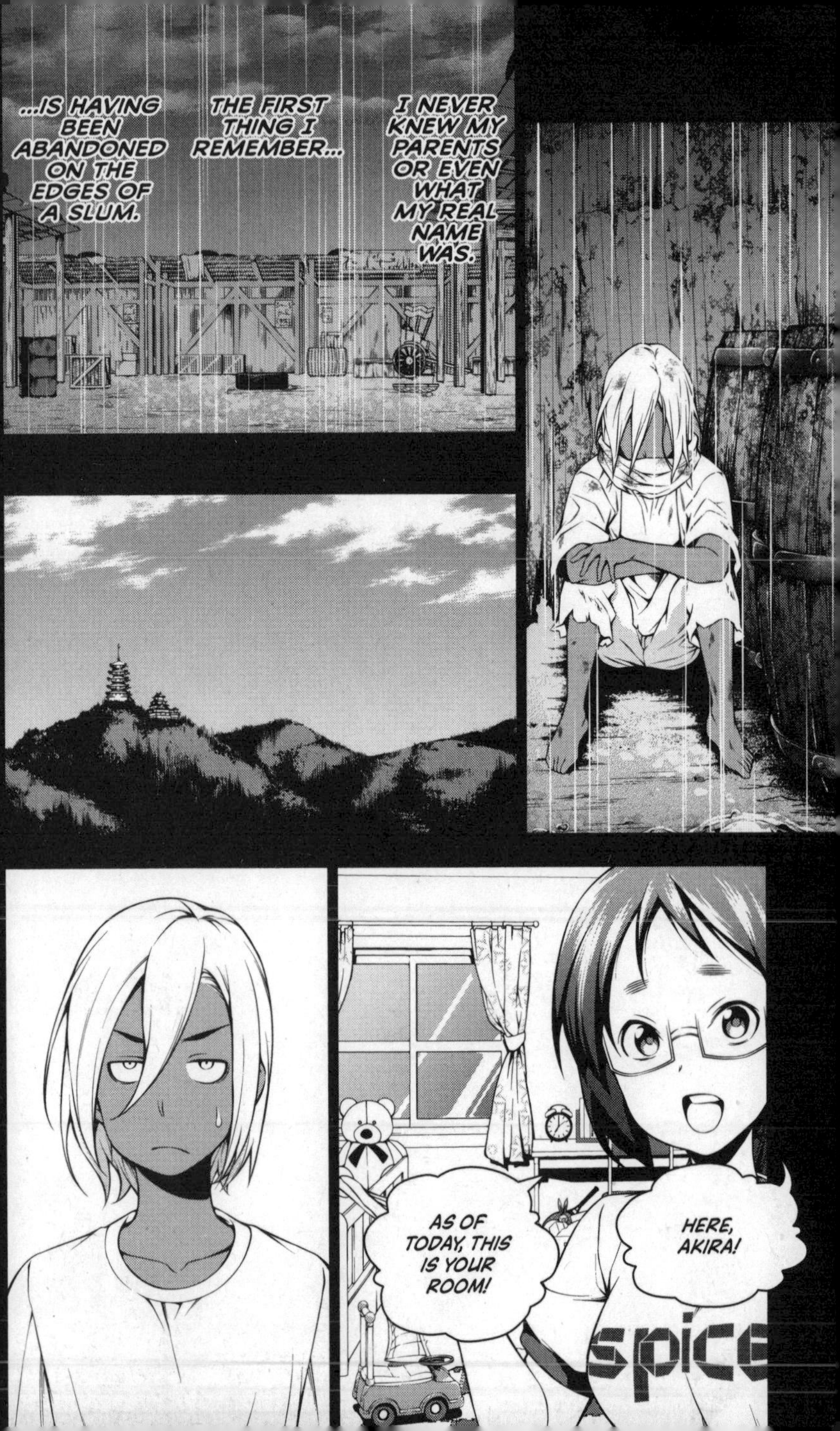
I NEVER KNEW MY PARENTS OR EVEN WHAT MY REAL NAME WAS.
THE FIRST THING I REMEMBER...
...IS HAVING BEEN ABANDONED ON THE EDGES OF A SLUM.
HERE, AKIRA!
spice
AS OF TODAY, THIS IS YOUR ROOM!

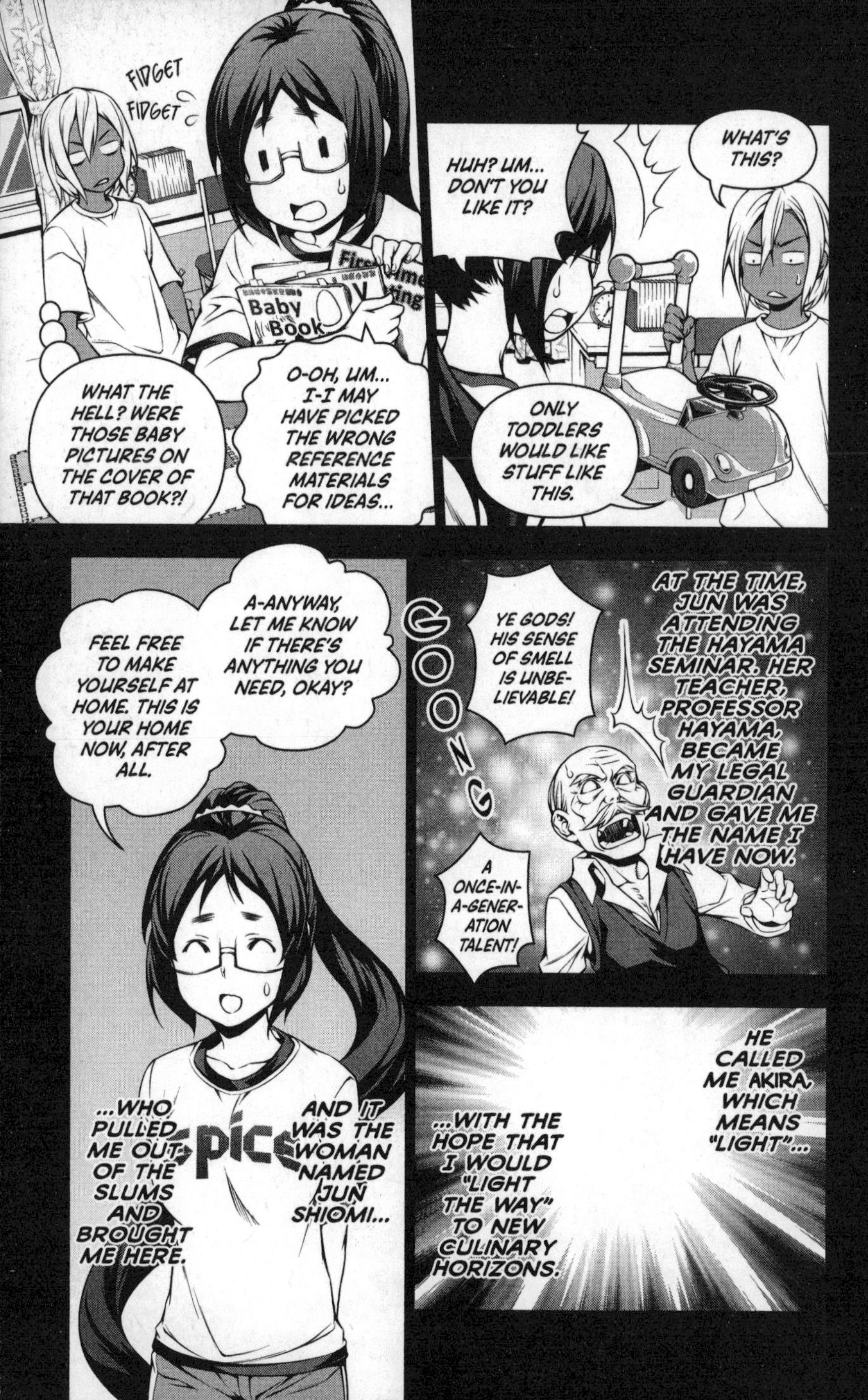
FIDGET
FIDGET
Baby Book
WHAT THE HELL? WERE THOSE BABY PICTURES ON THE COVER OF THAT BOOK?!
O-OH, UM... I-I MAY HAVE PICKED THE WRONG REFERENCE MATERIALS FOR IDEAS...
WHAT'S THIS?
HUH? UM... DON'T YOU LIKE IT?
ONLY TODDLERS WOULD LIKE STUFF LIKE THIS.
A-ANYWAY, LET ME KNOW IF THERE'S ANYTHING YOU NEED, OKAY?
FEEL FREE TO MAKE YOURSELF AT HOME. THIS IS YOUR HOME NOW, AFTER ALL.
AND IT WAS THE WOMAN NAMED JUN SHIOMI...
...WHO PULLED ME OUT OF THE SLUMS AND BROUGHT ME HERE.
Spice
AT THE TIME, JUN WAS ATTENDING THE HAYAMA SEMINAR. HER TEACHER, PROFESSOR HAYAMA, BECAME MY LEGAL GUARDIAN AND GAVE ME THE NAME I HAVE NOW.
GOOONG
YE GODS! HIS SENSE OF SMELL IS UNBE-LIEVABLE!
A ONCE-IN-A-GENER-ATION TALENT!
HE CALLED ME AKIRA, WHICH MEANS "LIGHT"...
...WITH THE HOPE THAT I WOULD "LIGHT THE WAY" TO NEW CULINARY HORIZONS.

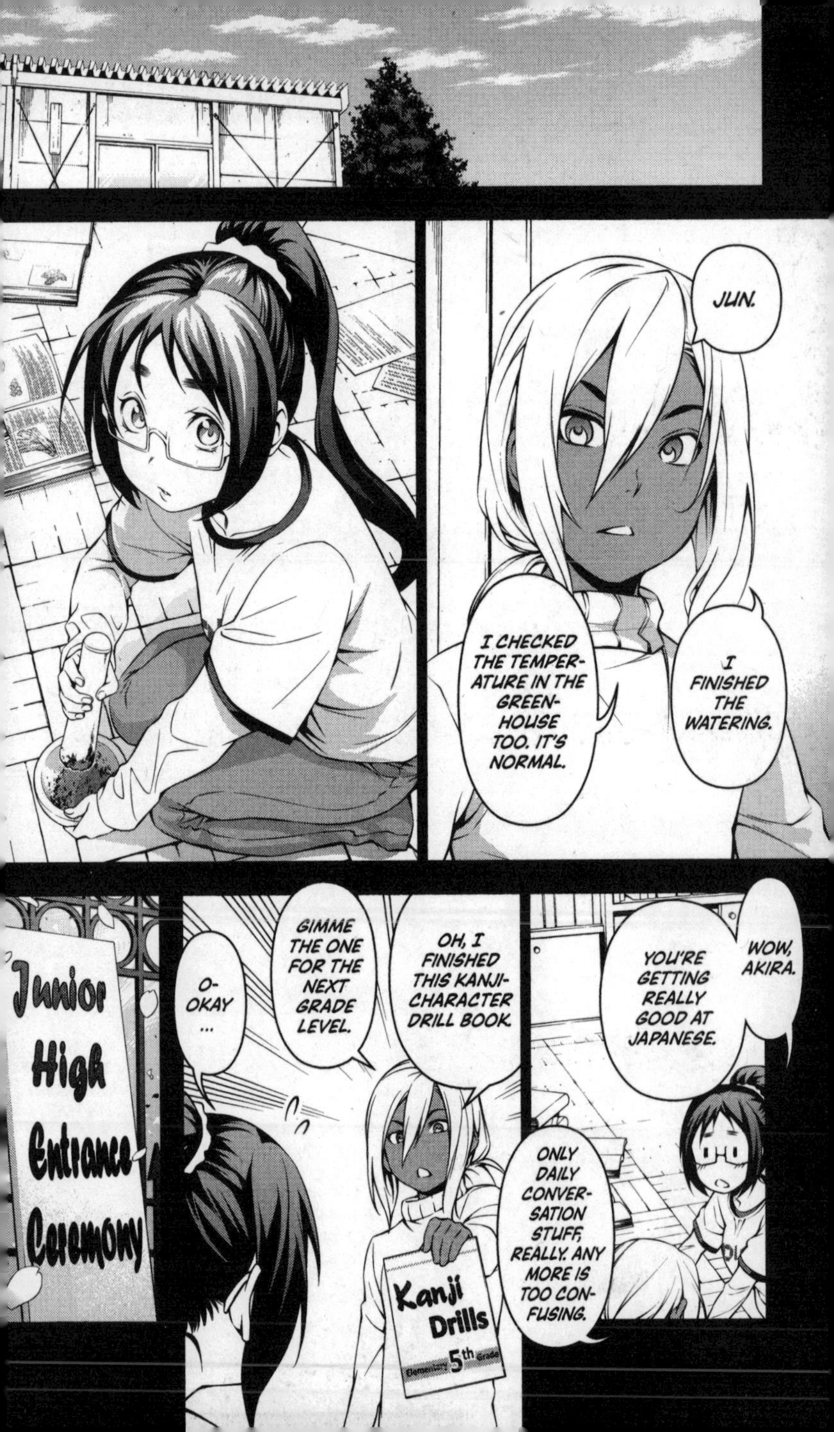

JUN.
I FINISHED THE WATERING.
I CHECKED THE TEMPERATURE IN THE GREENHOUSE TOO. IT'S NORMAL.
WOW, AKIRA.
YOU'RE GETTING REALLY GOOD AT JAPANESE.
ONLY DAILY CONVERSATION STUFF, REALLY. ANY MORE IS TOO CONFUSING.
OH, I FINISHED THIS KANJI-CHARACTER DRILL BOOK.
GIMME THE ONE FOR THE NEXT GRADE LEVEL.
O-OKAY...
Kanji Drills
Elementary 5th Grade
Junior High Entrance Ceremony

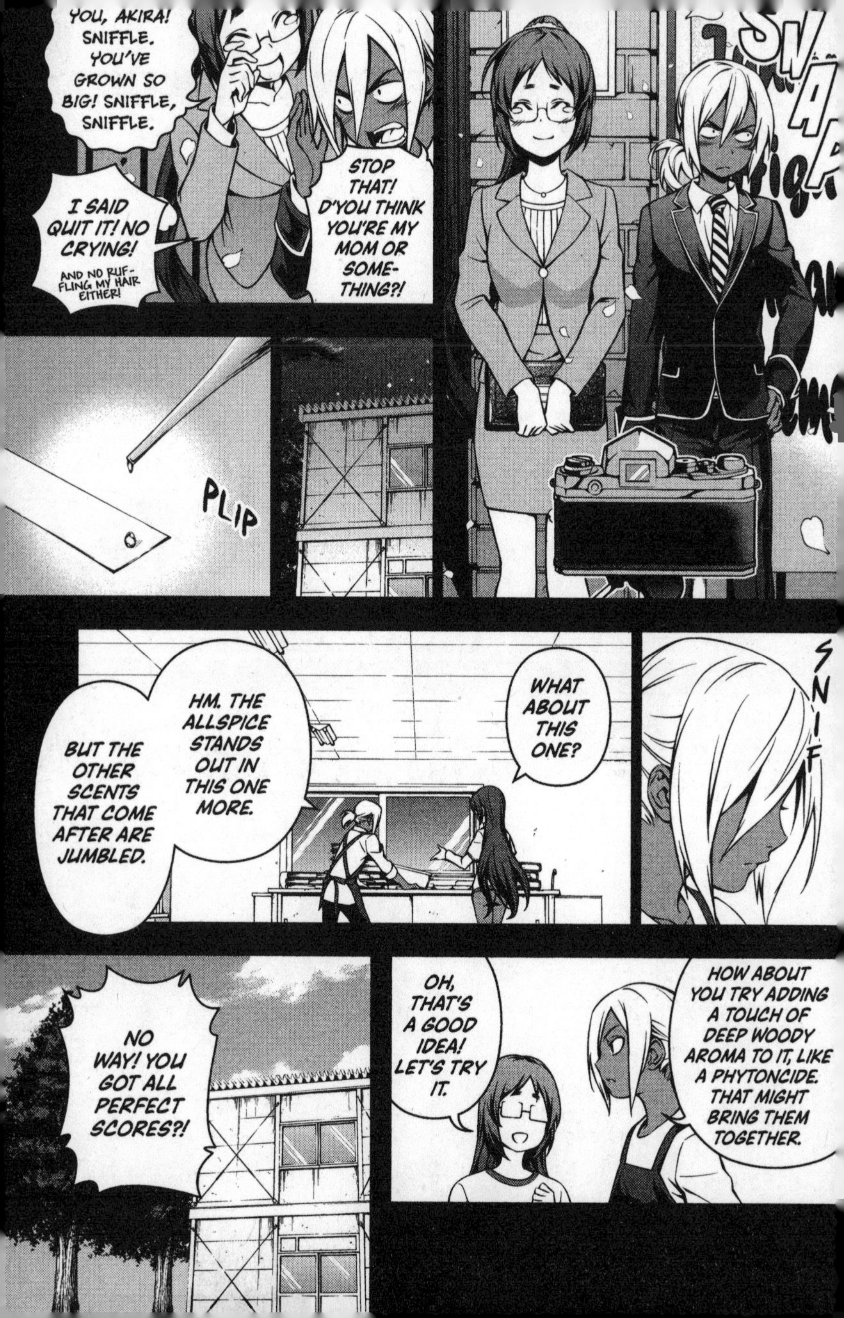
YOU, AKIRA! SNIFFLE. YOU'VE GROWN SO BIG! SNIFFLE, SNIFFLE.
STOP THAT! D'YOU THINK YOU'RE MY MOM OR SOME-THING?!
I SAID QUIT IT! NO CRYING!
AND NO RUF-FLING MY HAIR EITHER!
PLIP
SNIF
WHAT ABOUT THIS ONE?
HM. THE ALLSPICE STANDS OUT IN THIS ONE MORE.
BUT THE OTHER SCENTS THAT COME AFTER ARE JUMBLED.
HOW ABOUT YOU TRY ADDING A TOUCH OF DEEP WOODY AROMA TO IT, LIKE A PHYTONCIDE. THAT MIGHT BRING THEM TOGETHER.
OH, THAT'S A GOOD IDEA! LET'S TRY IT.
NO WAY! YOU GOT ALL PERFECT SCORES?!

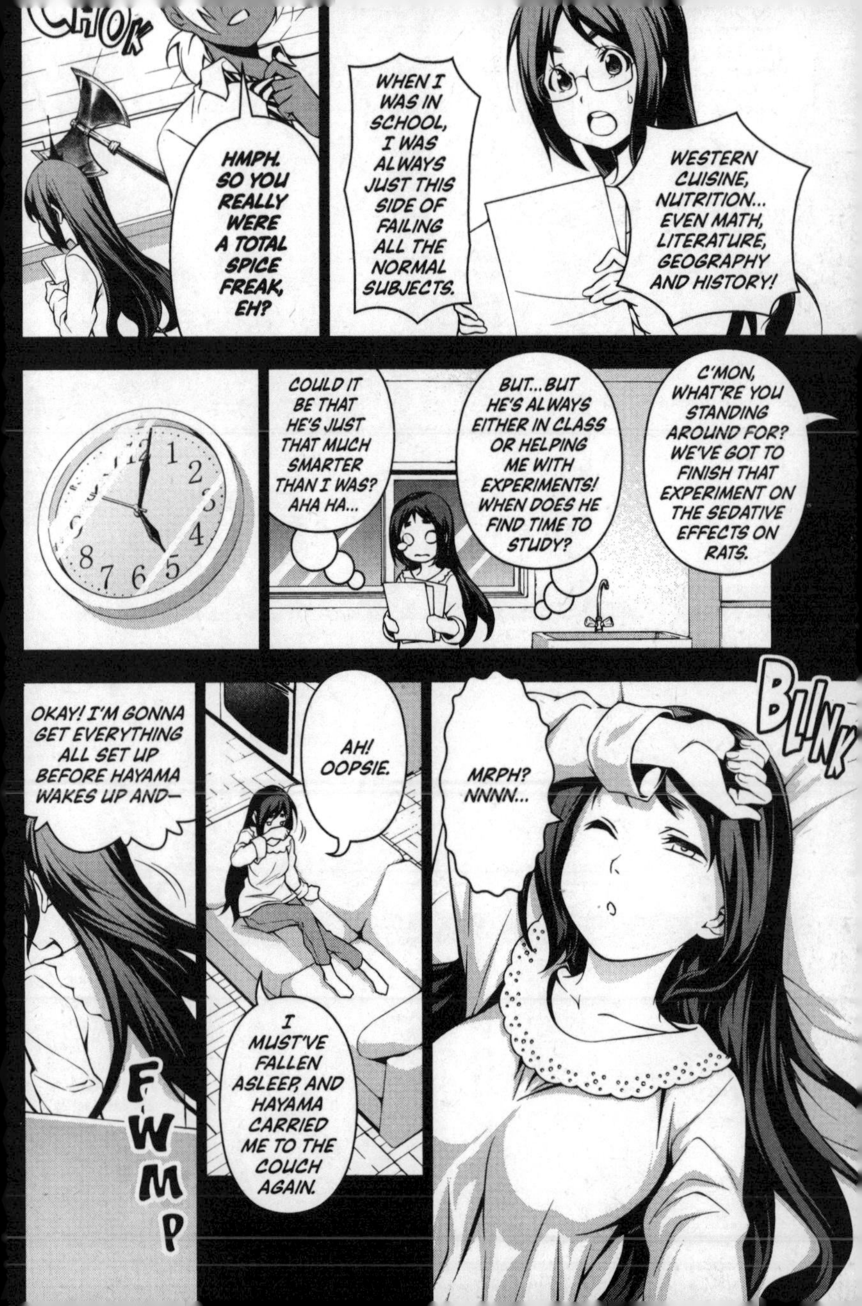
WHEN I WAS IN SCHOOL, I WAS ALWAYS JUST THIS SIDE OF FAILING ALL THE NORMAL SUBJECTS.
WESTERN CUISINE, NUTRITION... EVEN MATH, LITERATURE, GEOGRAPHY AND HISTORY!
CHOK
HMPH. SO YOU REALLY WERE A TOTAL SPICE FREAK, EH?
C'MON, WHAT'RE YOU STANDING AROUND FOR? WE'VE GOT TO FINISH THAT EXPERIMENT ON THE SEDATIVE EFFECTS ON RATS.
BUT...BUT HE'S ALWAYS EITHER IN CLASS OR HELPING ME WITH EXPERIMENTS! WHEN DOES HE FIND TIME TO STUDY?
COULD IT BE THAT HE'S JUST THAT MUCH SMARTER THAN I WAS? AHA HA...
BLINK
MRPH? NNNN...
AH! OOPSIE.
I MUST'VE FALLEN ASLEEP, AND HAYAMA CARRIED ME TO THE COUCH AGAIN.
OKAY! I'M GONNA GET EVERYTHING ALL SET UP BEFORE HAYAMA WAKES UP AND—
FWMP

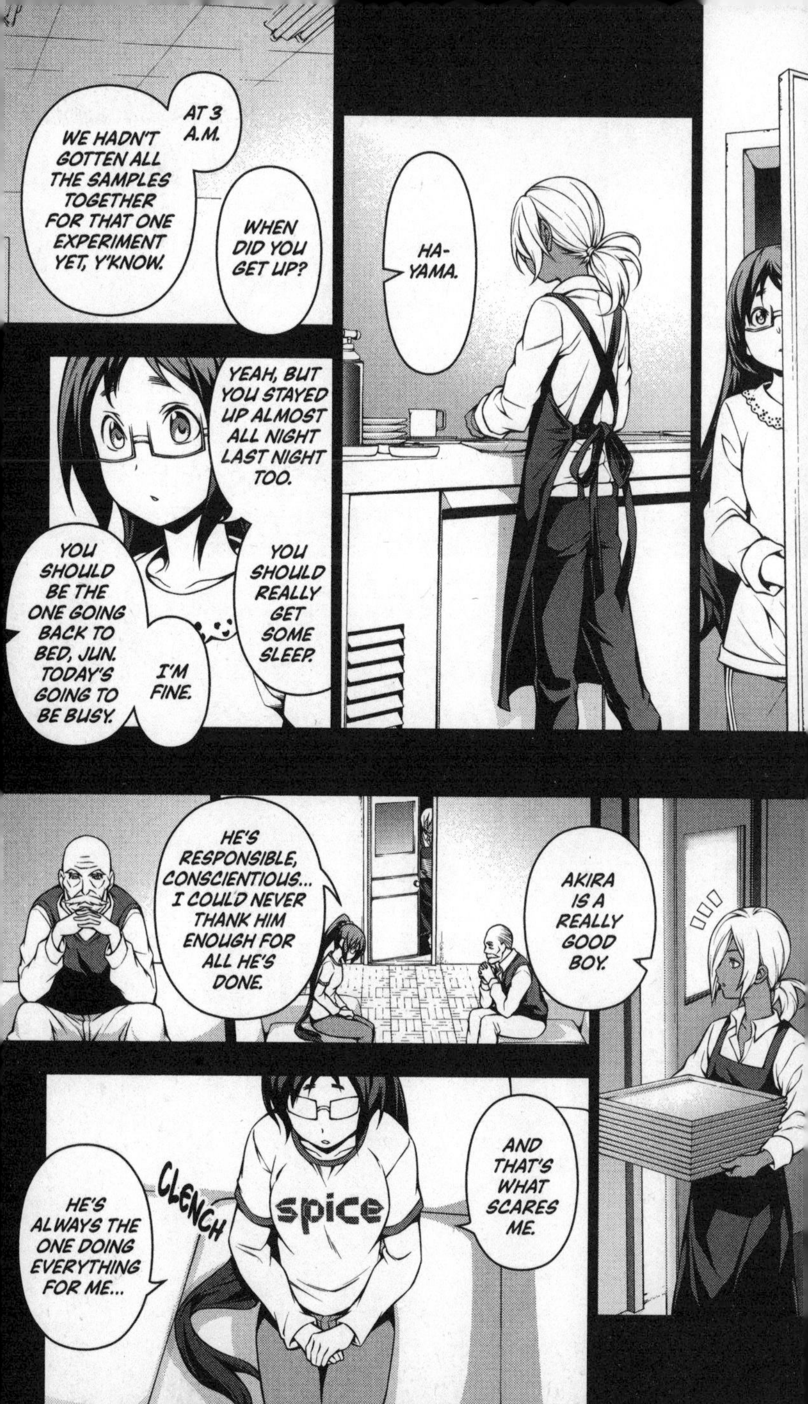
HA-YAMA.
WHEN DID YOU GET UP?
AT 3 A.M.
WE HADN'T GOTTEN ALL THE SAMPLES TOGETHER FOR THAT ONE EXPERIMENT YET, Y'KNOW.
YEAH, BUT YOU STAYED UP ALMOST ALL NIGHT LAST NIGHT TOO.
YOU SHOULD REALLY GET SOME SLEEP.
I'M FINE.
YOU SHOULD BE THE ONE GOING BACK TO BED, JUN. TODAY'S GOING TO BE BUSY.
AKIRA IS A REALLY GOOD BOY.
HE'S RESPONSIBLE, CONSCIENTIOUS... I COULD NEVER THANK HIM ENOUGH FOR ALL HE'S DONE.
AND THAT'S WHAT SCARES ME.
CLENCH
HE'S ALWAYS THE ONE DOING EVERYTHING FOR ME...

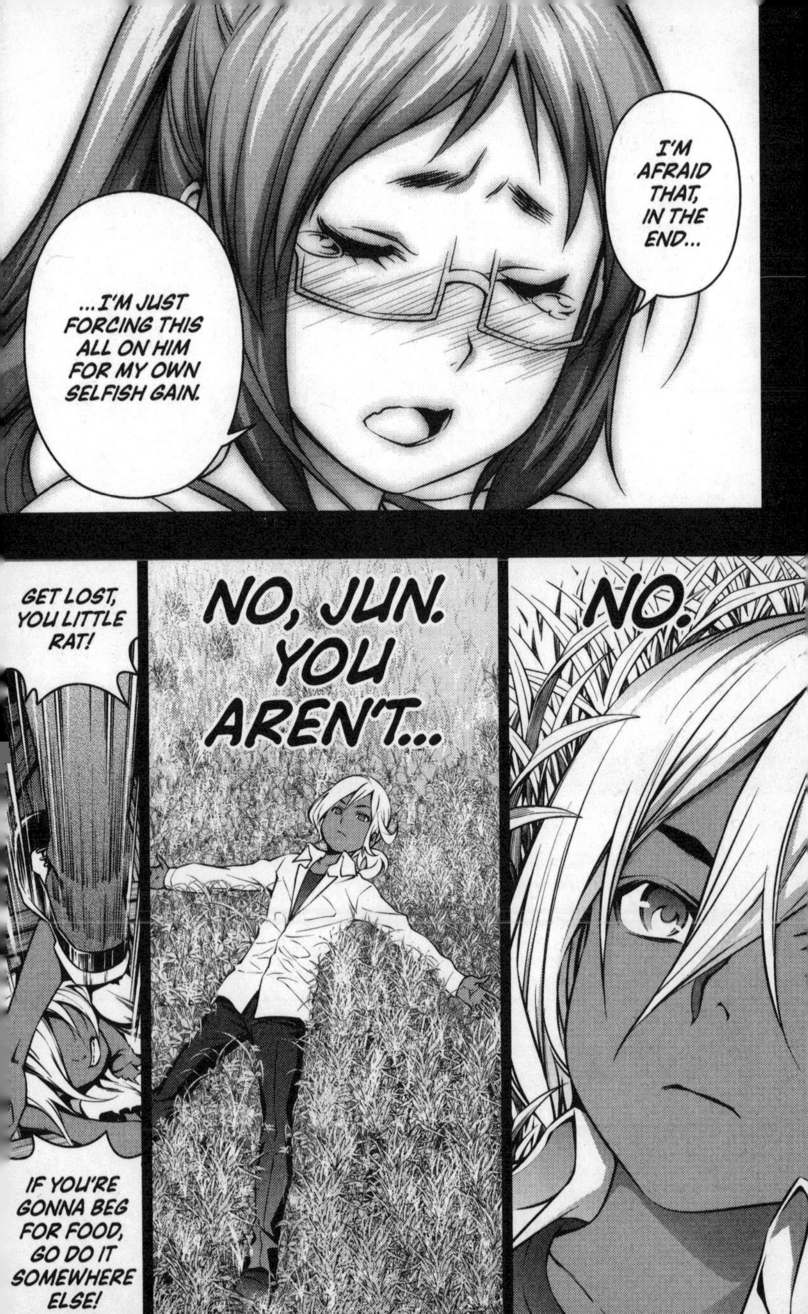
I'M AFRAID THAT, IN THE END...
...I'M JUST FORCING THIS ALL ON HIM FOR MY OWN SELFISH GAIN.
NO.
NO, JUN. YOU AREN'T...
GET LOST, YOU LITTLE RAT!
IF YOU'RE GONNA BEG FOR FOOD, GO DO IT SOMEWHERE ELSE!

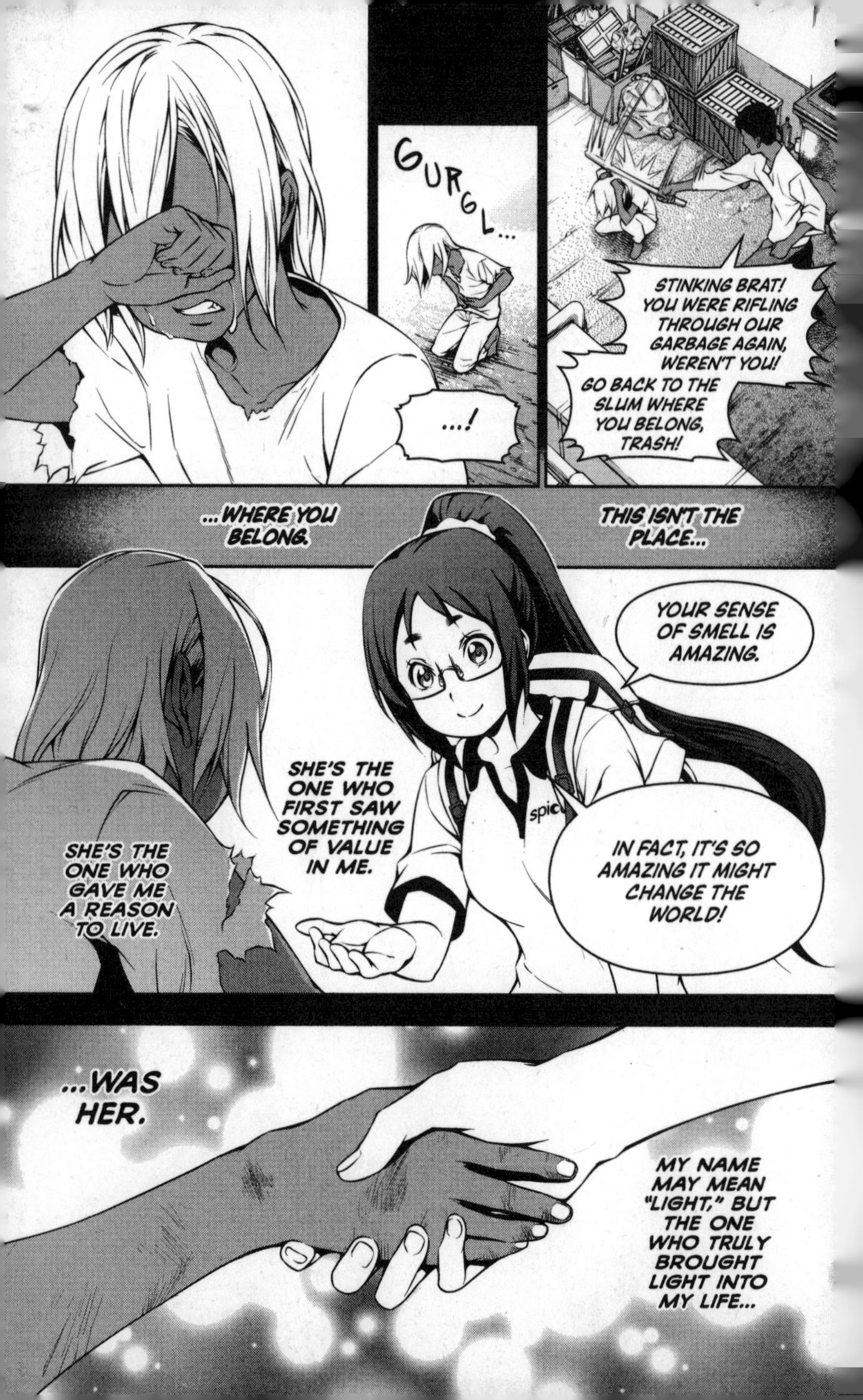
STINKING BRAT! YOU WERE RIFLING THROUGH OUR GARBAGE AGAIN, WEREN'T YOU!
GO BACK TO THE SLUM WHERE YOU BELONG, TRASH!
GURGL...
...!
THIS ISN'T THE PLACE...
...WHERE YOU BELONG.
YOUR SENSE OF SMELL IS AMAZING.
IN FACT, IT'S SO AMAZING IT MIGHT CHANGE THE WORLD!
SHE'S THE ONE WHO FIRST SAW SOMETHING OF VALUE IN ME.
SHE'S THE ONE WHO GAVE ME A REASON TO LIVE.
MY NAME MAY MEAN "LIGHT," BUT THE ONE WHO TRULY BROUGHT LIGHT INTO MY LIFE...
...WAS HER.

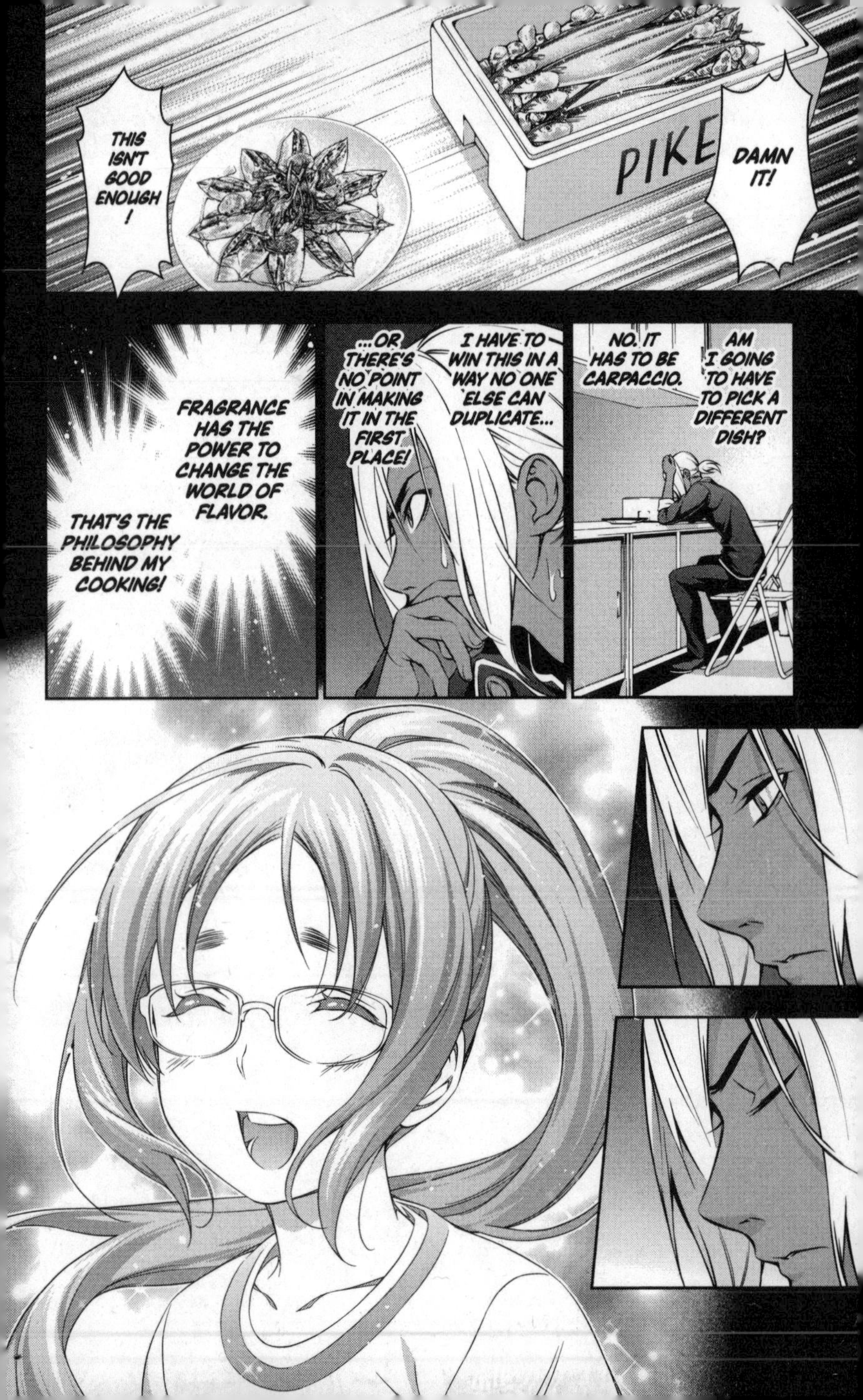
PIKE
DAMN IT!
THIS ISN'T GOOD ENOUGH!
AM I GOING TO HAVE TO PICK A DIFFERENT DISH?
NO. IT HAS TO BE CARPACCIO.
I HAVE TO WIN THIS IN A WAY NO ONE ELSE CAN DUPLICATE...
...OR THERE'S NO POINT IN MAKING IT IN THE FIRST PLACE!
FRAGRANCE HAS THE POWER TO CHANGE THE WORLD OF FLAVOR.
THAT'S THE PHILOSOPHY BEHIND MY COOKING!

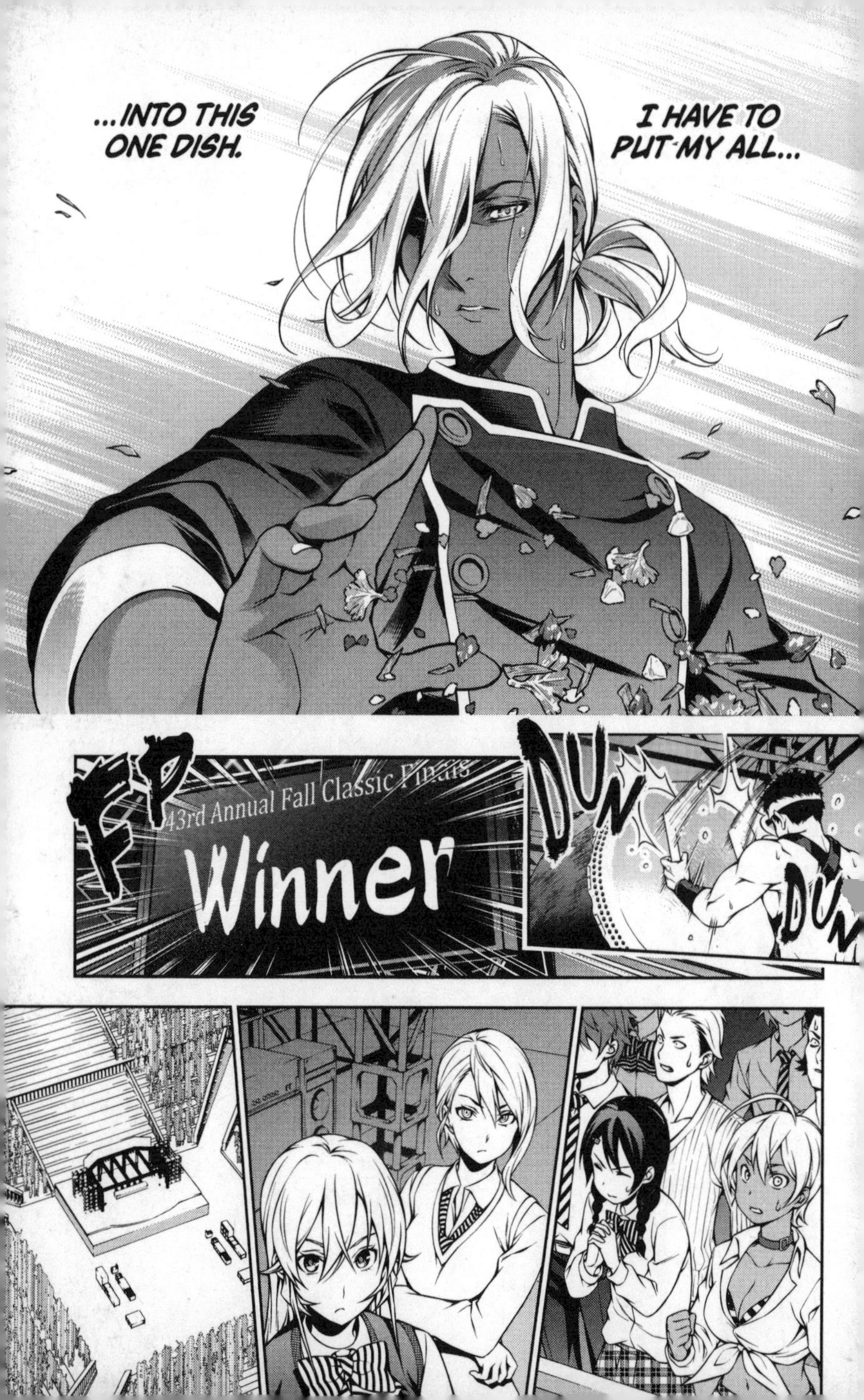
I HAVE TO PUT MY ALL...
...INTO THIS ONE DISH.
DUN
DUN
43rd Annual Fall Classic
Winner

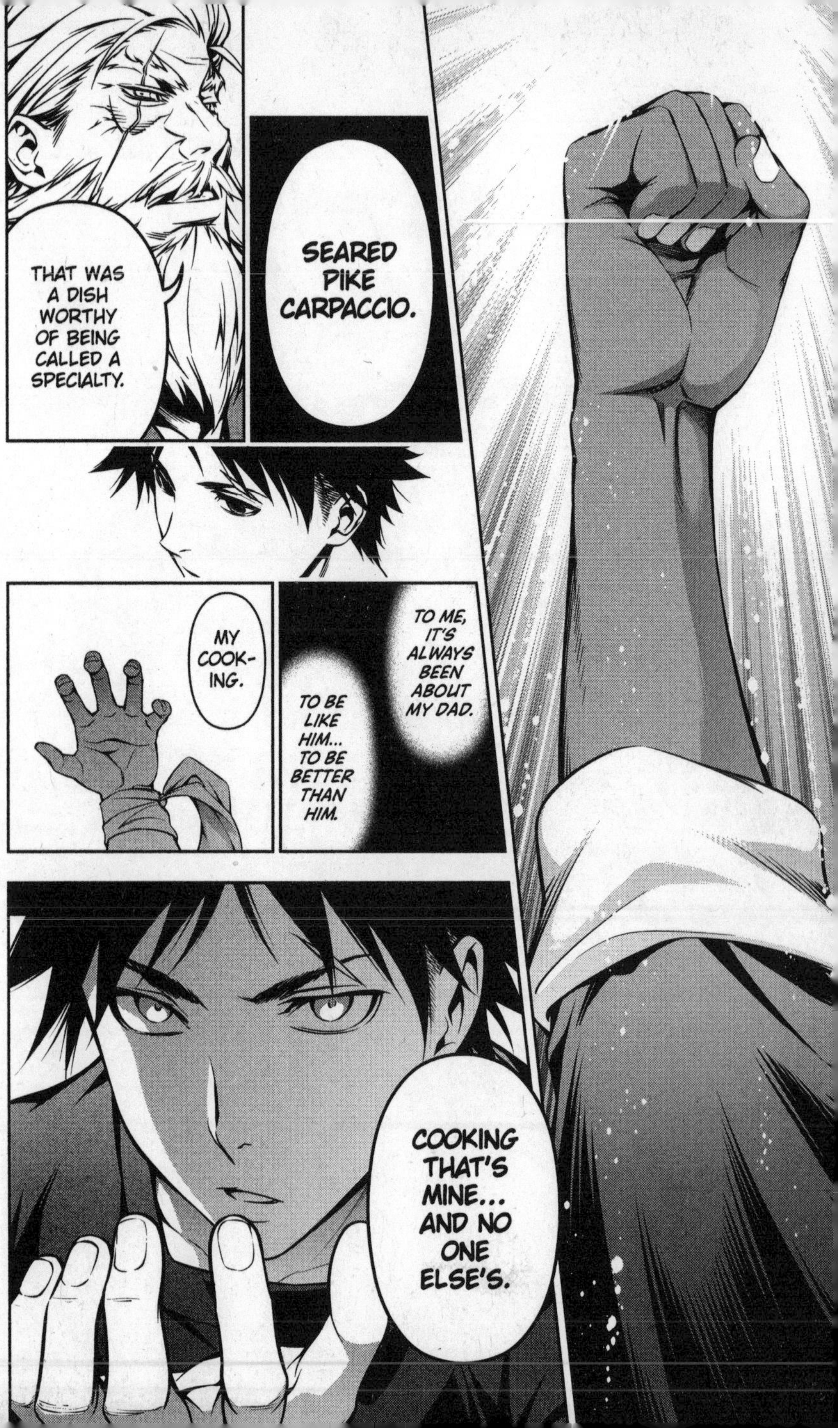
SEARED PIKE CARPACCIO.
THAT WAS A DISH WORTHY OF BEING CALLED A SPECIALTY.
TO ME, IT'S ALWAYS BEEN ABOUT MY DAD.
TO BE LIKE HIM... TO BE BETTER THAN HIM.
MY COOKING.
COOKING THAT'S MINE... AND NO ONE ELSE'S.

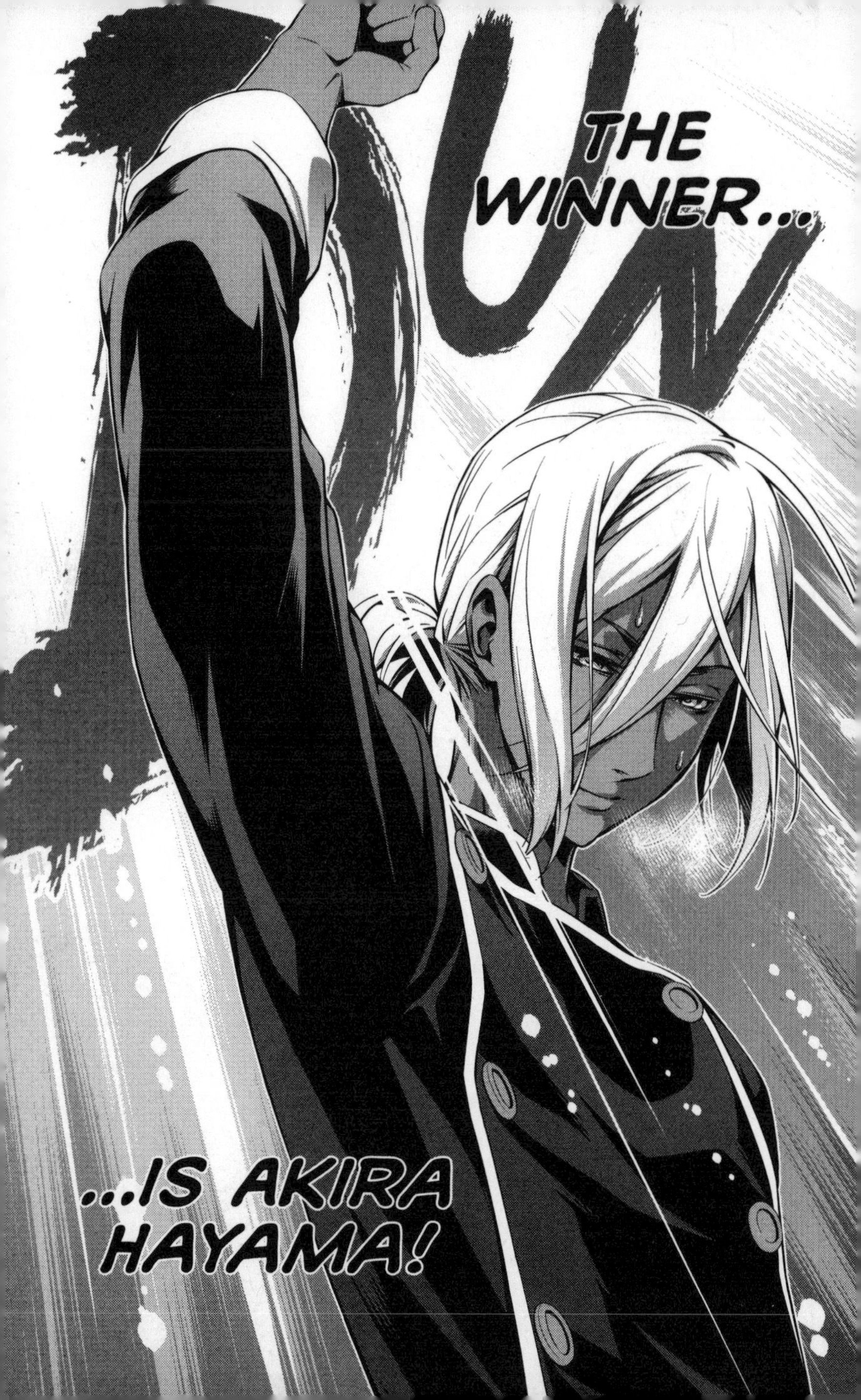
THE WINNER...
...IS AKIRA HAYAMA!

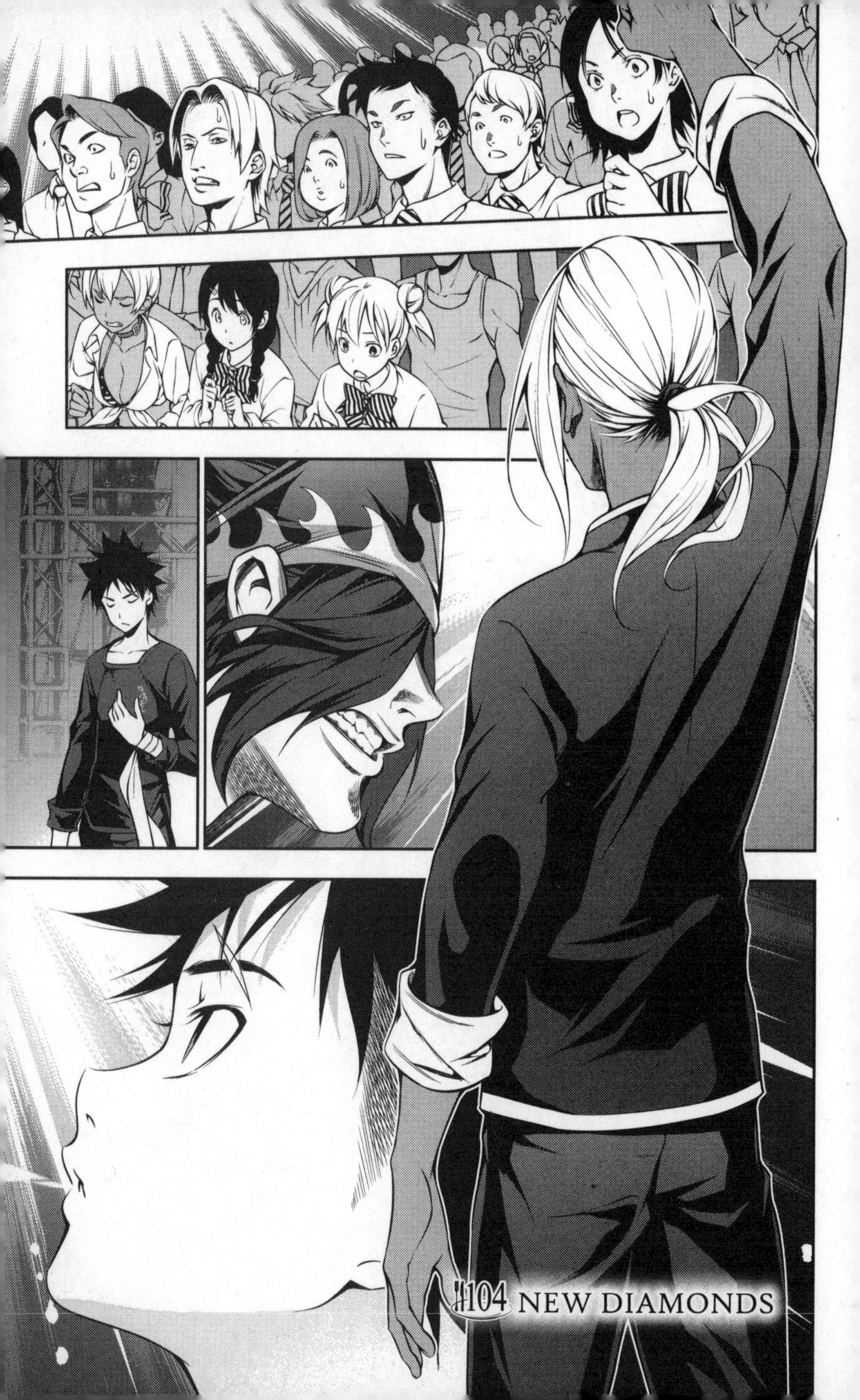
#104 NEW DIAMONDS

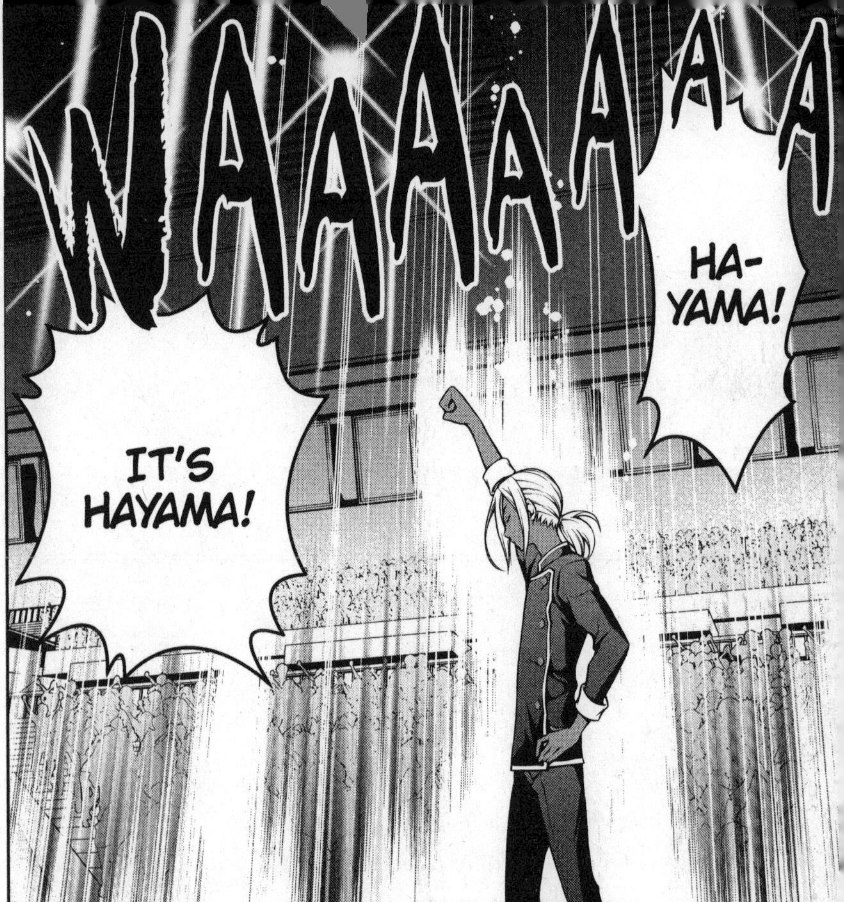
WAAAAAAA
HA-YAMA!
IT'S HAYAMA!

104 NEW DIAMONDS

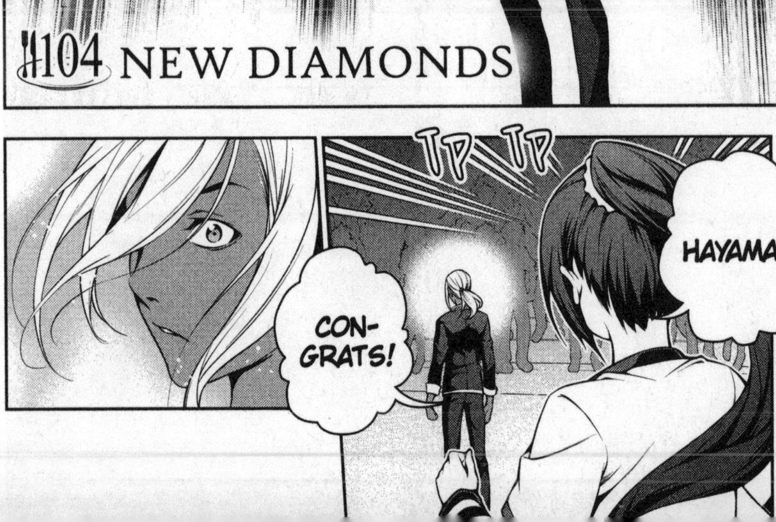
TP TP
HAYAMA!
CON-GRATS!

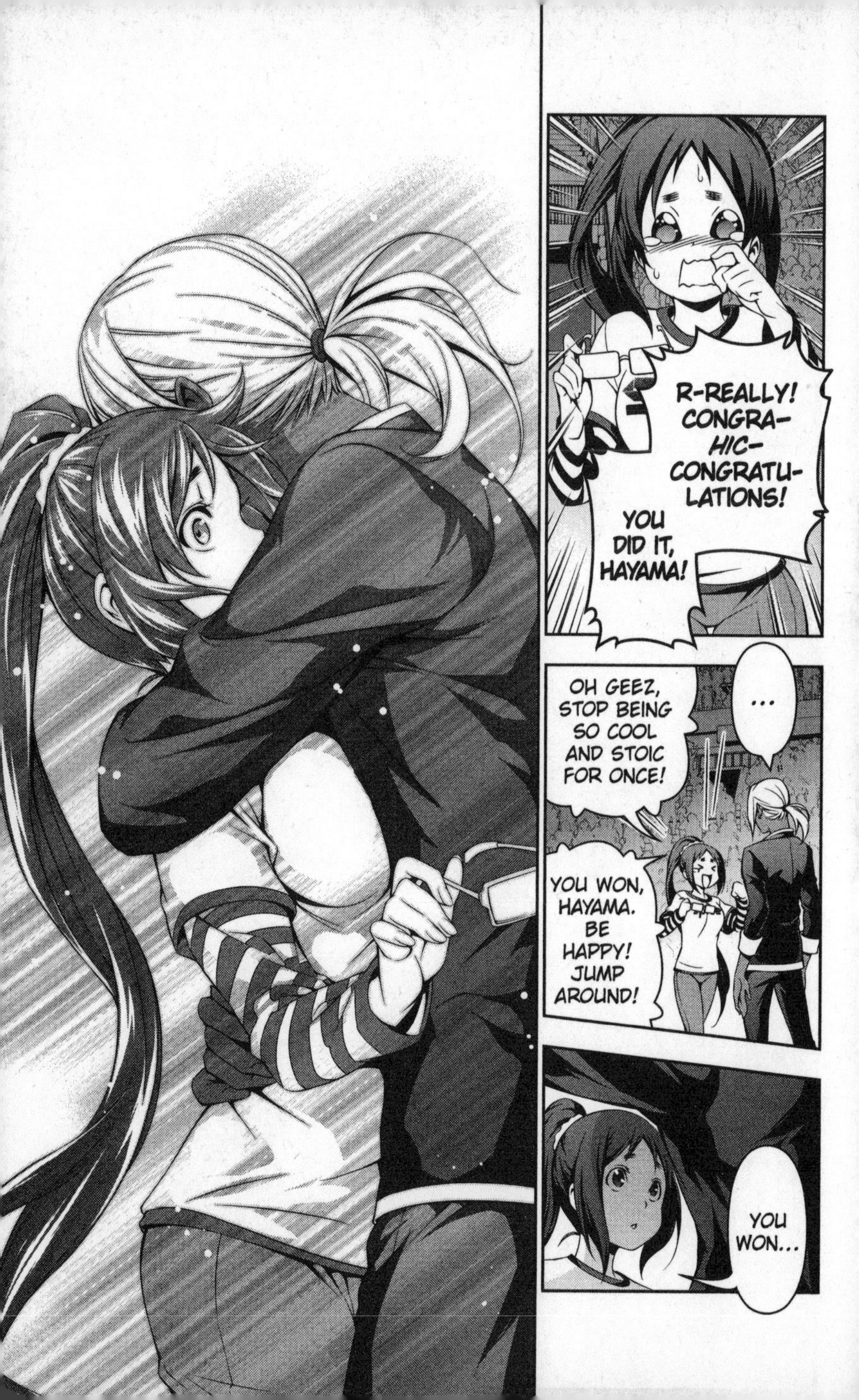
R-REALLY! CONGRA- HIC- CONGRATU- LATIONS!
YOU DID IT, HAYAMA!
...
OH GEEZ, STOP BEING SO COOL AND STOIC FOR ONCE!
YOU WON, HAYAMA. BE HAPPY! JUMP AROUND!
YOU WON...

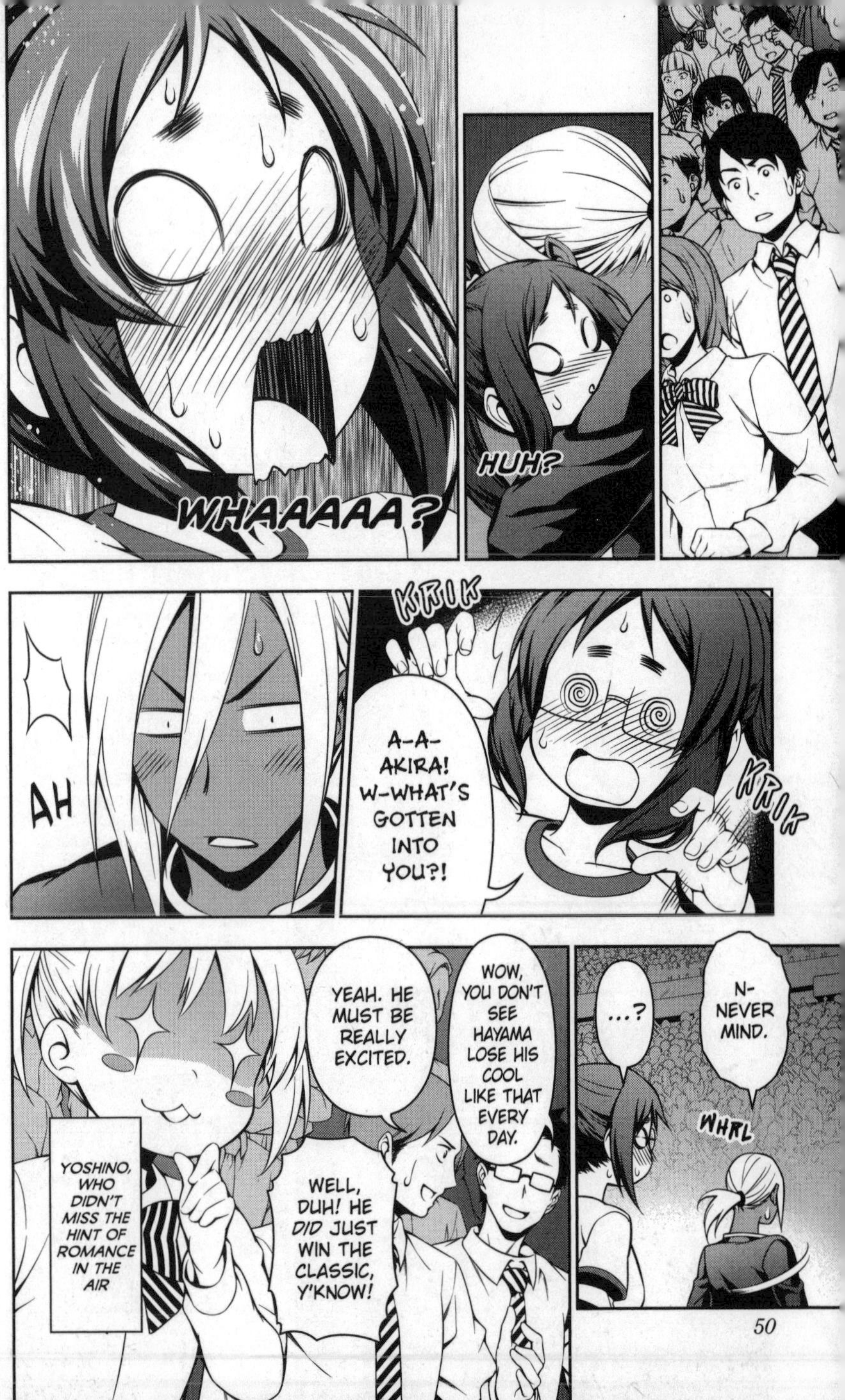
HUH?
WHAAAAAA?
KRIK
A-A-AKIRA! W-WHAT'S GOTTEN INTO YOU?!
KRIK
AH
N-NEVER MIND.
...?
WHRL
WOW, YOU DON'T SEE HAYAMA LOSE HIS COOL LIKE THAT EVERY DAY.
YEAH. HE MUST BE REALLY EXCITED.
WELL, DUH! HE *DID* JUST WIN THE CLASSIC, Y'KNOW!
YOSHINO, WHO DIDN'T MISS THE HINT OF ROMANCE IN THE AIR

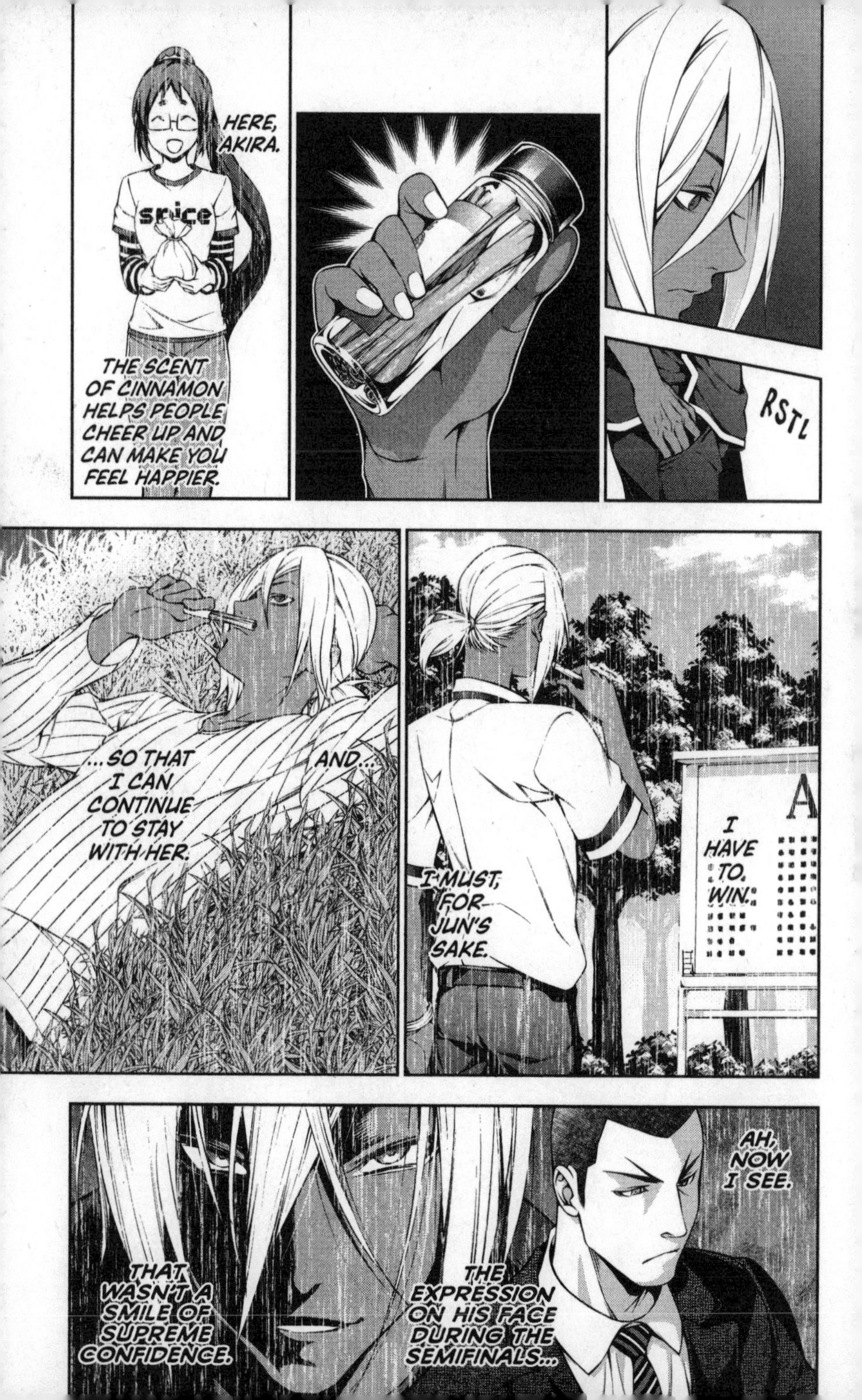
RSTL
HERE, AKIRA.
THE SCENT OF CINNAMON HELPS PEOPLE CHEER UP AND CAN MAKE YOU FEEL HAPPIER.
I HAVE TO WIN.
I MUST, FOR JUN'S SAKE.
AND...
...SO THAT I CAN CONTINUE TO STAY WITH HER.
AH, NOW I SEE.
THE EXPRESSION ON HIS FACE DURING THE SEMIFINALS...
THAT WASN'T A SMILE OF SUPREME CONFIDENCE.

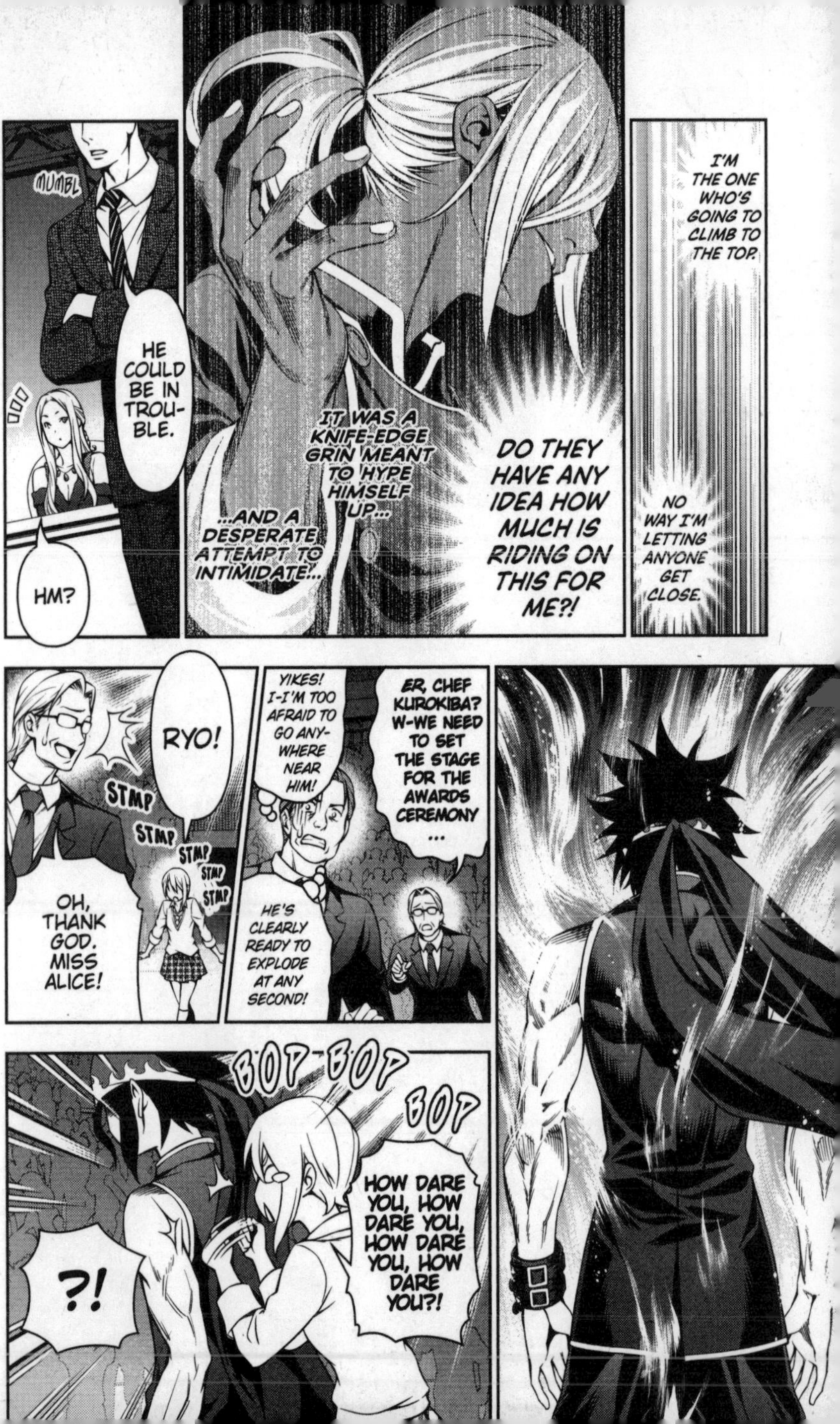
I'M THE ONE WHO'S GOING TO CLIMB TO THE TOP.
NO WAY I'M LETTING ANYONE GET CLOSE.
DO THEY HAVE ANY IDEA HOW MUCH IS RIDING ON THIS FOR ME?!
IT WAS A KNIFE-EDGE GRIN MEANT TO HYPE HIMSELF UP...
...AND A DESPERATE ATTEMPT TO INTIMIDATE...
MUMBL
HE COULD BE IN TROU-BLE.
HM?
ER, CHEF KUROKIBA? W-WE NEED TO SET THE STAGE FOR THE AWARDS CEREMONY...
YIKES! I-I'M TOO AFRAID TO GO ANY-WHERE NEAR HIM!
HE'S CLEARLY READY TO EXPLODE AT ANY SECOND!
RYO!
STMP STMP STMP STMP STMP
OH, THANK GOD. MISS ALICE!
BOP-BOP
BOP
HOW DARE YOU, HOW DARE YOU, HOW DARE YOU, HOW DARE YOU?!
?!

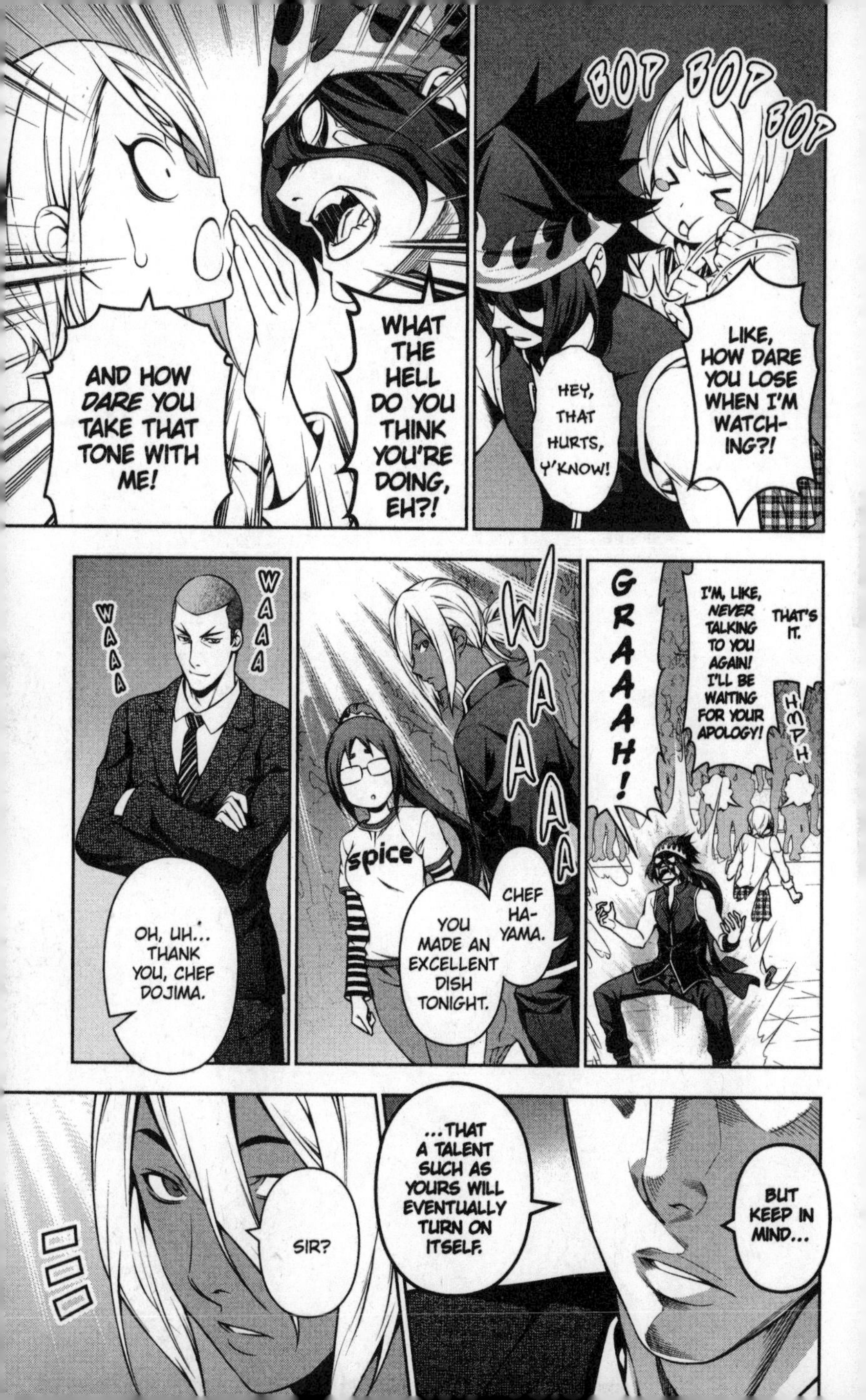
BOP BOP BOP BOP
LIKE, HOW DARE YOU LOSE WHEN I'M WATCHING?!
HEY, THAT HURTS, Y'KNOW!
WHAT THE HELL DO YOU THINK YOU'RE DOING, EH?!
AND HOW DARE YOU TAKE THAT TONE WITH ME!
THAT'S IT.
I'M, LIKE, NEVER TALKING TO YOU AGAIN! I'LL BE WAITING FOR YOUR APOLOGY!
HMPH
GRAAAAH!
WAAAAAA
CHEF HAYAMA.
YOU MADE AN EXCELLENT DISH TONIGHT.
spice
WAAAA
WAAAA
OH, UH... THANK YOU, CHEF DOJIMA.
BUT KEEP IN MIND...
...THAT A TALENT SUCH AS YOURS WILL EVENTUALLY TURN ON ITSELF.
SIR?

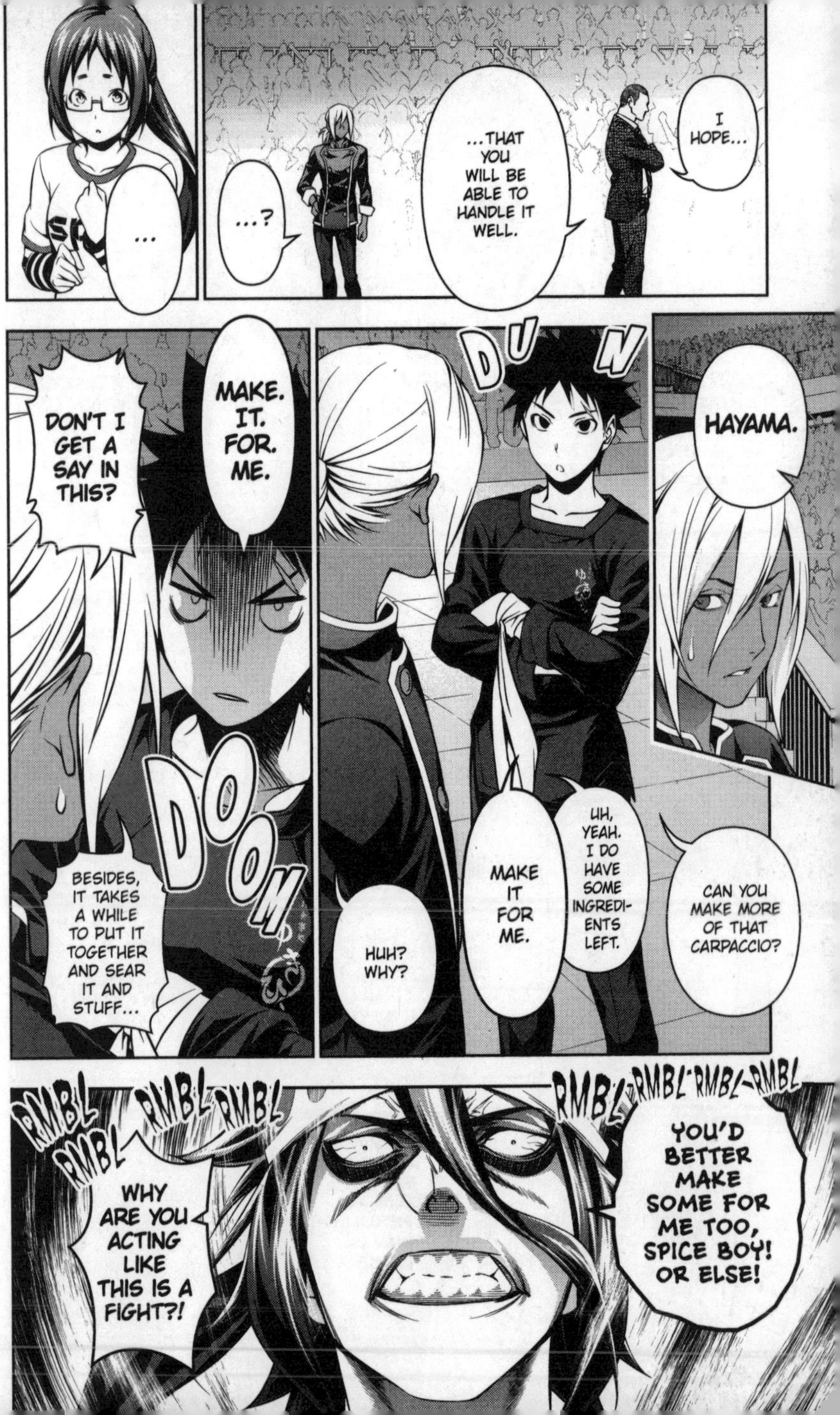
I HOPE...
...THAT YOU WILL BE ABLE TO HANDLE IT WELL.
...?
...
HAYAMA.
CAN YOU MAKE MORE OF THAT CARPACCIO?
DUN
UH, YEAH. I DO HAVE SOME INGREDI-ENTS LEFT.
MAKE IT FOR ME.
HUH? WHY?
MAKE. IT. FOR. ME.
DOOM
DON'T I GET A SAY IN THIS?
BESIDES, IT TAKES A WHILE TO PUT IT TOGETHER AND SEAR IT AND STUFF...
RMBL RMBL RMBL RMBL
YOU'D BETTER MAKE SOME FOR ME TOO, SPICE BOY! OR ELSE!
WHY ARE YOU ACTING LIKE THIS IS A FIGHT?!
RMBL RMBL RMBL RMBL

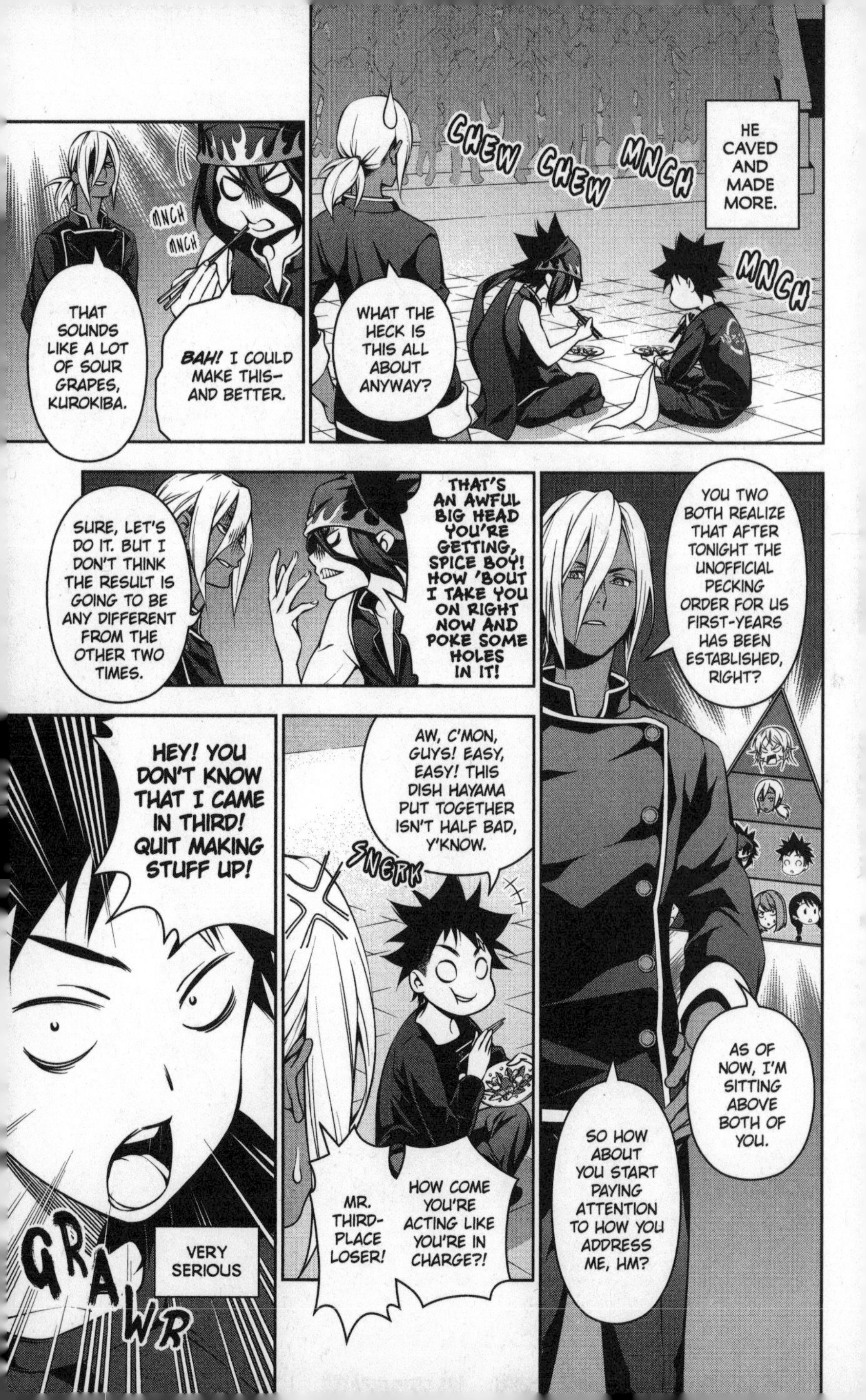
HE CAVED AND MADE MORE.
CHEW CHEW
MNCH
MNCH
WHAT THE HECK IS THIS ALL ABOUT ANYWAY?
MNCH
MNCH
BAH! I COULD MAKE THIS— AND BETTER.
THAT SOUNDS LIKE A LOT OF SOUR GRAPES, KUROKIBA.
YOU TWO BOTH REALIZE THAT AFTER TONIGHT THE UNOFFICIAL PECKING ORDER FOR US FIRST-YEARS HAS BEEN ESTABLISHED, RIGHT?
AS OF NOW, I'M SITTING ABOVE BOTH OF YOU.
SO HOW ABOUT YOU START PAYING ATTENTION TO HOW YOU ADDRESS ME, HM?
THAT'S AN AWFUL BIG HEAD YOU'RE GETTING, SPICE BOY! HOW 'BOUT I TAKE YOU ON RIGHT NOW AND POKE SOME HOLES IN IT!
SURE, LET'S DO IT. BUT I DON'T THINK THE RESULT IS GOING TO BE ANY DIFFERENT FROM THE OTHER TWO TIMES.
AW, C'MON, GUYS! EASY, EASY! THIS DISH HAYAMA PUT TOGETHER ISN'T HALF BAD, Y'KNOW.
SNERK
HOW COME YOU'RE ACTING LIKE YOU'RE IN CHARGE?!
MR. THIRD-PLACE LOSER!
HEY! YOU DON'T KNOW THAT I CAME IN THIRD! QUIT MAKING STUFF UP!
VERY SERIOUS
GRAWR

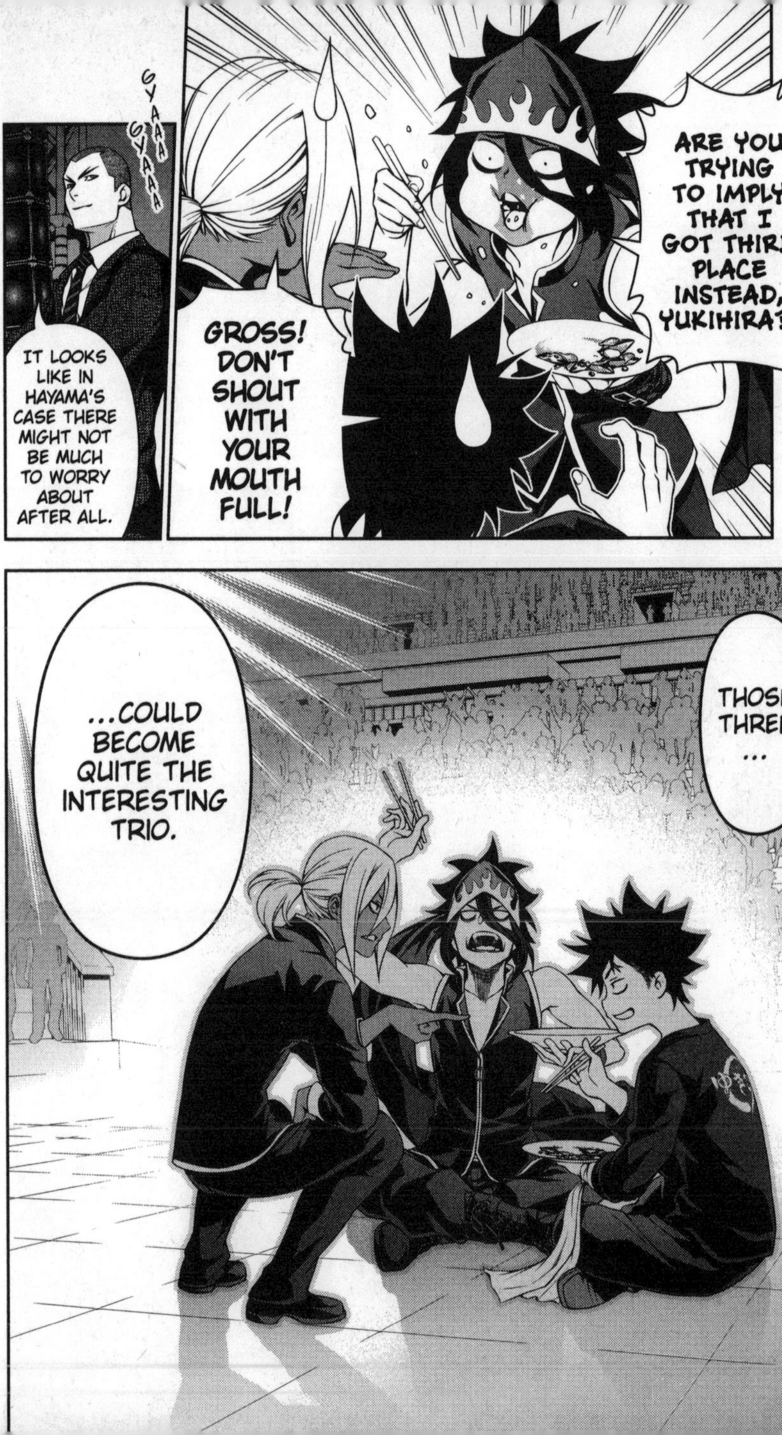
ARE YOU TRYING TO IMPLY THAT I GOT THIRD PLACE INSTEAD, YUKIHIRA?!
GROSS! DON'T SHOUT WITH YOUR MOUTH FULL!
GYAAA GYAAA
IT LOOKS LIKE IN HAYAMA'S CASE THERE MIGHT NOT BE MUCH TO WORRY ABOUT AFTER ALL.
THOSE THREE...
...COULD BECOME QUITE THE INTERESTING TRIO.

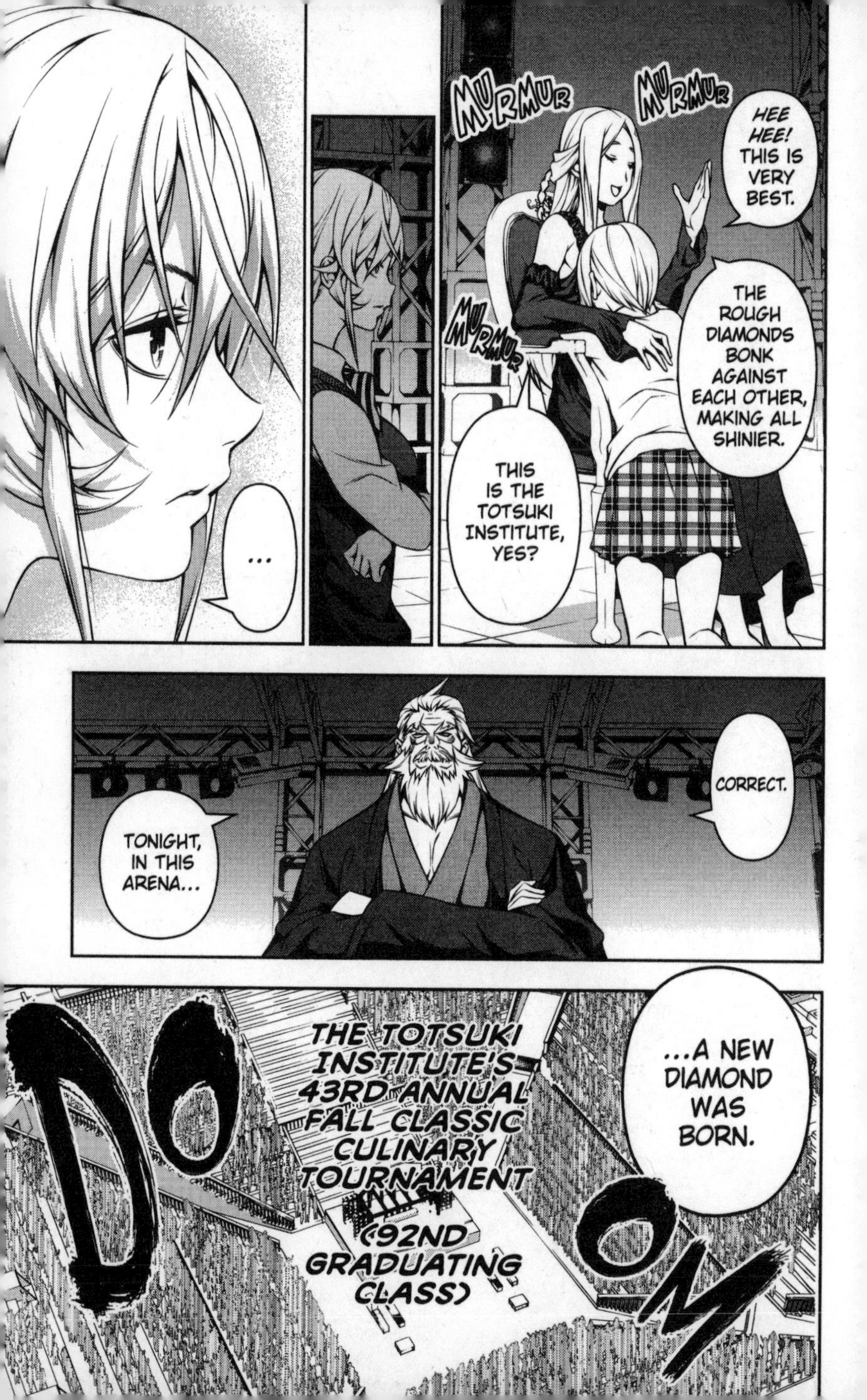
MURMUR
MURMUR
HEE HEE! THIS IS VERY BEST.
THE ROUGH DIAMONDS BONK AGAINST EACH OTHER, MAKING ALL SHINIER.
MURMUR
THIS IS THE TOTSUKI INSTITUTE, YES?
...
CORRECT.
TONIGHT, IN THIS ARENA...
...A NEW DIAMOND WAS BORN.
DOOM
THE TOTSUKI INSTITUTE'S 43RD ANNUAL FALL CLASSIC CULINARY TOURNAMENT (92ND GRADUATING CLASS)

60 STUDENTS QUALIFIED

A AND B BLOCK: 30 STUDENTS EACH

PRELIMINARIES FINAL STANDINGS BY BLOCK

[A BLOCK]
1ST	AKIRA HAYAMA
2ND (TIE)	RYO KUROKIBA
2ND (TIE)	SOMA YUKIHIRA
4TH	SUBARU MIMASAKA
5TH (TIE)	SHUN IBUSAKI
5TH (TIE)	ZENJI MARUI
7TH (TIE)	IKUMI MITO
7TH (TIE)	RYOKO SAKAKI

[B BLOCK]
1ST	ALICE NAKIRI
2ND	HISAKO ARATO
3RD	TAKUMI ALDINI
4TH	MEGUMI TADOKORO
5TH	MIYOKO HOJO
6TH	ISAMI ALDINI
7TH	YUKI YOSHINO
8TH	NAO SADATSUKA

FINALS QUALIFIERS

ALICE NAKIRI
SOMA YUKIHIRA
RYO KUROKIBA
MEGUMI TADOKORO

AKIRA HAYAMA
HISAKO ARATO
TAKUMI ALDINI
SUBARU MIMASAKA

RUNNERS-UP: SOMA YUKIHIRA
RYO KUROKIBA

WINNER

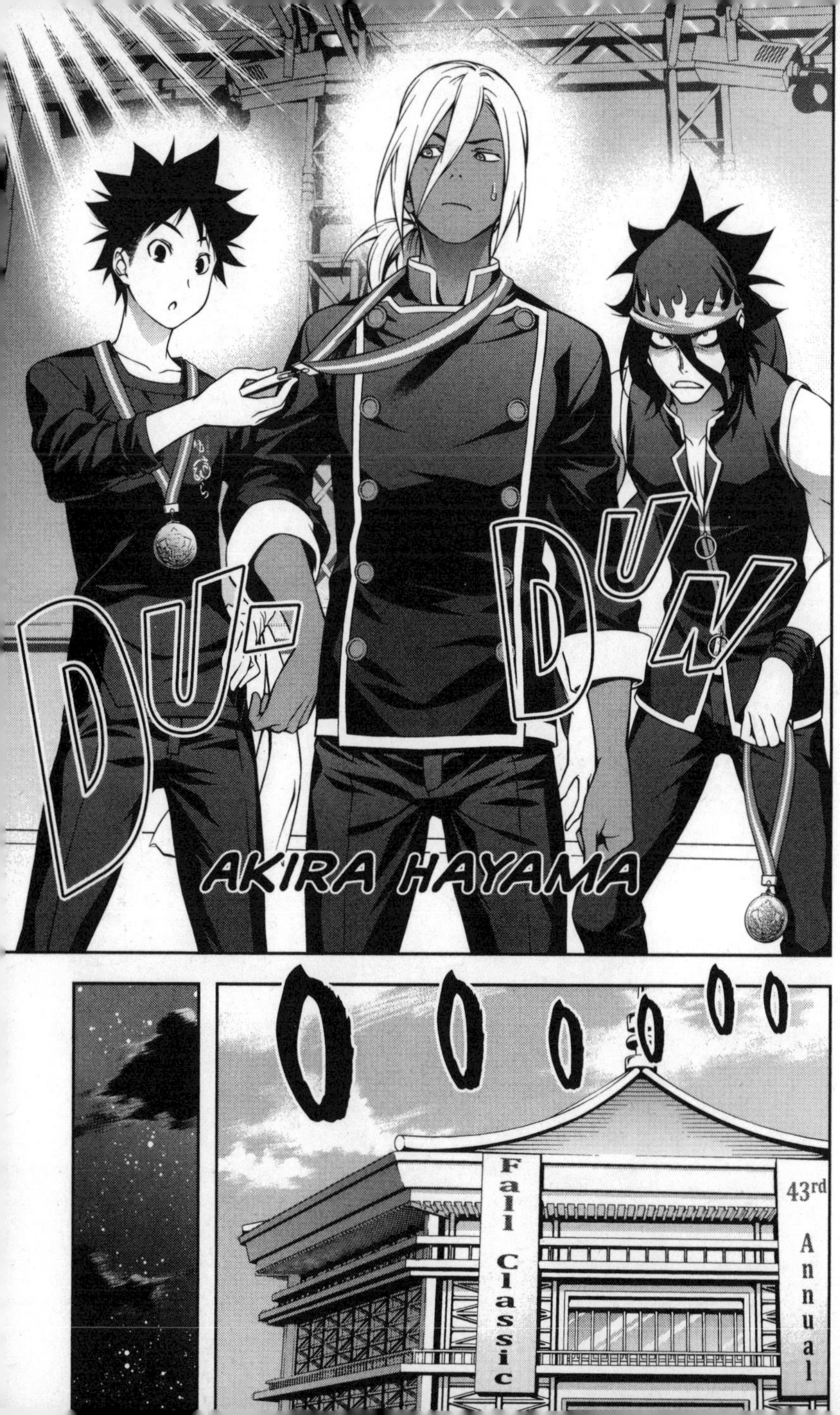
DU-DUN
AKIRA HAYAMA
OOOOO
43rd Annual
Fall Classic

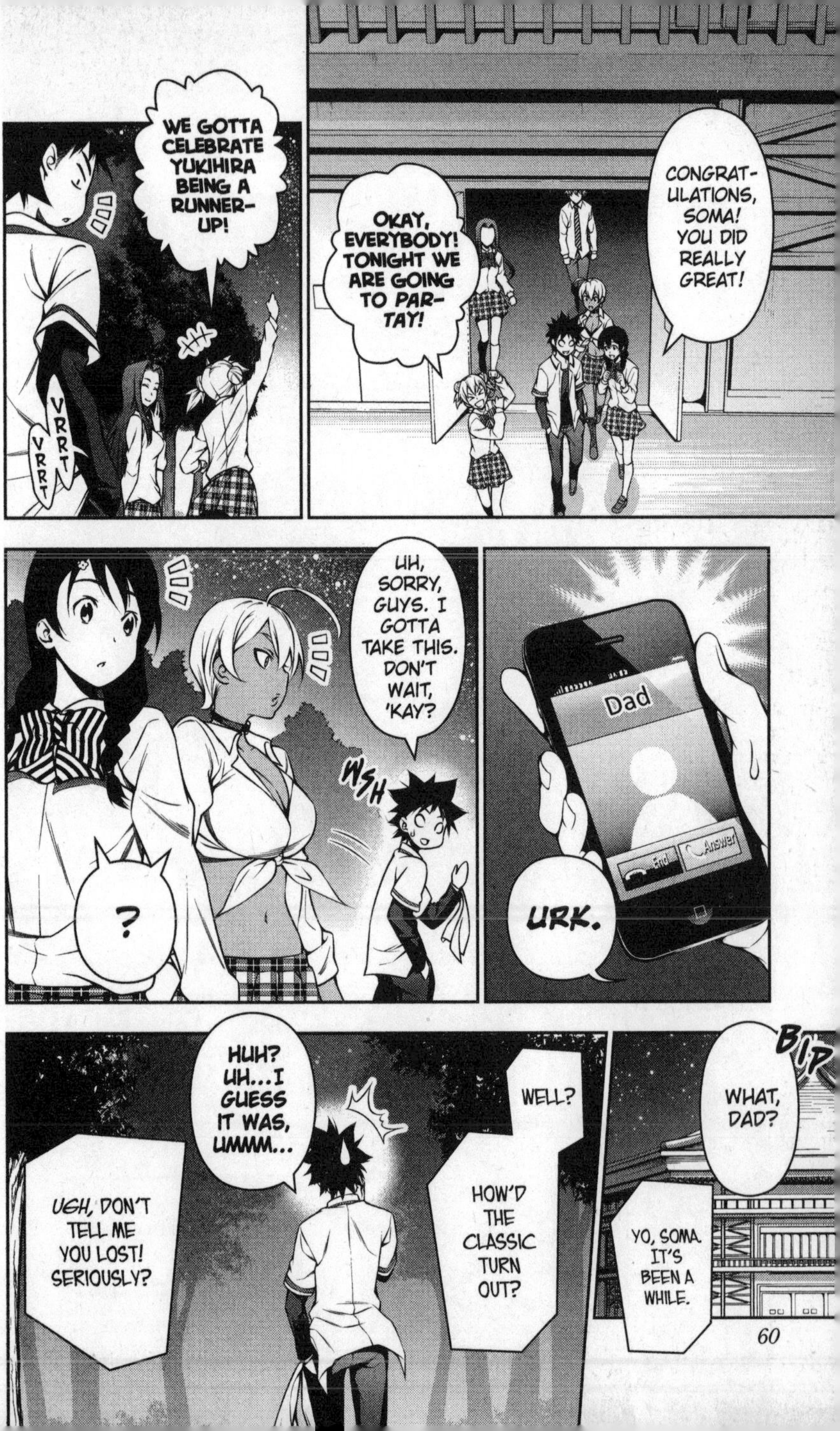
CONGRAT-ULATIONS, SOMA! YOU DID REALLY GREAT!
OKAY, EVERYBODY! TONIGHT WE ARE GOING TO PAR-TAY!
WE GOTTA CELEBRATE YUKIHIRA BEING A RUNNER-UP!
VRRT
VRRT
Dad
End
Answer
URK.
UH, SORRY, GUYS. I GOTTA TAKE THIS. DON'T WAIT, 'KAY?
WSH
?
BIP
WHAT, DAD?
YO, SOMA. IT'S BEEN A WHILE.
WELL?
HOW'D THE CLASSIC TURN OUT?
HUH? UH...I GUESS IT WAS, UMMM...
UGH, DON'T TELL ME YOU LOST! SERIOUSLY?

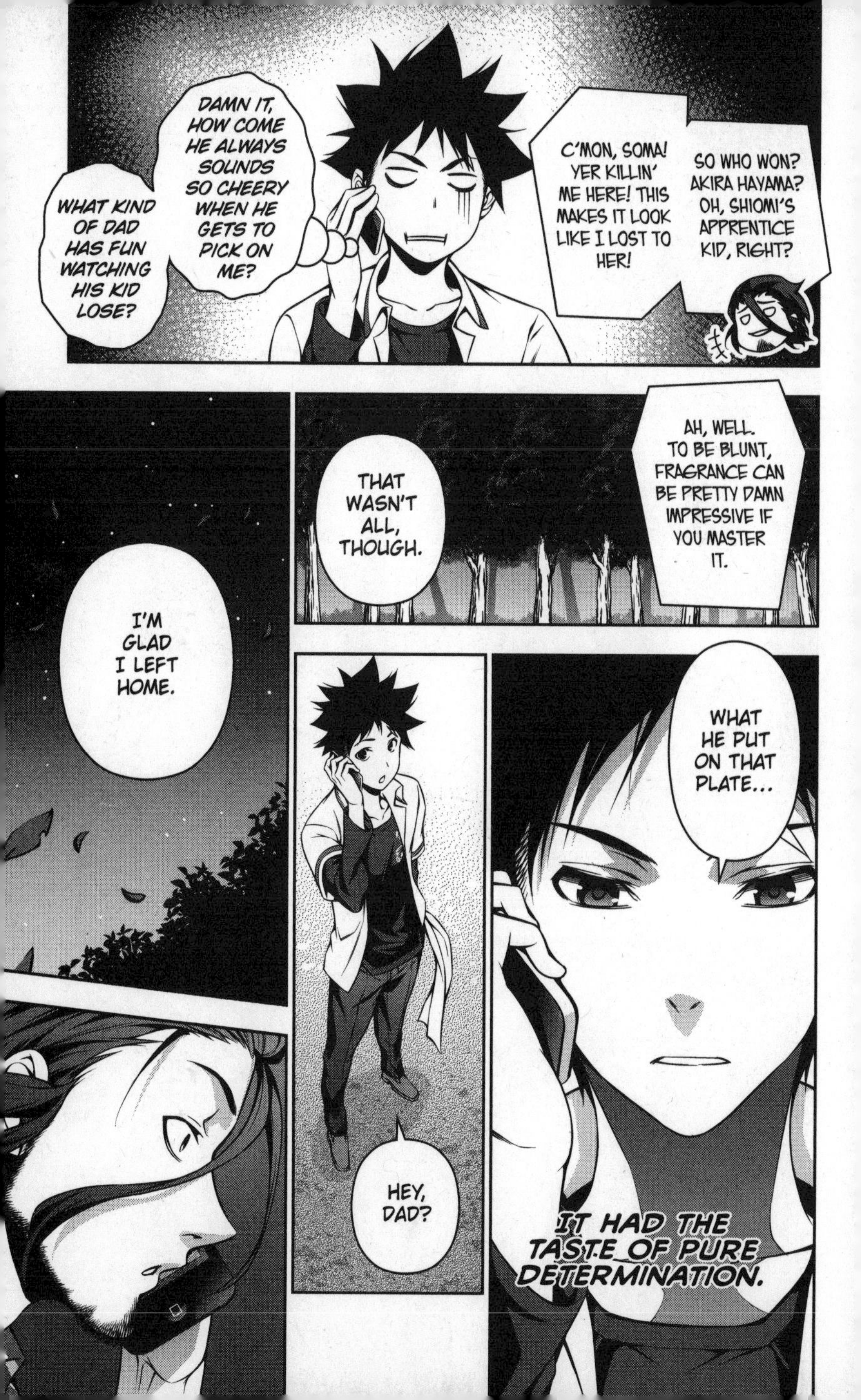
SO WHO WON? AKIRA HAYAMA? OH, SHIOMI'S APPRENTICE KID, RIGHT?
C'MON, SOMA! YER KILLIN' ME HERE! THIS MAKES IT LOOK LIKE I LOST TO HER!
DAMN IT, HOW COME HE ALWAYS SOUNDS SO CHEERY WHEN HE GETS TO PICK ON ME?
WHAT KIND OF DAD HAS FUN WATCHING HIS KID LOSE?
AH, WELL. TO BE BLUNT, FRAGRANCE CAN BE PRETTY DAMN IMPRESSIVE IF YOU MASTER IT.
THAT WASN'T ALL, THOUGH.
WHAT HE PUT ON THAT PLATE...
IT HAD THE TASTE OF PURE DETERMINATION.
HEY, DAD?
I'M GLAD I LEFT HOME.

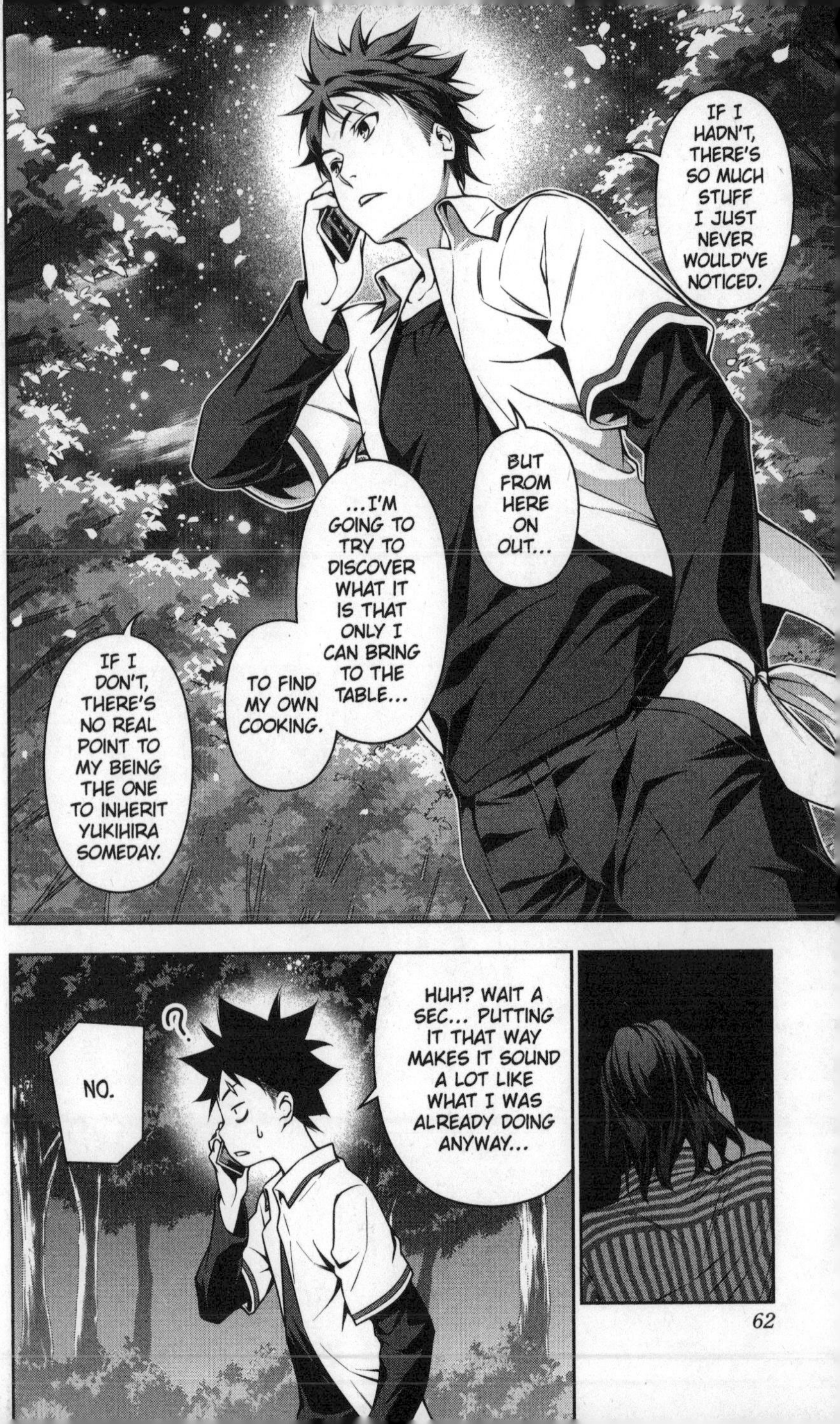
IF I HADN'T, THERE'S SO MUCH STUFF I JUST NEVER WOULD'VE NOTICED.
BUT FROM HERE ON OUT...
...I'M GOING TO TRY TO DISCOVER WHAT IT IS THAT ONLY I CAN BRING TO THE TABLE...
TO FIND MY OWN COOKING.
IF I DON'T, THERE'S NO REAL POINT TO MY BEING THE ONE TO INHERIT YUKIHIRA SOMEDAY.
HUH? WAIT A SEC... PUTTING IT THAT WAY MAKES IT SOUND A LOT LIKE WHAT I WAS ALREADY DOING ANYWAY...
?
NO.

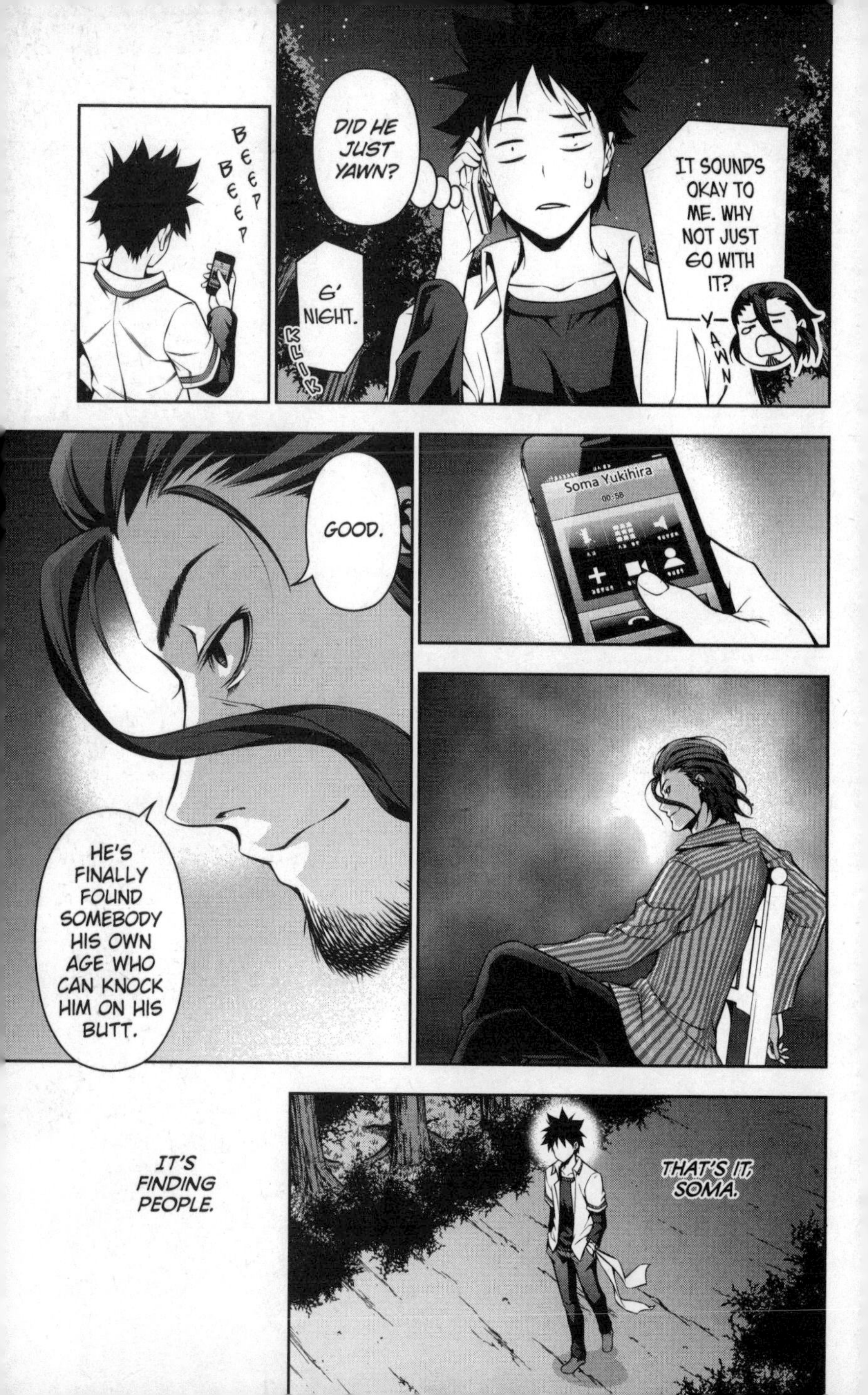
IT SOUNDS OKAY TO ME. WHY NOT JUST GO WITH IT?
Y-AWN
DID HE JUST YAWN?
G' NIGHT.
KLIK
BEEP BEEP
Soma Yukihira
00:58
GOOD.
HE'S FINALLY FOUND SOMEBODY HIS OWN AGE WHO CAN KNOCK HIM ON HIS BUTT.
THAT'S IT, SOMA.
IT'S FINDING PEOPLE.

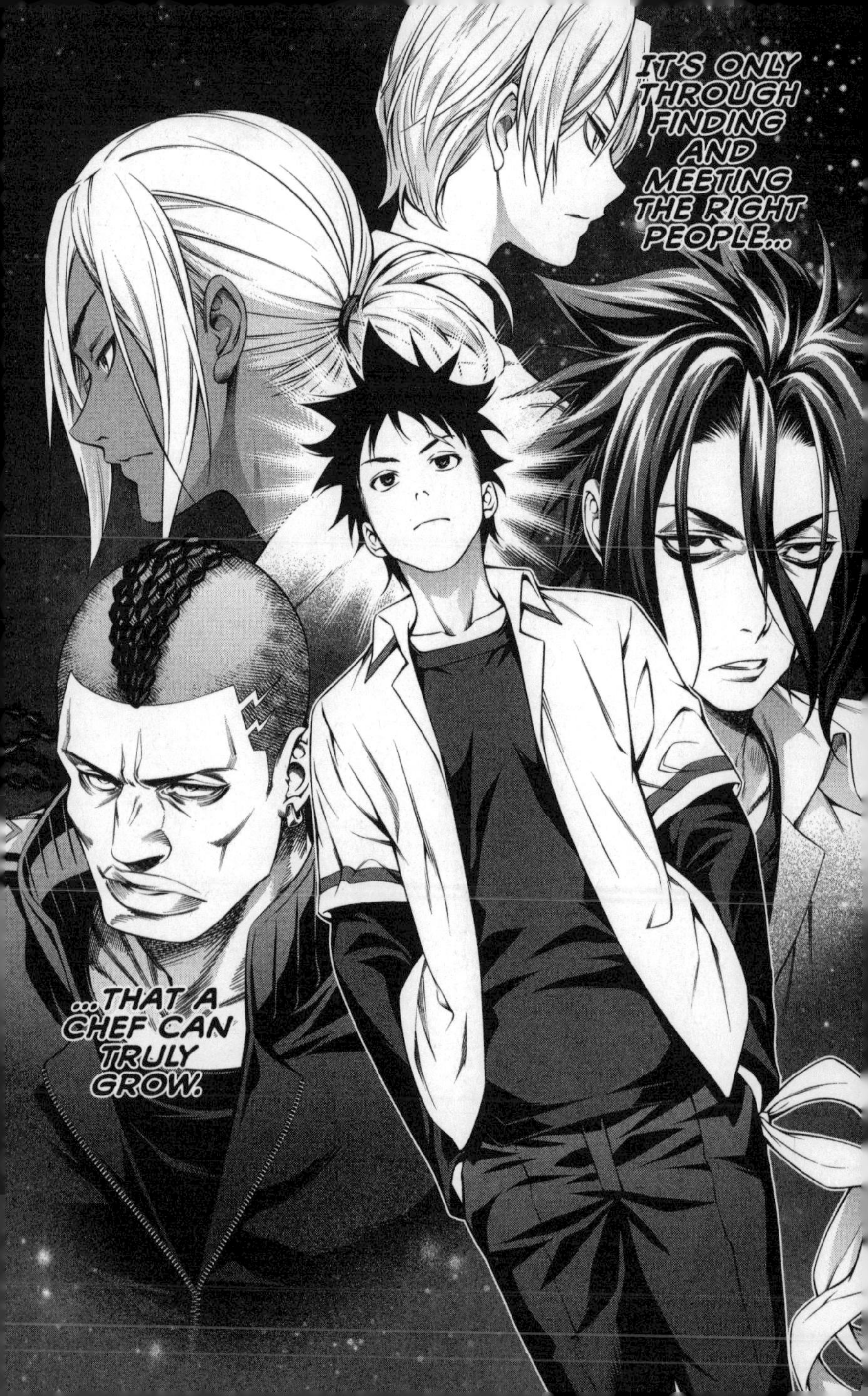
IT'S ONLY THROUGH FINDING AND MEETING THE RIGHT PEOPLE...
...THAT A CHEF CAN TRULY GROW.

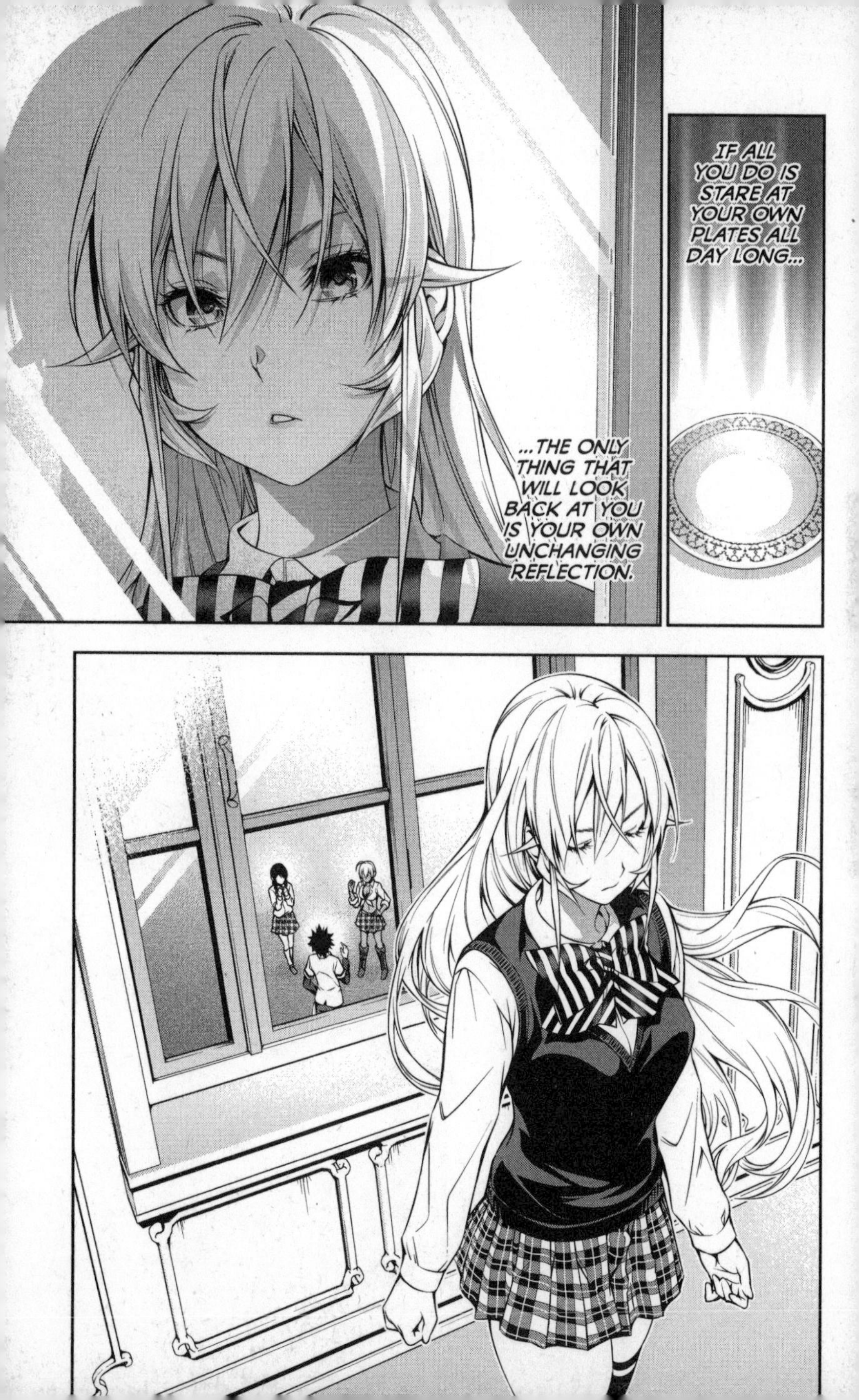
IF ALL YOU DO IS STARE AT YOUR OWN PLATES ALL DAY LONG...
...THE ONLY THING THAT WILL LOOK BACK AT YOU IS YOUR OWN UNCHANGING REFLECTION.

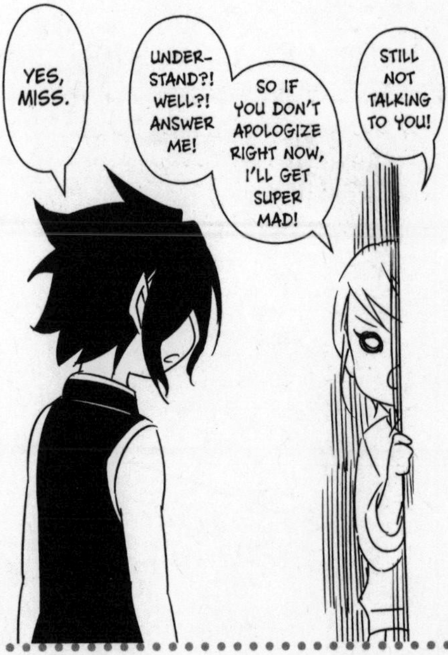
STILL NOT TALKING TO YOU!
SO IF YOU DON'T APOLOGIZE RIGHT NOW, I'LL GET SUPER MAD!
UNDER-STAND?! WELL?! ANSWER ME!
YES, MISS.

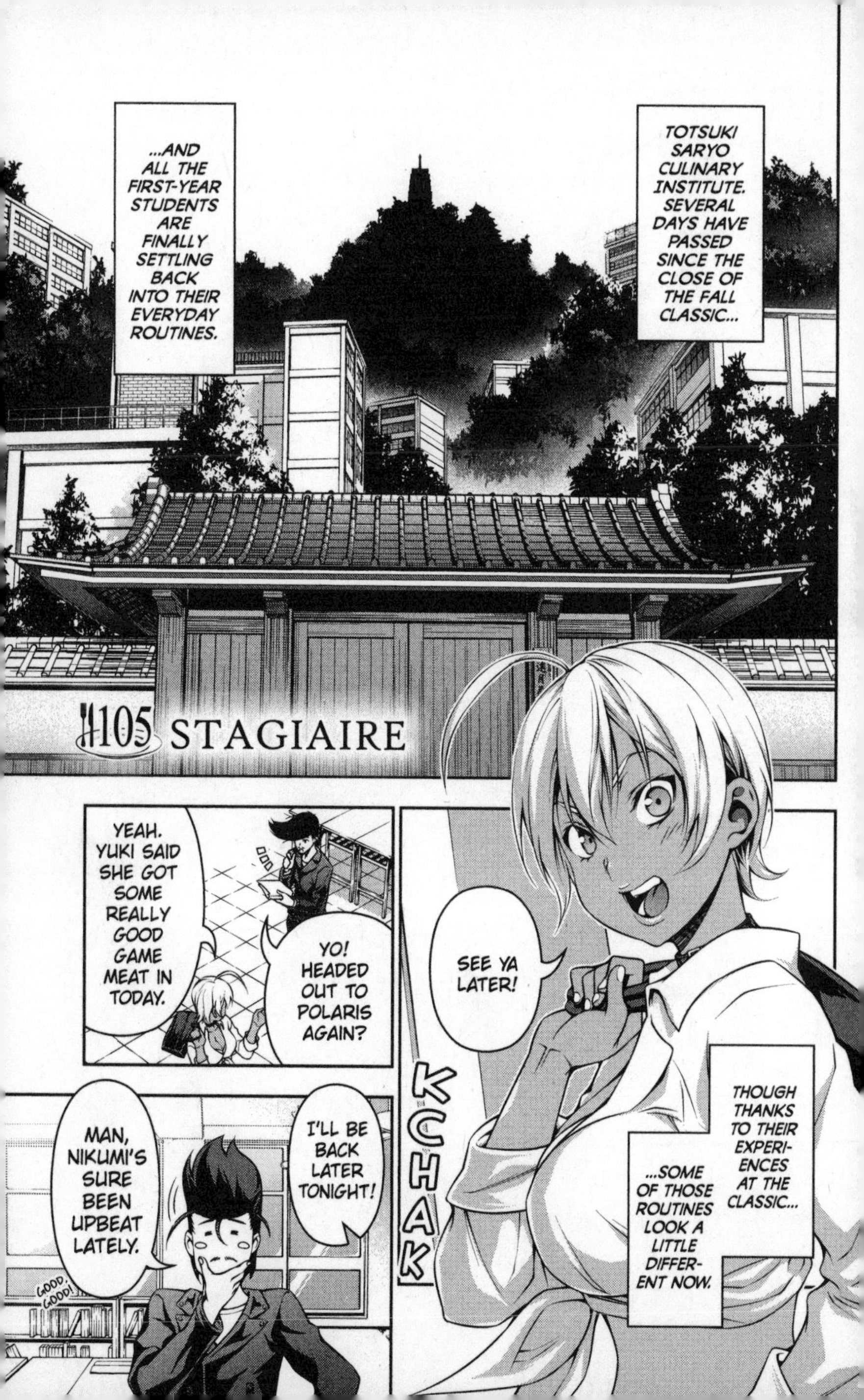
TOTSUKI SARYO CULINARY INSTITUTE. SEVERAL DAYS HAVE PASSED SINCE THE CLOSE OF THE FALL CLASSIC...
...AND ALL THE FIRST-YEAR STUDENTS ARE FINALLY SETTLING BACK INTO THEIR EVERYDAY ROUTINES.
105 STAGIAIRE
SEE YA LATER!
KCHAK
THOUGH THANKS TO THEIR EXPERIENCES AT THE CLASSIC...
...SOME OF THOSE ROUTINES LOOK A LITTLE DIFFERENT NOW.
YO! HEADED OUT TO POLARIS AGAIN?
YEAH. YUKI SAID SHE GOT SOME REALLY GOOD GAME MEAT IN TODAY.
I'LL BE BACK LATER TONIGHT!
MAN, NIKUMI'S SURE BEEN UPBEAT LATELY.
GOOD, GOOD!

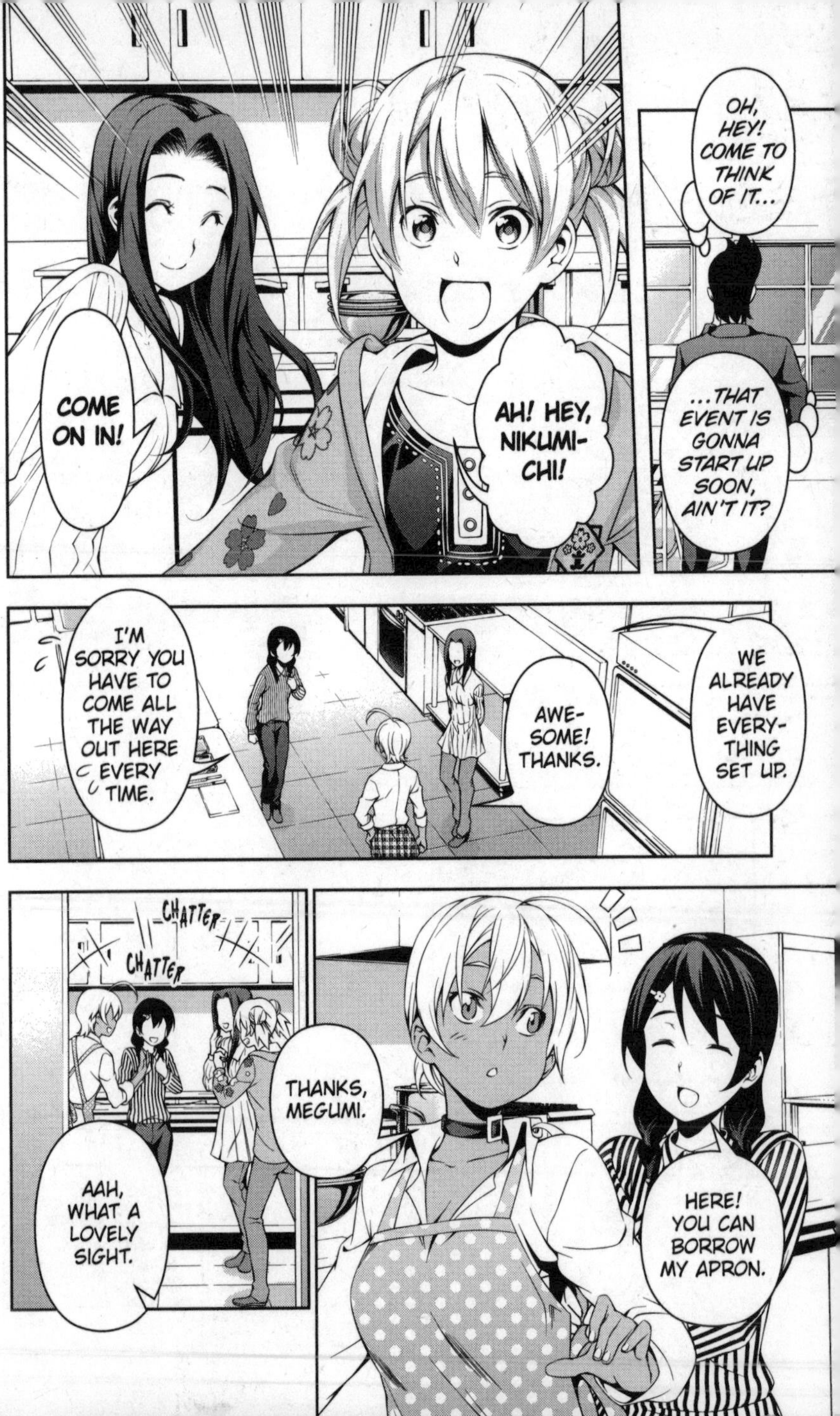
OH, HEY! COME TO THINK OF IT...
...THAT EVENT IS GONNA START UP SOON, AIN'T IT?
AH! HEY, NIKUMI-CHI!
COME ON IN!
WE ALREADY HAVE EVERYTHING SET UP.
AWESOME! THANKS.
I'M SORRY YOU HAVE TO COME ALL THE WAY OUT HERE EVERY TIME.
HERE! YOU CAN BORROW MY APRON.
THANKS, MEGUMI.
CHATTER
CHATTER
AAH, WHAT A LOVELY SIGHT.

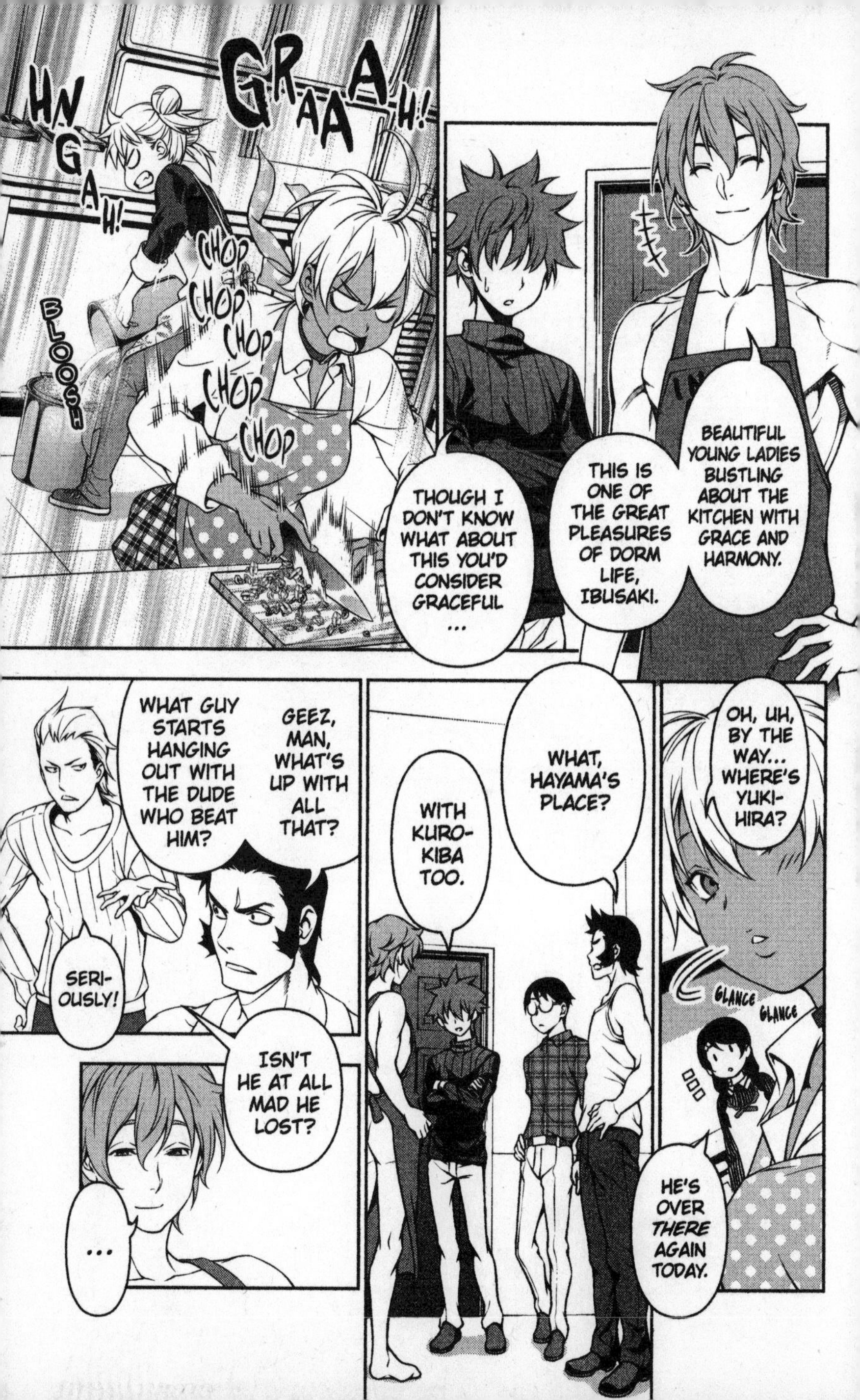

BEAUTIFUL YOUNG LADIES BUSTLING ABOUT THE KITCHEN WITH GRACE AND HARMONY.
THIS IS ONE OF THE GREAT PLEASURES OF DORM LIFE, IBUSAKI.
THOUGH I DON'T KNOW WHAT ABOUT THIS YOU'D CONSIDER GRACEFUL...
GRAAAH!
HNGAAH!
CHOP CHOP CHOP CHOP CHOP
BLOOSH
OH, UH, BY THE WAY... WHERE'S YUKIHIRA?
GLANCE GLANCE
HE'S OVER *THERE* AGAIN TODAY.
WHAT, HAYAMA'S PLACE?
WITH KUROKIBA TOO.
GEEZ, MAN, WHAT'S UP WITH ALL THAT?
WHAT GUY STARTS HANGING OUT WITH THE DUDE WHO BEAT HIM?
SERIOUSLY!
ISN'T HE AT ALL MAD HE LOST?
...

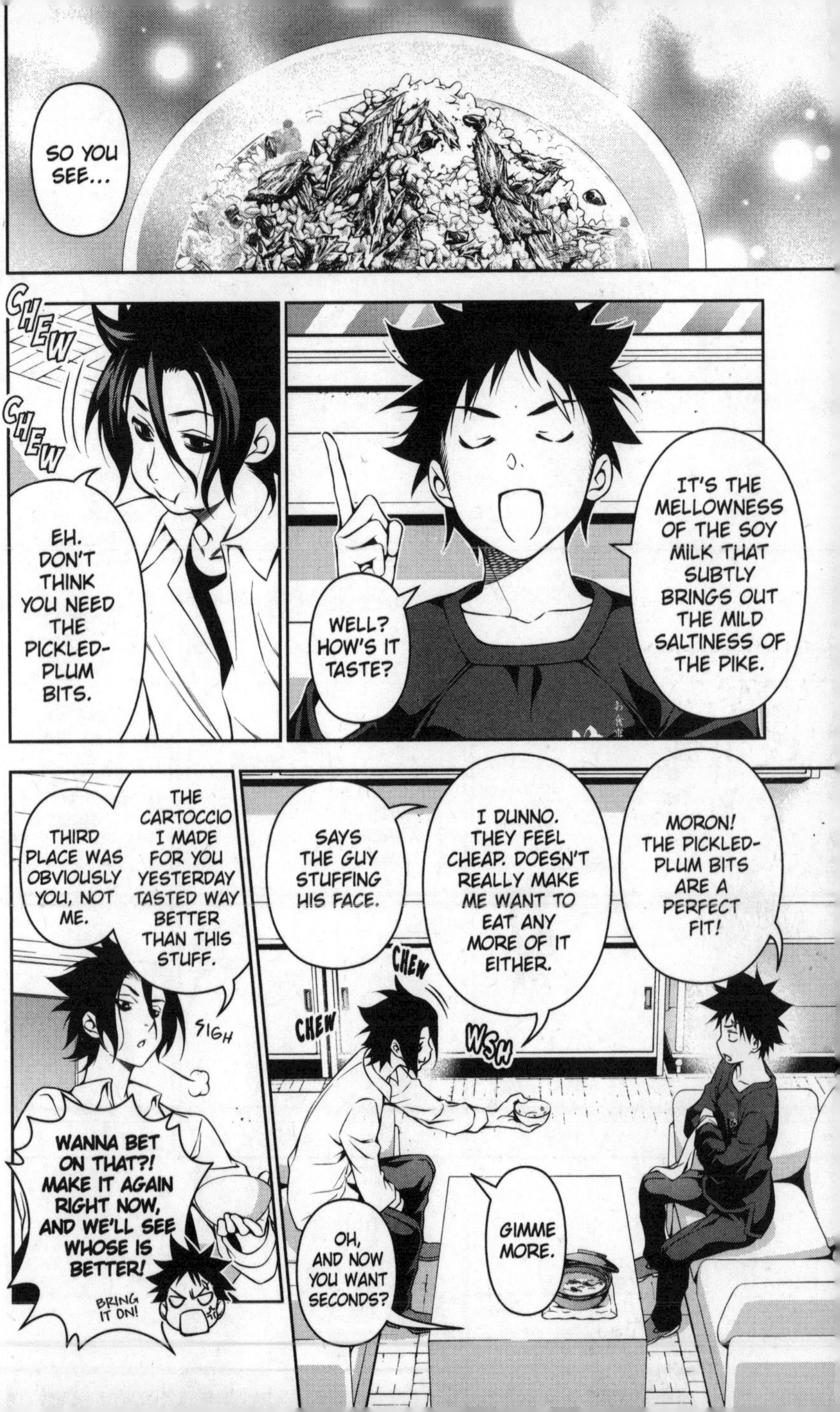
SO YOU SEE...
IT'S THE MELLOWNESS OF THE SOY MILK THAT SUBTLY BRINGS OUT THE MILD SALTINESS OF THE PIKE.
WELL? HOW'S IT TASTE?
CHEW CHEW
EH. DON'T THINK YOU NEED THE PICKLED-PLUM BITS.
MORON! THE PICKLED-PLUM BITS ARE A PERFECT FIT!
I DUNNO. THEY FEEL CHEAP. DOESN'T REALLY MAKE ME WANT TO EAT ANY MORE OF IT EITHER.
CHEW
SAYS THE GUY STUFFING HIS FACE.
CHEW
WSH
GIMME MORE.
OH, AND NOW YOU WANT SECONDS?
THE CARTOCCIO I MADE FOR YOU YESTERDAY TASTED WAY BETTER THAN THIS STUFF.
THIRD PLACE WAS OBVIOUSLY YOU, NOT ME.
SIGH
WANNA BET ON THAT?! MAKE IT AGAIN RIGHT NOW, AND WE'LL SEE WHOSE IS BETTER!
BRING IT ON!

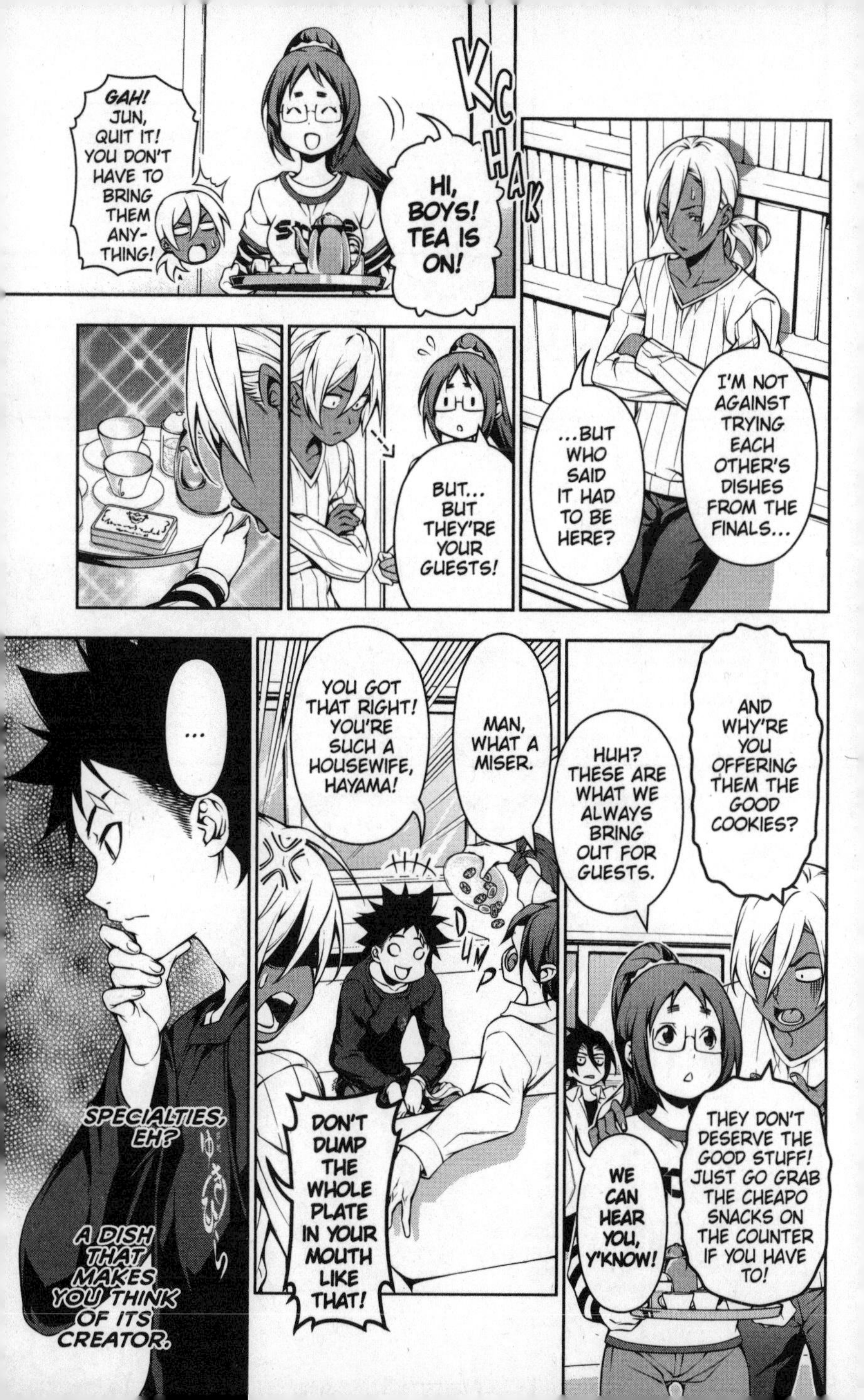
HI, BOYS! TEA IS ON!
GAH! JUN, QUIT IT! YOU DON'T HAVE TO BRING THEM ANY-THING!
KCHAK
I'M NOT AGAINST TRYING EACH OTHER'S DISHES FROM THE FINALS...
...BUT WHO SAID IT HAD TO BE HERE?
BUT... BUT THEY'RE YOUR GUESTS!
AND WHY'RE YOU OFFERING THEM THE GOOD COOKIES?
HUH? THESE ARE WHAT WE ALWAYS BRING OUT FOR GUESTS.
THEY DON'T DESERVE THE GOOD STUFF! JUST GO GRAB THE CHEAPO SNACKS ON THE COUNTER IF YOU HAVE TO!
WE CAN HEAR YOU, Y'KNOW!
MAN, WHAT A MISER.
YOU GOT THAT RIGHT! YOU'RE SUCH A HOUSEWIFE, HAYAMA!
DUMP
DON'T DUMP THE WHOLE PLATE IN YOUR MOUTH LIKE THAT!
...
SPECIALTIES, EH?
A DISH THAT MAKES YOU THINK OF ITS CREATOR.

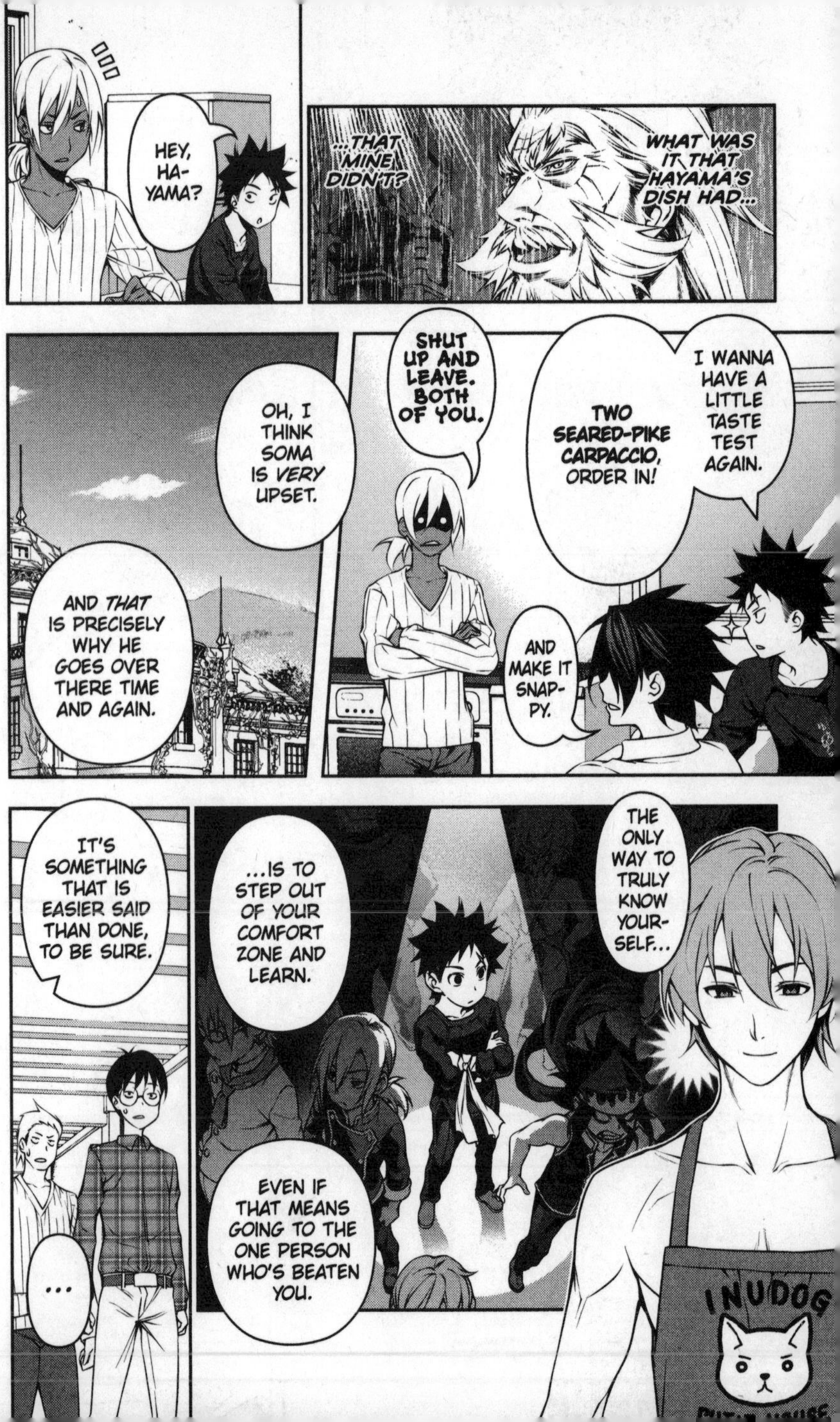
WHAT WAS IT THAT HAYAMA'S DISH HAD...
...THAT MINE DIDN'T?
HEY, HA-YAMA?
I WANNA HAVE A LITTLE TASTE TEST AGAIN.
TWO SEARED-PIKE CARPACCIO, ORDER IN!
AND MAKE IT SNAP-PY.
SHUT UP AND LEAVE. BOTH OF YOU.
OH, I THINK SOMA IS *VERY* UPSET.
AND *THAT* IS PRECISELY WHY HE GOES OVER THERE TIME AND AGAIN.
THE ONLY WAY TO TRULY KNOW YOUR-SELF...
...IS TO STEP OUT OF YOUR COMFORT ZONE AND LEARN.
EVEN IF THAT MEANS GOING TO THE ONE PERSON WHO'S BEATEN YOU.
INUDOG
IT'S SOMETHING THAT IS EASIER SAID THAN DONE, TO BE SURE.
...

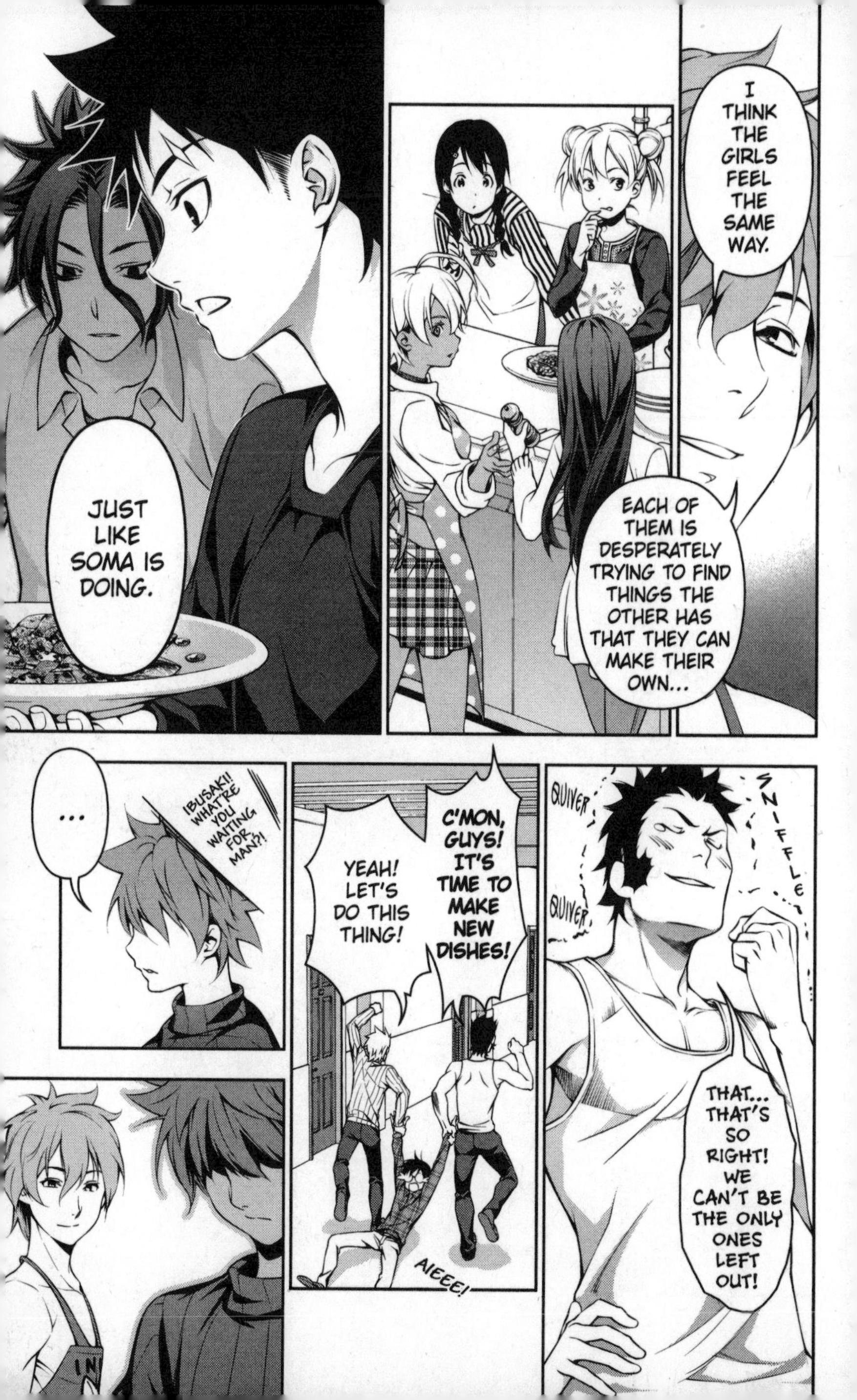
I THINK THE GIRLS FEEL THE SAME WAY.
EACH OF THEM IS DESPERATELY TRYING TO FIND THINGS THE OTHER HAS THAT THEY CAN MAKE THEIR OWN...
JUST LIKE SOMA IS DOING.
QUIVER
SNIFFLE
QUIVER
THAT... THAT'S SO RIGHT! WE CAN'T BE THE ONLY ONES LEFT OUT!
C'MON, GUYS! IT'S TIME TO MAKE NEW DISHES!
YEAH! LET'S DO THIS THING!
AIEEE!
IBUSAKI! WHAT'RE YOU WAITING FOR, MAN?!
...

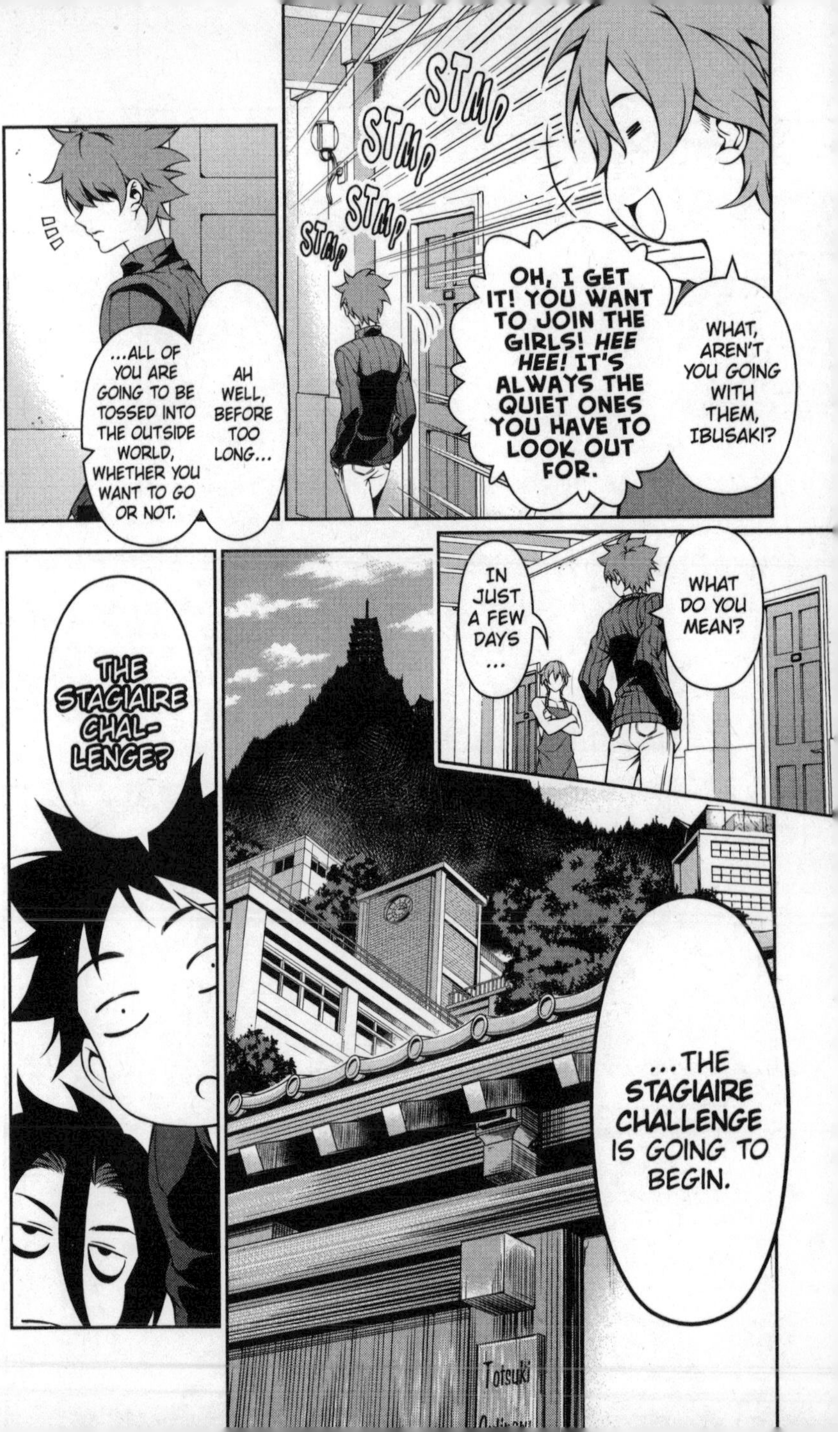

STMP
STMP
STMP
STMP
WHAT, AREN'T YOU GOING WITH THEM, IBUSAKI?
OH, I GET IT! YOU WANT TO JOIN THE GIRLS! *HEE HEE!* IT'S ALWAYS THE QUIET ONES YOU HAVE TO LOOK OUT FOR.
AH WELL, BEFORE TOO LONG...
...ALL OF YOU ARE GOING TO BE TOSSED INTO THE OUTSIDE WORLD, WHETHER YOU WANT TO GO OR NOT.
WHAT DO YOU MEAN?
IN JUST A FEW DAYS...
...THE STAGIAIRE CHALLENGE IS GOING TO BEGIN.
Totsuki
THE STAGIAIRE CHAL-LENGE?

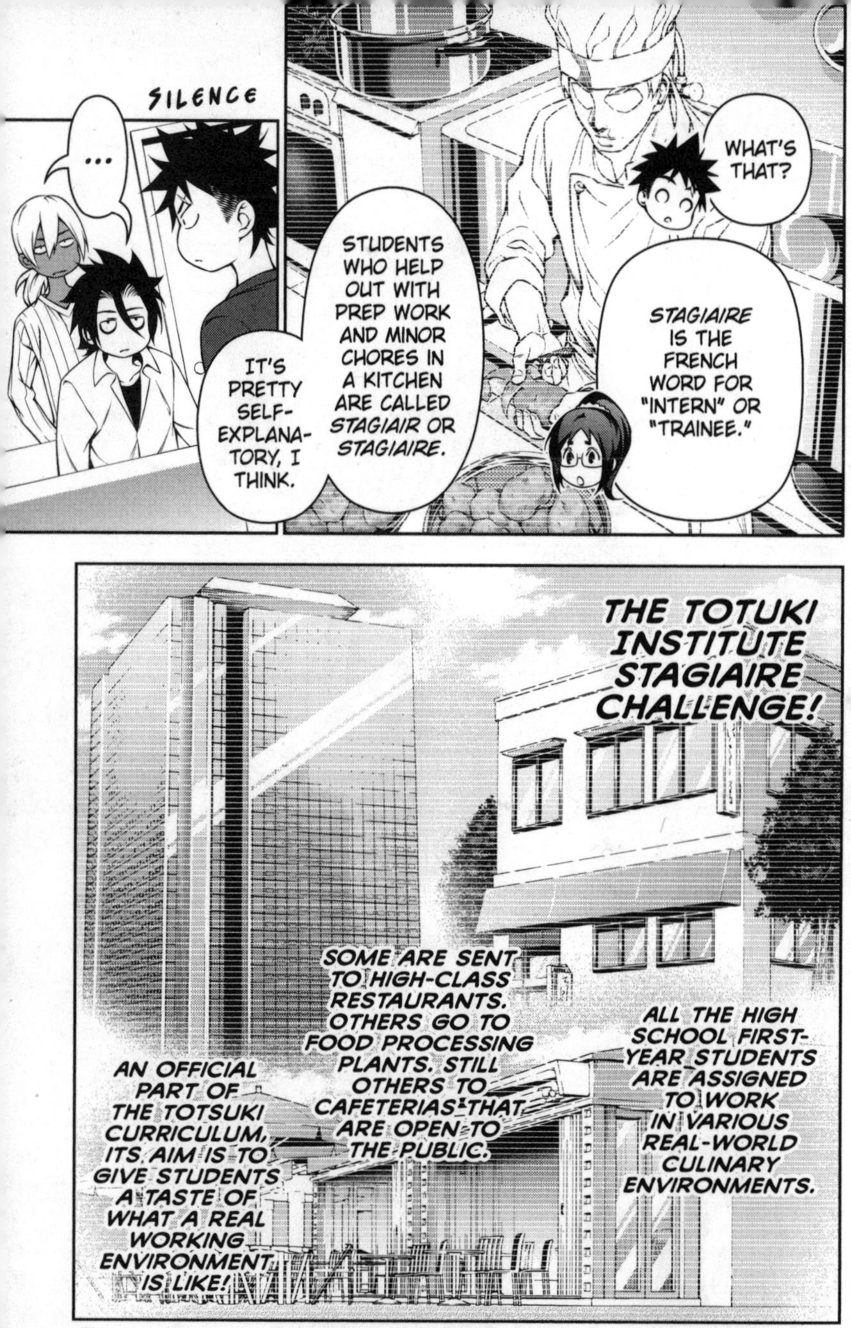
WHAT'S THAT?
STAGIAIRE IS THE FRENCH WORD FOR "INTERN" OR "TRAINEE."
STUDENTS WHO HELP OUT WITH PREP WORK AND MINOR CHORES IN A KITCHEN ARE CALLED STAGIAIR OR STAGIAIRE.
IT'S PRETTY SELF-EXPLANATORY, I THINK.
SILENCE
...
THE TOTUKI INSTITUTE STAGIAIRE CHALLENGE!
ALL THE HIGH SCHOOL FIRST-YEAR STUDENTS ARE ASSIGNED TO WORK IN VARIOUS REAL-WORLD CULINARY ENVIRONMENTS.
SOME ARE SENT TO HIGH-CLASS RESTAURANTS. OTHERS GO TO FOOD PROCESSING PLANTS. STILL OTHERS TO CAFETERIAS THAT ARE OPEN TO THE PUBLIC.
AN OFFICIAL PART OF THE TOTSUKI CURRICULUM, ITS AIM IS TO GIVE STUDENTS A TASTE OF WHAT A REAL WORKING ENVIRONMENT IS LIKE!

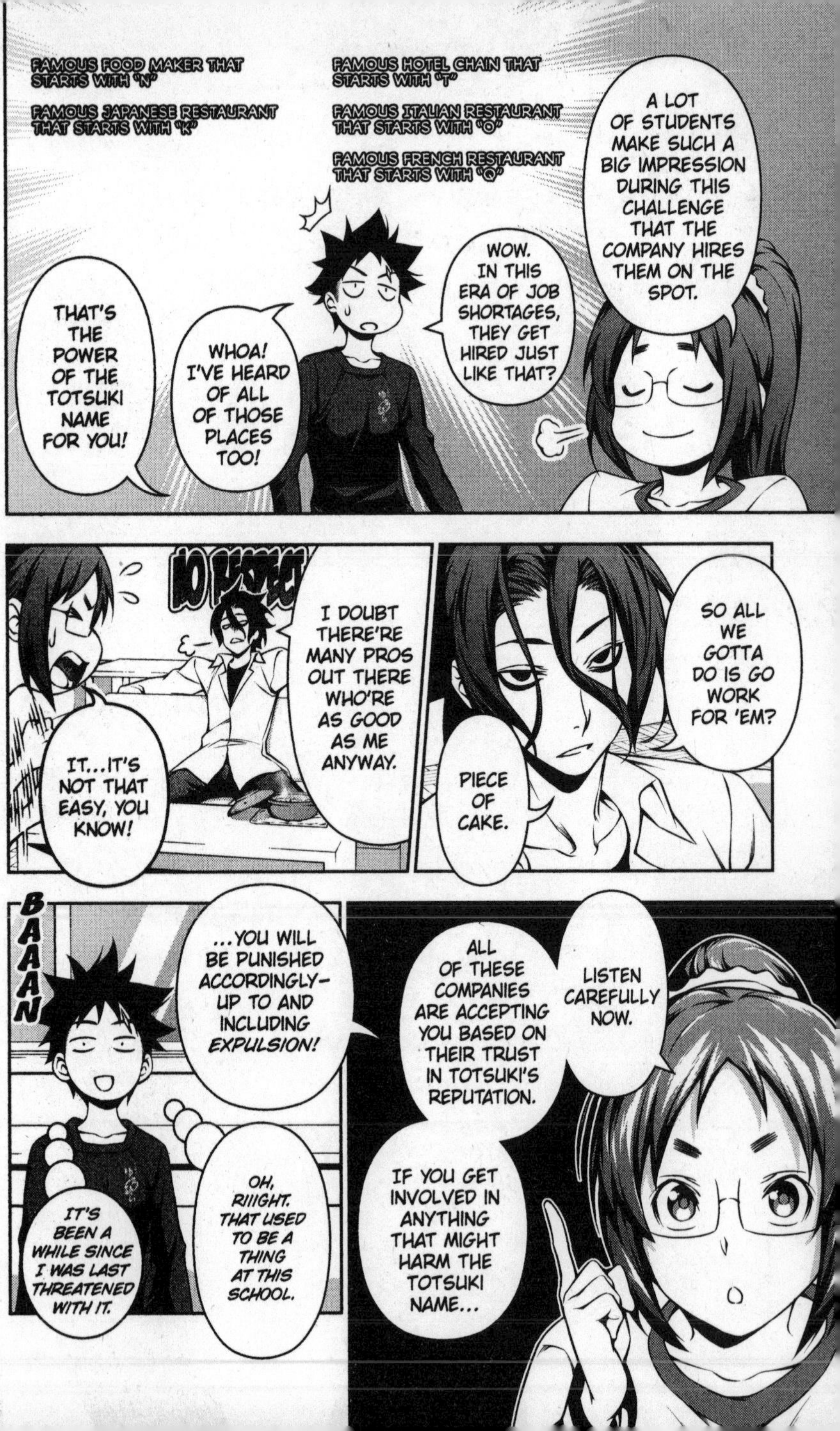

A LOT OF STUDENTS MAKE SUCH A BIG IMPRESSION DURING THIS CHALLENGE THAT THE COMPANY HIRES THEM ON THE SPOT.
FAMOUS HOTEL CHAIN THAT STARTS WITH "T"
FAMOUS ITALIAN RESTAURANT THAT STARTS WITH "O"
FAMOUS FRENCH RESTAURANT THAT STARTS WITH "Q"
FAMOUS FOOD MAKER THAT STARTS WITH "N"
FAMOUS JAPANESE RESTAURANT THAT STARTS WITH "K"
WOW. IN THIS ERA OF JOB SHORTAGES, THEY GET HIRED JUST LIKE THAT?
WHOA! I'VE HEARD OF ALL OF THOSE PLACES TOO!
THAT'S THE POWER OF THE TOTSUKI NAME FOR YOU!
SO ALL WE GOTTA DO IS GO WORK FOR 'EM?
PIECE OF CAKE.
I DOUBT THERE'RE MANY PROS OUT THERE WHO'RE AS GOOD AS ME ANYWAY.
IT...IT'S NOT THAT EASY, YOU KNOW!
LISTEN CAREFULLY NOW.
ALL OF THESE COMPANIES ARE ACCEPTING YOU BASED ON THEIR TRUST IN TOTSUKI'S REPUTATION.
IF YOU GET INVOLVED IN ANYTHING THAT MIGHT HARM THE TOTSUKI NAME...
...YOU WILL BE PUNISHED ACCORDINGLY–UP TO AND INCLUDING *EXPULSION!*
BAAAAN
OH, RIIIGHT. THAT USED TO BE A THING AT THIS SCHOOL.
IT'S BEEN A WHILE SINCE I WAS LAST THREATENED WITH IT.

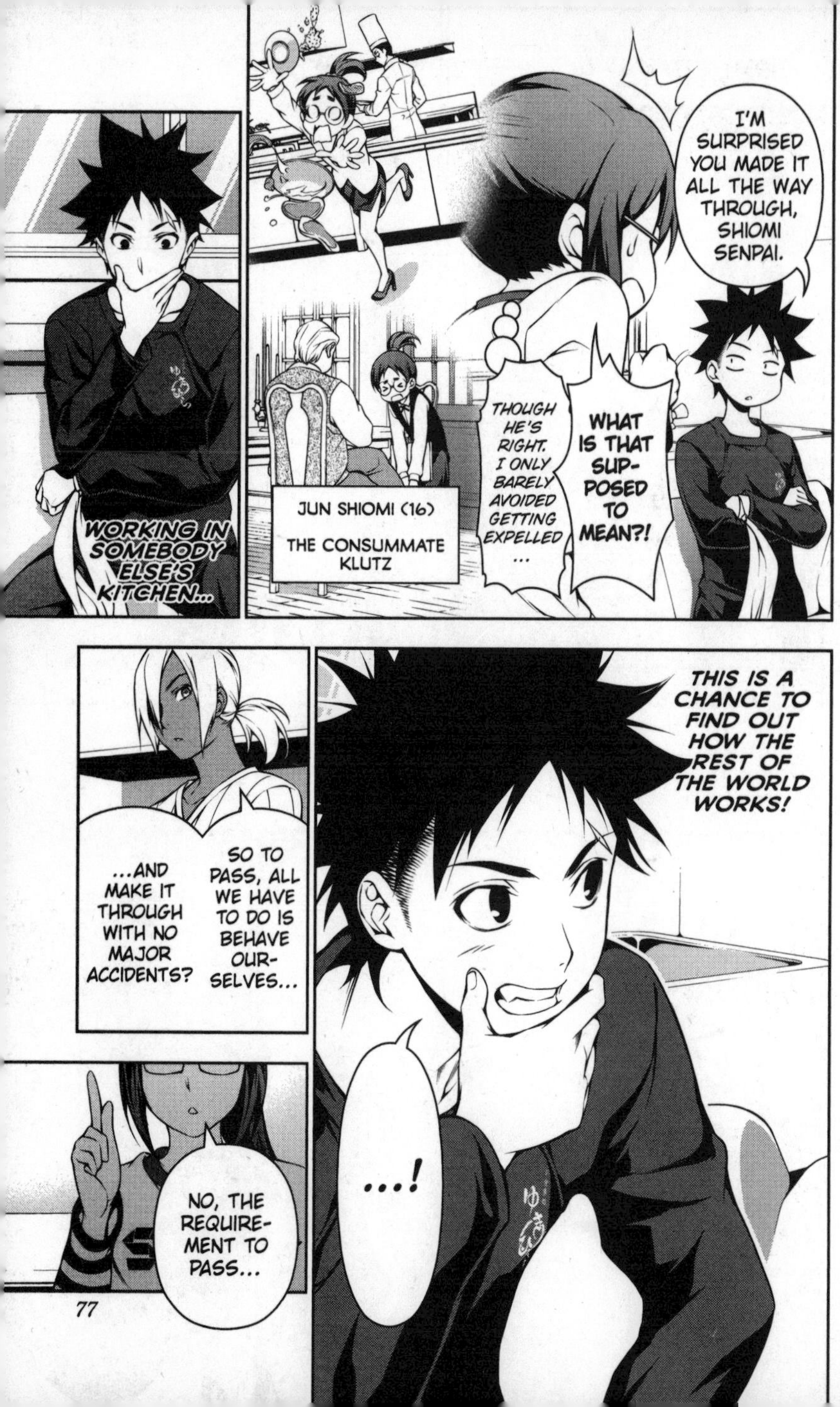
I'M SURPRISED YOU MADE IT ALL THE WAY THROUGH, SHIOMI SENPAI.
WHAT IS THAT SUP-POSED TO MEAN?!
THOUGH HE'S RIGHT. I ONLY BARELY AVOIDED GETTING EXPELLED ...
JUN SHIOMI (16)
THE CONSUMMATE KLUTZ
WORKING IN SOMEBODY ELSE'S KITCHEN...
THIS IS A CHANCE TO FIND OUT HOW THE REST OF THE WORLD WORKS!
...!
SO TO PASS, ALL WE HAVE TO DO IS BEHAVE OUR-SELVES...
...AND MAKE IT THROUGH WITH NO MAJOR ACCIDENTS?
NO, THE REQUIRE-MENT TO PASS...

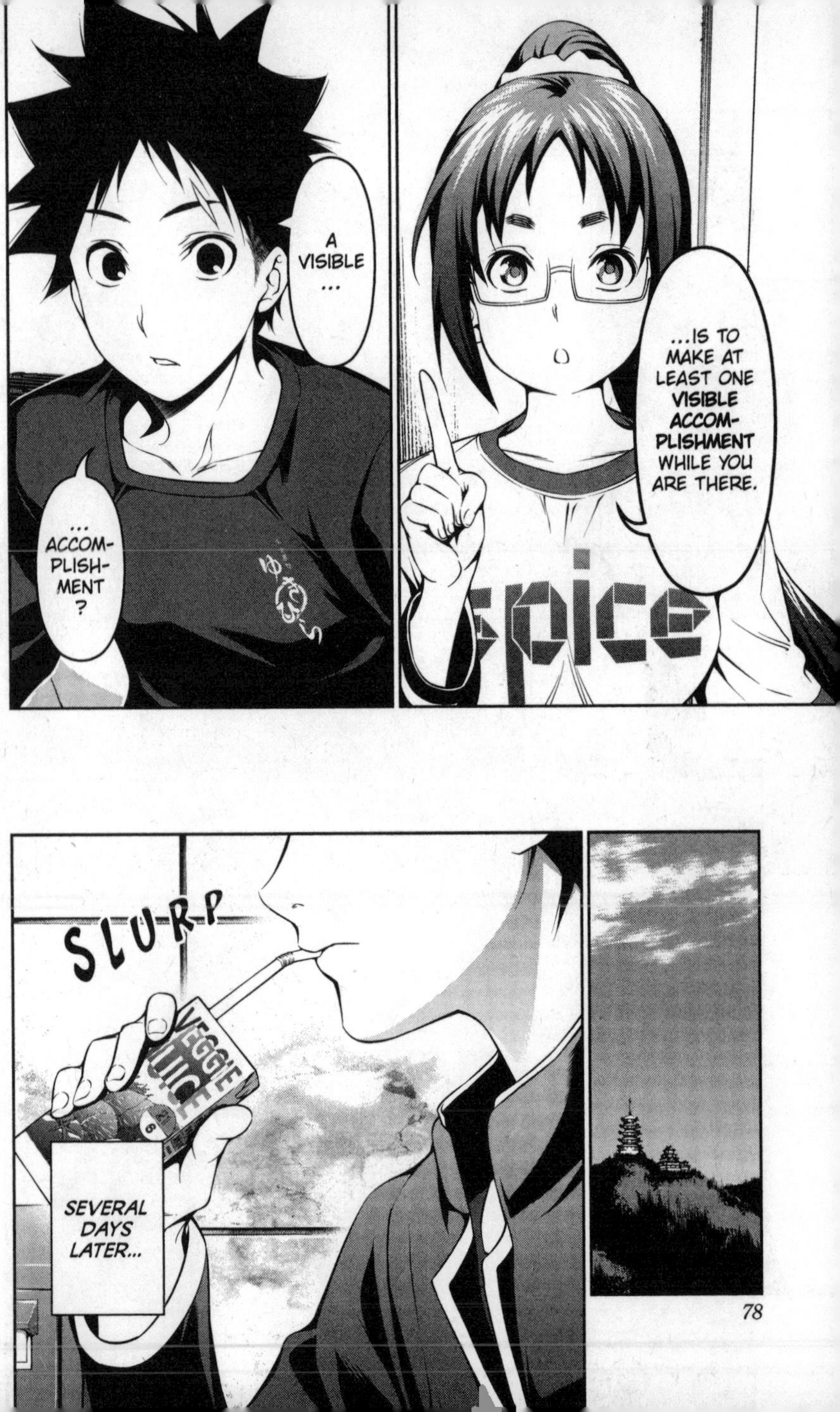
...IS TO MAKE AT LEAST ONE VISIBLE ACCOMPLISHMENT WHILE YOU ARE THERE.
spice
A VISIBLE ...
... ACCOMPLISHMENT?
SEVERAL DAYS LATER...
SLURP
VEGGIE JUICE

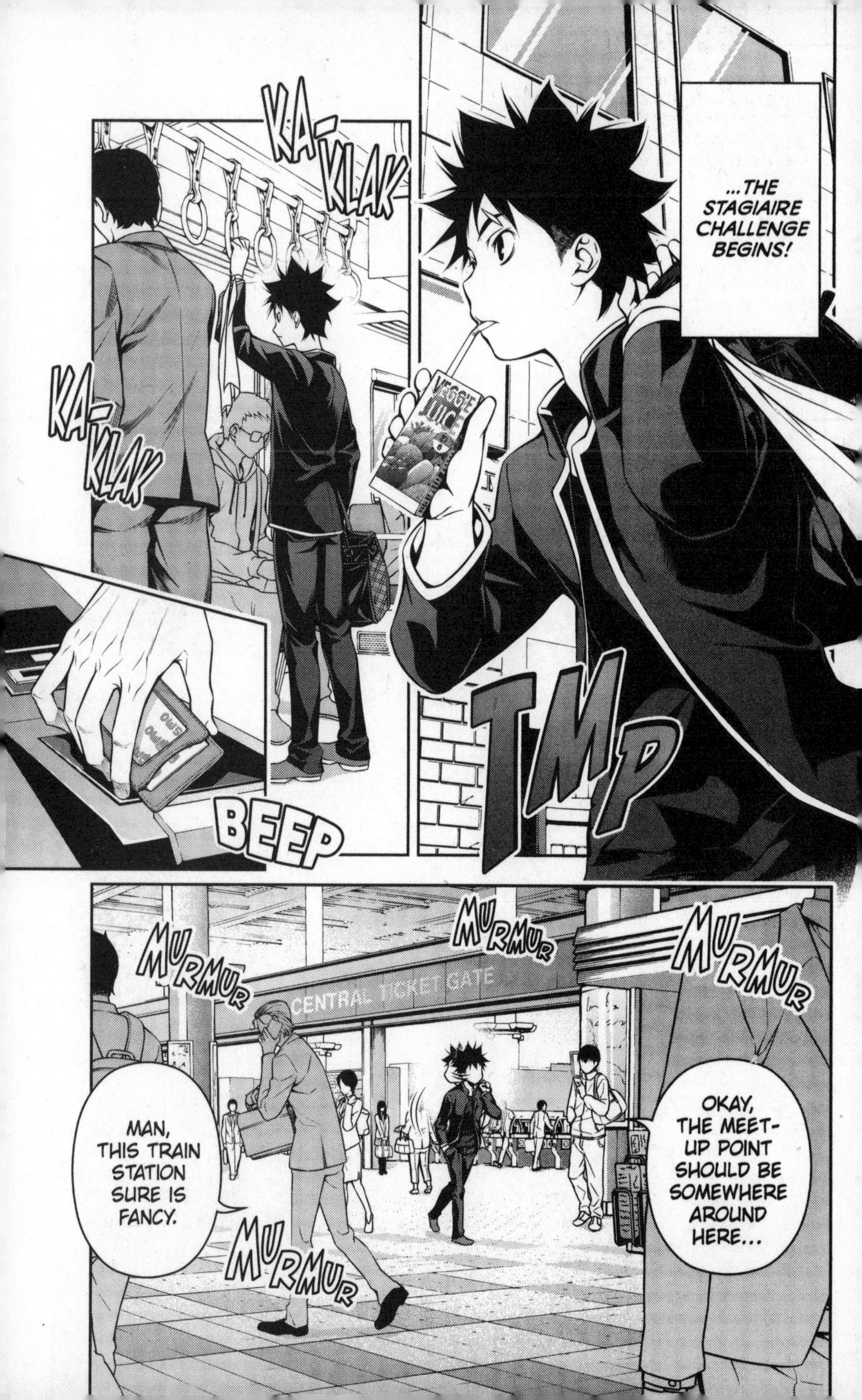
...THE STAGIAIRE CHALLENGE BEGINS!
VEGGIE JUICE
TMP
KA-KLAK
KA-KLAK
BEEP
MURMUR
MURMUR
OKAY, THE MEET-UP POINT SHOULD BE SOMEWHERE AROUND HERE...
CENTRAL TICKET GATE
MURMUR
MAN, THIS TRAIN STATION SURE IS FANCY.
MURMUR

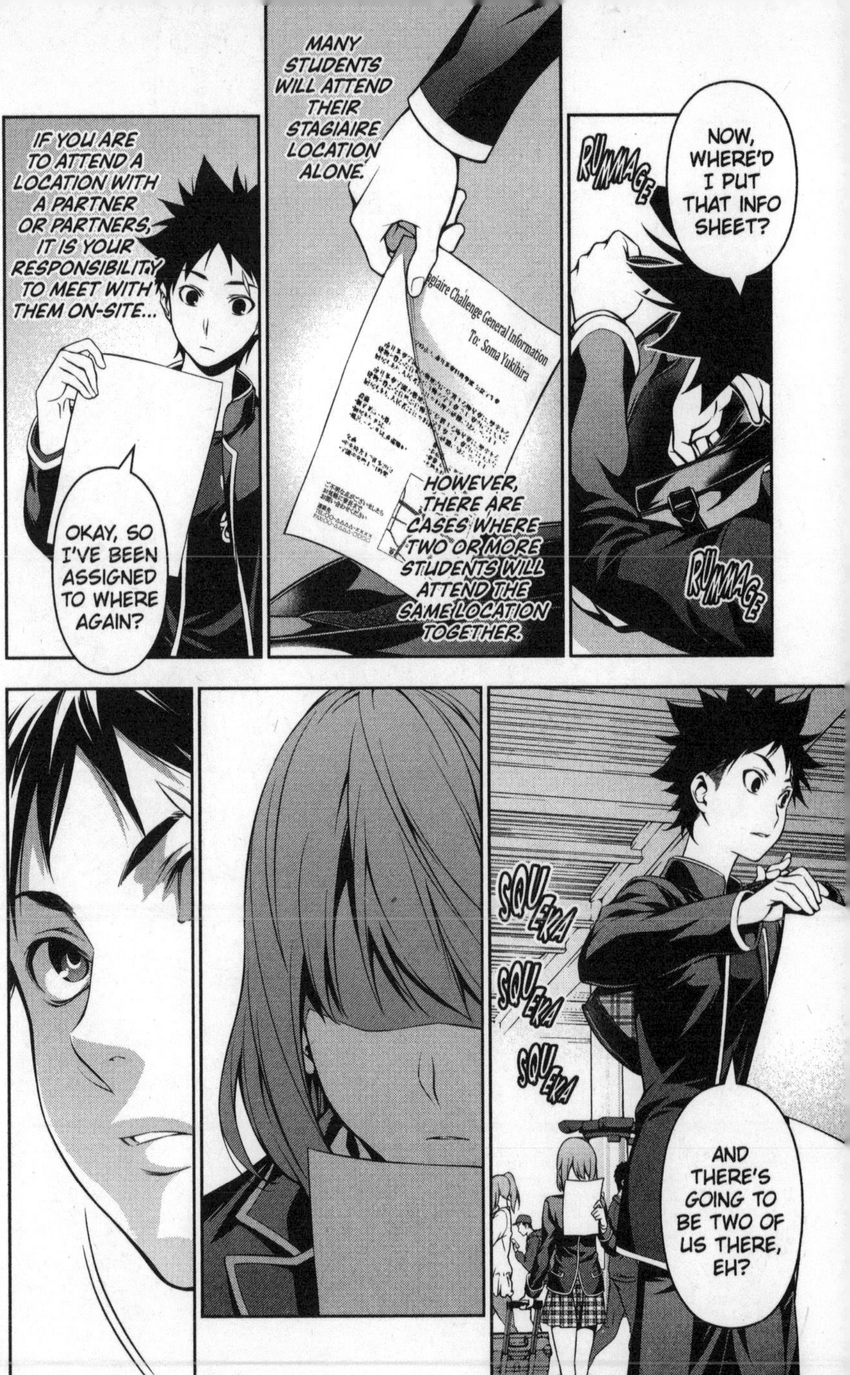
RUMMAGE
NOW, WHERE'D I PUT THAT INFO SHEET?
RUMMAGE
MANY STUDENTS WILL ATTEND THEIR STAGIAIRE LOCATION ALONE.
Challenge General Information
To: Soma Yukihira
HOWEVER, THERE ARE CASES WHERE TWO OR MORE STUDENTS WILL ATTEND THE SAME LOCATION TOGETHER.
IF YOU ARE TO ATTEND A LOCATION WITH A PARTNER OR PARTNERS, IT IS YOUR RESPONSIBILITY TO MEET WITH THEM ON-SITE...
OKAY, SO I'VE BEEN ASSIGNED TO WHERE AGAIN?
SQUEKA
SQUEKA
SQUEKA
AND THERE'S GOING TO BE TWO OF US THERE, EH?

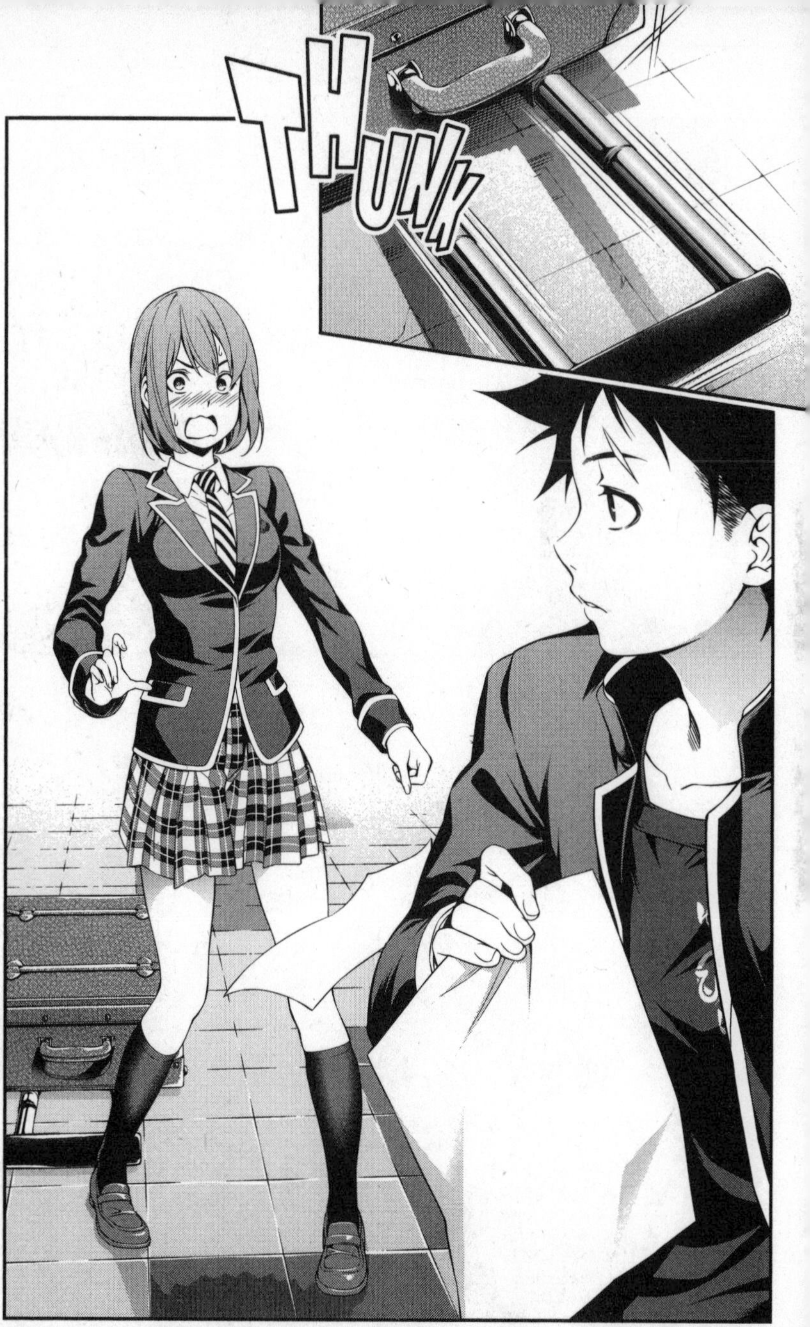
THUNK

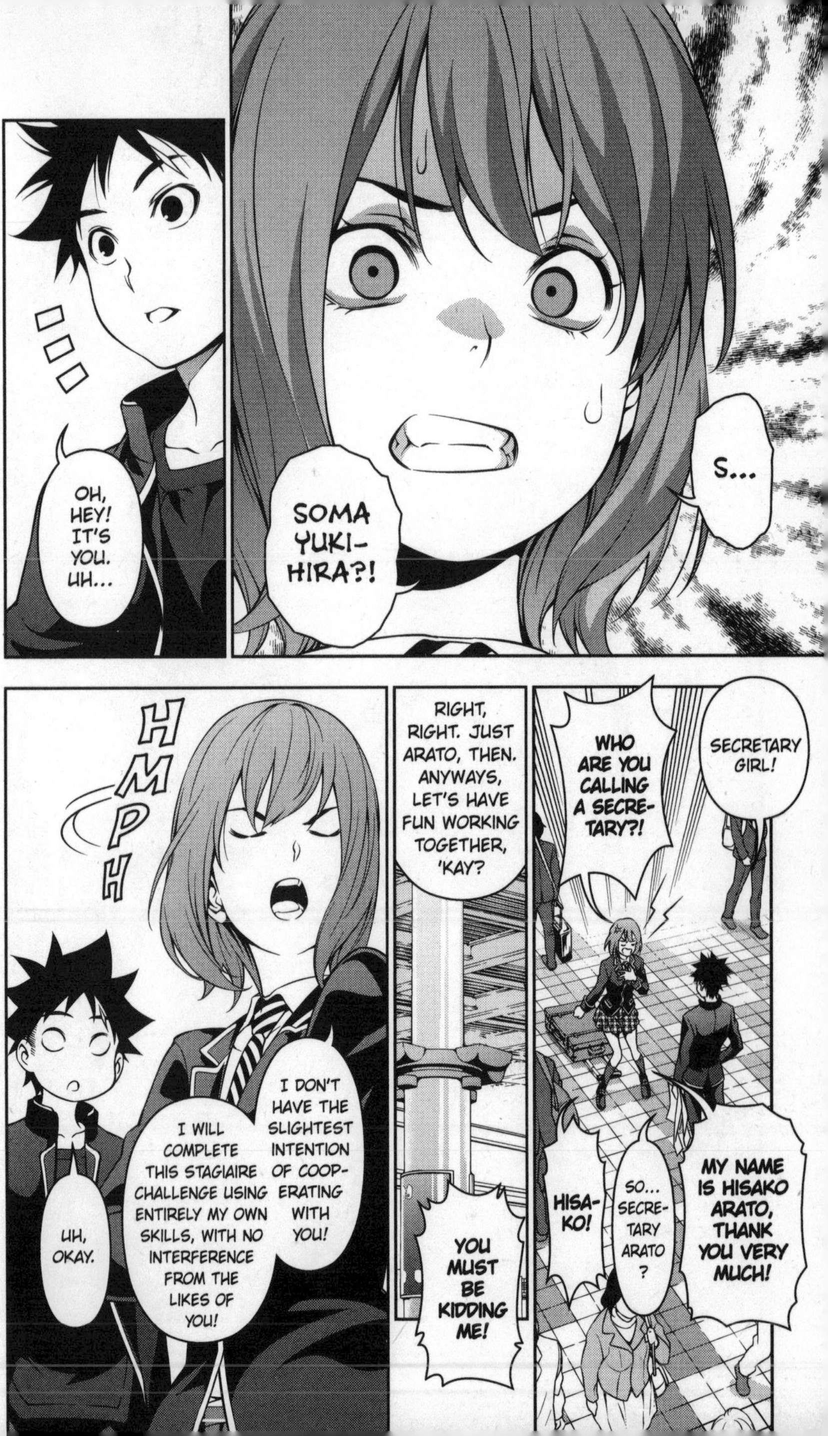
S...
SOMA YUKIHIRA?!
...
OH, HEY! IT'S YOU. UH...
SECRETARY GIRL!
WHO ARE YOU CALLING A SECRETARY?!
MY NAME IS HISAKO ARATO, THANK YOU VERY MUCH!
SO... SECRETARY ARATO?
HISAKO!
RIGHT, RIGHT. JUST ARATO, THEN. ANYWAYS, LET'S HAVE FUN WORKING TOGETHER, 'KAY?
YOU MUST BE KIDDING ME!
HMPH
I DON'T HAVE THE SLIGHTEST INTENTION OF COOPERATING WITH YOU!
I WILL COMPLETE THIS STAGIAIRE CHALLENGE USING ENTIRELY MY OWN SKILLS, WITH NO INTERFERENCE FROM THE LIKES OF YOU!
UH, OKAY.

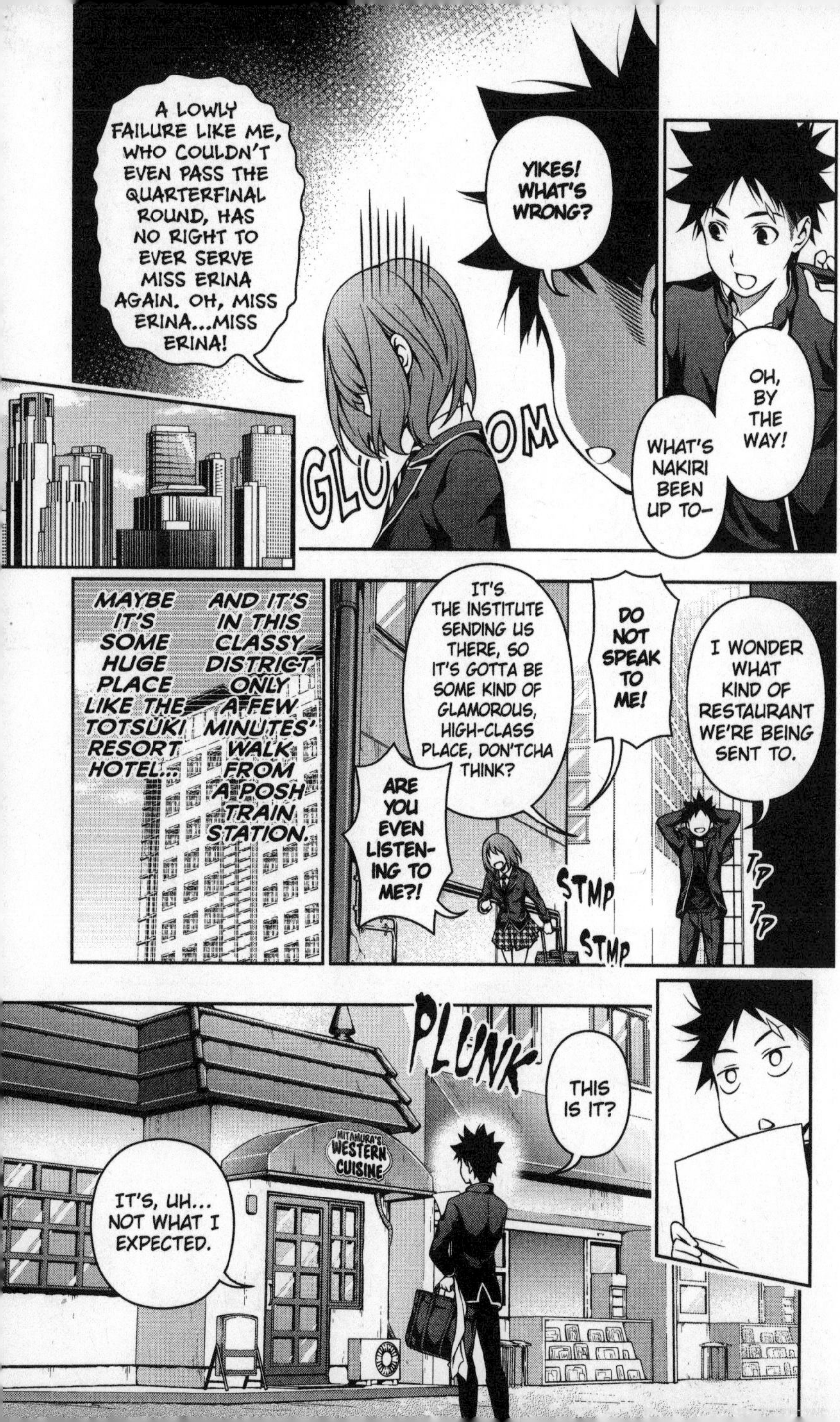
OH, BY THE WAY!
WHAT'S NAKIRI BEEN UP TO–
GLOOM
A LOWLY FAILURE LIKE ME, WHO COULDN'T EVEN PASS THE QUARTERFINAL ROUND, HAS NO RIGHT TO EVER SERVE MISS ERINA AGAIN. OH, MISS ERINA...MISS ERINA!
YIKES! WHAT'S WRONG?
I WONDER WHAT KIND OF RESTAURANT WE'RE BEING SENT TO.
DO NOT SPEAK TO ME!
IT'S THE INSTITUTE SENDING US THERE, SO IT'S GOTTA BE SOME KIND OF GLAMOROUS, HIGH-CLASS PLACE, DON'TCHA THINK?
ARE YOU EVEN LISTENING TO ME?!
STMP
STMP
TP
TP
MAYBE IT'S SOME HUGE PLACE LIKE THE TOTSUKI RESORT HOTEL...
AND IT'S IN THIS CLASSY DISTRICT ONLY A FEW MINUTES' WALK FROM A POSH TRAIN STATION.
THIS IS IT?
PLUNK
MITAMURA'S WESTERN CUISINE
IT'S, UH... NOT WHAT I EXPECTED.

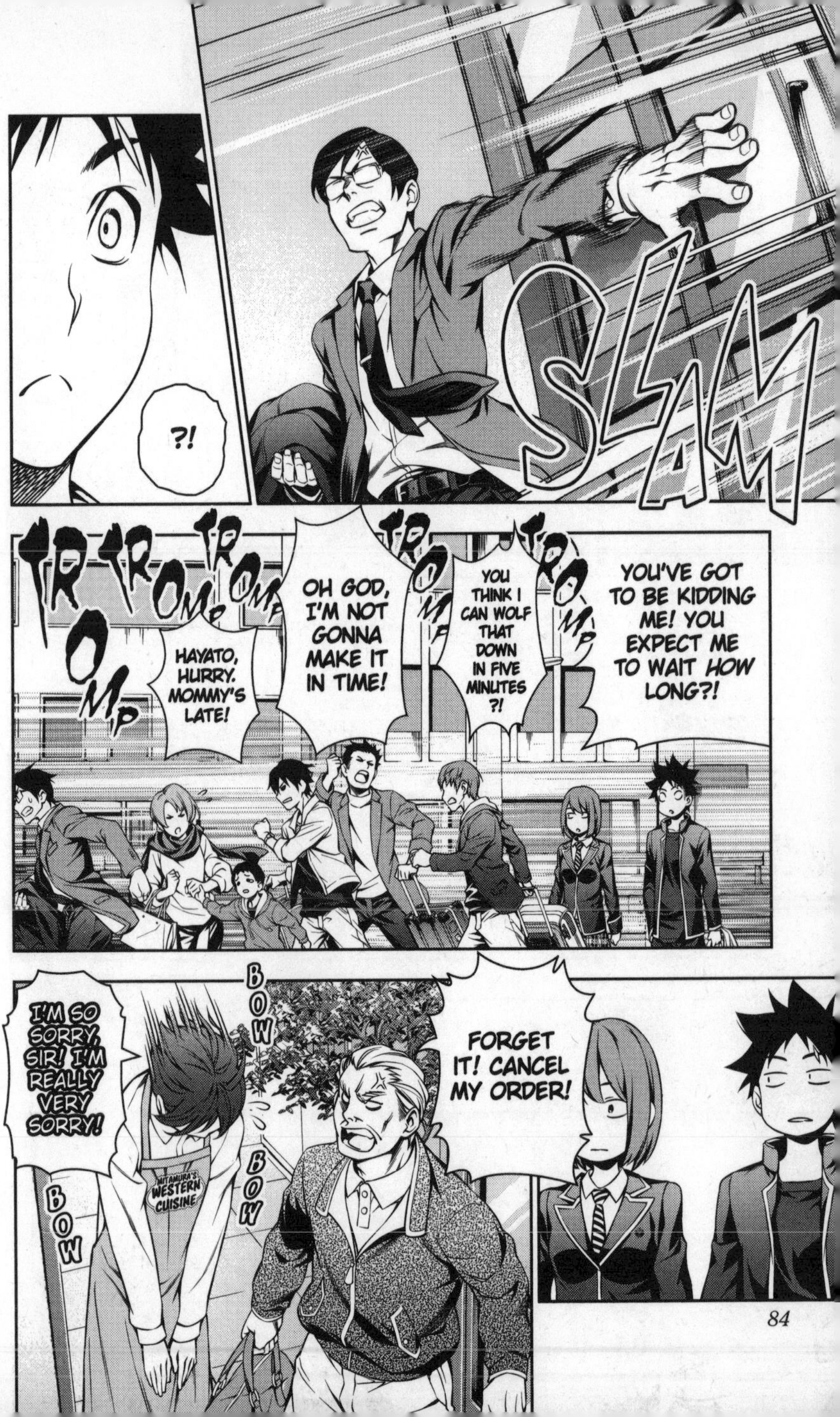
SLAM
?!
TROMP TROMP
YOU'VE GOT TO BE KIDDING ME! YOU EXPECT ME TO WAIT HOW LONG?!
YOU THINK I CAN WOLF THAT DOWN IN FIVE MINUTES?!
OH GOD, I'M NOT GONNA MAKE IT IN TIME!
HAYATO, HURRY. MOMMY'S LATE!
TROMP TROMP TROMP
FORGET IT! CANCEL MY ORDER!
BOW BOW
I'M SO SORRY, SIR! I'M REALLY VERY SORRY!
MITAMURA'S WESTERN CUISINE
BOW

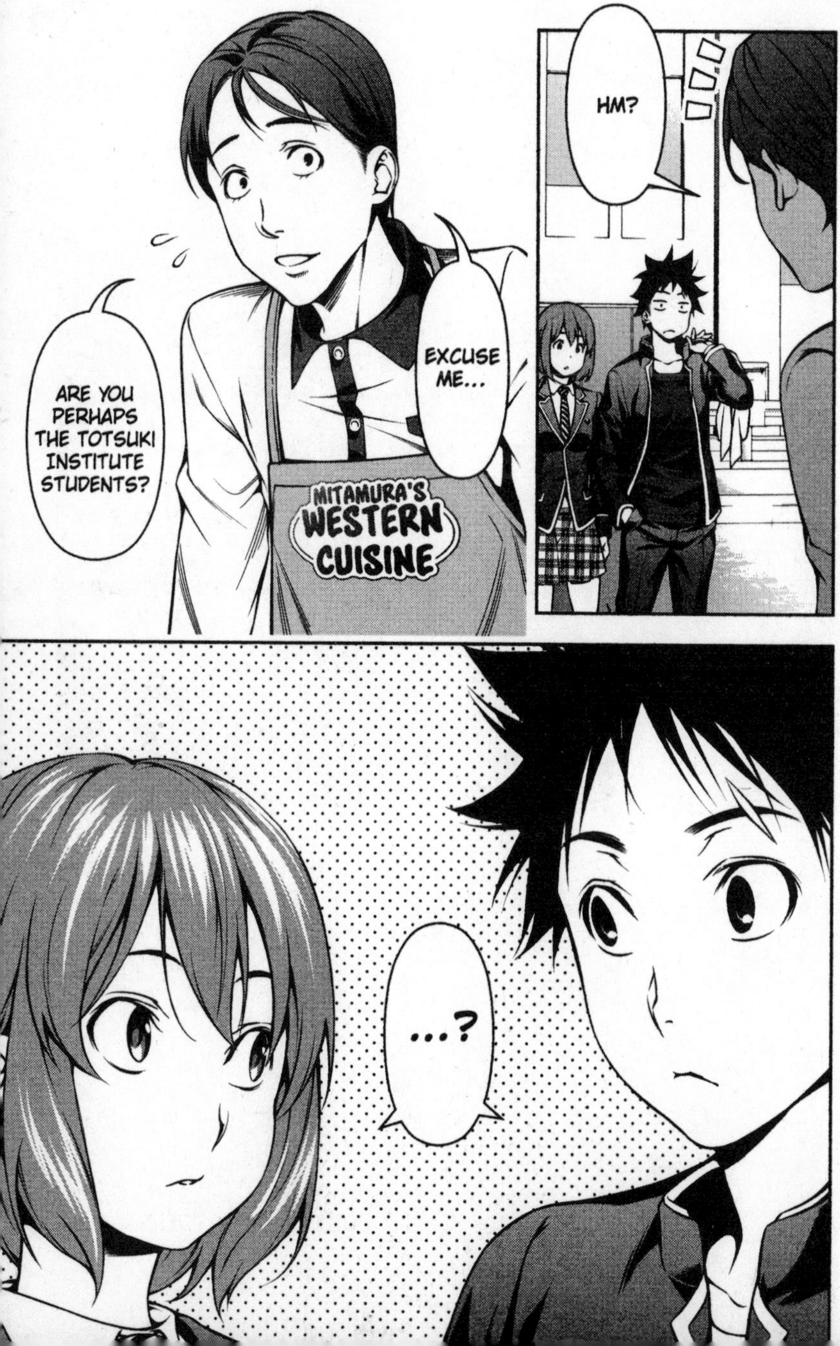
HM?
EXCUSE ME...
ARE YOU PERHAPS THE TOTSUKI INSTITUTE STUDENTS?
MITAMURA'S WESTERN CUISINE
...?

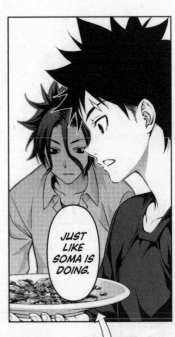

JUST LIKE SOMA IS DOING.
HAYAMA REALLY DID MAKE IT FOR THEM.
THEY WOULDN'T LEAVE. I HAD TO.

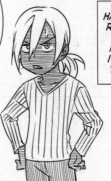

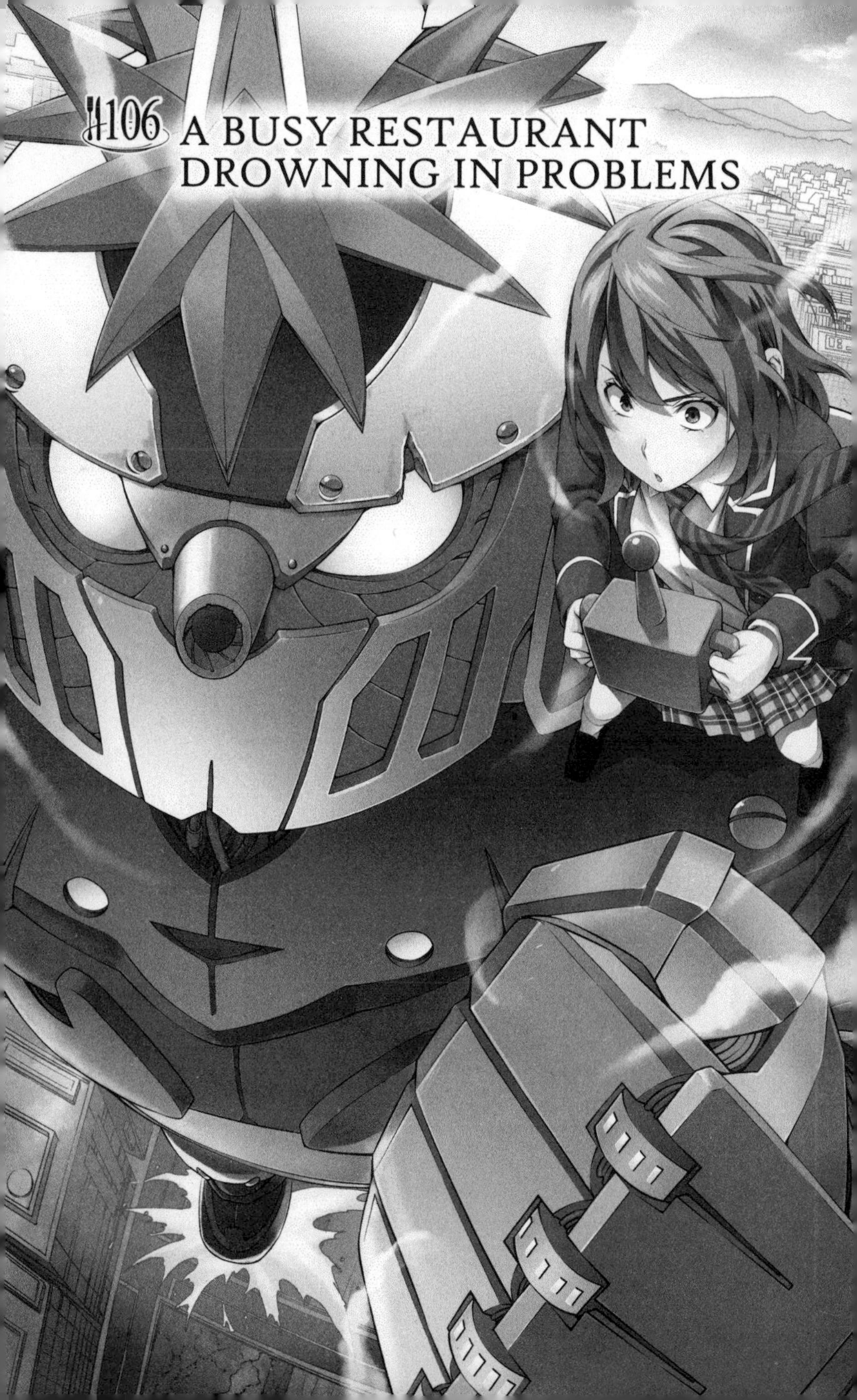
#106 A BUSY RESTAURANT
DROWNING IN PROBLEMS

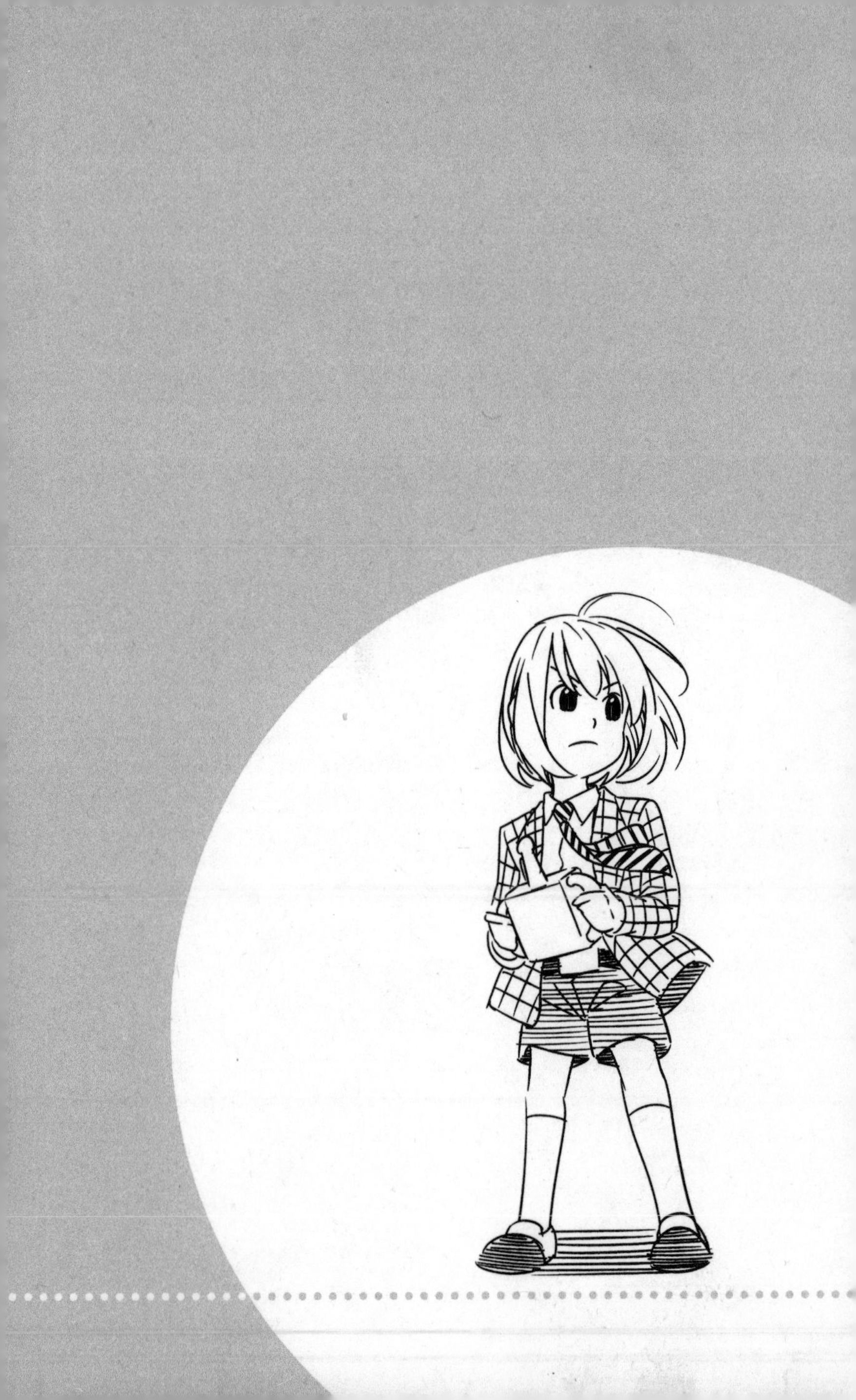

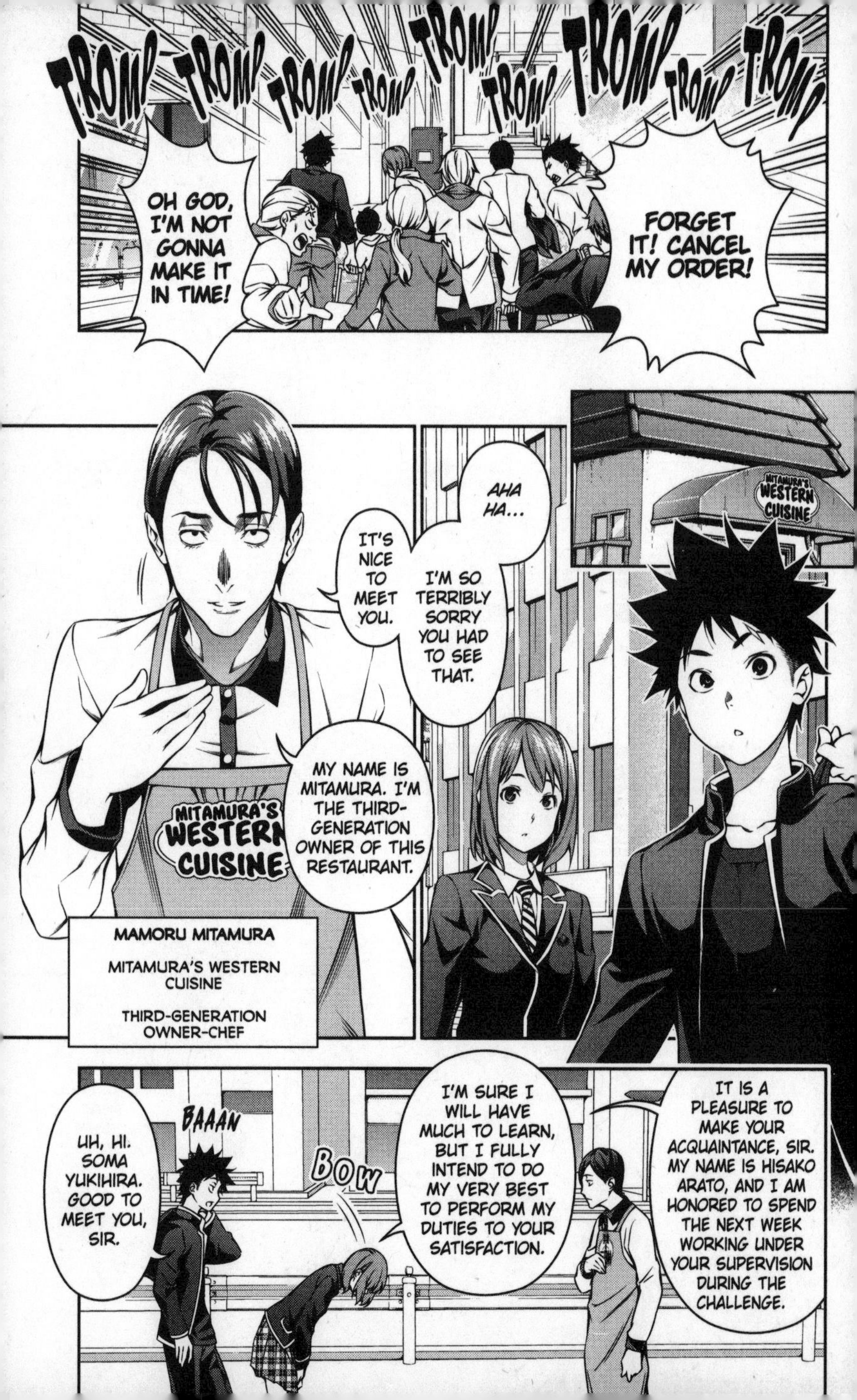
TROMP TROMP TROMP TROMP TROMP TROMP TROMP TROMP TROMP
FORGET IT! CANCEL MY ORDER!
OH GOD, I'M NOT GONNA MAKE IT IN TIME!
MITAMURA'S WESTERN CUISINE
AHA HA...
I'M SO TERRIBLY SORRY YOU HAD TO SEE THAT.
IT'S NICE TO MEET YOU.
MY NAME IS MITAMURA. I'M THE THIRD-GENERATION OWNER OF THIS RESTAURANT.
MITAMURA'S WESTERN CUISINE
MAMORU MITAMURA
MITAMURA'S WESTERN CUISINE
THIRD-GENERATION OWNER-CHEF
IT IS A PLEASURE TO MAKE YOUR ACQUAINTANCE, SIR. MY NAME IS HISAKO ARATO, AND I AM HONORED TO SPEND THE NEXT WEEK WORKING UNDER YOUR SUPERVISION DURING THE CHALLENGE.
I'M SURE I WILL HAVE MUCH TO LEARN, BUT I FULLY INTEND TO DO MY VERY BEST TO PERFORM MY DUTIES TO YOUR SATISFACTION.
BOW
BAAAN
UH, HI. SOMA YUKIHIRA. GOOD TO MEET YOU, SIR.

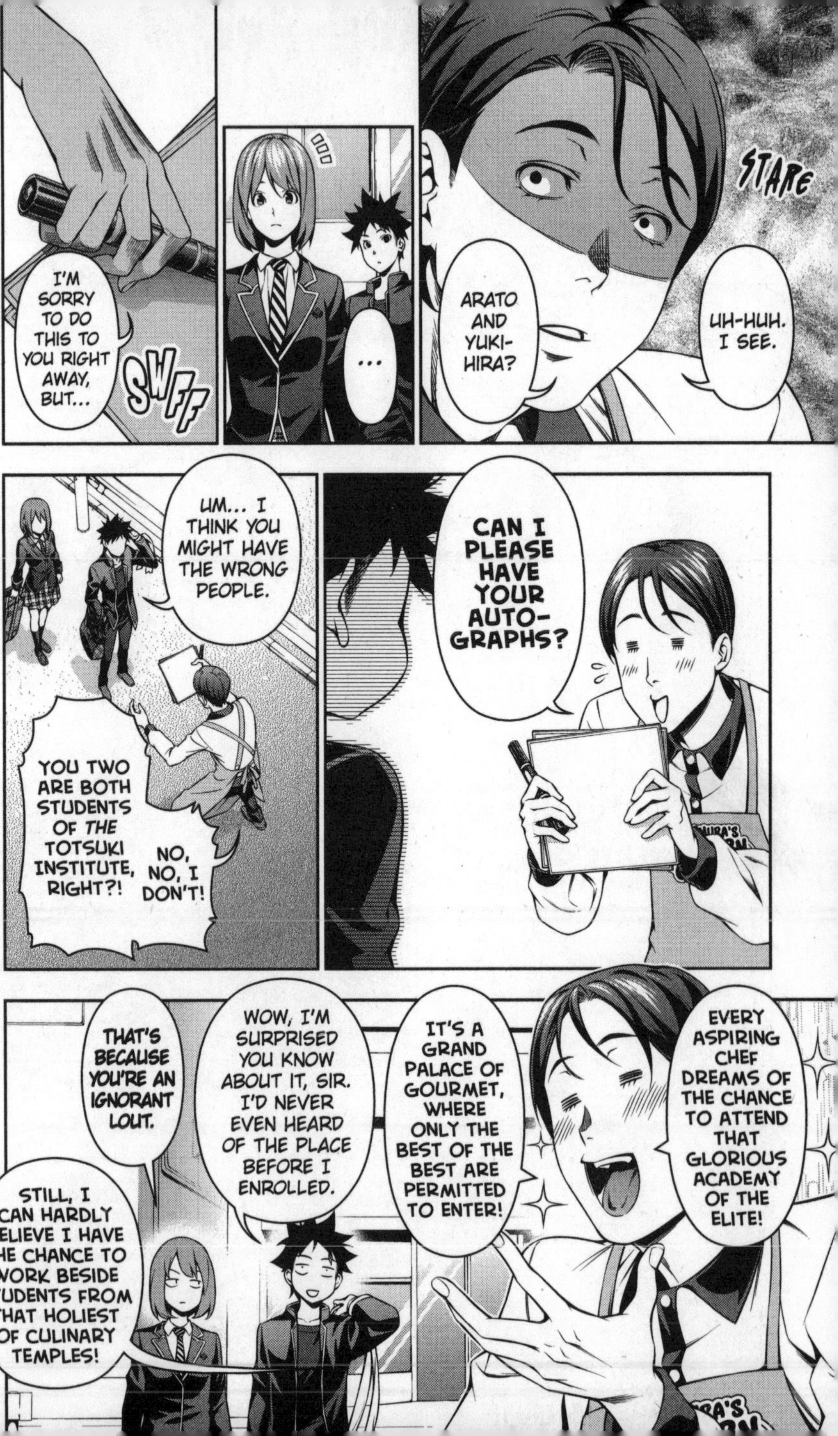
STARE
UH-HUH. I SEE.
ARATO AND YUKI-HIRA?
...
I'M SORRY TO DO THIS TO YOU RIGHT AWAY, BUT...
SWFF
CAN I PLEASE HAVE YOUR AUTO-GRAPHS?
UM... I THINK YOU MIGHT HAVE THE WRONG PEOPLE.
NO, NO, I DON'T!
YOU TWO ARE BOTH STUDENTS OF *THE* TOTSUKI INSTITUTE, RIGHT?!
EVERY ASPIRING CHEF DREAMS OF THE CHANCE TO ATTEND THAT GLORIOUS ACADEMY OF THE ELITE!
IT'S A GRAND PALACE OF GOURMET, WHERE ONLY THE BEST OF THE BEST ARE PERMITTED TO ENTER!
WOW, I'M SURPRISED YOU KNOW ABOUT IT, SIR. I'D NEVER EVEN HEARD OF THE PLACE BEFORE I ENROLLED.
THAT'S BECAUSE YOU'RE AN IGNORANT LOUT.
STILL, I CAN HARDLY BELIEVE I HAVE THE CHANCE TO WORK BESIDE STUDENTS FROM THAT HOLIEST OF CULINARY TEMPLES!

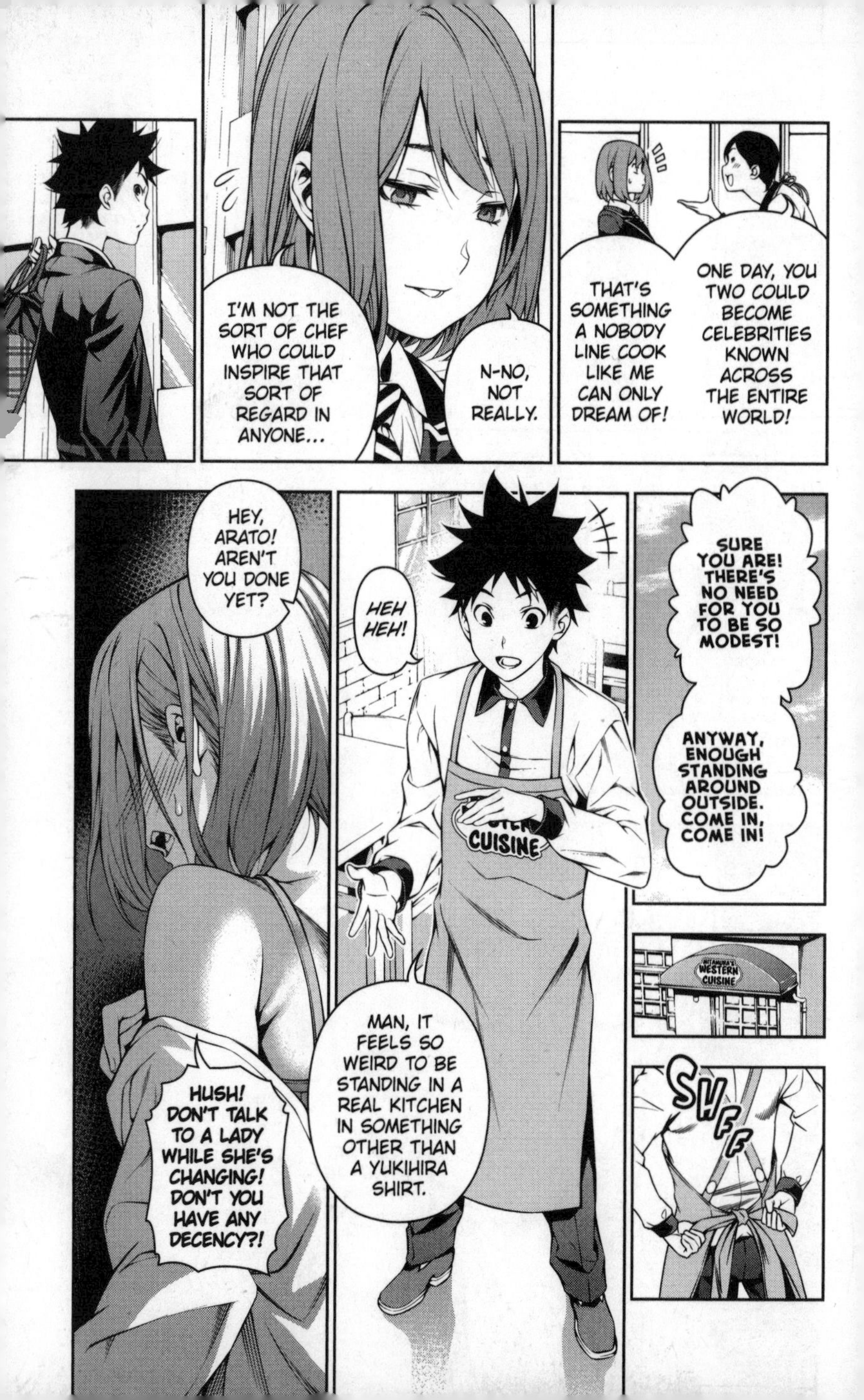

ONE DAY, YOU TWO COULD BECOME CELEBRITIES KNOWN ACROSS THE ENTIRE WORLD!
THAT'S SOMETHING A NOBODY LINE COOK LIKE ME CAN ONLY DREAM OF!
N-NO, NOT REALLY.
I'M NOT THE SORT OF CHEF WHO COULD INSPIRE THAT SORT OF REGARD IN ANYONE...
SURE YOU ARE! THERE'S NO NEED FOR YOU TO BE SO MODEST!
ANYWAY, ENOUGH STANDING AROUND OUTSIDE. COME IN, COME IN!
MITAMURA'S WESTERN CUISINE
SHFF
HEH HEH!
CUISINE
MAN, IT FEELS SO WEIRD TO BE STANDING IN A REAL KITCHEN IN SOMETHING OTHER THAN A YUKIHIRA SHIRT.
HEY, ARATO! AREN'T YOU DONE YET?
HUSH! DON'T TALK TO A LADY WHILE SHE'S CHANGING! DON'T YOU HAVE ANY DECENCY?!

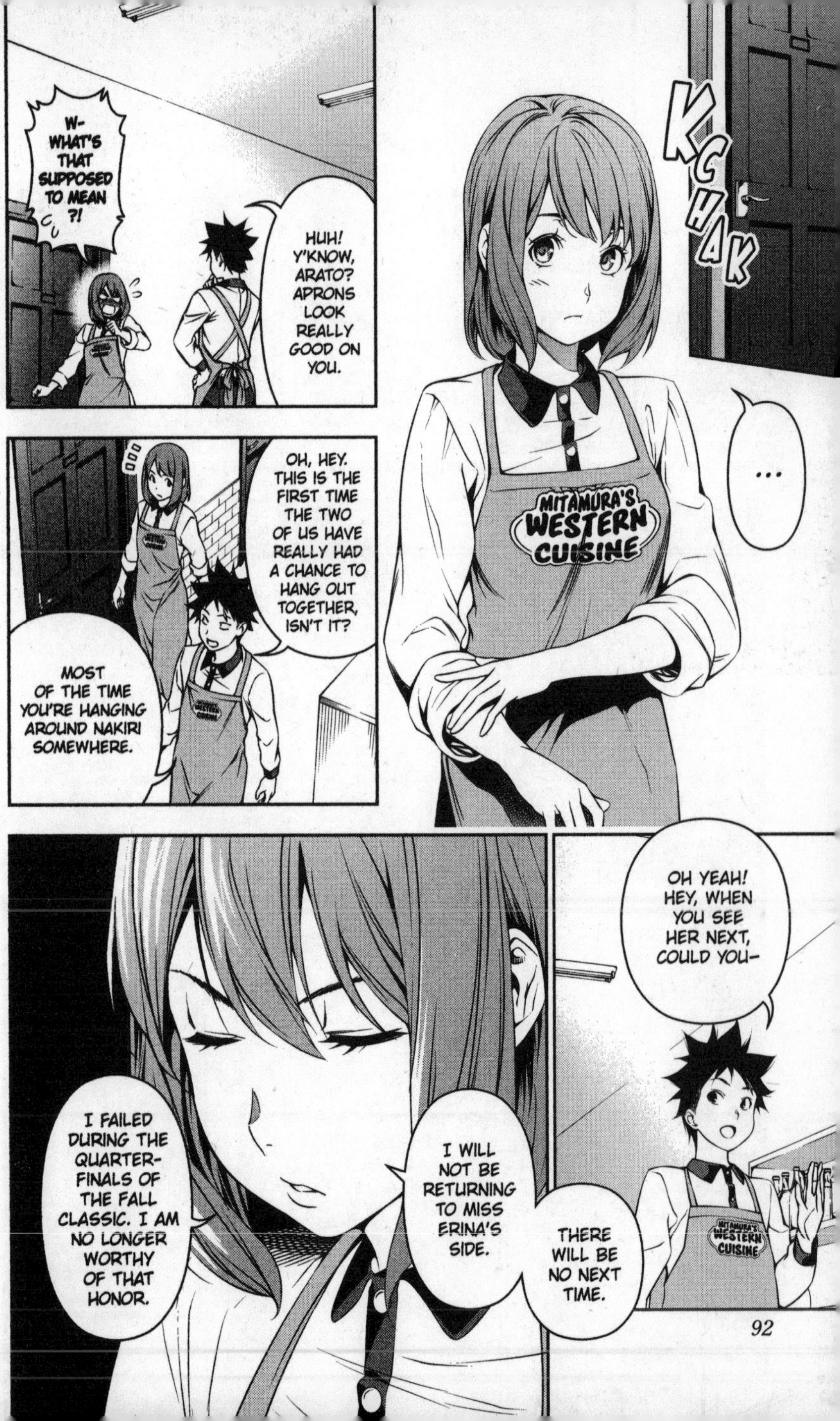
KCHAK
...
HUH! Y'KNOW, ARATO? APRONS LOOK REALLY GOOD ON YOU.
W-WHAT'S THAT SUPPOSED TO MEAN ?!
OH, HEY. THIS IS THE FIRST TIME THE TWO OF US HAVE REALLY HAD A CHANCE TO HANG OUT TOGETHER, ISN'T IT?
MOST OF THE TIME YOU'RE HANGING AROUND NAKIRI SOMEWHERE.
MITAMURA'S WESTERN CUISINE
OH YEAH! HEY, WHEN YOU SEE HER NEXT, COULD YOU-
I WILL NOT BE RETURNING TO MISS ERINA'S SIDE.
I FAILED DURING THE QUARTER-FINALS OF THE FALL CLASSIC. I AM NO LONGER WORTHY OF THAT HONOR.
THERE WILL BE NO NEXT TIME.

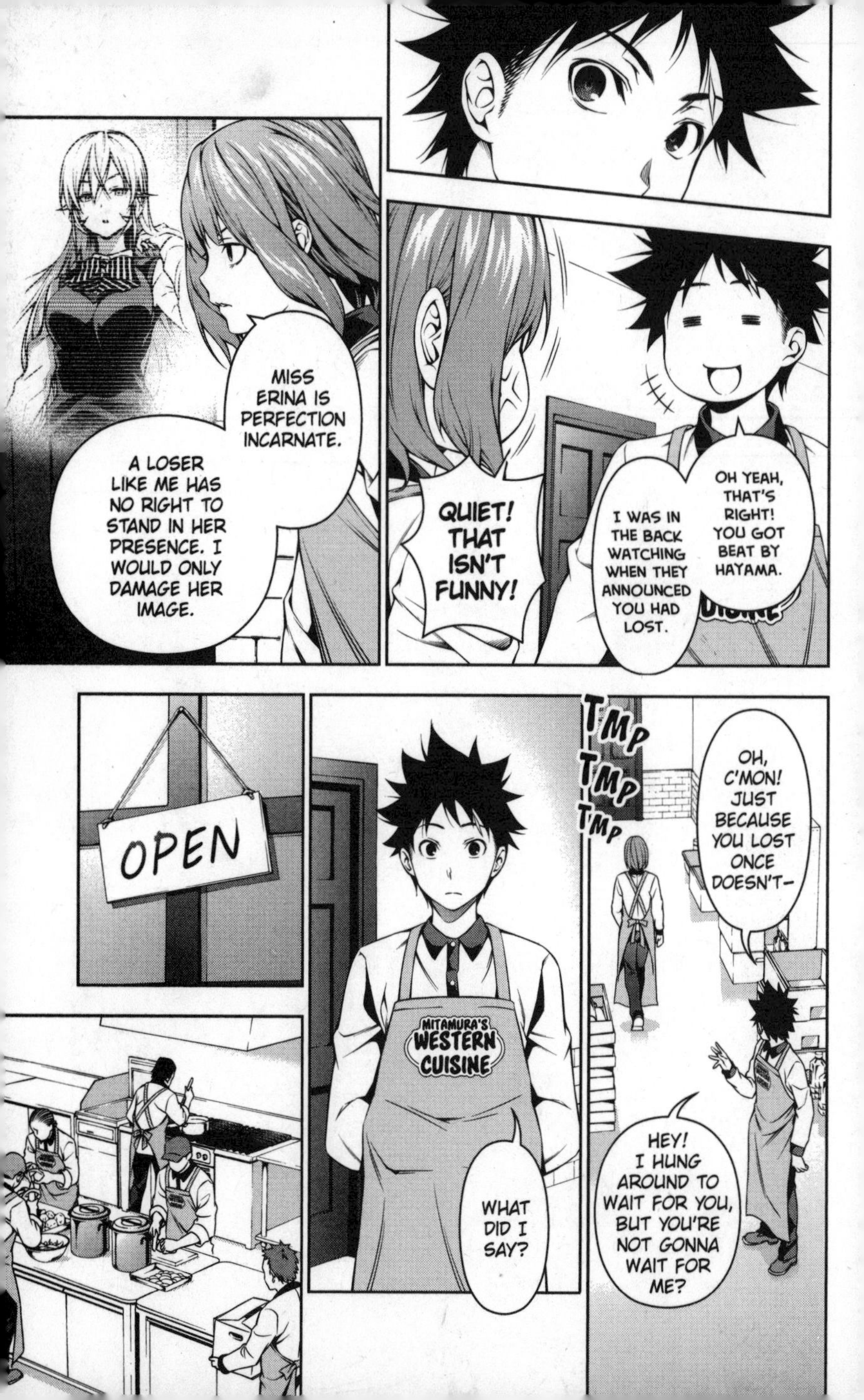

OH YEAH, THAT'S RIGHT! YOU GOT BEAT BY HAYAMA.
I WAS IN THE BACK WATCHING WHEN THEY ANNOUNCED YOU HAD LOST.
QUIET! THAT ISN'T FUNNY!
MISS ERINA IS PERFECTION INCARNATE.
A LOSER LIKE ME HAS NO RIGHT TO STAND IN HER PRESENCE. I WOULD ONLY DAMAGE HER IMAGE.
TMP TMP TMP
OH, C'MON! JUST BECAUSE YOU LOST ONCE DOESN'T—
WHAT DID I SAY?
MITAMURA'S WESTERN CUISINE
HEY! I HUNG AROUND TO WAIT FOR YOU, BUT YOU'RE NOT GONNA WAIT FOR ME?
OPEN

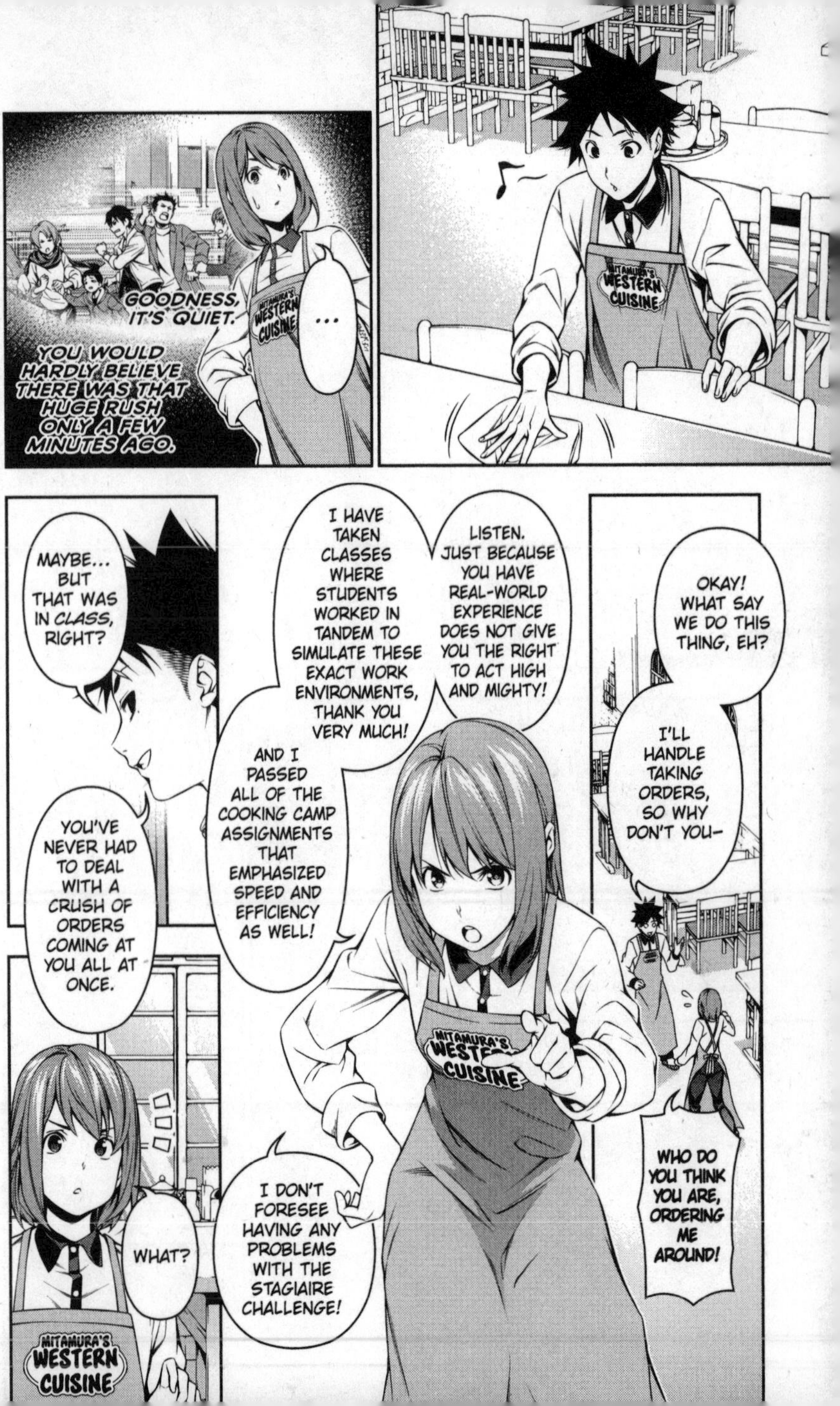
...
GOODNESS, IT'S QUIET.
YOU WOULD HARDLY BELIEVE THERE WAS THAT HUGE RUSH ONLY A FEW MINUTES AGO.
OKAY! WHAT SAY WE DO THIS THING, EH?
I'LL HANDLE TAKING ORDERS, SO WHY DON'T YOU–
WHO DO YOU THINK YOU ARE, ORDERING ME AROUND!
LISTEN. JUST BECAUSE YOU HAVE REAL-WORLD EXPERIENCE DOES NOT GIVE YOU THE RIGHT TO ACT HIGH AND MIGHTY!
I HAVE TAKEN CLASSES WHERE STUDENTS WORKED IN TANDEM TO SIMULATE THESE EXACT WORK ENVIRONMENTS, THANK YOU VERY MUCH!
AND I PASSED ALL OF THE COOKING CAMP ASSIGNMENTS THAT EMPHASIZED SPEED AND EFFICIENCY AS WELL!
I DON'T FORESEE HAVING ANY PROBLEMS WITH THE STAGIAIRE CHALLENGE!
MAYBE... BUT THAT WAS IN *CLASS*, RIGHT?
YOU'VE NEVER HAD TO DEAL WITH A CRUSH OF ORDERS COMING AT YOU ALL AT ONCE.
WHAT?

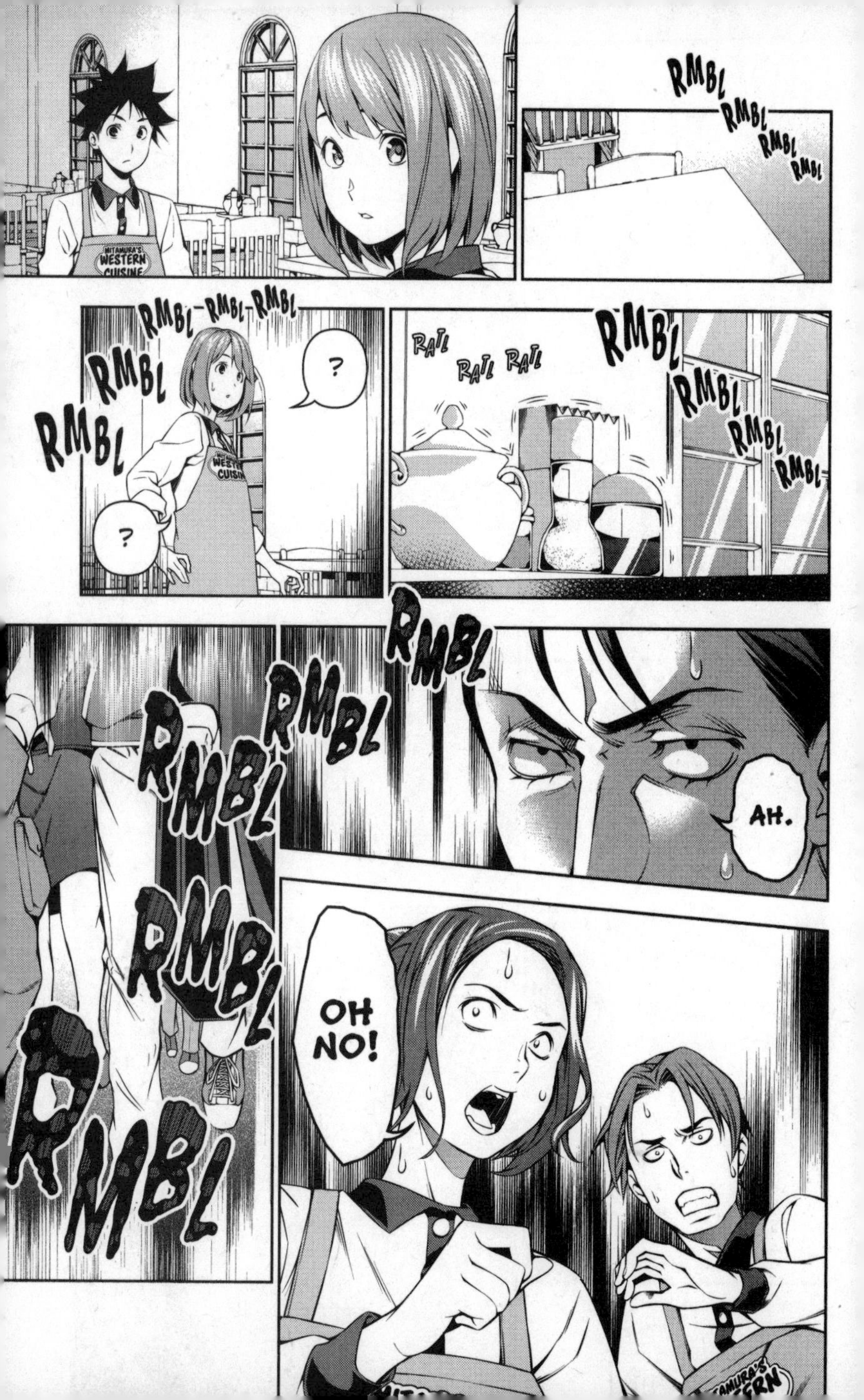
RMBL
RMBL
RMBL
RMBL
MITAMURA'S WESTERN CUISINE
RMBL
RMBL
RMBL
RMBL
RATL
RATL
RATL
RMBL-RMBL-RMBL
RMBL
RMBL
?
?
RMBL
AH.
RMBL
OH NO!
RMBL
RMBL
RMBL

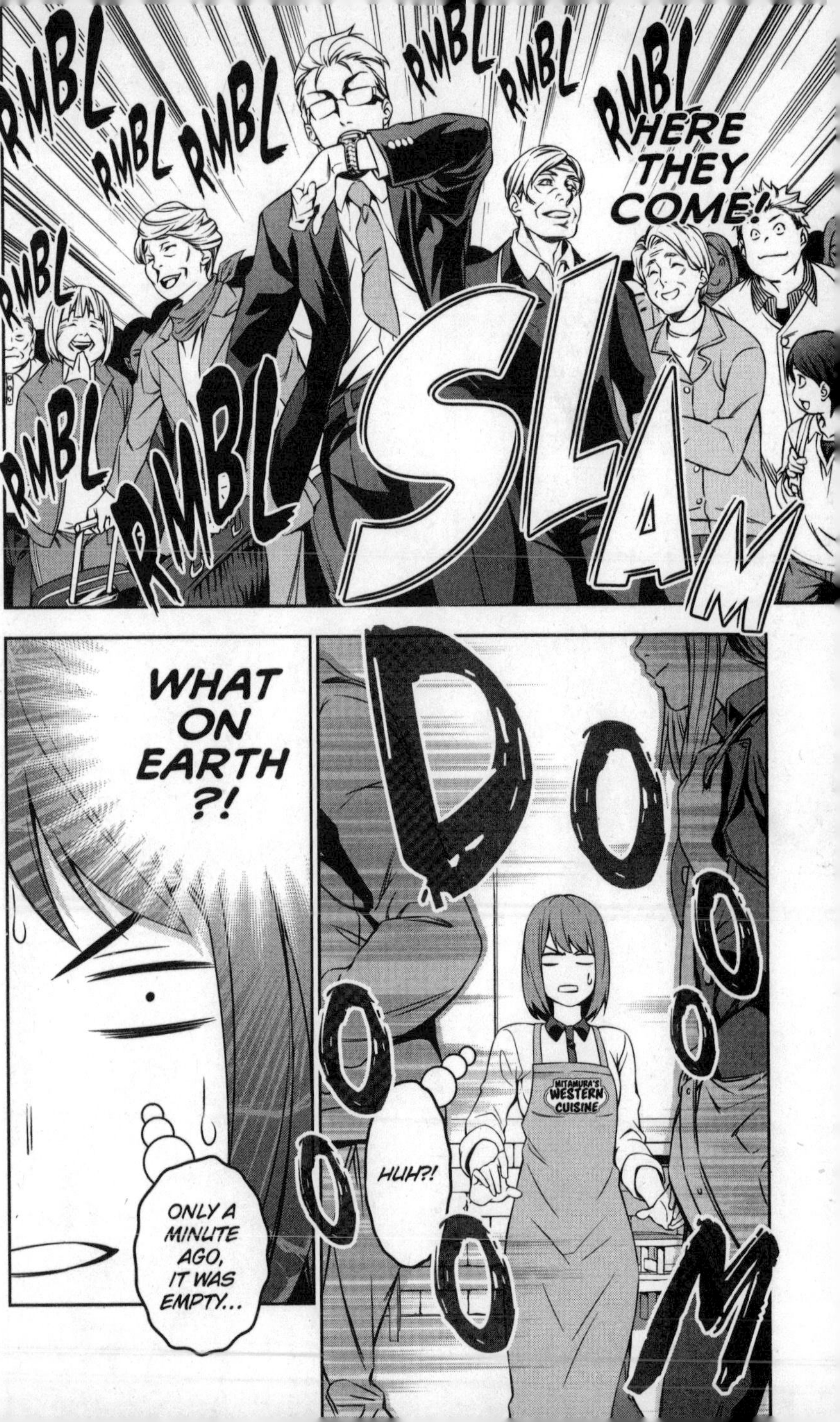
RMBL RMBL RMBL RMBL
HERE THEY COME!
RMBL RMBL RMBL RMBL
SLAM
DOOOOOOM
MITAMURA'S WESTERN CUISINE
HUH?!
WHAT ON EARTH ?!
ONLY A MINUTE AGO, IT WAS EMPTY...

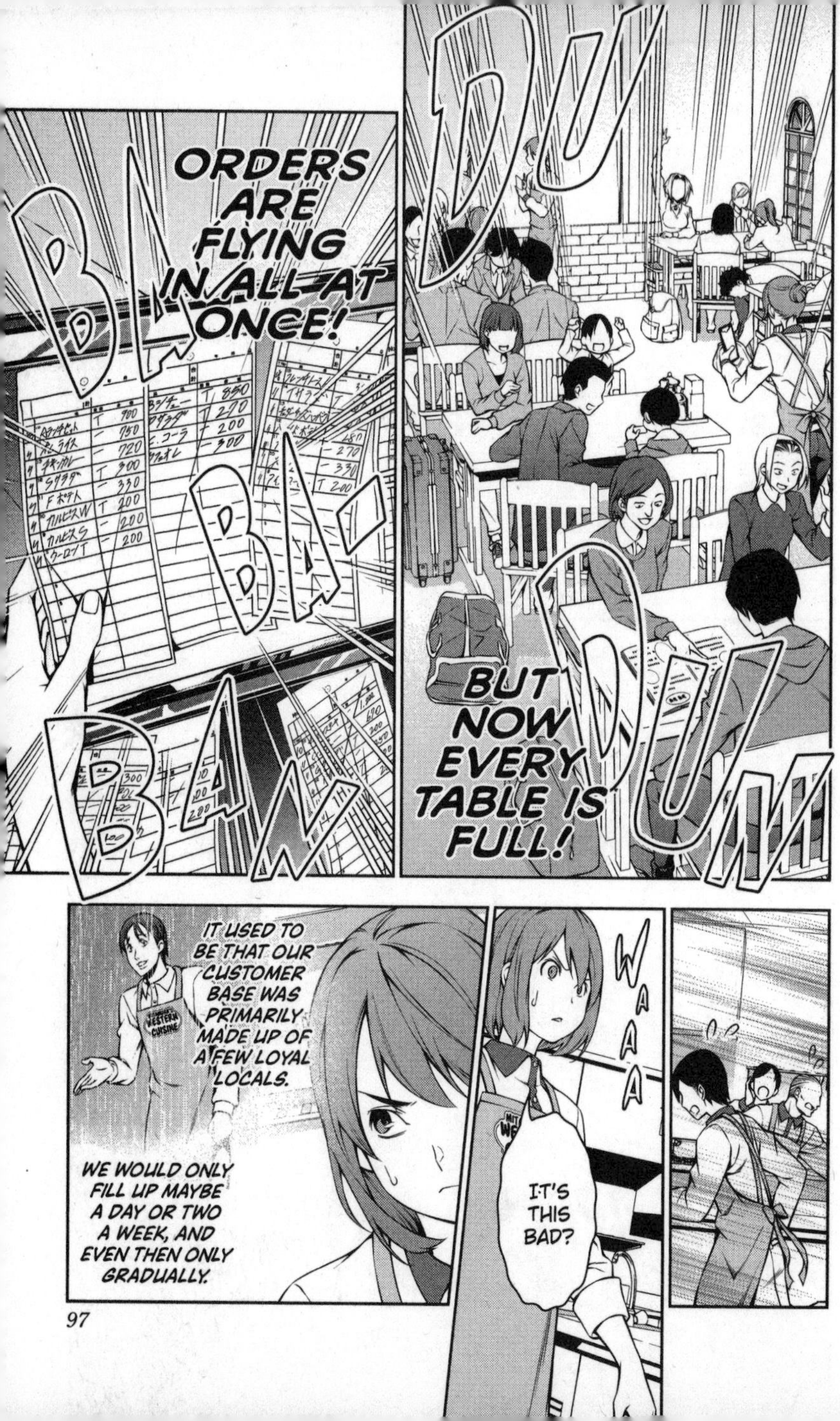
DU
DUM
BUT NOW EVERY TABLE IS FULL!
ORDERS ARE FLYING IN ALL AT ONCE!
BA-
BA-
BAM
WAAAA
IT'S THIS BAD?
IT USED TO BE THAT OUR CUSTOMER BASE WAS PRIMARILY MADE UP OF A FEW LOYAL LOCALS.
WESTERN CUISINE
WE WOULD ONLY FILL UP MAYBE A DAY OR TWO A WEEK, AND EVEN THEN ONLY GRADUALLY.

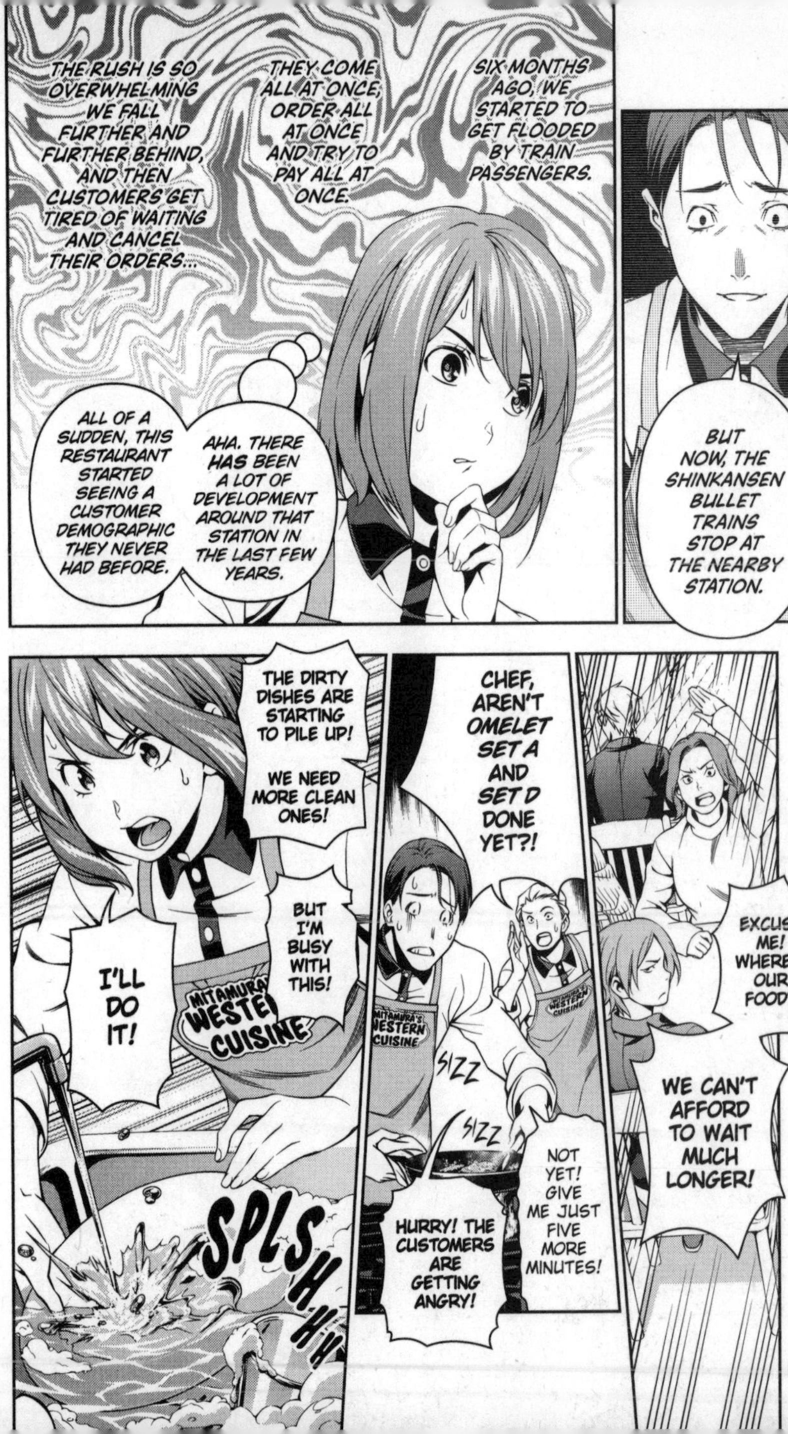
BUT NOW, THE SHINKANSEN BULLET TRAINS STOP AT THE NEARBY STATION.
SIX MONTHS AGO, WE STARTED TO GET FLOODED BY TRAIN PASSENGERS.
THEY COME ALL AT ONCE, ORDER ALL AT ONCE AND TRY TO PAY ALL AT ONCE.
THE RUSH IS SO OVERWHELMING WE FALL FURTHER AND FURTHER BEHIND, AND THEN CUSTOMERS GET TIRED OF WAITING AND CANCEL THEIR ORDERS...
AHA. THERE HAS BEEN A LOT OF DEVELOPMENT AROUND THAT STATION IN THE LAST FEW YEARS.
ALL OF A SUDDEN, THIS RESTAURANT STARTED SEEING A CUSTOMER DEMOGRAPHIC THEY NEVER HAD BEFORE.
EXCUSE ME! WHERE'S OUR FOOD?
WE CAN'T AFFORD TO WAIT MUCH LONGER!
CHEF, AREN'T OMELET SET A AND SET D DONE YET?!
MITAMURA'S WESTERN CUISINE
MITAMURA'S WESTERN CUISINE
SIZZ
SIZZ
NOT YET! GIVE ME JUST FIVE MORE MINUTES!
HURRY! THE CUSTOMERS ARE GETTING ANGRY!
THE DIRTY DISHES ARE STARTING TO PILE UP!
WE NEED MORE CLEAN ONES!
BUT I'M BUSY WITH THIS!
I'LL DO IT!
SPLSHHH

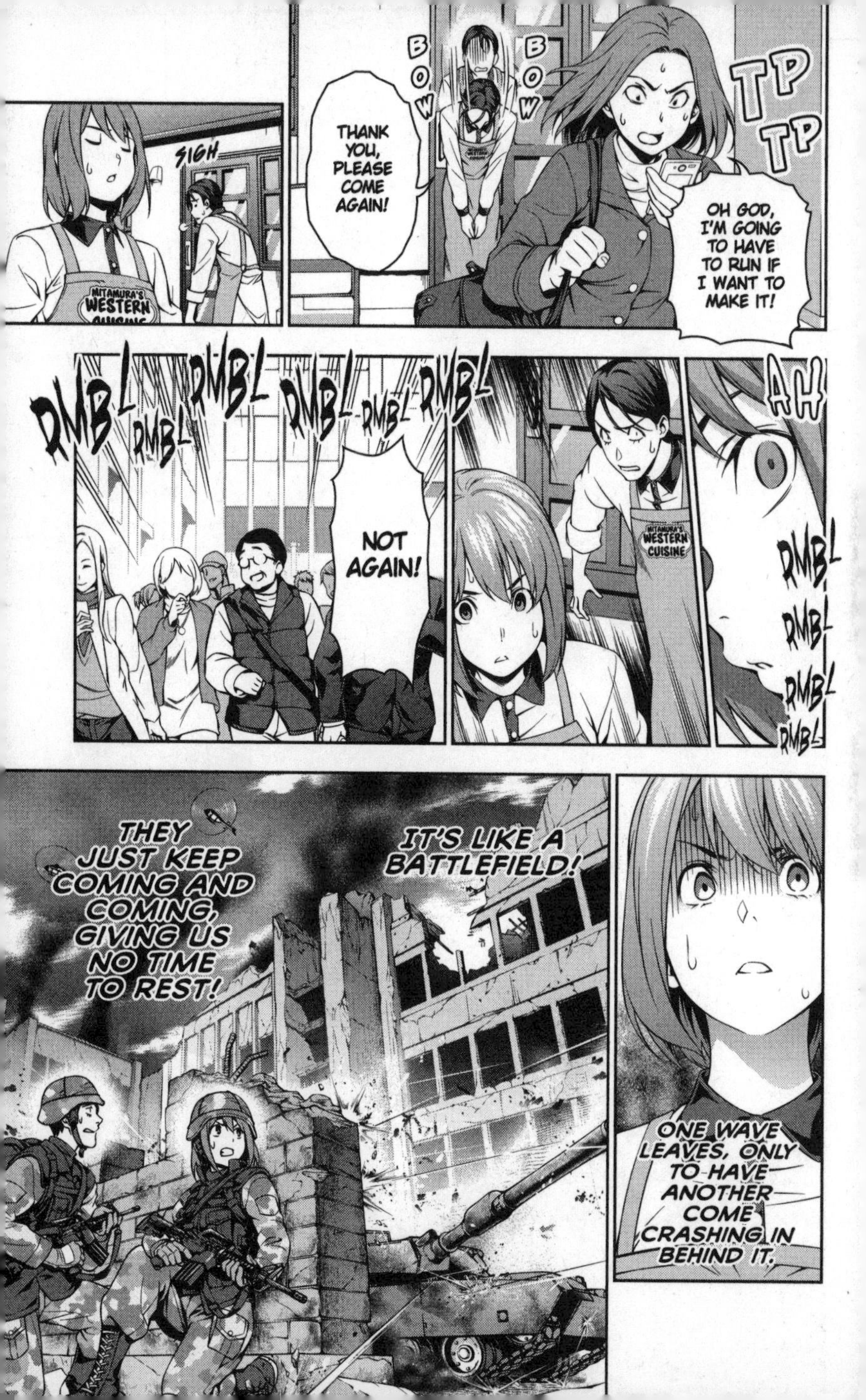
TP TP
OH GOD, I'M GOING TO HAVE TO RUN IF I WANT TO MAKE IT!
BOW BOW
THANK YOU, PLEASE COME AGAIN!
SIGH
MITAMURA'S WESTERN
AH
RMBL RMBL RMBL RMBL
MITAMURA'S WESTERN CUISINE
RMBL RMBL RMBL RMBL RMBL RMBL RMBL
NOT AGAIN!
ONE WAVE LEAVES, ONLY TO HAVE ANOTHER COME CRASHING IN BEHIND IT.
IT'S LIKE A BATTLEFIELD!
THEY JUST KEEP COMING AND COMING, GIVING US NO TIME TO REST!

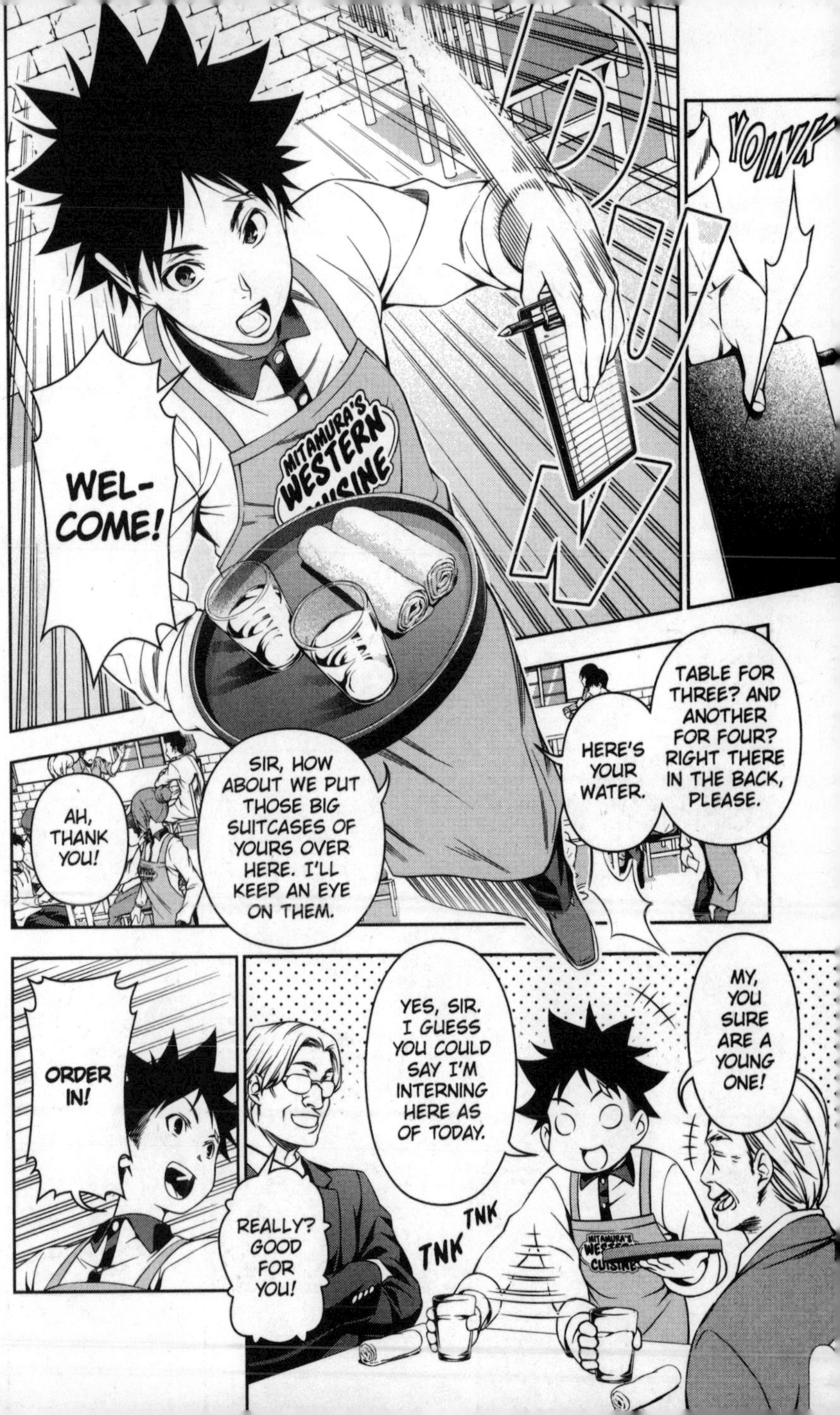
YOINK
WEL-COME!
MITAMURA'S WESTERN CUISINE
TABLE FOR THREE? AND ANOTHER FOR FOUR? RIGHT THERE IN THE BACK, PLEASE.
HERE'S YOUR WATER.
SIR, HOW ABOUT WE PUT THOSE BIG SUITCASES OF YOURS OVER HERE. I'LL KEEP AN EYE ON THEM.
AH, THANK YOU!
MY, YOU SURE ARE A YOUNG ONE!
YES, SIR. I GUESS YOU COULD SAY I'M INTERNING HERE AS OF TODAY.
TNK
TNK
REALLY? GOOD FOR YOU!
ORDER IN!

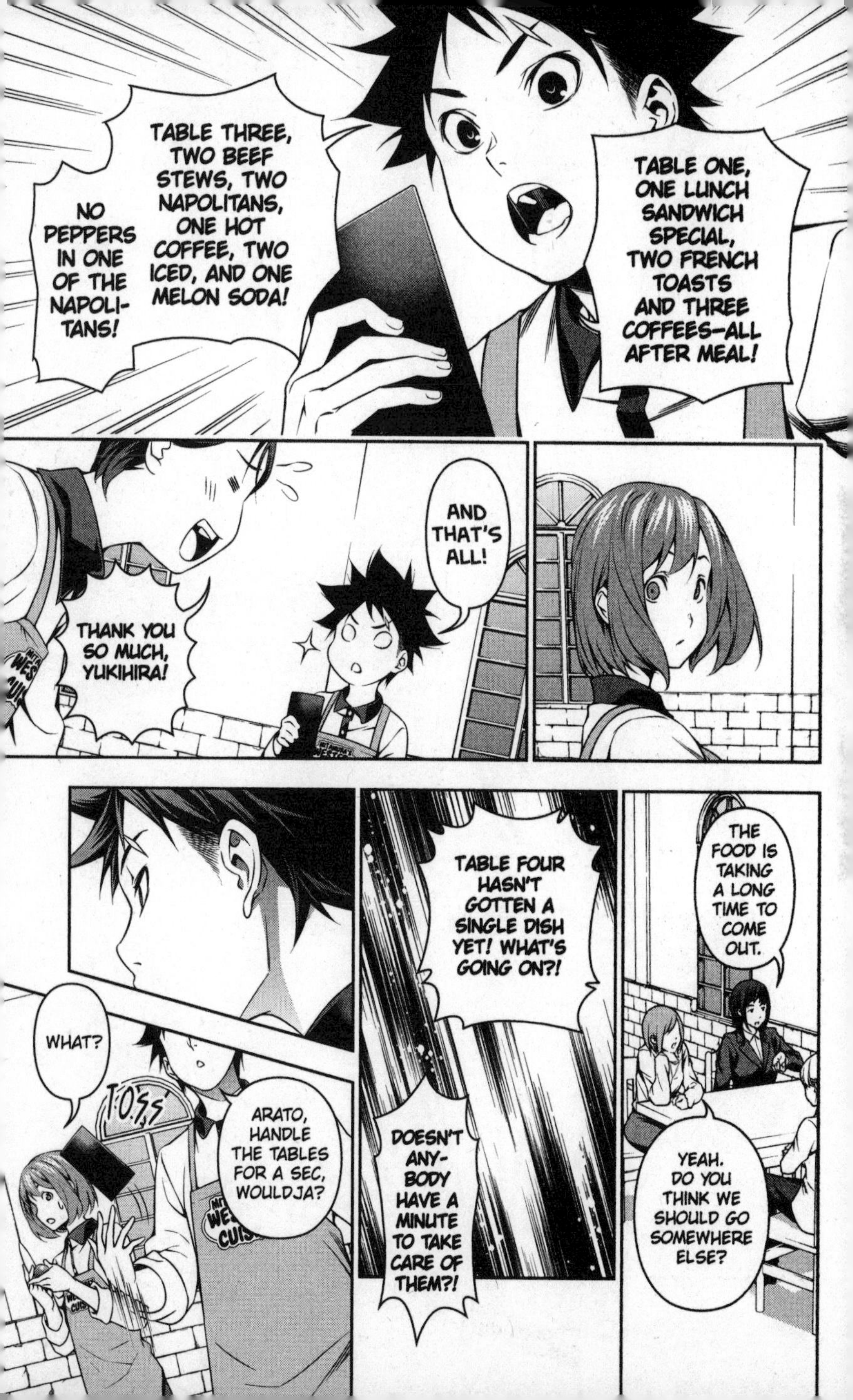
TABLE ONE, ONE LUNCH SANDWICH SPECIAL, TWO FRENCH TOASTS AND THREE COFFEES—ALL AFTER MEAL!
TABLE THREE, TWO BEEF STEWS, TWO NAPOLITANS, ONE HOT COFFEE, TWO ICED, AND ONE MELON SODA!
NO PEPPERS IN ONE OF THE NAPOLI-TANS!
AND THAT'S ALL!
THANK YOU SO MUCH, YUKIHIRA!
THE FOOD IS TAKING A LONG TIME TO COME OUT.
YEAH. DO YOU THINK WE SHOULD GO SOMEWHERE ELSE?
TABLE FOUR HASN'T GOTTEN A SINGLE DISH YET! WHAT'S GOING ON?!
DOESN'T ANY-BODY HAVE A MINUTE TO TAKE CARE OF THEM?!
WHAT?
TOSS
ARATO, HANDLE THE TABLES FOR A SEC, WOULDJA?

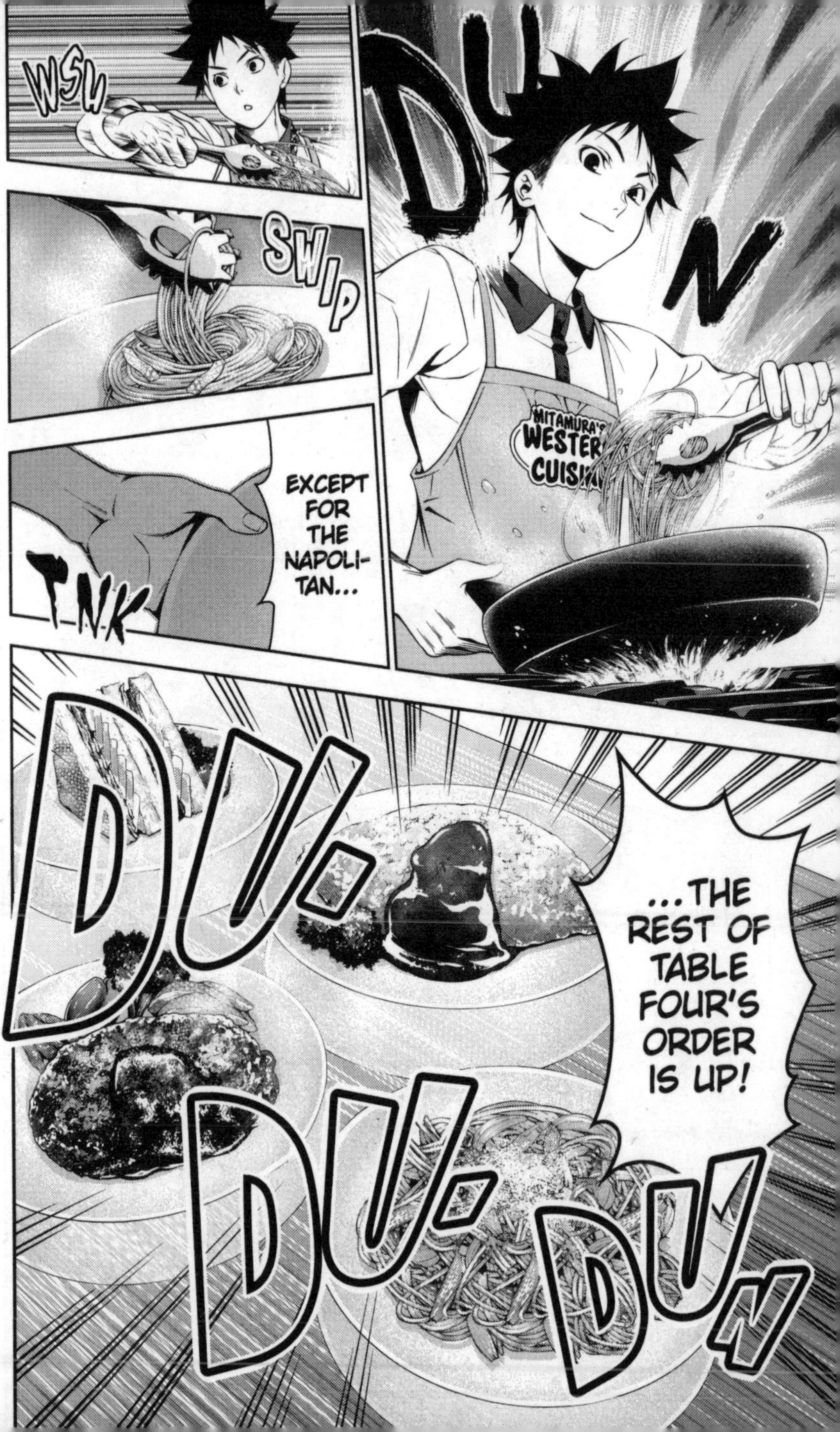
DUN
MITAMURA'S WESTER CUISIN
WSH
SWIP
EXCEPT FOR THE NAPOLI-TAN...
TNK
...THE REST OF TABLE FOUR'S ORDER IS UP!
DU- DU- DUN

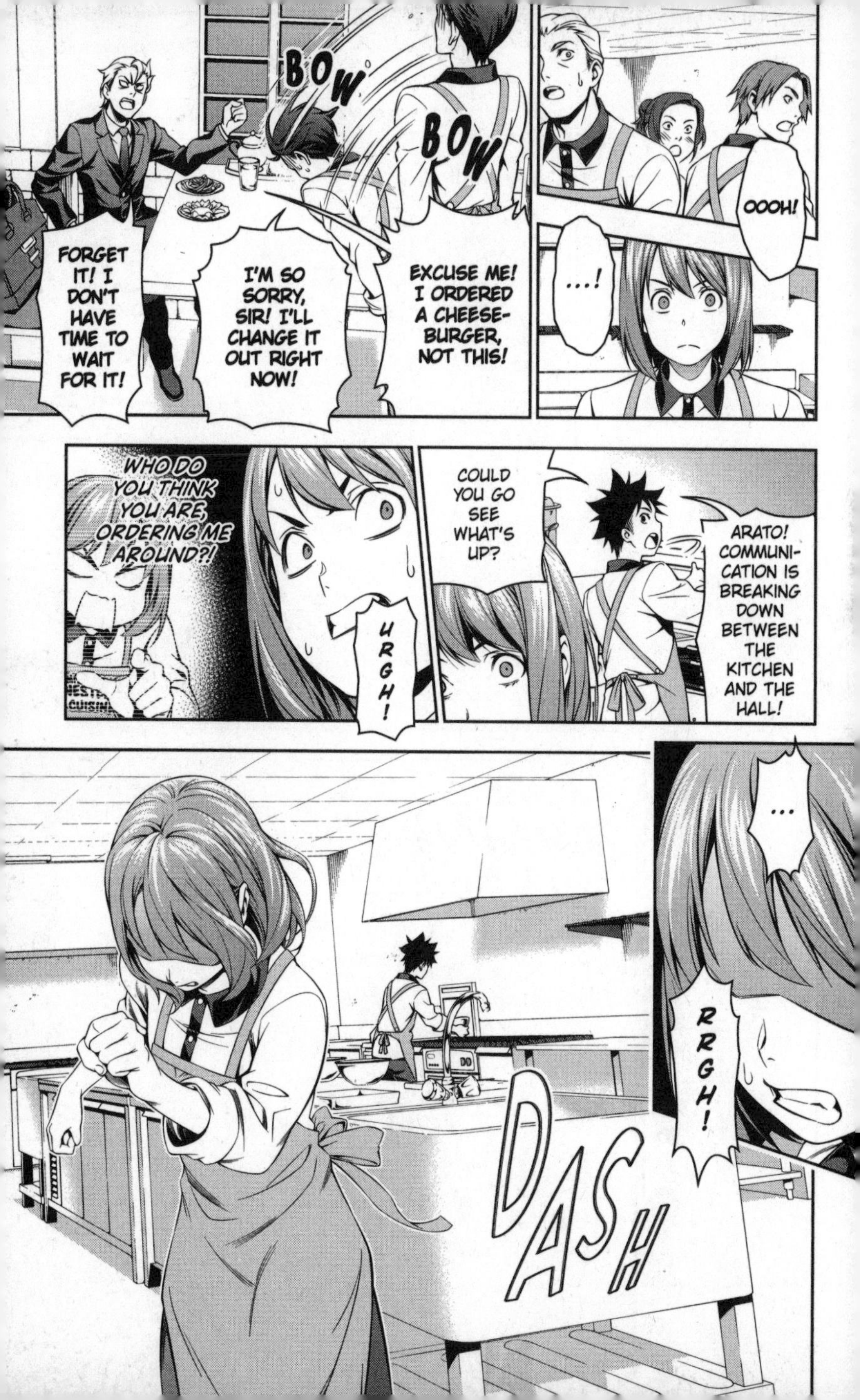
OOOH!
...!
EXCUSE ME! I ORDERED A CHEESE-BURGER, NOT THIS!
BOW BOW
I'M SO SORRY, SIR! I'LL CHANGE IT OUT RIGHT NOW!
FORGET IT! I DON'T HAVE TIME TO WAIT FOR IT!
ARATO! COMMUNICATION IS BREAKING DOWN BETWEEN THE KITCHEN AND THE HALL!
COULD YOU GO SEE WHAT'S UP?
URGH!
WHO DO YOU THINK YOU ARE, ORDERING ME AROUND?!
...
RRGH!
DASH

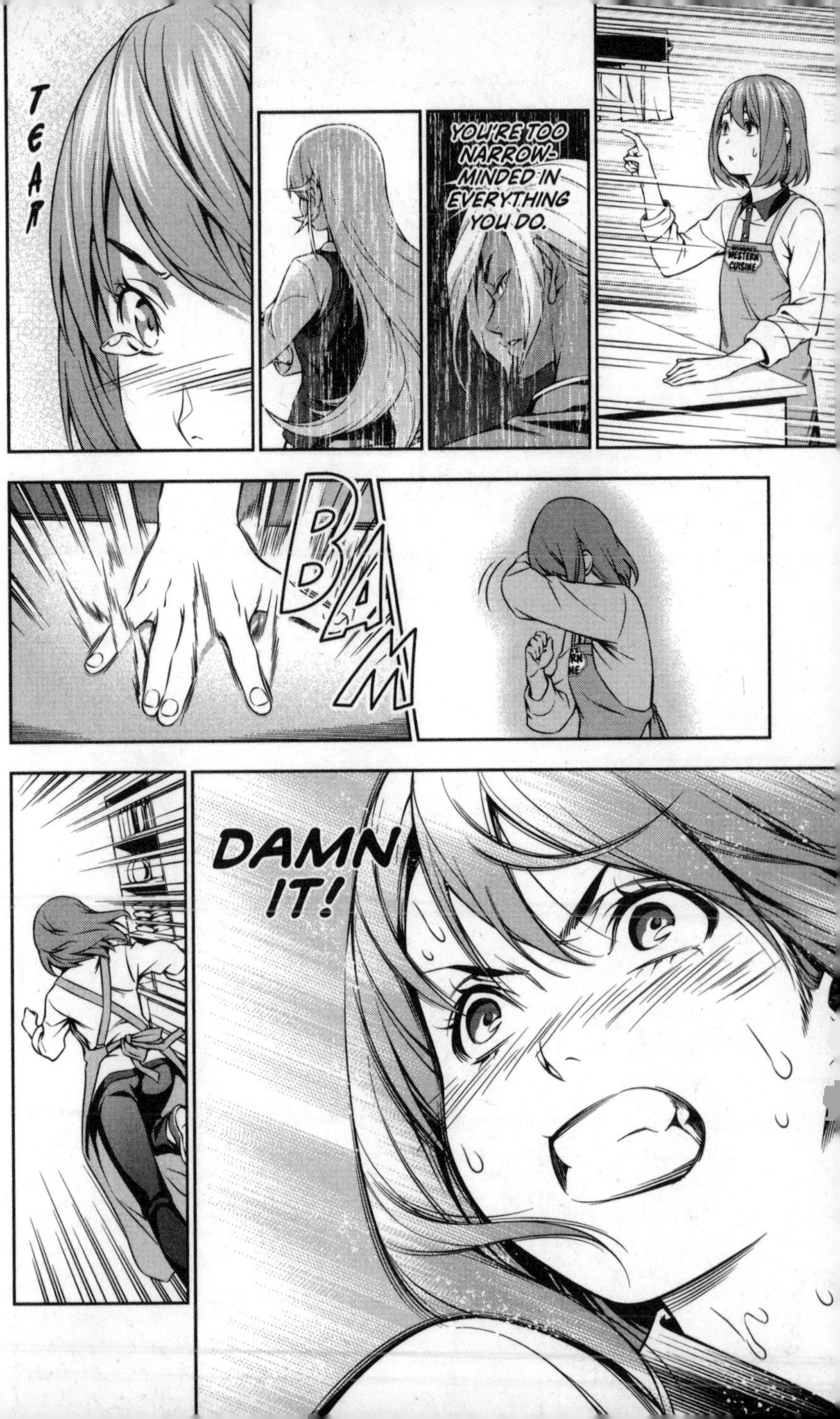
WESTERN CUISINE
YOU'RE TOO NARROW-MINDED IN EVERYTHING YOU DO.
TEAR
BAM
DAMN IT!

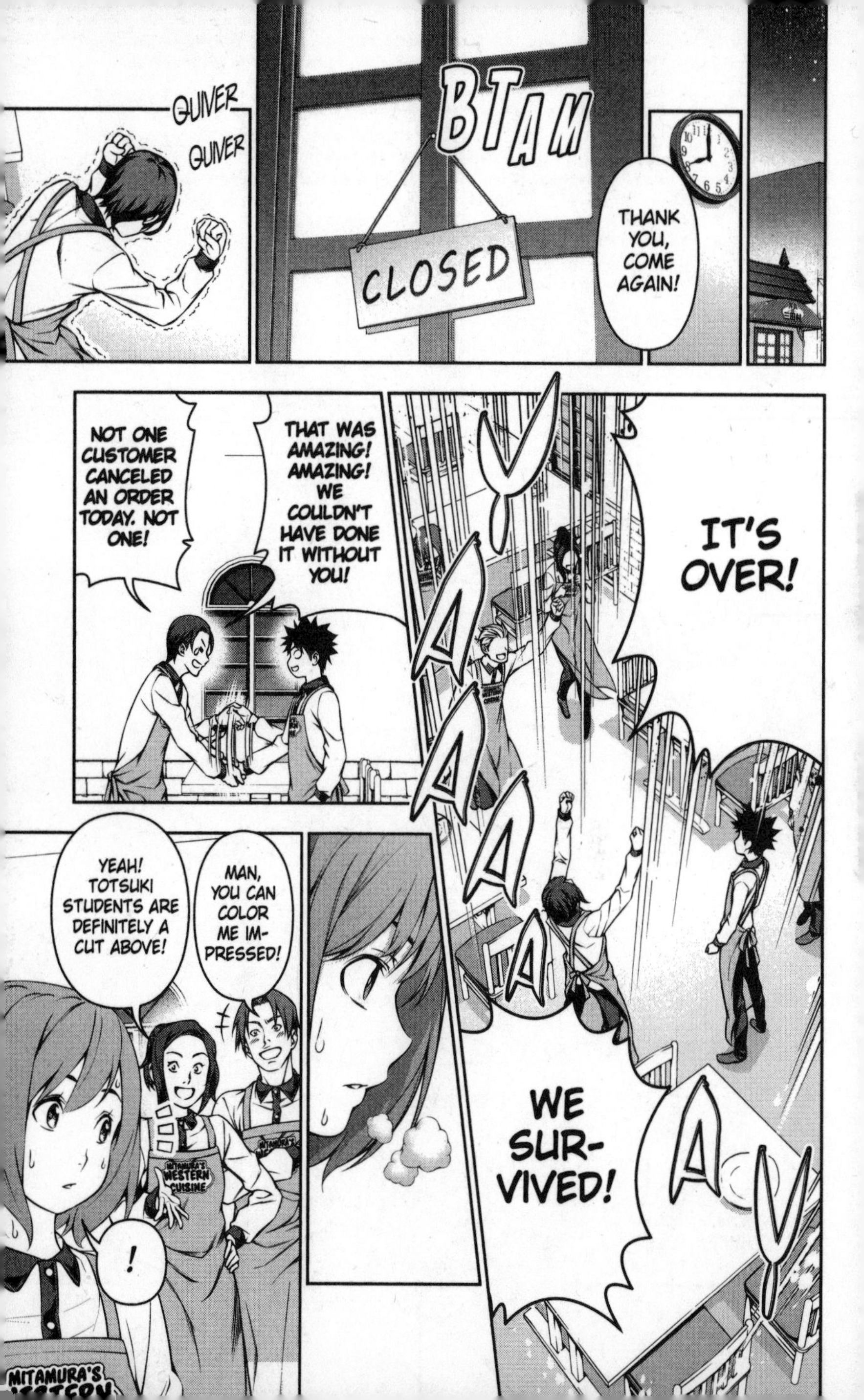

THANK YOU, COME AGAIN!
BTAM
CLOSED
QUIVER
QUIVER
YAAAAAAAAY
IT'S OVER!
WE SURVIVED!
THAT WAS AMAZING! AMAZING! WE COULDN'T HAVE DONE IT WITHOUT YOU!
NOT ONE CUSTOMER CANCELED AN ORDER TODAY. NOT ONE!
MAN, YOU CAN COLOR ME IM-PRESSED!
YEAH! TOTSUKI STUDENTS ARE DEFINITELY A CUT ABOVE!
MITAMURA'S WESTERN CUISINE
!

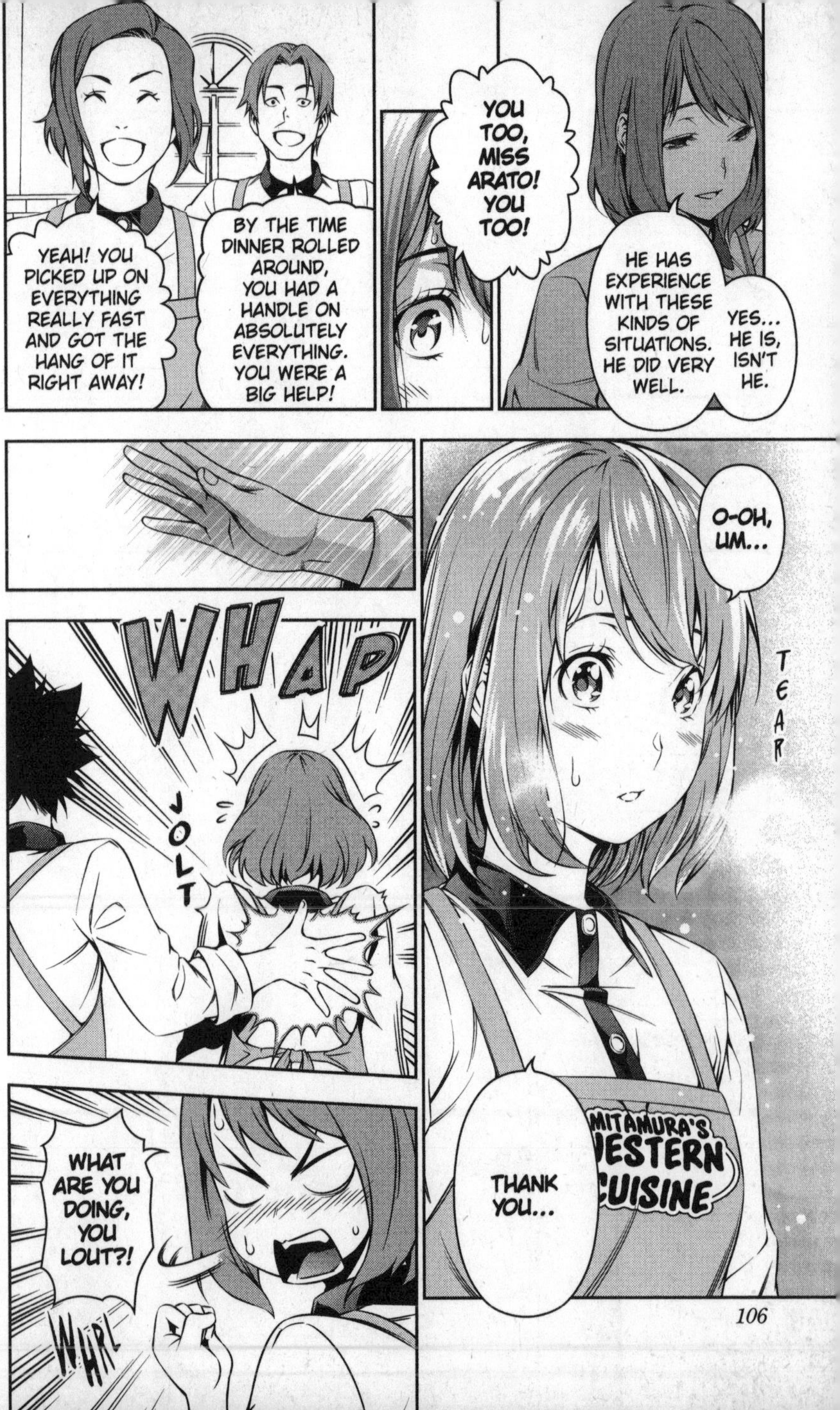
YES... HE IS, ISN'T HE.
HE HAS EXPERIENCE WITH THESE KINDS OF SITUATIONS. HE DID VERY WELL.
YOU TOO, MISS ARATO! YOU TOO!
BY THE TIME DINNER ROLLED AROUND, YOU HAD A HANDLE ON ABSOLUTELY EVERYTHING. YOU WERE A BIG HELP!
YEAH! YOU PICKED UP ON EVERYTHING REALLY FAST AND GOT THE HANG OF IT RIGHT AWAY!
O-OH, UM...
TEAR
MITAMURA'S WESTERN CUISINE
THANK YOU...
WHAP
JOLT
WHAT ARE YOU DOING, YOU LOUT?!
WHIRL

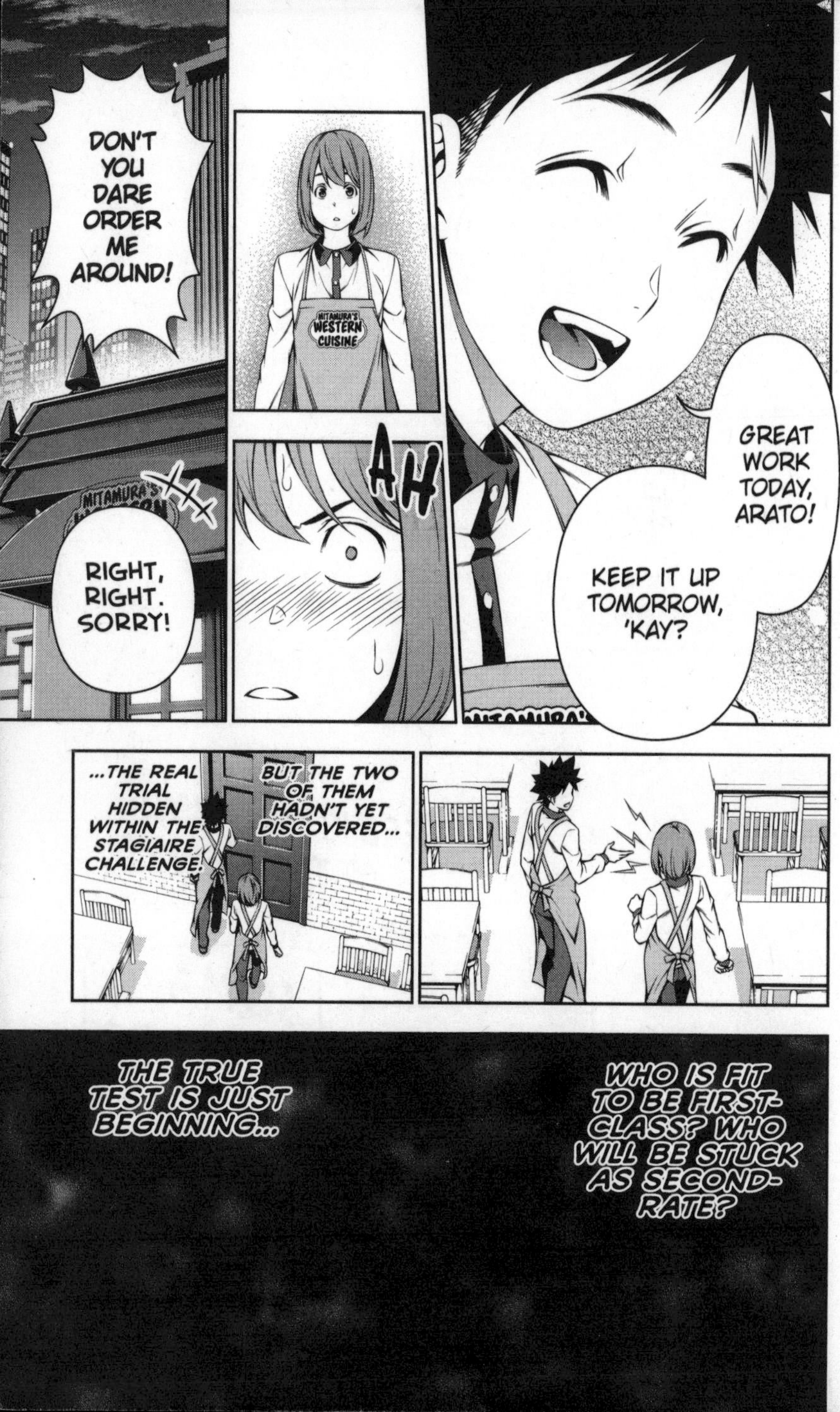
GREAT WORK TODAY, ARATO!
KEEP IT UP TOMORROW, 'KAY?
MITAMURA'S WESTERN CUISINE
AH
DON'T YOU DARE ORDER ME AROUND!
MITAMURA'S
RIGHT, RIGHT. SORRY!
BUT THE TWO OF THEM HADN'T YET DISCOVERED...
...THE REAL TRIAL HIDDEN WITHIN THE STAGIAIRE CHALLENGE.
WHO IS FIT TO BE FIRST-CLASS? WHO WILL BE STUCK AS SECOND-RATE?
THE TRUE TEST IS JUST BEGINNING...

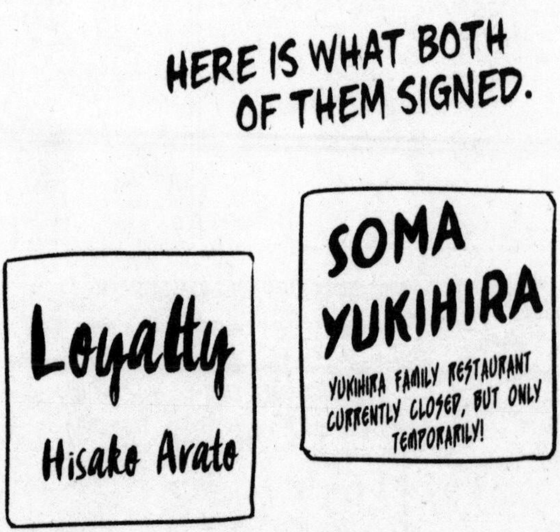
HERE IS WHAT BOTH OF THEM SIGNED.
Loyalty
Hisako Arato
SOMA YUKIHIRA
YUKIHIRA FAMILY RESTAURANT CURRENTLY CLOSED, BUT ONLY TEMPORARILY!

107 IDEAL DISTANCE

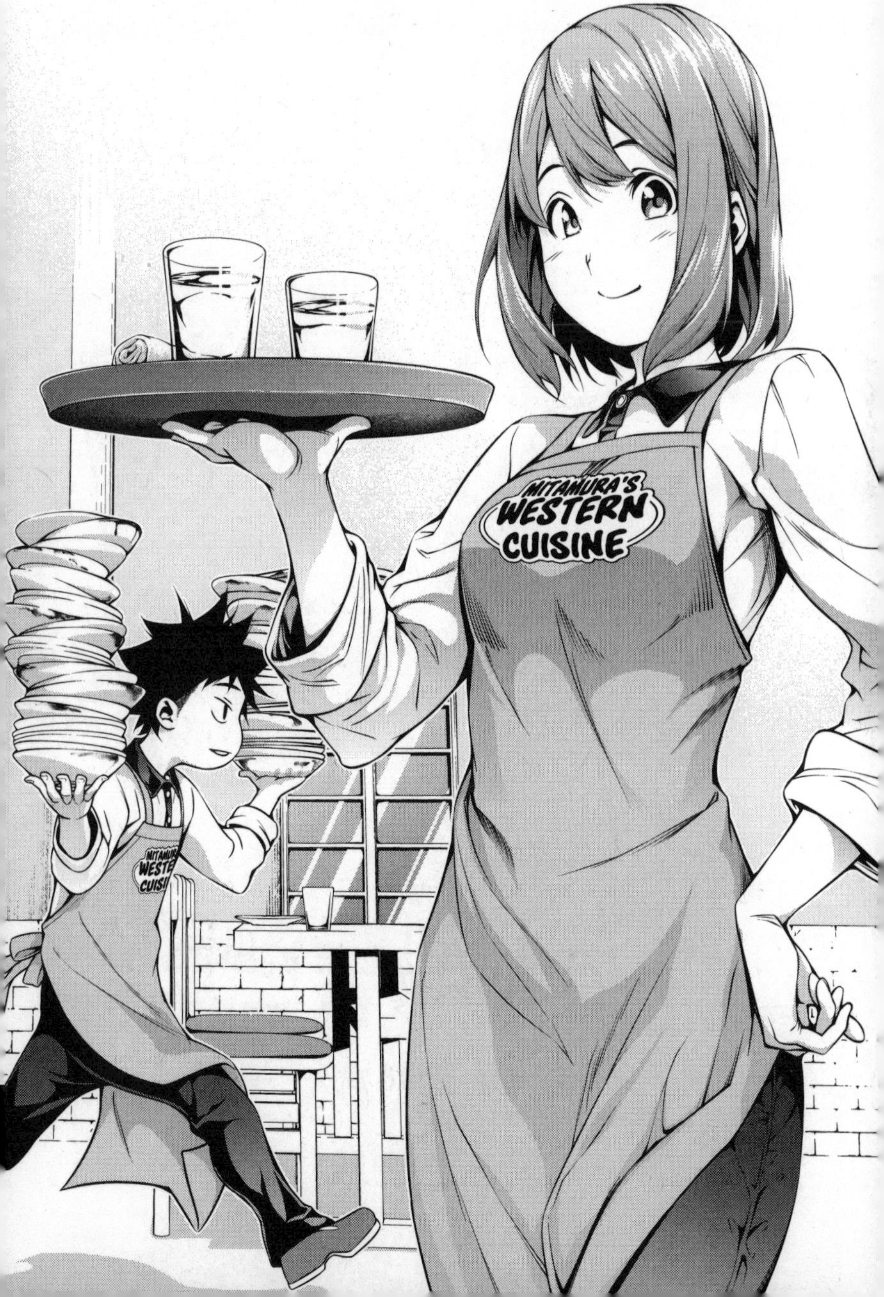
MITAMURA'S WESTERN CUISINE

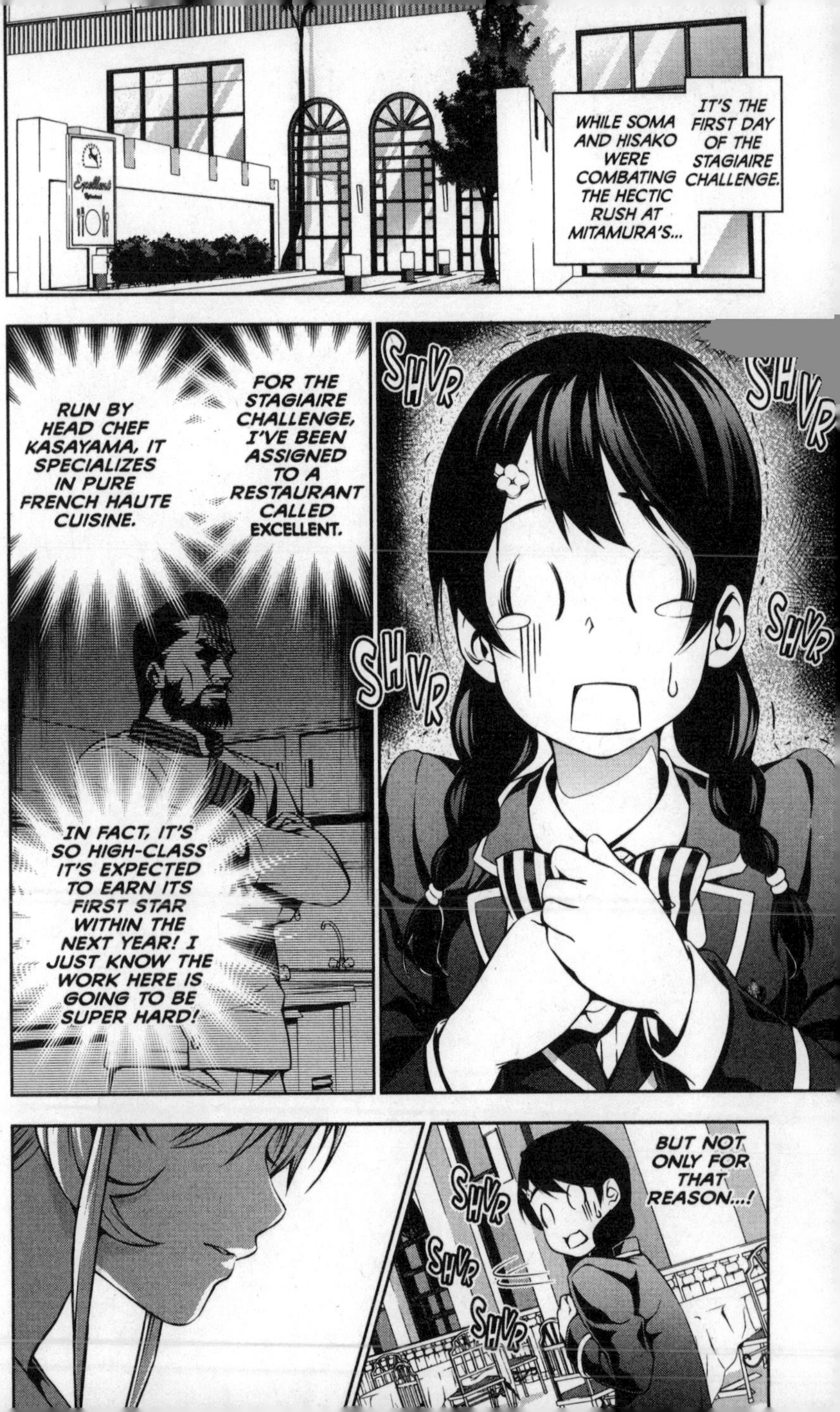

IT'S THE FIRST DAY OF THE STAGIAIRE CHALLENGE.
WHILE SOMA AND HISAKO WERE COMBATING THE HECTIC RUSH AT MITAMURA'S...
SHVR
SHVR
SHVR
SHVR
FOR THE STAGIAIRE CHALLENGE, I'VE BEEN ASSIGNED TO A RESTAURANT CALLED EXCELLENT.
RUN BY HEAD CHEF KASAYAMA, IT SPECIALIZES IN PURE FRENCH HAUTE CUISINE.
IN FACT, IT'S SO HIGH-CLASS IT'S EXPECTED TO EARN ITS FIRST STAR WITHIN THE NEXT YEAR! I JUST KNOW THE WORK HERE IS GOING TO BE SUPER HARD!
BUT NOT ONLY FOR THAT REASON...!
SHVR
SHVR
SHVR

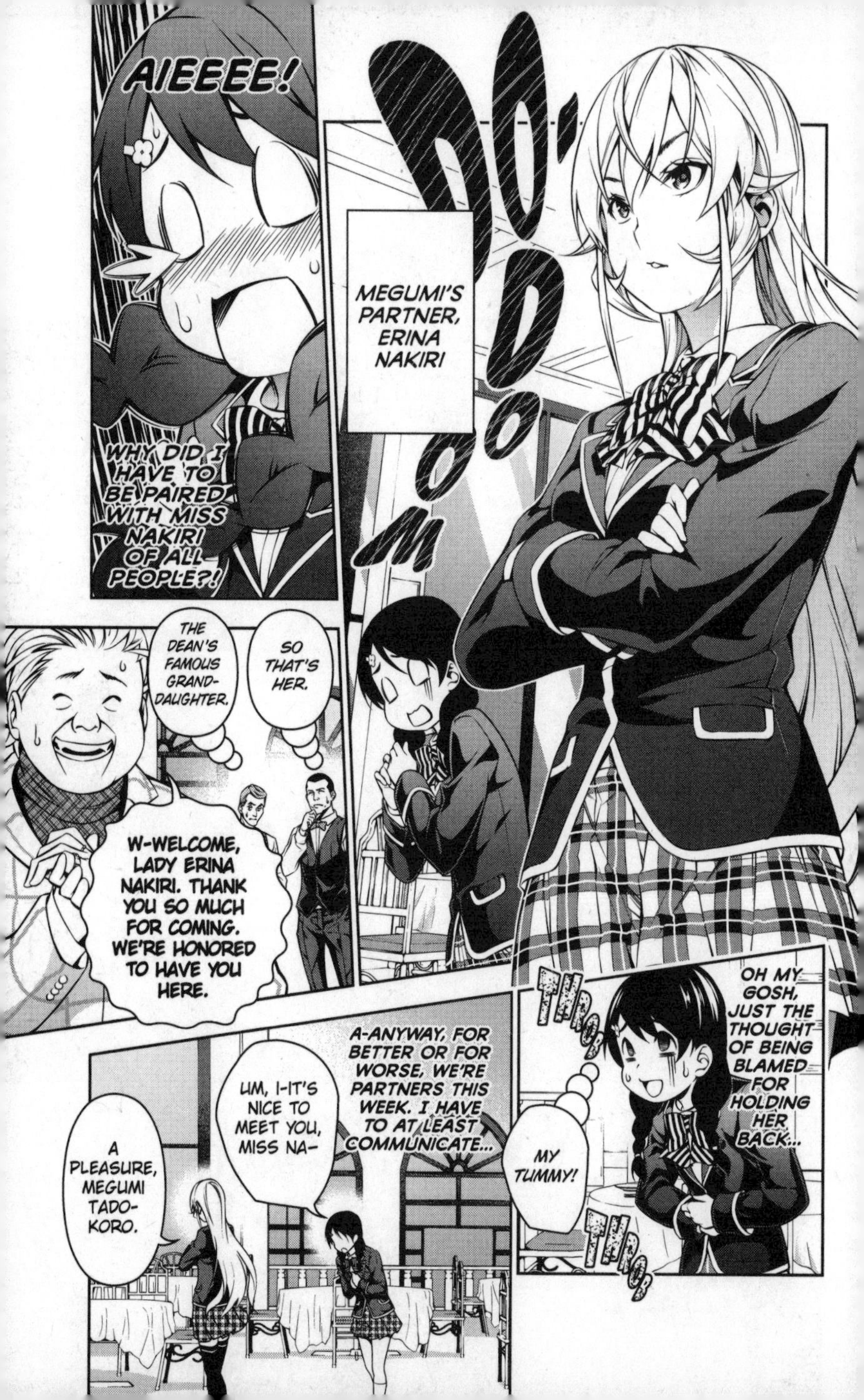
MEGUMI'S PARTNER, ERINA NAKIRI
DO-DO-DOOOOM
AIEEEE!
WHY DID I HAVE TO BE PAIRED WITH MISS NAKIRI OF ALL PEOPLE?!
SO THAT'S HER.
THE DEAN'S FAMOUS GRAND-DAUGHTER.
W-WELCOME, LADY ERINA NAKIRI. THANK YOU SO MUCH FOR COMING. WE'RE HONORED TO HAVE YOU HERE.
THROB
OH MY GOSH, JUST THE THOUGHT OF BEING BLAMED FOR HOLDING HER BACK...
MY TUMMY!
THROB
A-ANYWAY, FOR BETTER OR FOR WORSE, WE'RE PARTNERS THIS WEEK. I HAVE TO AT LEAST COMMUNICATE...
UM, I-IT'S NICE TO MEET YOU, MISS NA-
A PLEASURE, MEGUMI TADO-KORO.

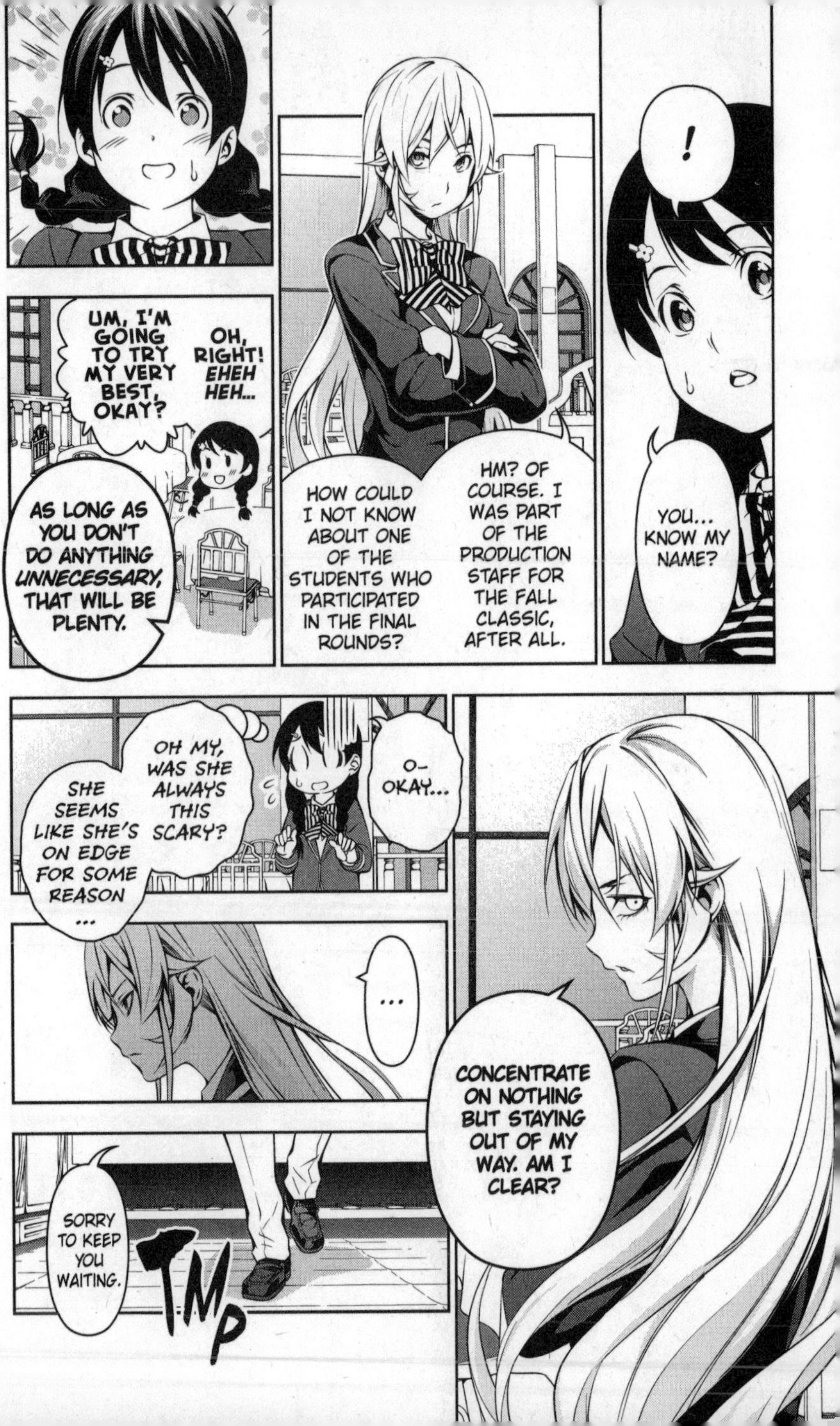
!
YOU... KNOW MY NAME?
HM? OF COURSE. I WAS PART OF THE PRODUCTION STAFF FOR THE FALL CLASSIC, AFTER ALL.
HOW COULD I NOT KNOW ABOUT ONE OF THE STUDENTS WHO PARTICIPATED IN THE FINAL ROUNDS?
OH, RIGHT! EHEH HEH...
UM, I'M GOING TO TRY MY VERY BEST, OKAY?
AS LONG AS YOU DON'T DO ANYTHING *UNNECESSARY*, THAT WILL BE PLENTY.
CONCENTRATE ON NOTHING BUT STAYING OUT OF MY WAY. AM I CLEAR?
O-OKAY...
OH MY, WAS SHE ALWAYS THIS SCARY?
SHE SEEMS LIKE SHE'S ON EDGE FOR SOME REASON...
...
TMP
SORRY TO KEEP YOU WAITING.

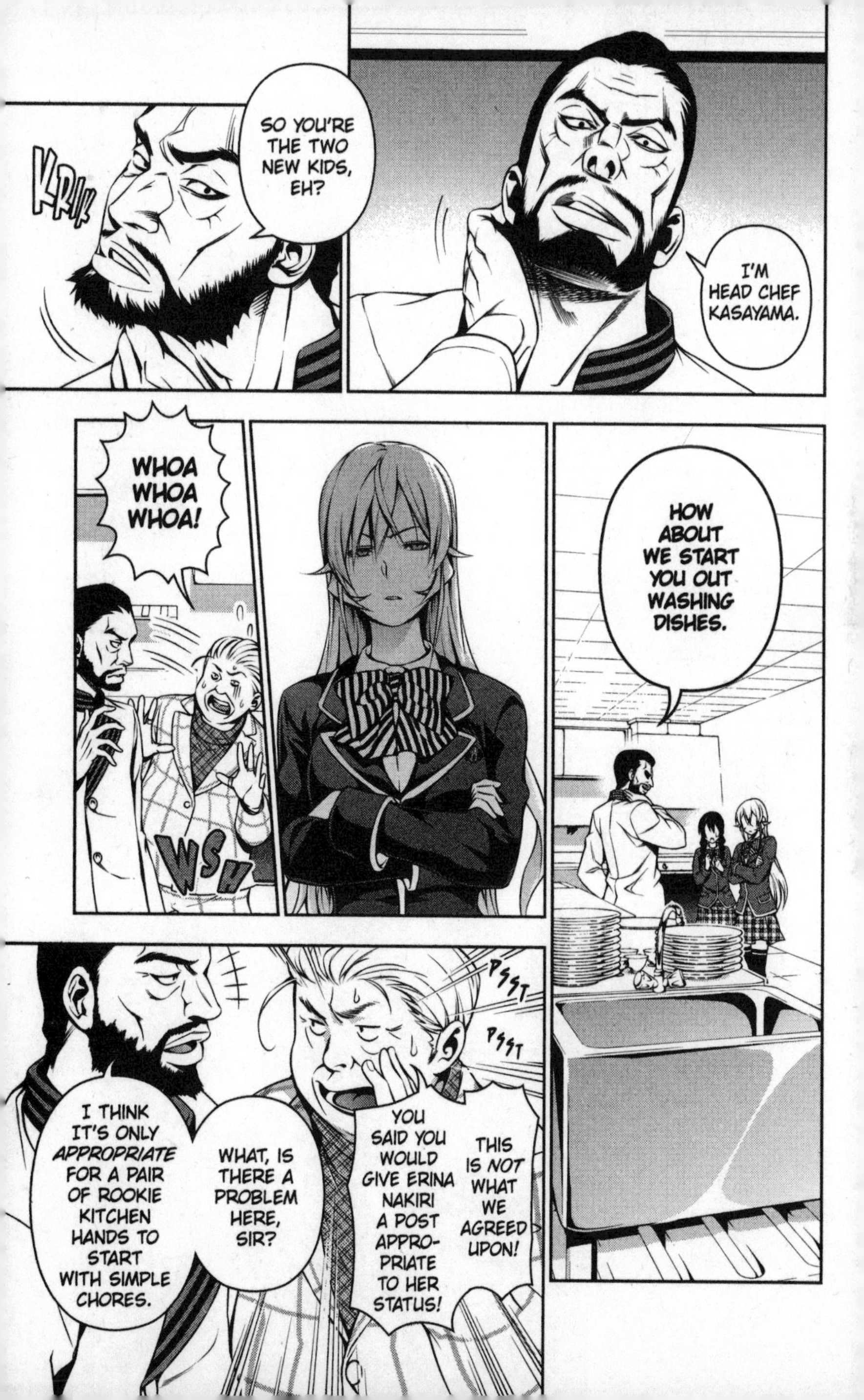
I'M HEAD CHEF KASAYAMA.
KRIK
SO YOU'RE THE TWO NEW KIDS, EH?
HOW ABOUT WE START YOU OUT WASHING DISHES.
WHOA WHOA WHOA!
WSH
PSST
PSST
THIS IS *NOT* WHAT WE AGREED UPON!
YOU SAID YOU WOULD GIVE ERINA NAKIRI A POST APPRO-PRIATE TO HER STATUS!
WHAT, IS THERE A PROBLEM HERE, SIR?
I THINK IT'S ONLY *APPROPRIATE* FOR A PAIR OF ROOKIE KITCHEN HANDS TO START WITH SIMPLE CHORES.

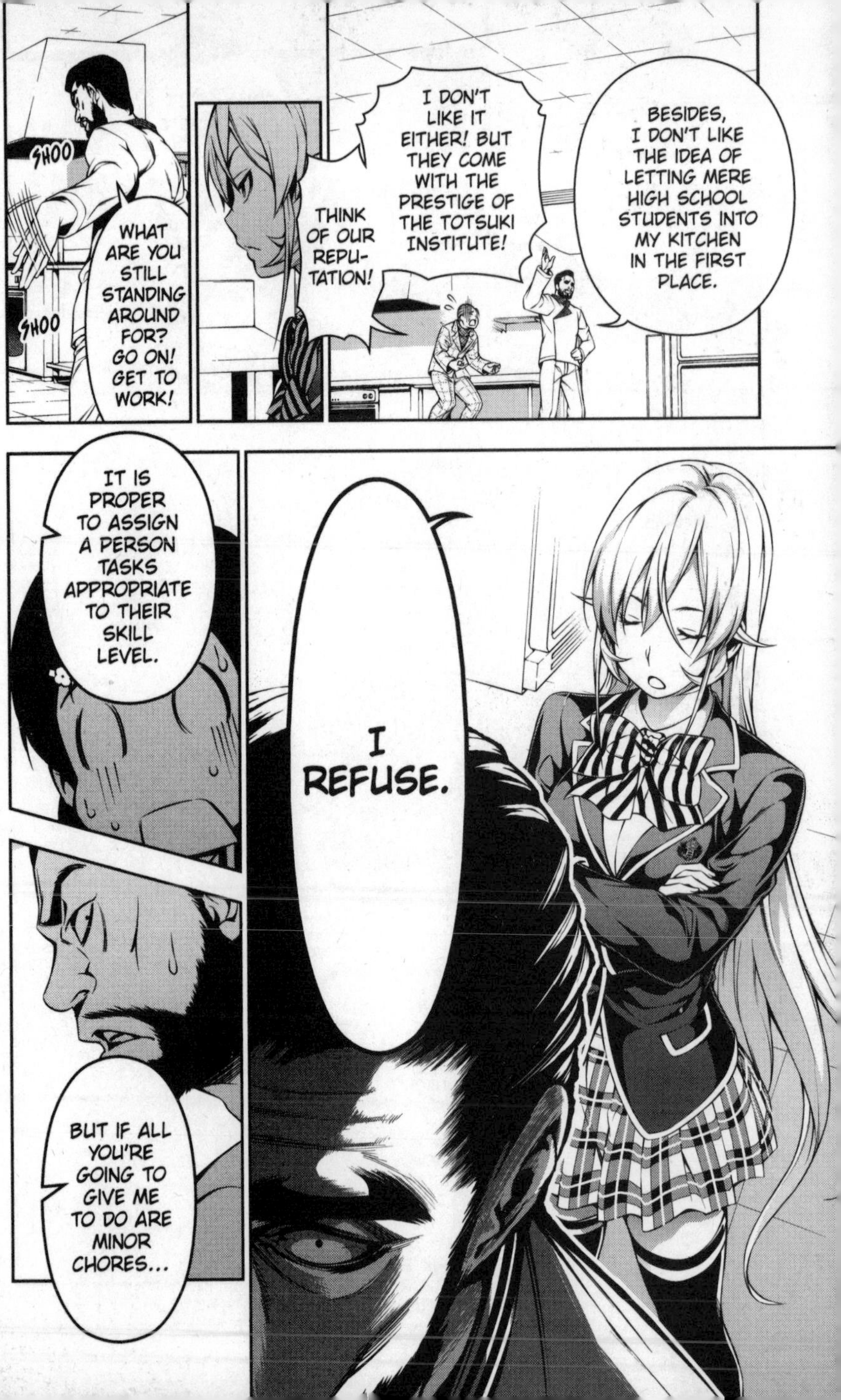
BESIDES, I DON'T LIKE THE IDEA OF LETTING MERE HIGH SCHOOL STUDENTS INTO MY KITCHEN IN THE FIRST PLACE.
I DON'T LIKE IT EITHER! BUT THEY COME WITH THE PRESTIGE OF THE TOTSUKI INSTITUTE!
THINK OF OUR REPUTATION!
WHAT ARE YOU STILL STANDING AROUND FOR? GO ON! GET TO WORK!
SHOO
SHOO
I REFUSE.
IT IS PROPER TO ASSIGN A PERSON TASKS APPROPRIATE TO THEIR SKILL LEVEL.
BUT IF ALL YOU'RE GOING TO GIVE ME TO DO ARE MINOR CHORES...

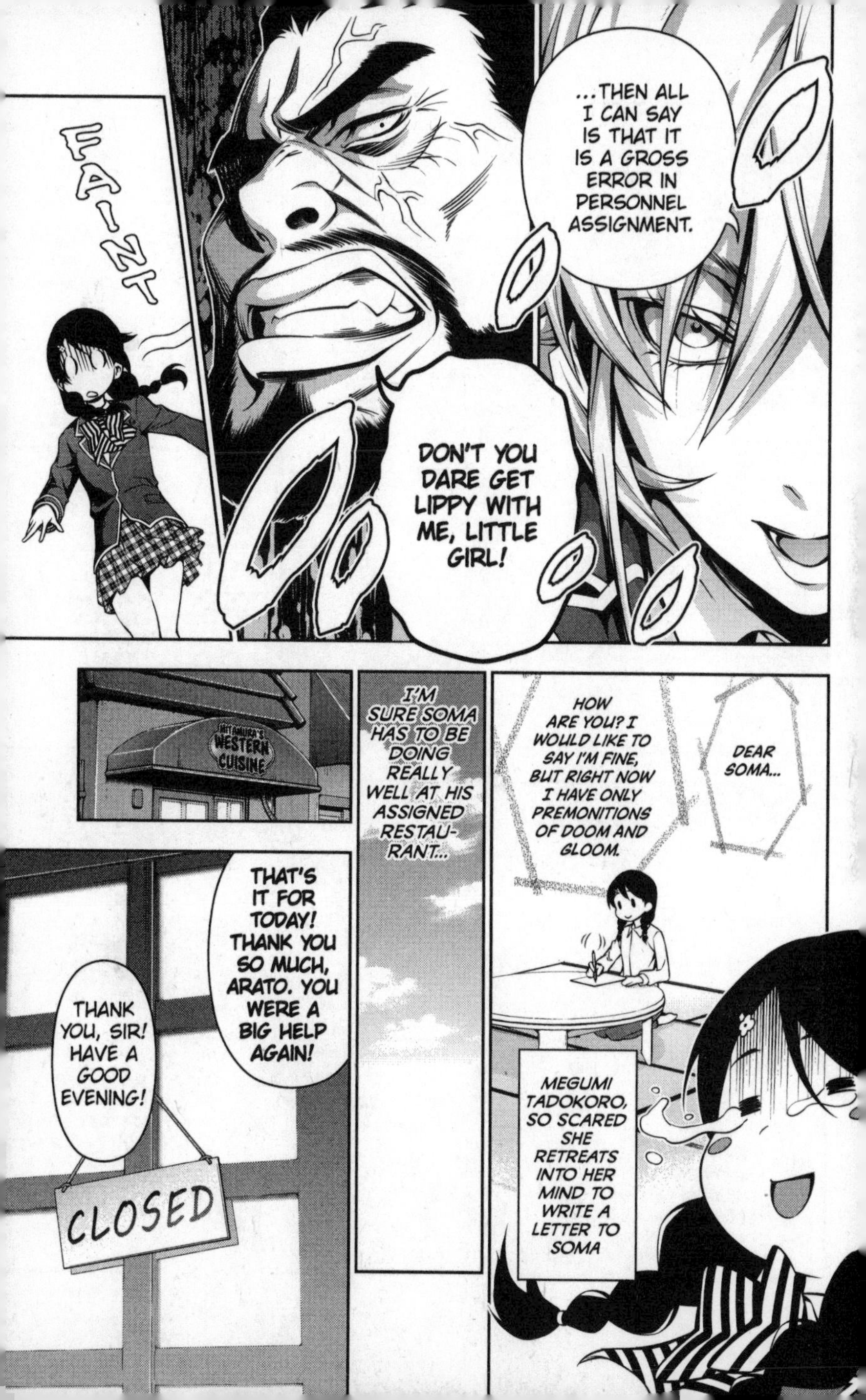
...THEN ALL I CAN SAY IS THAT IT IS A GROSS ERROR IN PERSONNEL ASSIGNMENT.
DON'T YOU DARE GET LIPPY WITH ME, LITTLE GIRL!
FAINT
DEAR SOMA...
HOW ARE YOU? I WOULD LIKE TO SAY I'M FINE, BUT RIGHT NOW I HAVE ONLY PREMONITIONS OF DOOM AND GLOOM.
MEGUMI TADOKORO, SO SCARED SHE RETREATS INTO HER MIND TO WRITE A LETTER TO SOMA
I'M SURE SOMA HAS TO BE DOING REALLY WELL AT HIS ASSIGNED RESTAU- RANT...
MITAMURA'S WESTERN CUISINE
THAT'S IT FOR TODAY! THANK YOU SO MUCH, ARATO. YOU WERE A BIG HELP AGAIN!
THANK YOU, SIR! HAVE A GOOD EVENING!
CLOSED

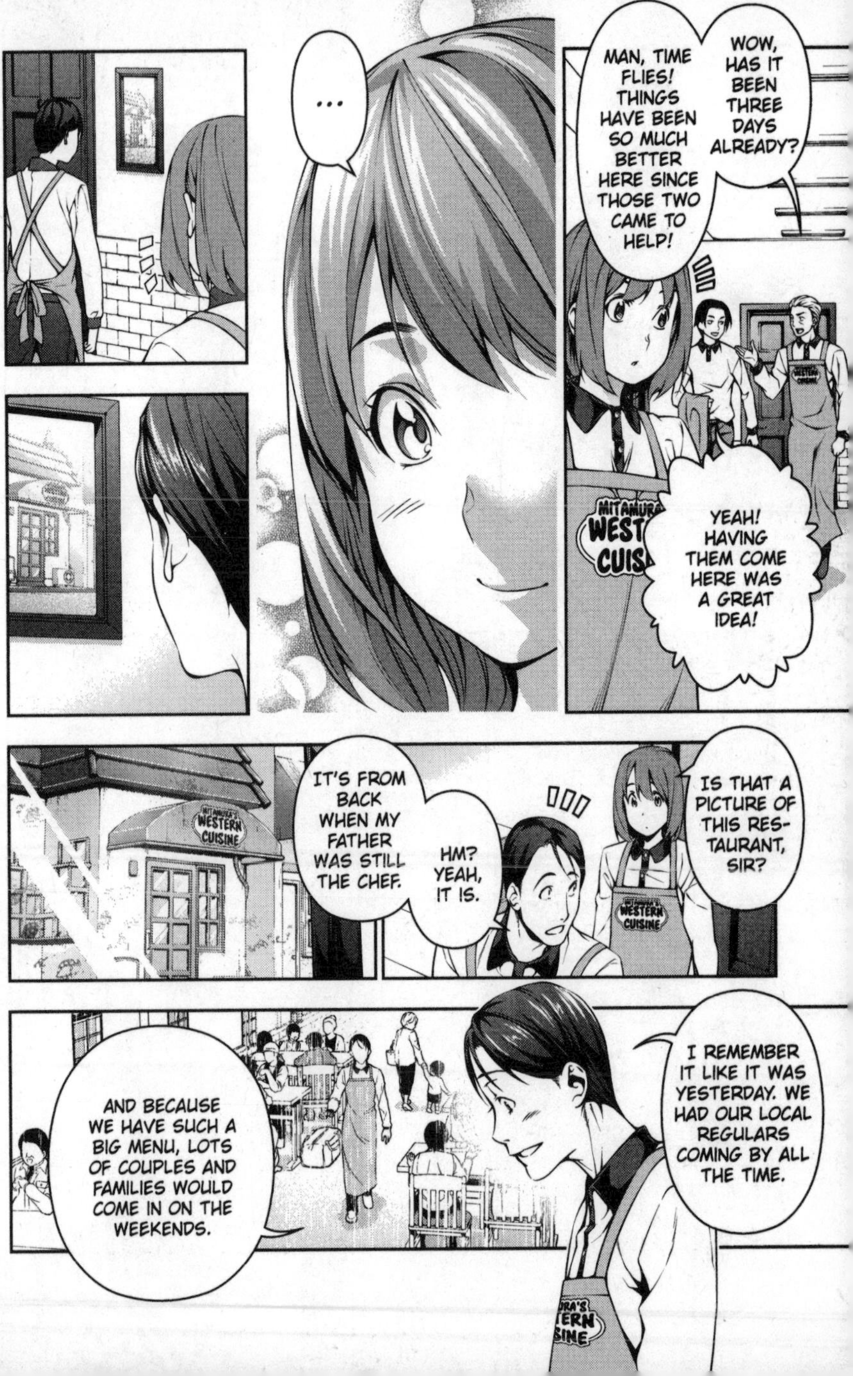
WOW, HAS IT BEEN THREE DAYS ALREADY?
MAN, TIME FLIES! THINGS HAVE BEEN SO MUCH BETTER HERE SINCE THOSE TWO CAME TO HELP!
YEAH! HAVING THEM COME HERE WAS A GREAT IDEA!
...
IS THAT A PICTURE OF THIS RES- TAURANT, SIR?
HM? YEAH, IT IS.
MITAMURA'S WESTERN CUISINE
IT'S FROM BACK WHEN MY FATHER WAS STILL THE CHEF.
I REMEMBER IT LIKE IT WAS YESTERDAY. WE HAD OUR LOCAL REGULARS COMING BY ALL THE TIME.
AND BECAUSE WE HAVE SUCH A BIG MENU, LOTS OF COUPLES AND FAMILIES WOULD COME IN ON THE WEEKENDS.

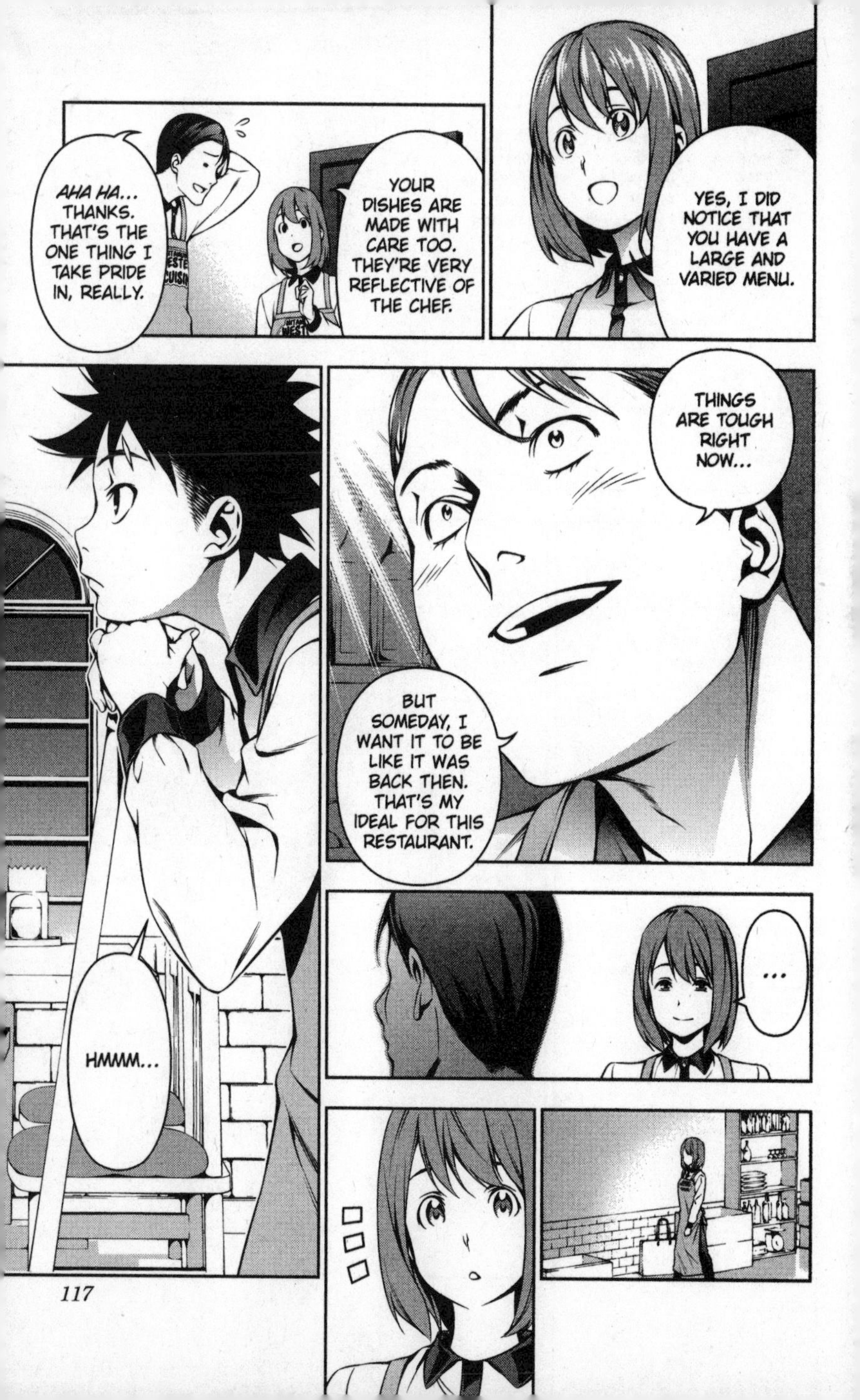
YES, I DID NOTICE THAT YOU HAVE A LARGE AND VARIED MENU.
YOUR DISHES ARE MADE WITH CARE TOO. THEY'RE VERY REFLECTIVE OF THE CHEF.
AHA HA... THANKS. THAT'S THE ONE THING I TAKE PRIDE IN, REALLY.
THINGS ARE TOUGH RIGHT NOW...
BUT SOMEDAY, I WANT IT TO BE LIKE IT WAS BACK THEN. THAT'S MY IDEAL FOR THIS RESTAURANT.
...
HMMM...

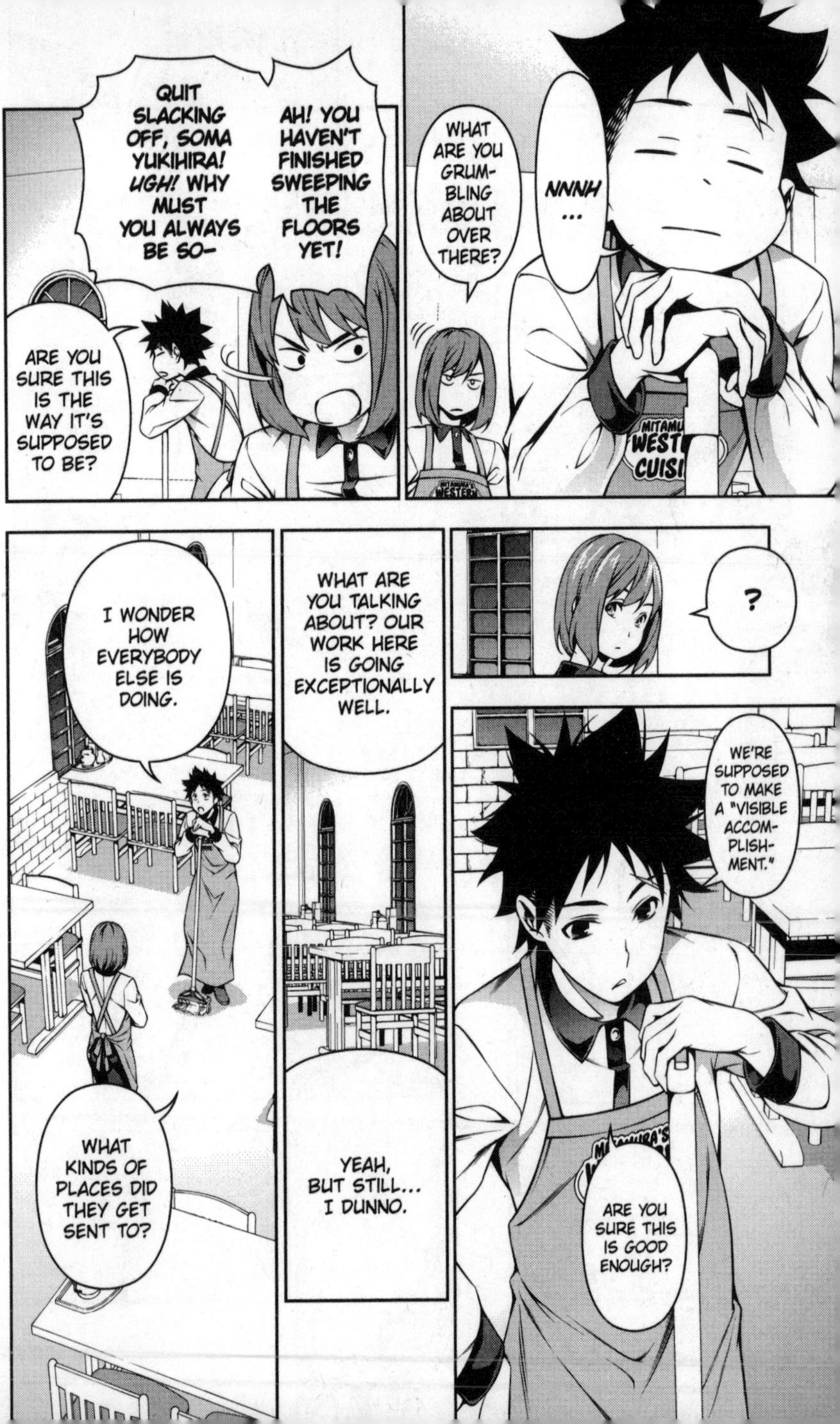
NNNH ...
WHAT ARE YOU GRUMBLING ABOUT OVER THERE?
MITAMU WESTE CUISI
AH! YOU HAVEN'T FINISHED SWEEPING THE FLOORS YET!
QUIT SLACKING OFF, SOMA YUKIHIRA! UGH! WHY MUST YOU ALWAYS BE SO-
ARE YOU SURE THIS IS THE WAY IT'S SUPPOSED TO BE?
?
WE'RE SUPPOSED TO MAKE A "VISIBLE ACCOMPLISHMENT."
ARE YOU SURE THIS IS GOOD ENOUGH?
WHAT ARE YOU TALKING ABOUT? OUR WORK HERE IS GOING EXCEPTIONALLY WELL.
YEAH, BUT STILL... I DUNNO.
I WONDER HOW EVERYBODY ELSE IS DOING.
WHAT KINDS OF PLACES DID THEY GET SENT TO?

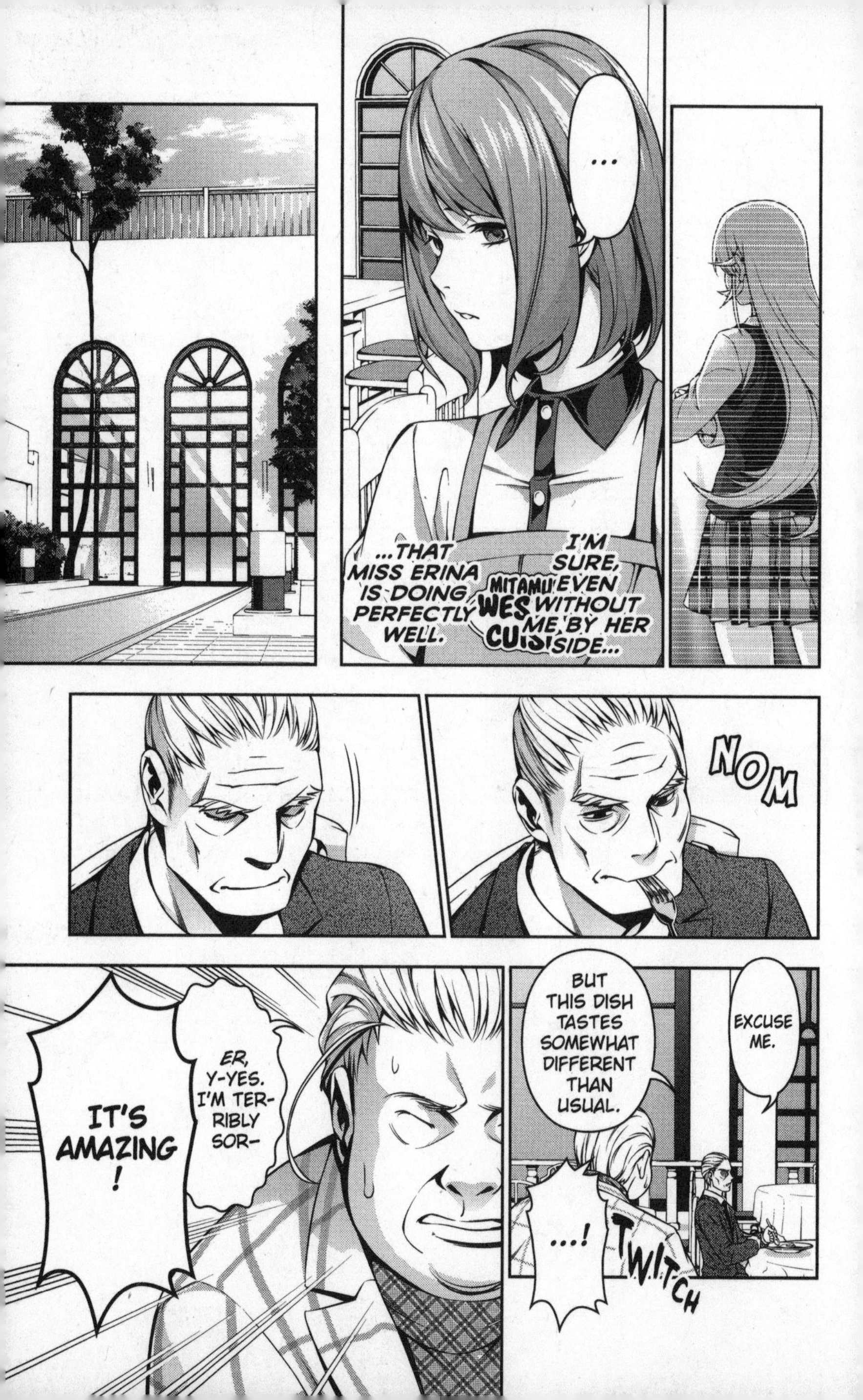
...
I'M SURE, EVEN WITHOUT ME BY HER SIDE...
...THAT MISS ERINA IS DOING PERFECTLY WELL.
NOM
EXCUSE ME.
BUT THIS DISH TASTES SOMEWHAT DIFFERENT THAN USUAL.
...!
TWITCH
ER, Y-YES. I'M TERRIBLY SOR-
IT'S AMAZING!

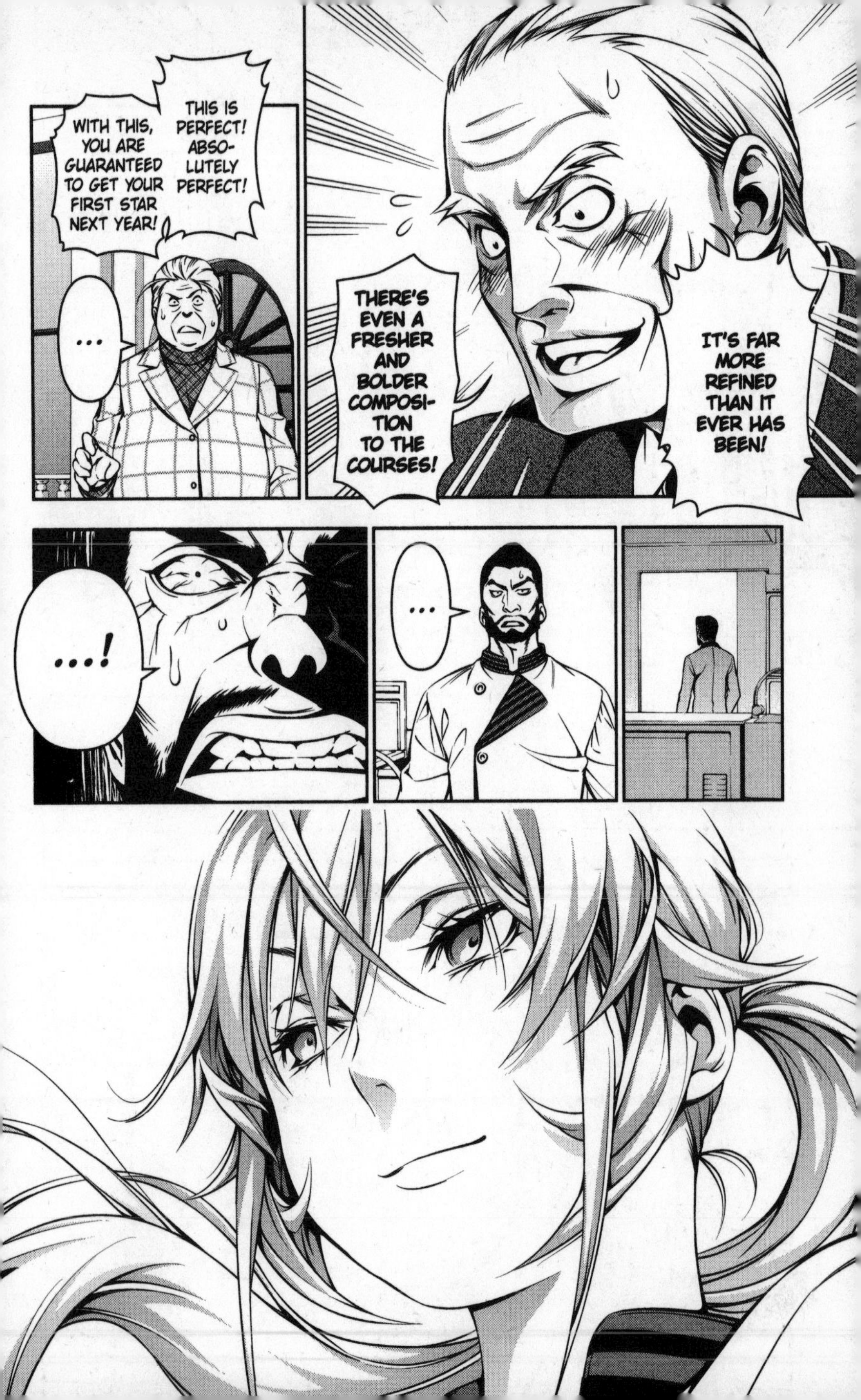
IT'S FAR MORE REFINED THAN IT EVER HAS BEEN!
THERE'S EVEN A FRESHER AND BOLDER COMPOSI-TION TO THE COURSES!
THIS IS PERFECT! ABSO-LUTELY PERFECT!
WITH THIS, YOU ARE GUARANTEED TO GET YOUR FIRST STAR NEXT YEAR!
...
...
...!

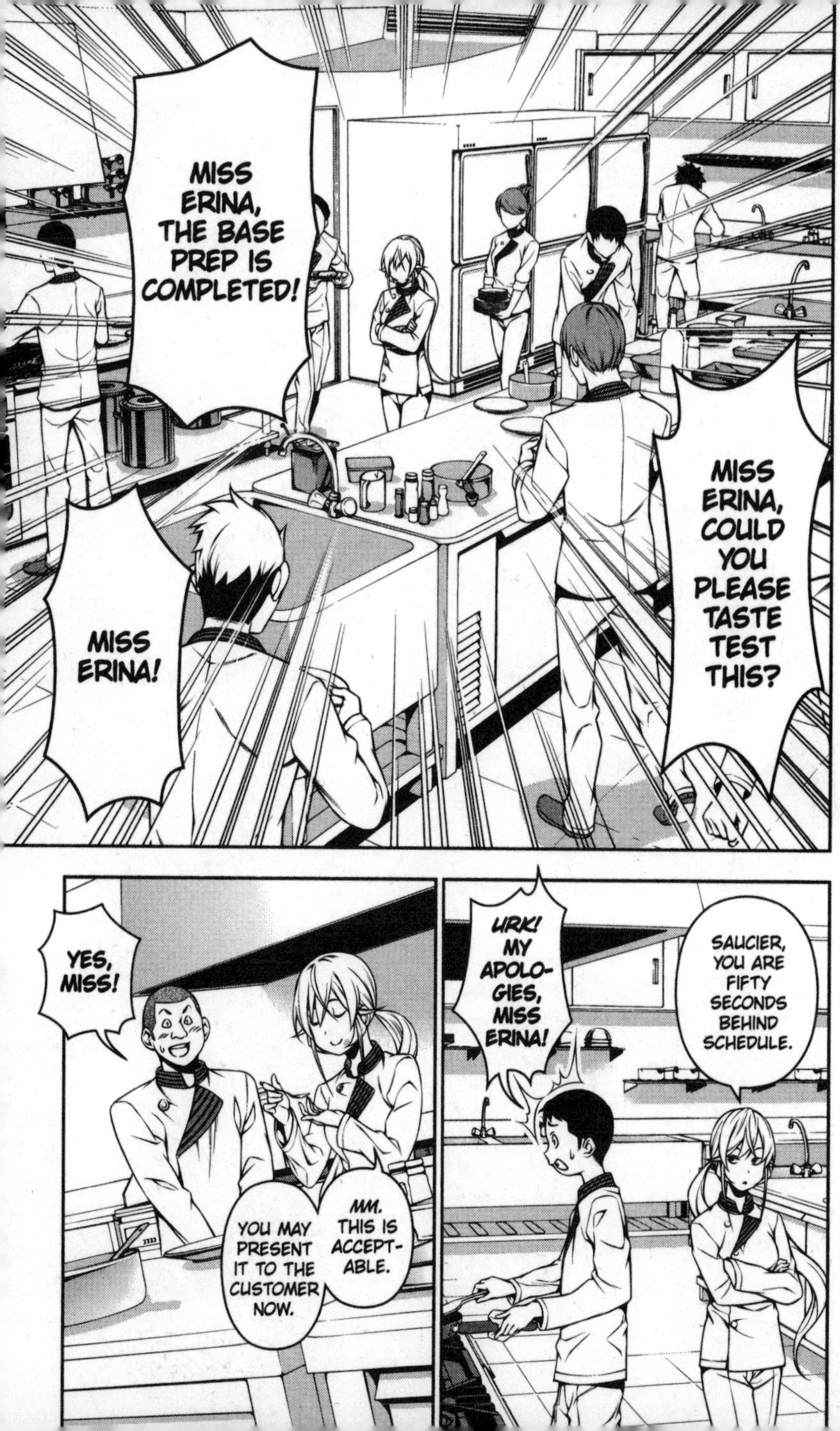
MISS ERINA, COULD YOU PLEASE TASTE TEST THIS?
MISS ERINA, THE BASE PREP IS COMPLETED!
MISS ERINA!
SAUCIER, YOU ARE FIFTY SECONDS BEHIND SCHEDULE.
URK! MY APOLOGIES, MISS ERINA!
MM. THIS IS ACCEPTABLE.
YOU MAY PRESENT IT TO THE CUSTOMER NOW.
YES, MISS!

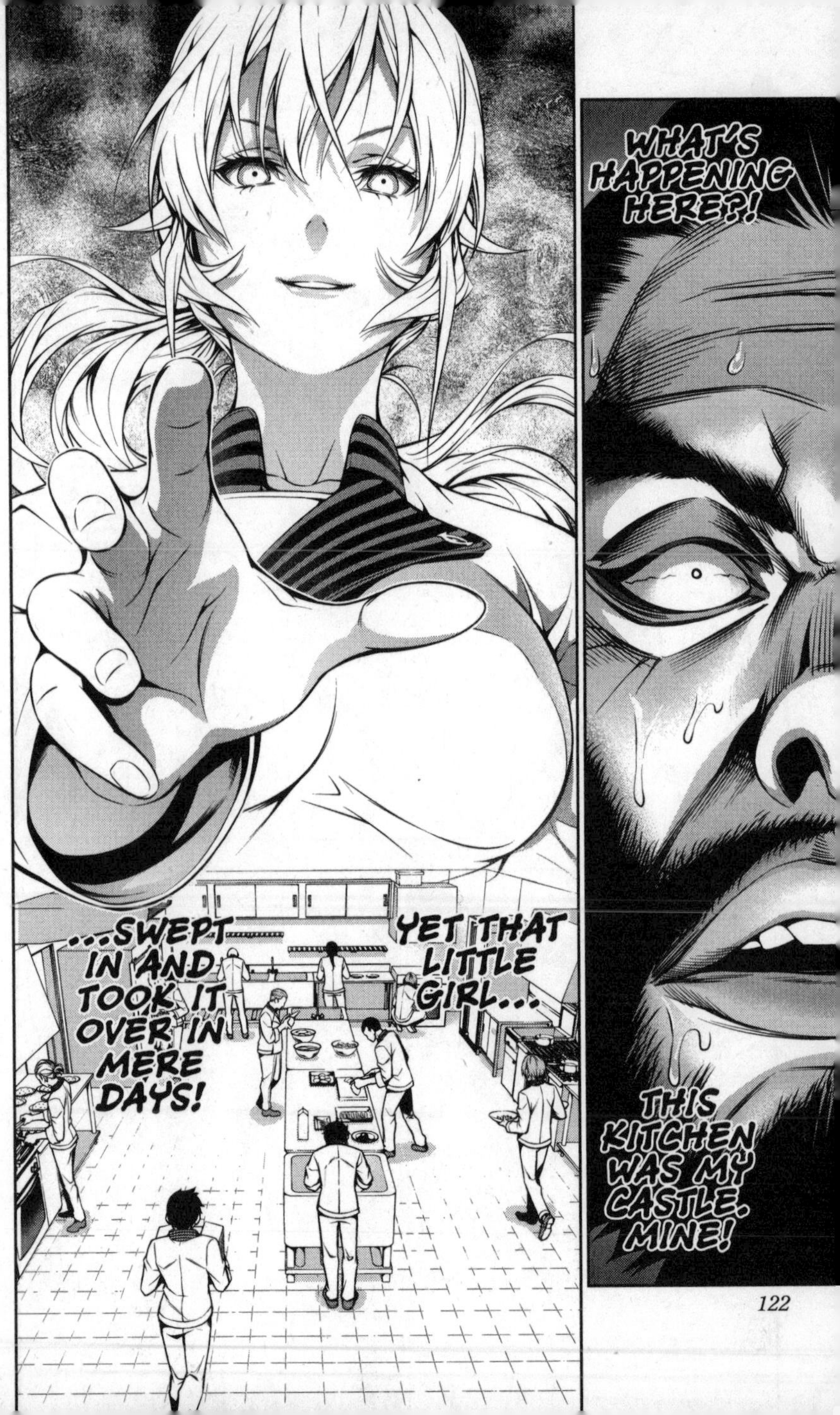
WHAT'S HAPPENING HERE?!
THIS KITCHEN WAS MY CASTLE. MINE!
YET THAT LITTLE GIRL...
...SWEPT IN AND TOOK IT OVER IN MERE DAYS!

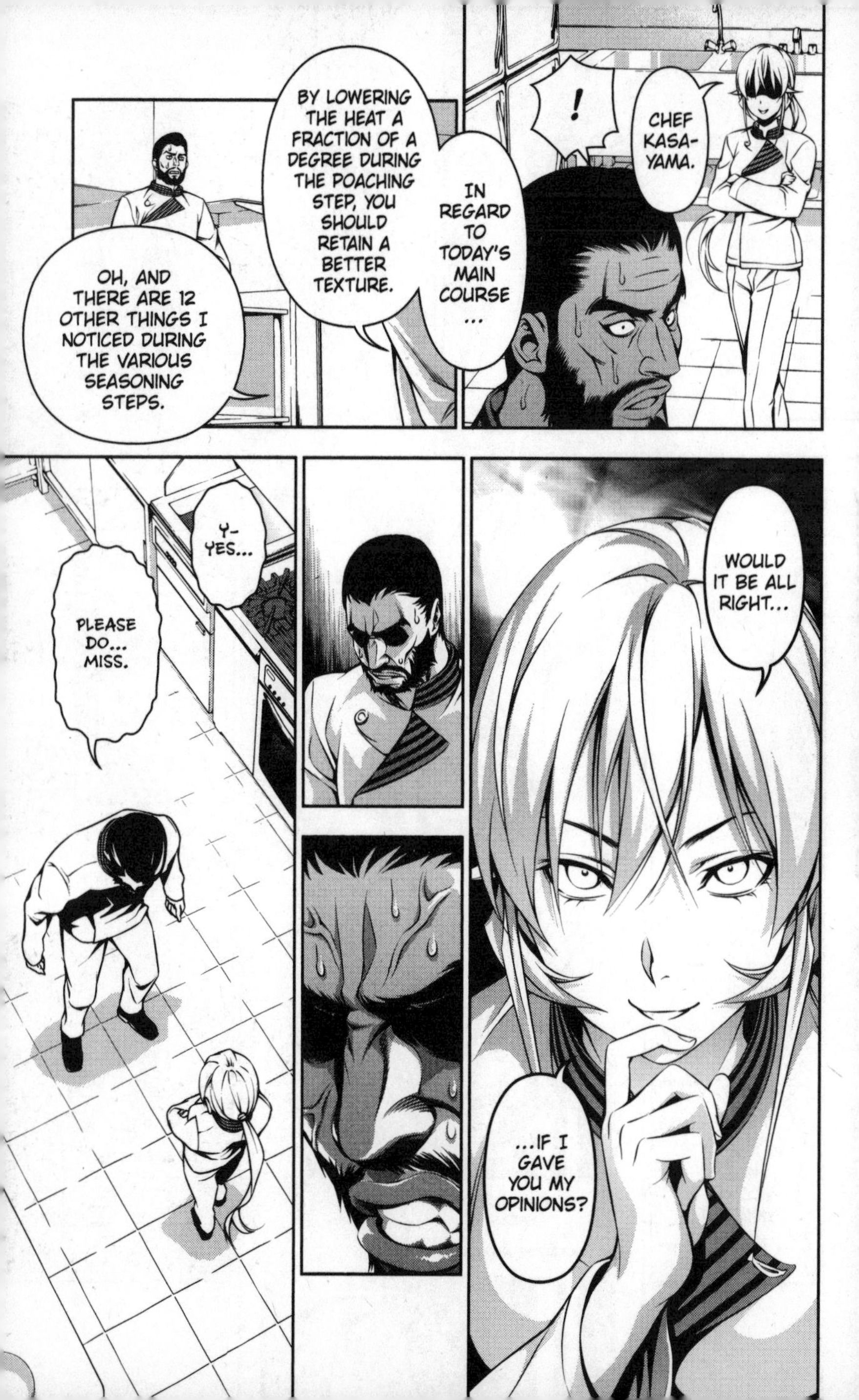
CHEF KASA-YAMA.
!
IN REGARD TO TODAY'S MAIN COURSE ...
BY LOWERING THE HEAT A FRACTION OF A DEGREE DURING THE POACHING STEP, YOU SHOULD RETAIN A BETTER TEXTURE.
OH, AND THERE ARE 12 OTHER THINGS I NOTICED DURING THE VARIOUS SEASONING STEPS.
WOULD IT BE ALL RIGHT...
...IF I GAVE YOU MY OPINIONS?
Y-YES...
PLEASE DO... MISS.

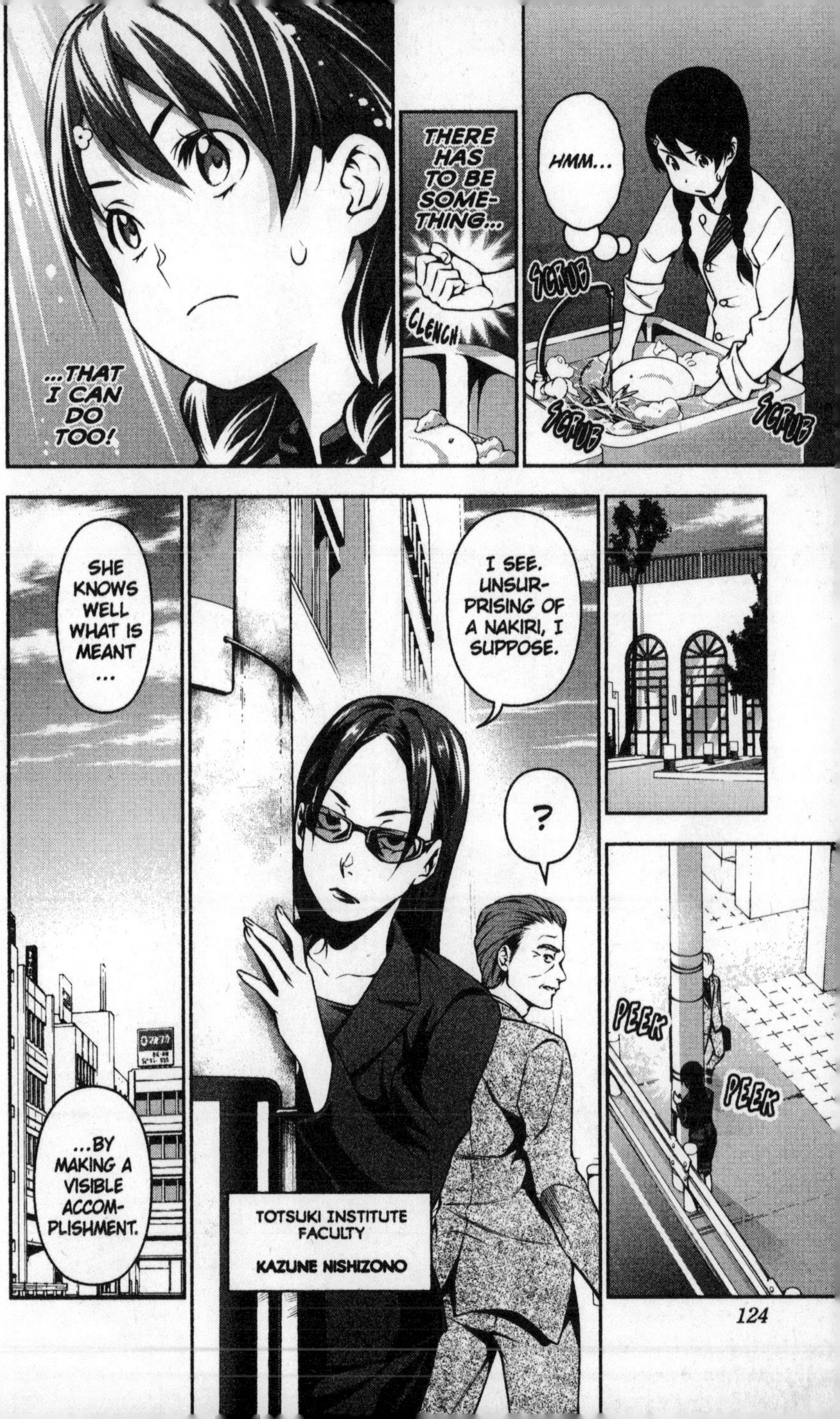
HMM...
SCRUB
SCRUB
SCRUB
THERE HAS TO BE SOME-THING...
CLENCH
...THAT I CAN DO TOO!
PEEK
PEEK
I SEE. UNSUR-PRISING OF A NAKIRI, I SUPPOSE.
?
TOTSUKI INSTITUTE FACULTY
KAZUNE NISHIZONO
SHE KNOWS WELL WHAT IS MEANT ...
...BY MAKING A VISIBLE ACCOM-PLISHMENT.

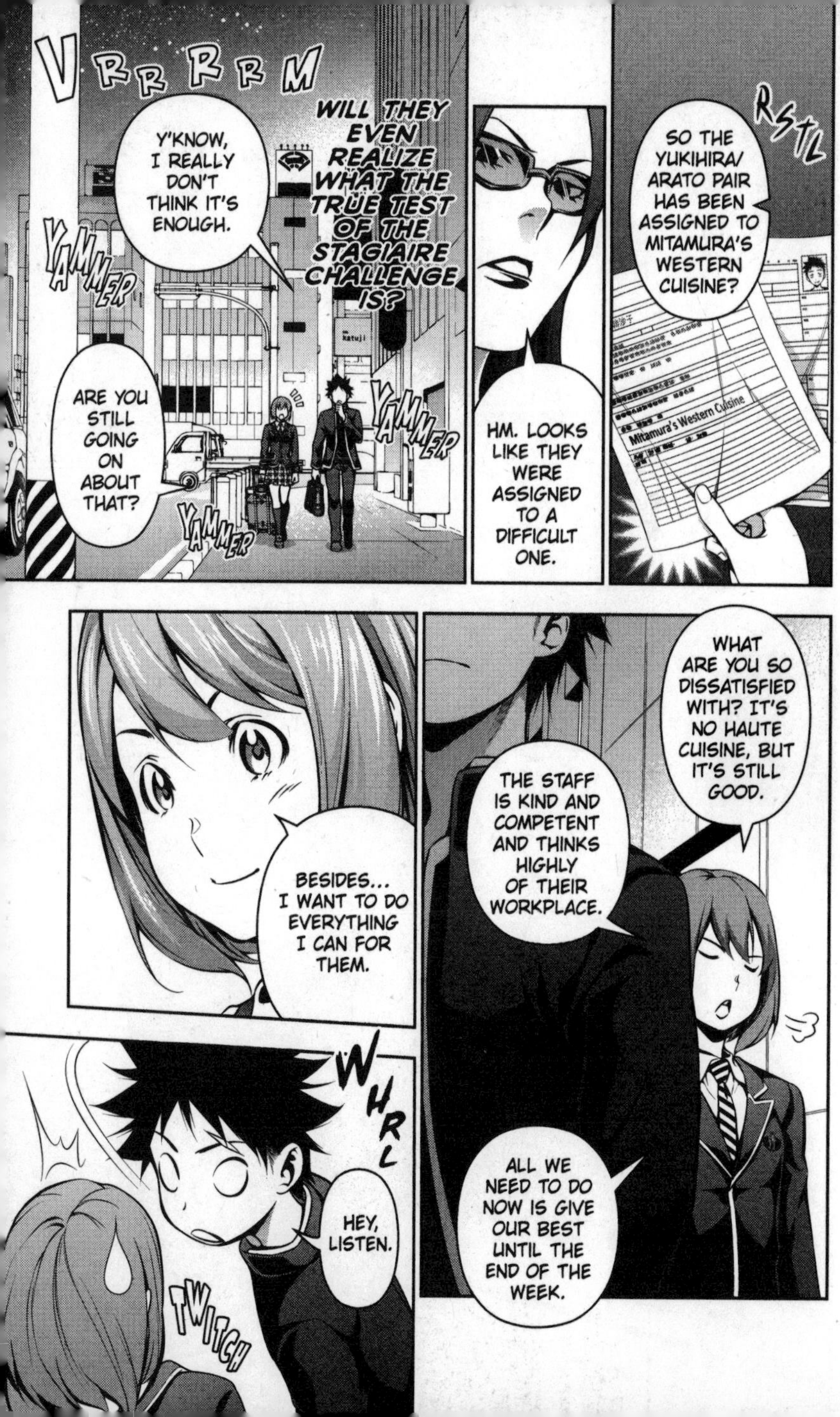
RSTL
SO THE YUKIHIRA/ ARATO PAIR HAS BEEN ASSIGNED TO MITAMURA'S WESTERN CUISINE?
Mitamura's Western Cuisine
HM. LOOKS LIKE THEY WERE ASSIGNED TO A DIFFICULT ONE.
VRRRRM
WILL THEY EVEN REALIZE WHAT THE TRUE TEST OF THE STAGIAIRE CHALLENGE IS?
Y'KNOW, I REALLY DON'T THINK IT'S ENOUGH.
YAMMER
katuji
YAMMER
ARE YOU STILL GOING ON ABOUT THAT?
YAMMER
WHAT ARE YOU SO DISSATISFIED WITH? IT'S NO HAUTE CUISINE, BUT IT'S STILL GOOD.
THE STAFF IS KIND AND COMPETENT AND THINKS HIGHLY OF THEIR WORKPLACE.
ALL WE NEED TO DO NOW IS GIVE OUR BEST UNTIL THE END OF THE WEEK.
BESIDES... I WANT TO DO EVERYTHING I CAN FOR THEM.
WHRL
HEY, LISTEN.
TWITCH

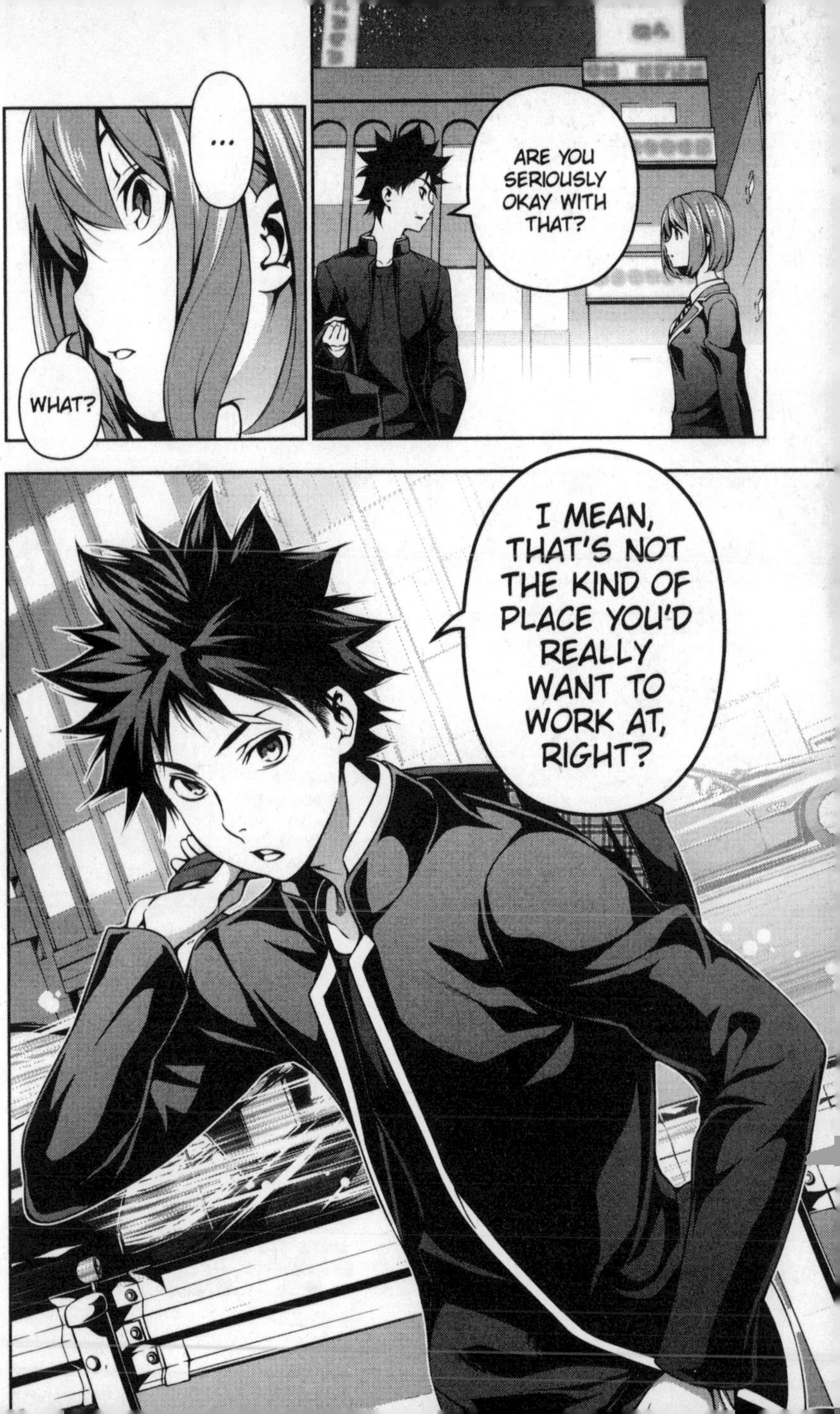
ARE YOU SERIOUSLY OKAY WITH THAT?
...
WHAT?
I MEAN, THAT'S NOT THE KIND OF PLACE YOU'D REALLY WANT TO WORK AT, RIGHT?

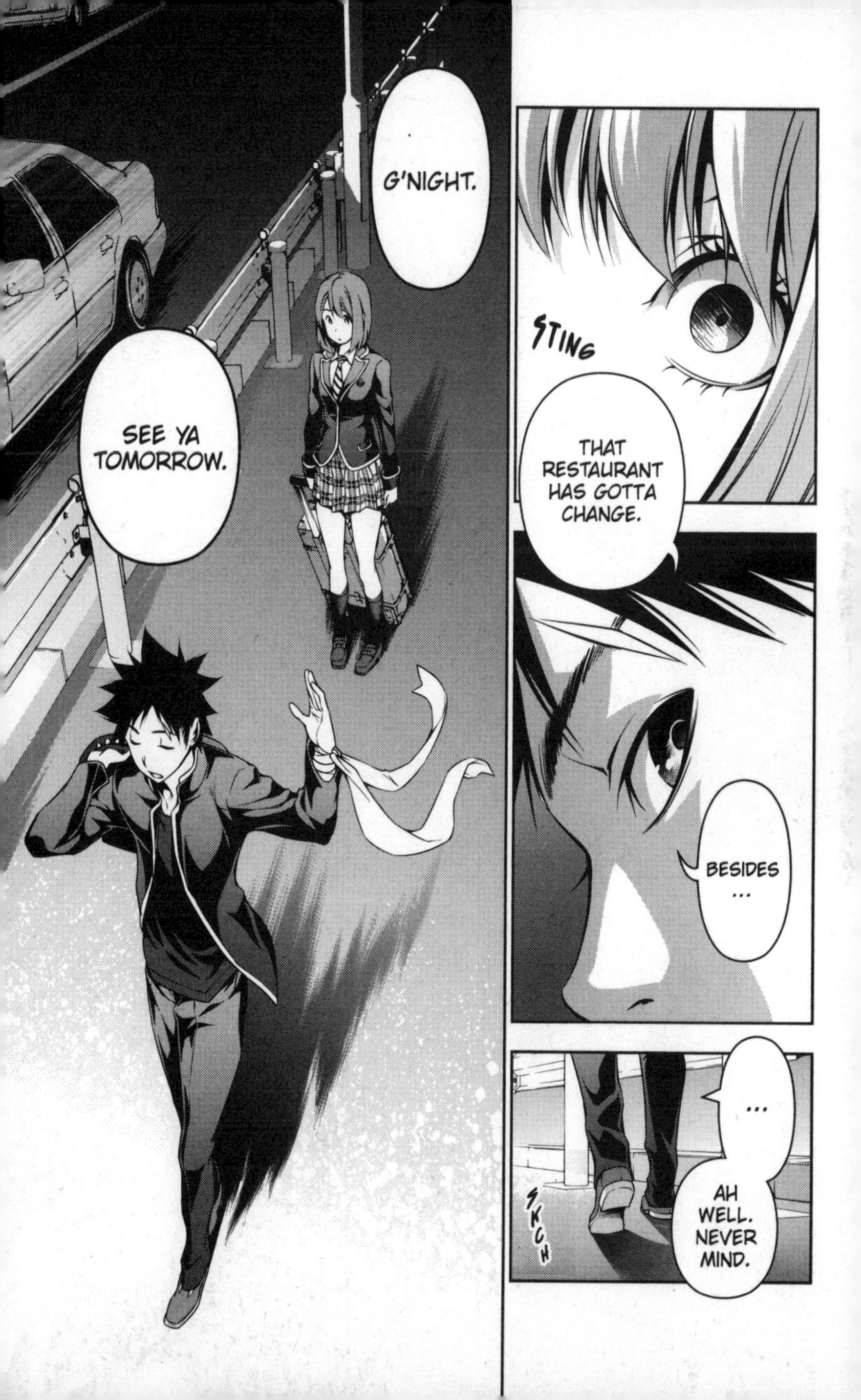
STING
THAT RESTAURANT HAS GOTTA CHANGE.
BESIDES ...
...
AH WELL. NEVER MIND.
SKCH
G'NIGHT.
SEE YA TOMORROW.

SWISH

#108 CHOOSE YOUR PATH

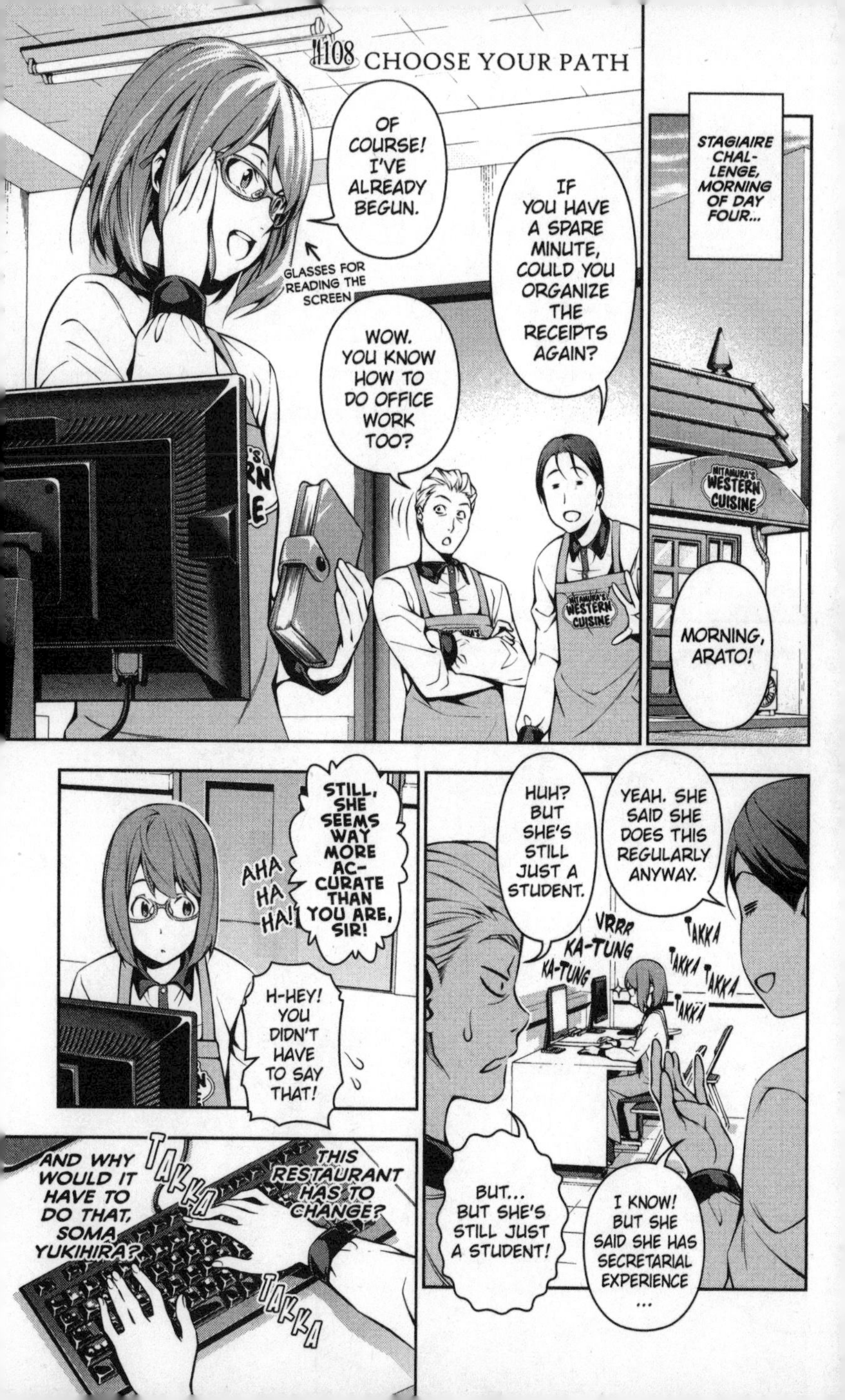
STAGIAIRE CHAL-LENGE, MORNING OF DAY FOUR...
NITAMURA'S WESTERN CUISINE
MORNING, ARATO!
IF YOU HAVE A SPARE MINUTE, COULD YOU ORGANIZE THE RECEIPTS AGAIN?
OF COURSE! I'VE ALREADY BEGUN.
GLASSES FOR READING THE SCREEN
WOW. YOU KNOW HOW TO DO OFFICE WORK TOO?
NITAMURA'S WESTERN CUISINE
YEAH. SHE SAID SHE DOES THIS REGULARLY ANYWAY.
HUH? BUT SHE'S STILL JUST A STUDENT.
VRRR
KA-TUNG
KA-TUNG
TAKKA
TAKKA
TAKKA
TAKKA
I KNOW! BUT SHE SAID SHE HAS SECRETARIAL EXPERIENCE ...
BUT... BUT SHE'S STILL JUST A STUDENT!
STILL, SHE SEEMS WAY MORE AC-CURATE THAN YOU ARE, SIR!
AHA HA HA!
H-HEY! YOU DIDN'T HAVE TO SAY THAT!
THIS RESTAURANT HAS TO CHANGE?
TAKKA
AND WHY WOULD IT HAVE TO DO THAT, SOMA YUKIHIRA?
TAKKA

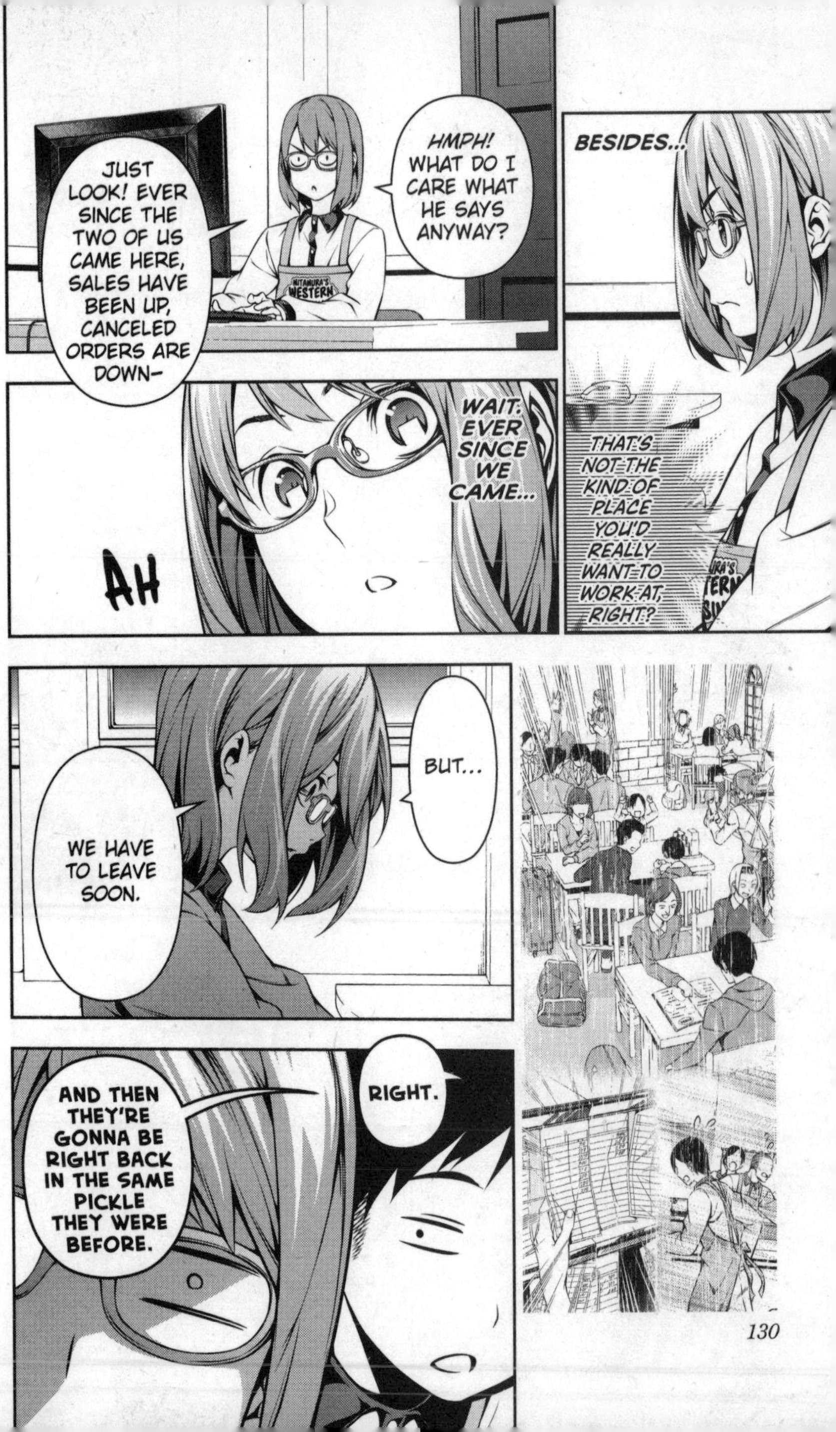

BESIDES...
THAT'S NOT THE KIND OF PLACE YOU'D REALLY WANT TO WORK AT, RIGHT?
HMPH! WHAT DO I CARE WHAT HE SAYS ANYWAY?
JUST LOOK! EVER SINCE THE TWO OF US CAME HERE, SALES HAVE BEEN UP, CANCELED ORDERS ARE DOWN-
MITAMURA'S WESTERN
WAIT. EVER SINCE WE CAME...
AH
BUT...
WE HAVE TO LEAVE SOON.
RIGHT.
AND THEN THEY'RE GONNA BE RIGHT BACK IN THE SAME PICKLE THEY WERE BEFORE.

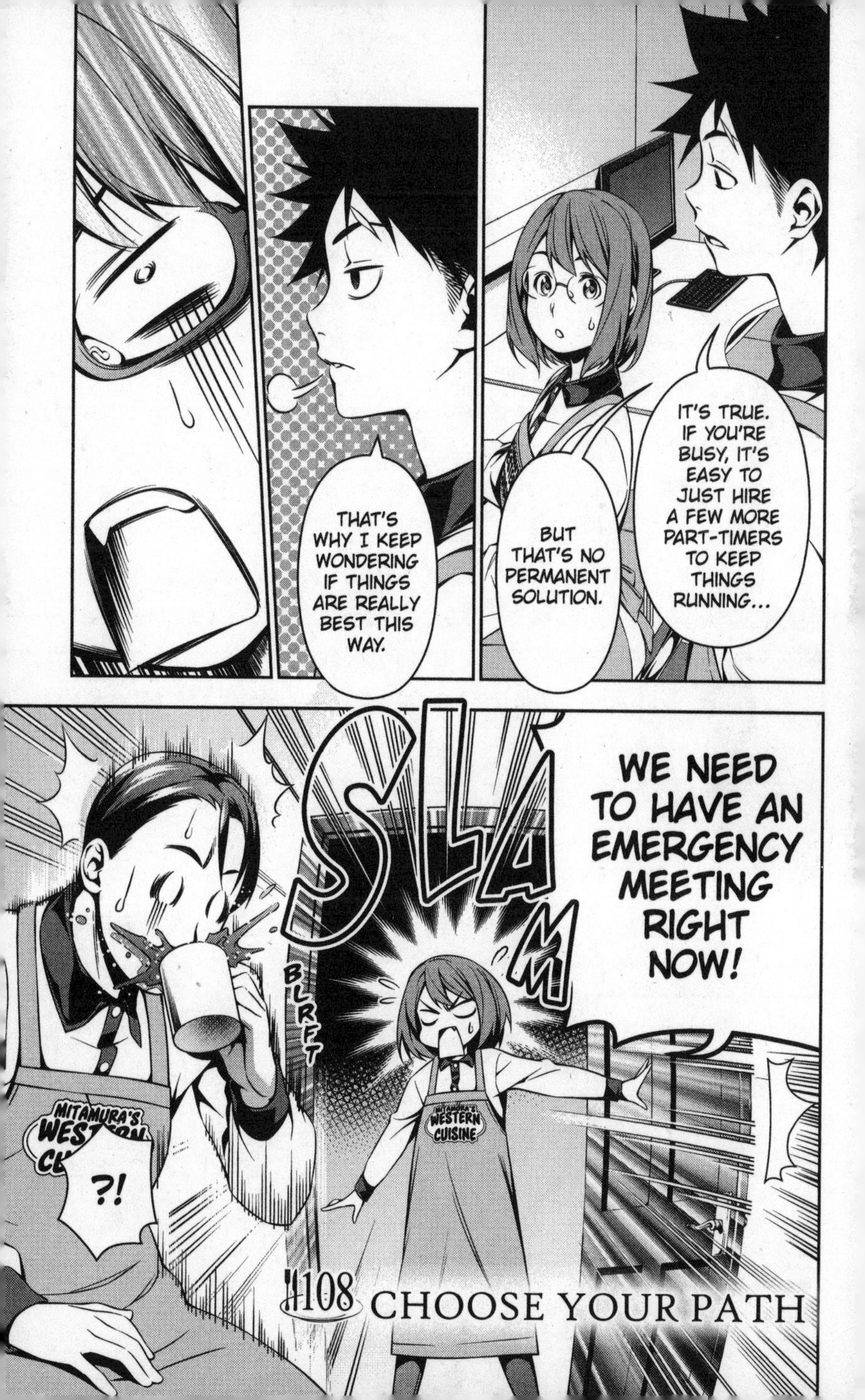
IT'S TRUE. IF YOU'RE BUSY, IT'S EASY TO JUST HIRE A FEW MORE PART-TIMERS TO KEEP THINGS RUNNING...
BUT THAT'S NO PERMANENT SOLUTION.
THAT'S WHY I KEEP WONDERING IF THINGS ARE REALLY BEST THIS WAY.
WE NEED TO HAVE AN EMERGENCY MEETING RIGHT NOW!
SLAM
MITAMURA'S WESTERN CUISINE
BLRFT
?!
108 CHOOSE YOUR PATH

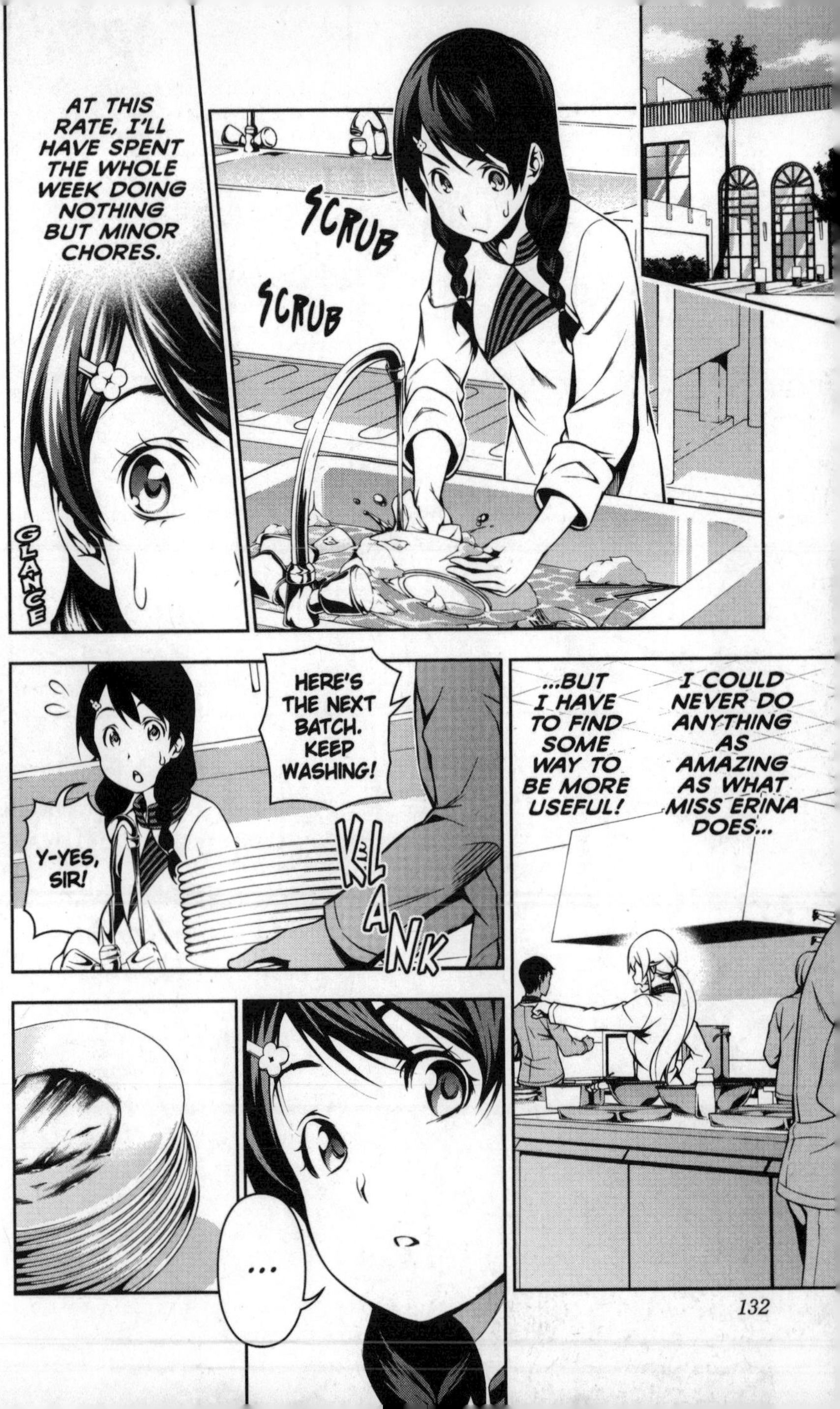
SCRUB
SCRUB
AT THIS RATE, I'LL HAVE SPENT THE WHOLE WEEK DOING NOTHING BUT MINOR CHORES.
GLANCE
I COULD NEVER DO ANYTHING AS AMAZING AS WHAT MISS ERINA DOES...
...BUT I HAVE TO FIND SOME WAY TO BE MORE USEFUL!
HERE'S THE NEXT BATCH. KEEP WASHING!
Y-YES, SIR!
KLANK
...

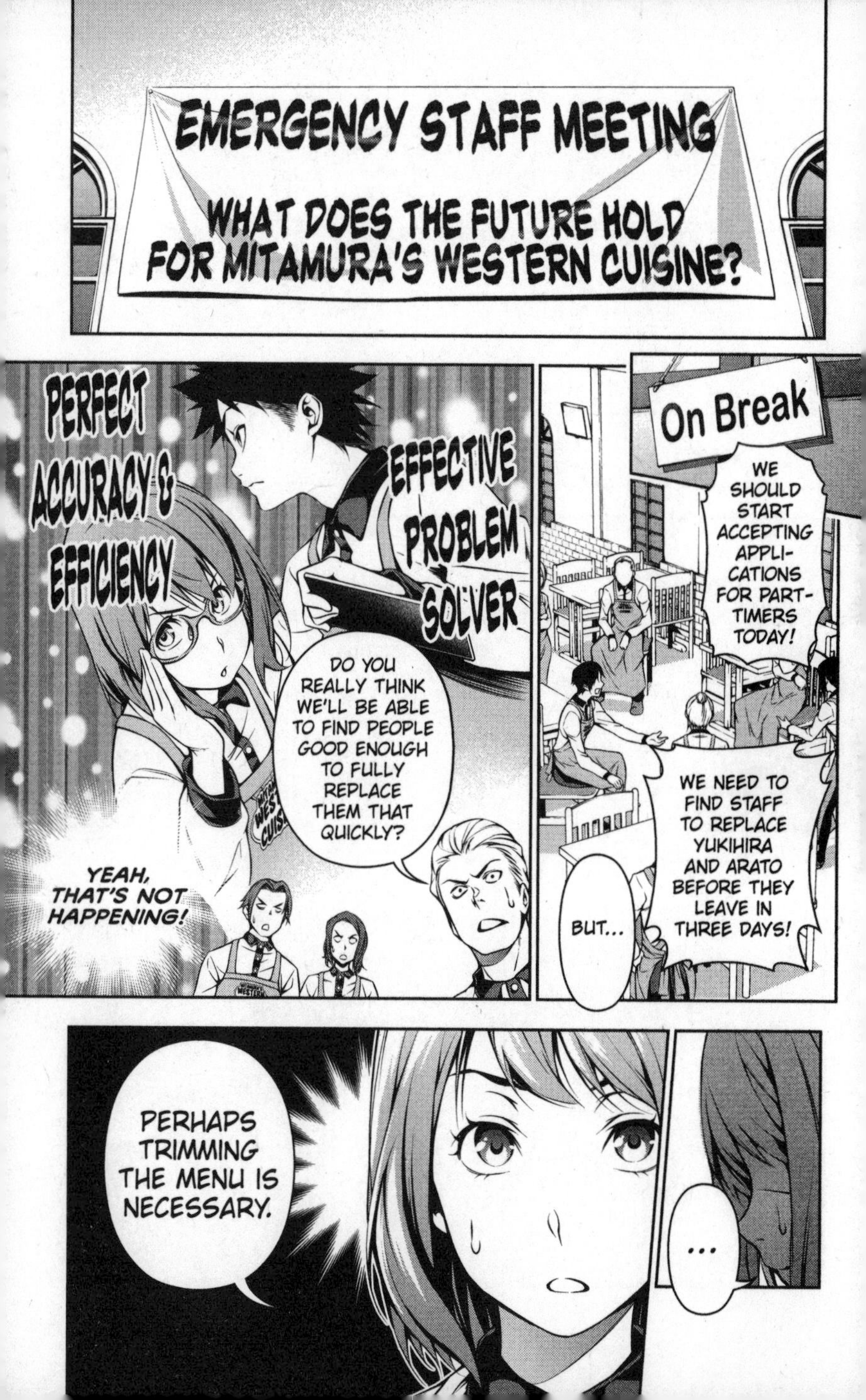
EMERGENCY STAFF MEETING
WHAT DOES THE FUTURE HOLD FOR MITAMURA'S WESTERN CUISINE?
On Break
WE SHOULD START ACCEPTING APPLI-CATIONS FOR PART-TIMERS TODAY!
WE NEED TO FIND STAFF TO REPLACE YUKIHIRA AND ARATO BEFORE THEY LEAVE IN THREE DAYS!
BUT...
EFFECTIVE PROBLEM SOLVER
PERFECT ACCURACY & EFFICIENCY
DO YOU REALLY THINK WE'LL BE ABLE TO FIND PEOPLE GOOD ENOUGH TO FULLY REPLACE THEM THAT QUICKLY?
YEAH, THAT'S NOT HAPPENING!
...
PERHAPS TRIMMING THE MENU IS NECESSARY.

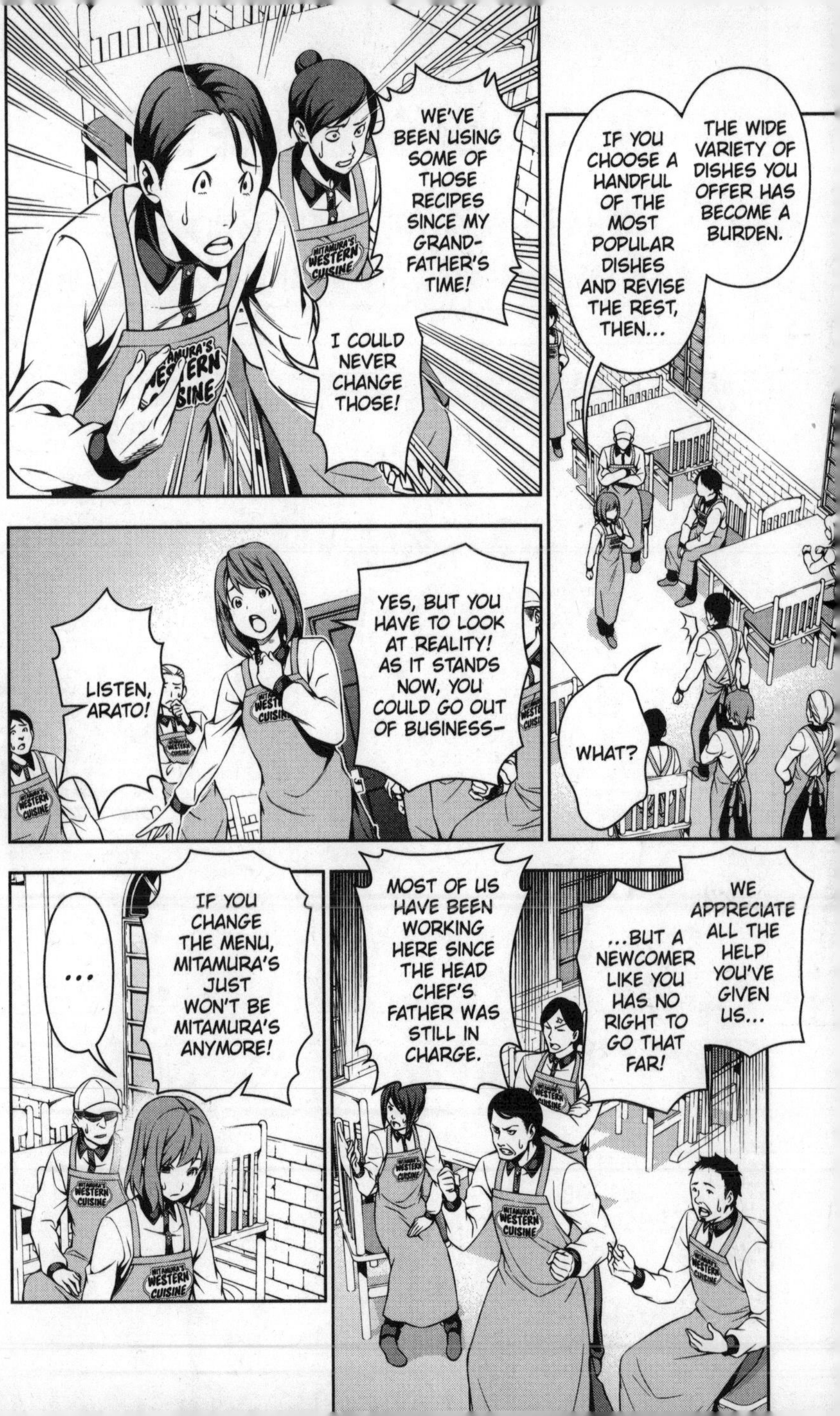
THE WIDE VARIETY OF DISHES YOU OFFER HAS BECOME A BURDEN.
IF YOU CHOOSE A HANDFUL OF THE MOST POPULAR DISHES AND REVISE THE REST, THEN...
WHAT?
WE'VE BEEN USING SOME OF THOSE RECIPES SINCE MY GRAND-FATHER'S TIME!
I COULD NEVER CHANGE THOSE!
YES, BUT YOU HAVE TO LOOK AT REALITY! AS IT STANDS NOW, YOU COULD GO OUT OF BUSINESS—
LISTEN, ARATO!
WE APPRECIATE ALL THE HELP YOU'VE GIVEN US...
...BUT A NEWCOMER LIKE YOU HAS NO RIGHT TO GO THAT FAR!
MOST OF US HAVE BEEN WORKING HERE SINCE THE HEAD CHEF'S FATHER WAS STILL IN CHARGE.
IF YOU CHANGE THE MENU, MITAMURA'S JUST WON'T BE MITAMURA'S ANYMORE!
...

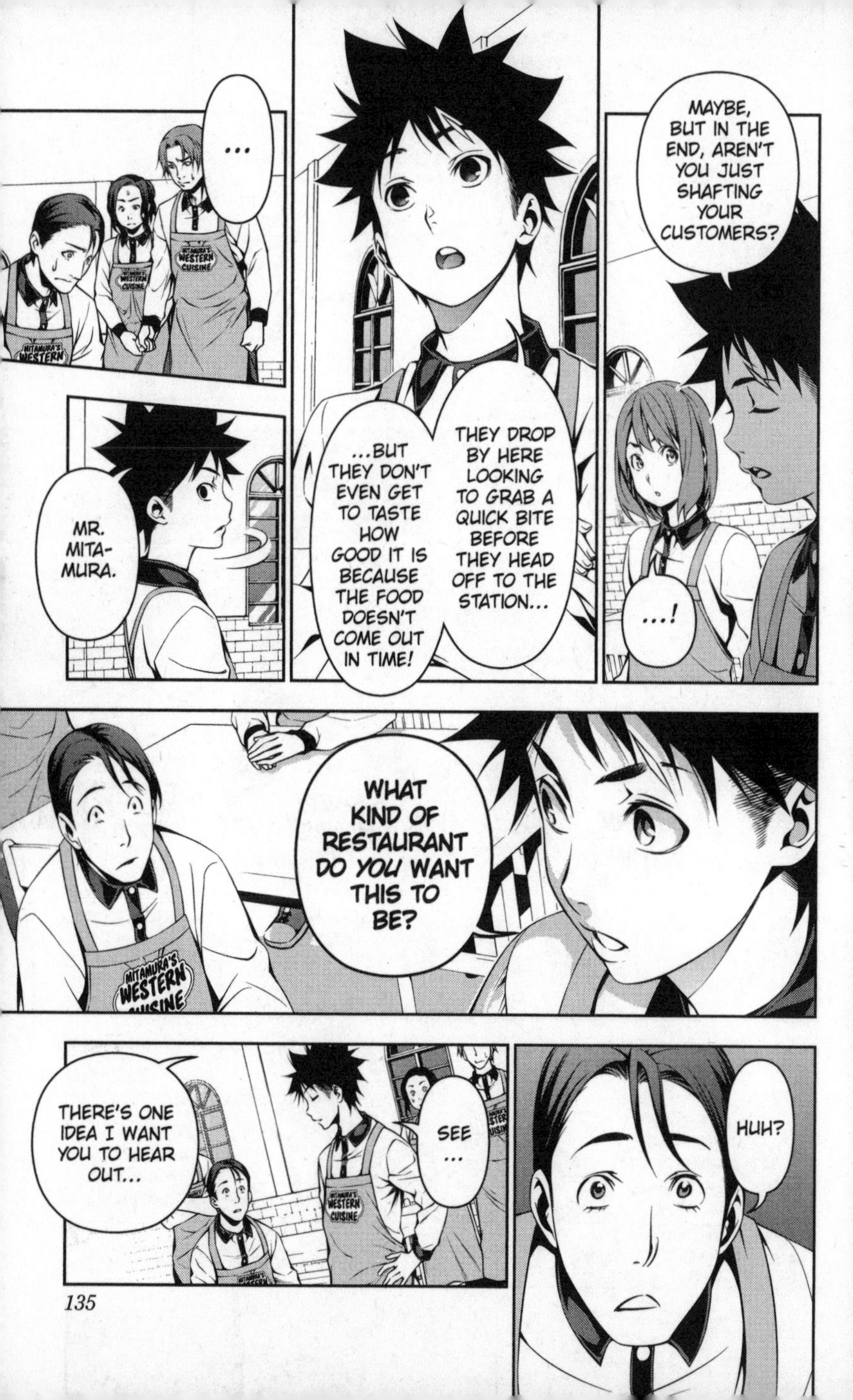
MAYBE, BUT IN THE END, AREN'T YOU JUST SHAFTING YOUR CUSTOMERS?
...!
THEY DROP BY HERE LOOKING TO GRAB A QUICK BITE BEFORE THEY HEAD OFF TO THE STATION...
...BUT THEY DON'T EVEN GET TO TASTE HOW GOOD IT IS BECAUSE THE FOOD DOESN'T COME OUT IN TIME!
...
MR. MITA-MURA.
WHAT KIND OF RESTAURANT DO *YOU* WANT THIS TO BE?
HUH?
SEE ...
THERE'S ONE IDEA I WANT YOU TO HEAR OUT...

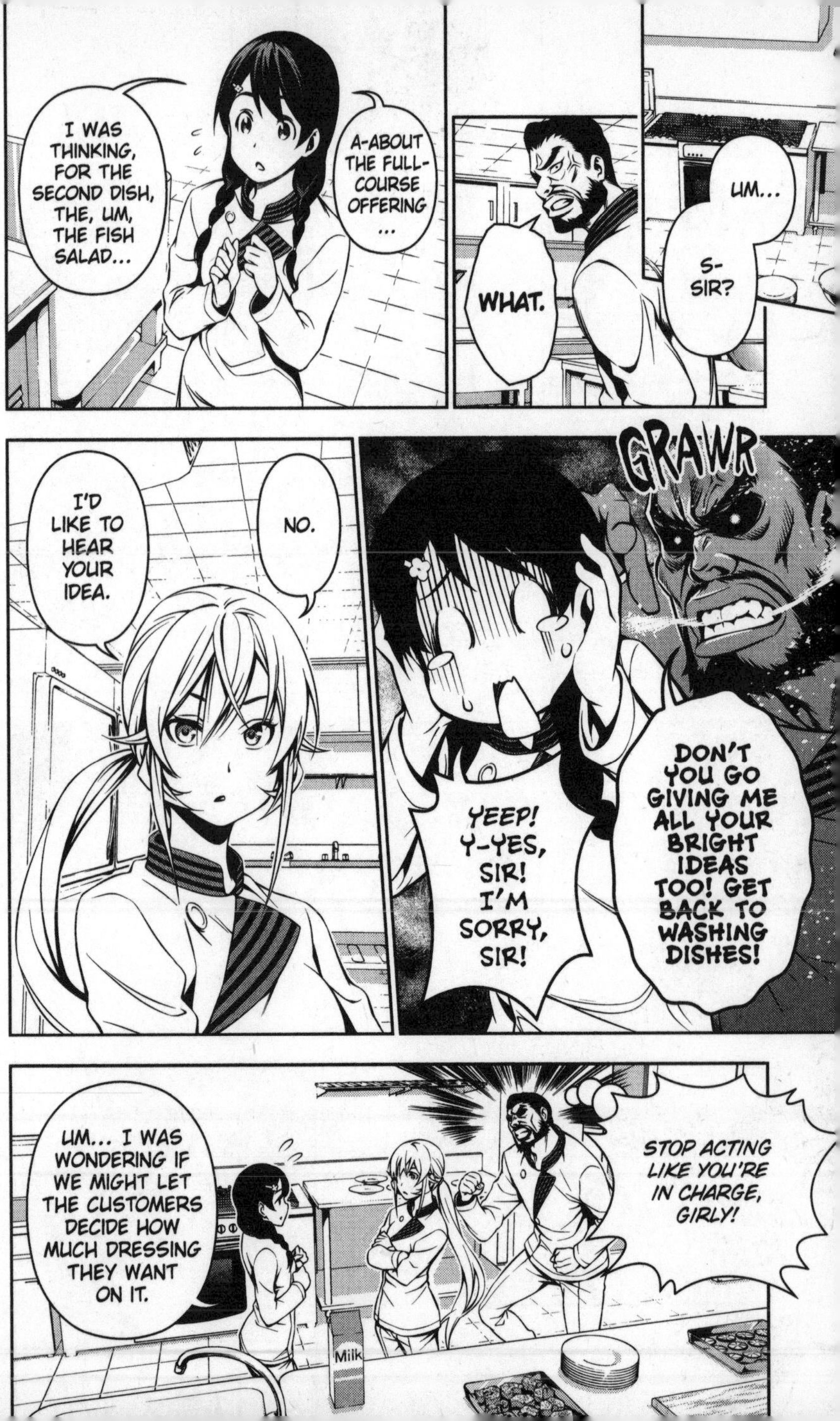
UM...
S-SIR?
WHAT.
A-ABOUT THE FULL-COURSE OFFERING...
I WAS THINKING, FOR THE SECOND DISH, THE, UM, THE FISH SALAD...
GRAWR
DON'T YOU GO GIVING ME ALL YOUR BRIGHT IDEAS TOO! GET BACK TO WASHING DISHES!
YEEP! Y-YES, SIR! I'M SORRY, SIR!
NO.
I'D LIKE TO HEAR YOUR IDEA.
STOP ACTING LIKE YOU'RE IN CHARGE, GIRLY!
UM... I WAS WONDERING IF WE MIGHT LET THE CUSTOMERS DECIDE HOW MUCH DRESSING THEY WANT ON IT.
Milk

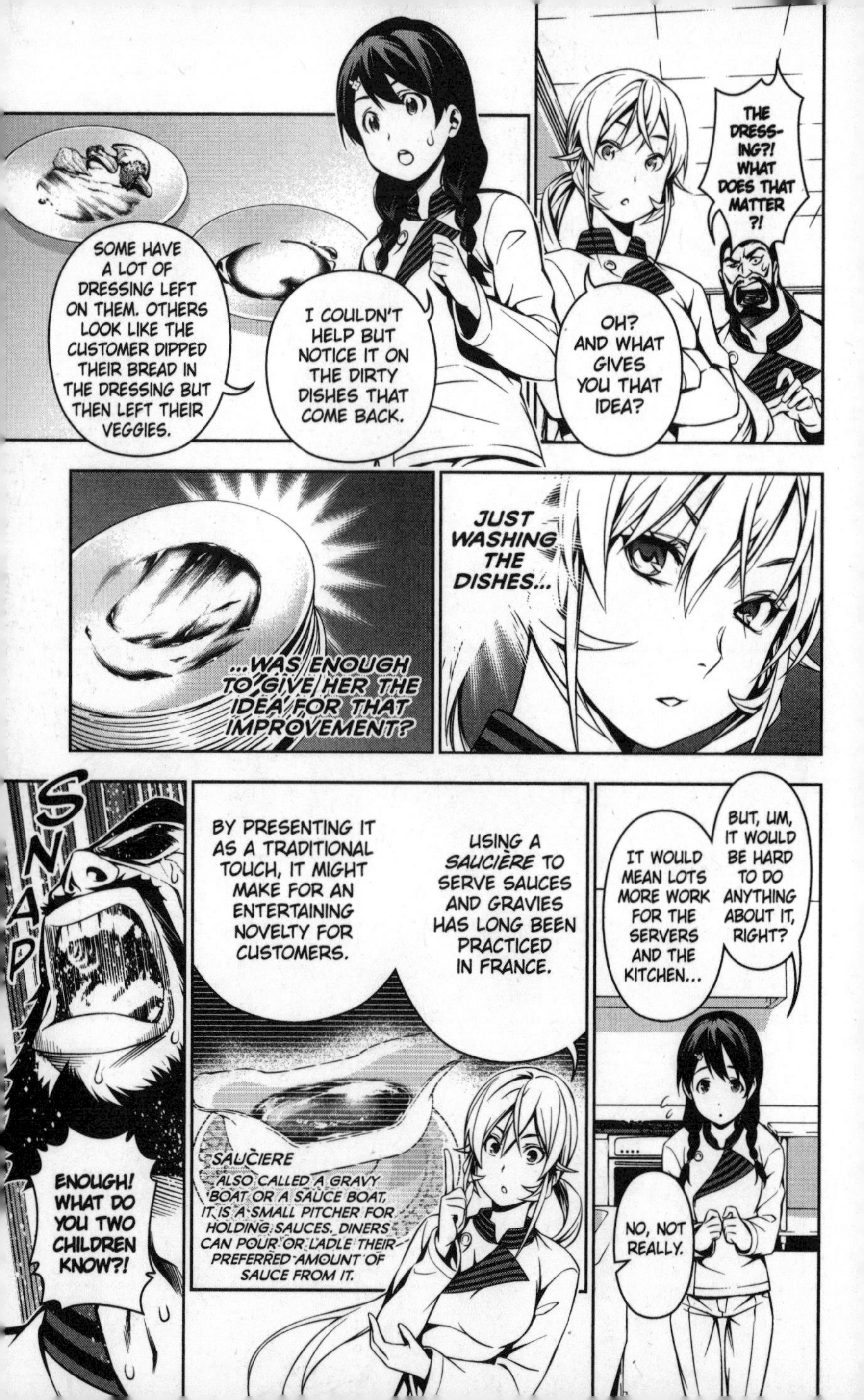
THE DRESSING?! WHAT DOES THAT MATTER?!
OH? AND WHAT GIVES YOU THAT IDEA?
I COULDN'T HELP BUT NOTICE IT ON THE DIRTY DISHES THAT COME BACK.
SOME HAVE A LOT OF DRESSING LEFT ON THEM. OTHERS LOOK LIKE THE CUSTOMER DIPPED THEIR BREAD IN THE DRESSING BUT THEN LEFT THEIR VEGGIES.
JUST WASHING THE DISHES...
...WAS ENOUGH TO GIVE HER THE IDEA FOR THAT IMPROVEMENT?
BUT, UM, IT WOULD BE HARD TO DO ANYTHING ABOUT IT, RIGHT?
IT WOULD MEAN LOTS MORE WORK FOR THE SERVERS AND THE KITCHEN...
NO, NOT REALLY.
USING A SAUCIÈRE TO SERVE SAUCES AND GRAVIES HAS LONG BEEN PRACTICED IN FRANCE.
BY PRESENTING IT AS A TRADITIONAL TOUCH, IT MIGHT MAKE FOR AN ENTERTAINING NOVELTY FOR CUSTOMERS.
SAUCIERE
ALSO CALLED A GRAVY BOAT OR A SAUCE BOAT, IT IS A SMALL PITCHER FOR HOLDING SAUCES. DINERS CAN POUR OR LADLE THEIR PREFERRED AMOUNT OF SAUCE FROM IT.
SNAP
ENOUGH! WHAT DO YOU TWO CHILDREN KNOW?!

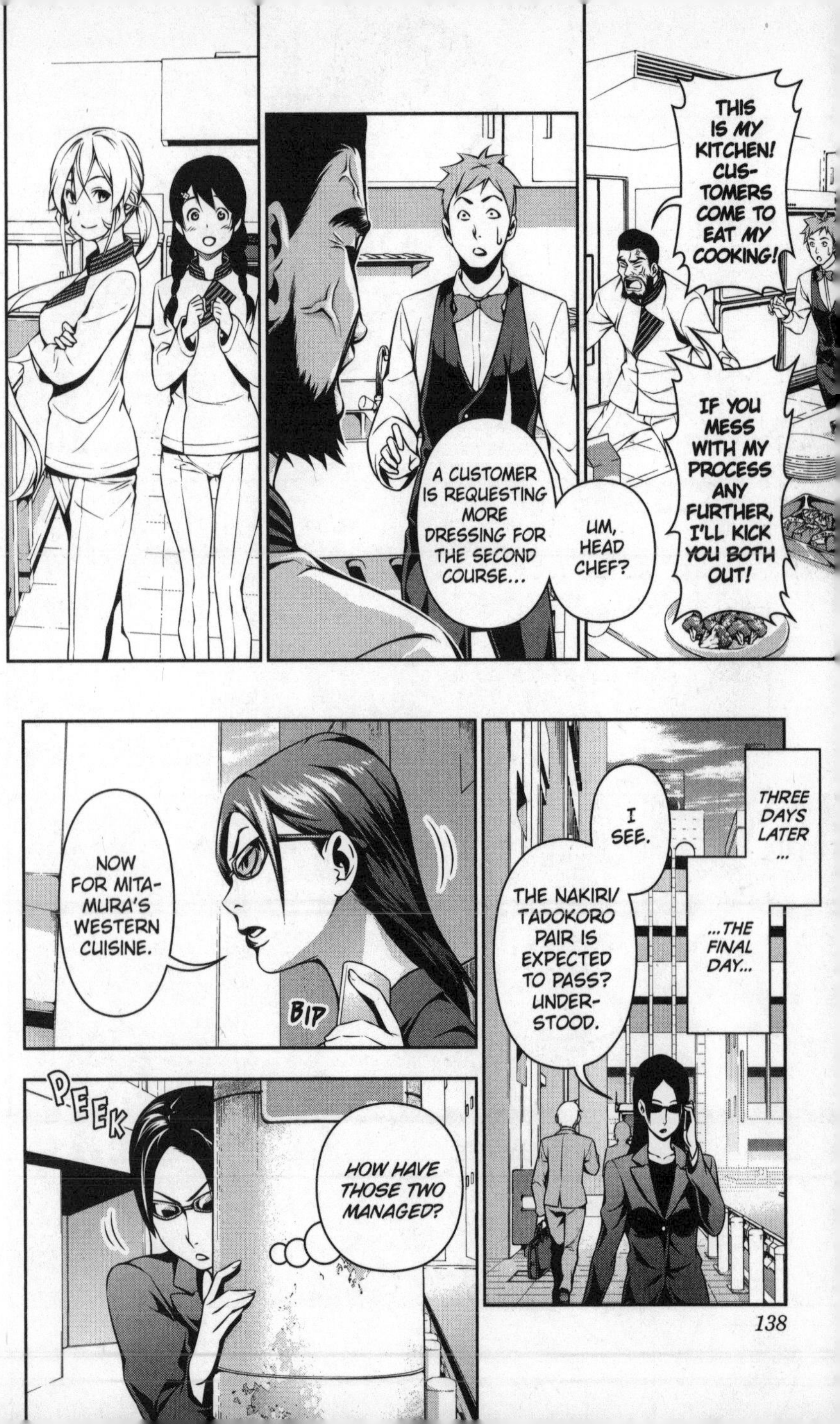
THIS IS MY KITCHEN! CUS-TOMERS COME TO EAT MY COOKING!
IF YOU MESS WITH MY PROCESS ANY FURTHER, I'LL KICK YOU BOTH OUT!
UM, HEAD CHEF?
A CUSTOMER IS REQUESTING MORE DRESSING FOR THE SECOND COURSE...
THREE DAYS LATER ...
...THE FINAL DAY...
I SEE.
THE NAKIRI/ TADOKORO PAIR IS EXPECTED TO PASS? UNDER-STOOD.
NOW FOR MITA-MURA'S WESTERN CUISINE.
BIP
PEEK
HOW HAVE THOSE TWO MANAGED?

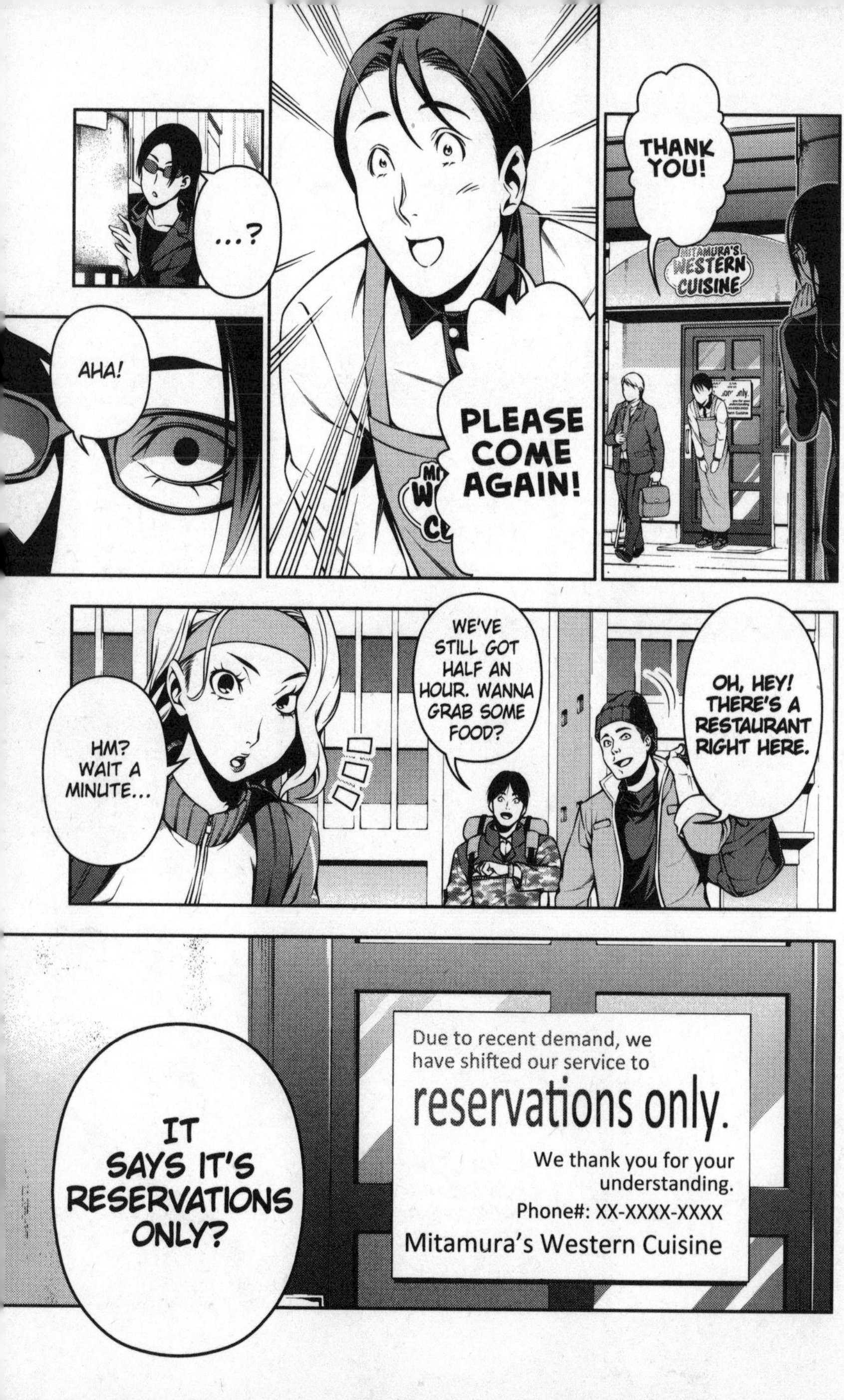
THANK YOU!
MITAMURA'S WESTERN CUISINE
PLEASE COME AGAIN!
...?
AHA!
OH, HEY! THERE'S A RESTAURANT RIGHT HERE.
WE'VE STILL GOT HALF AN HOUR. WANNA GRAB SOME FOOD?
HM? WAIT A MINUTE...
Due to recent demand, we have shifted our service to
reservations only.
We thank you for your understanding.
Phone#: XX-XXXX-XXXX
Mitamura's Western Cuisine
IT SAYS IT'S RESERVATIONS ONLY?

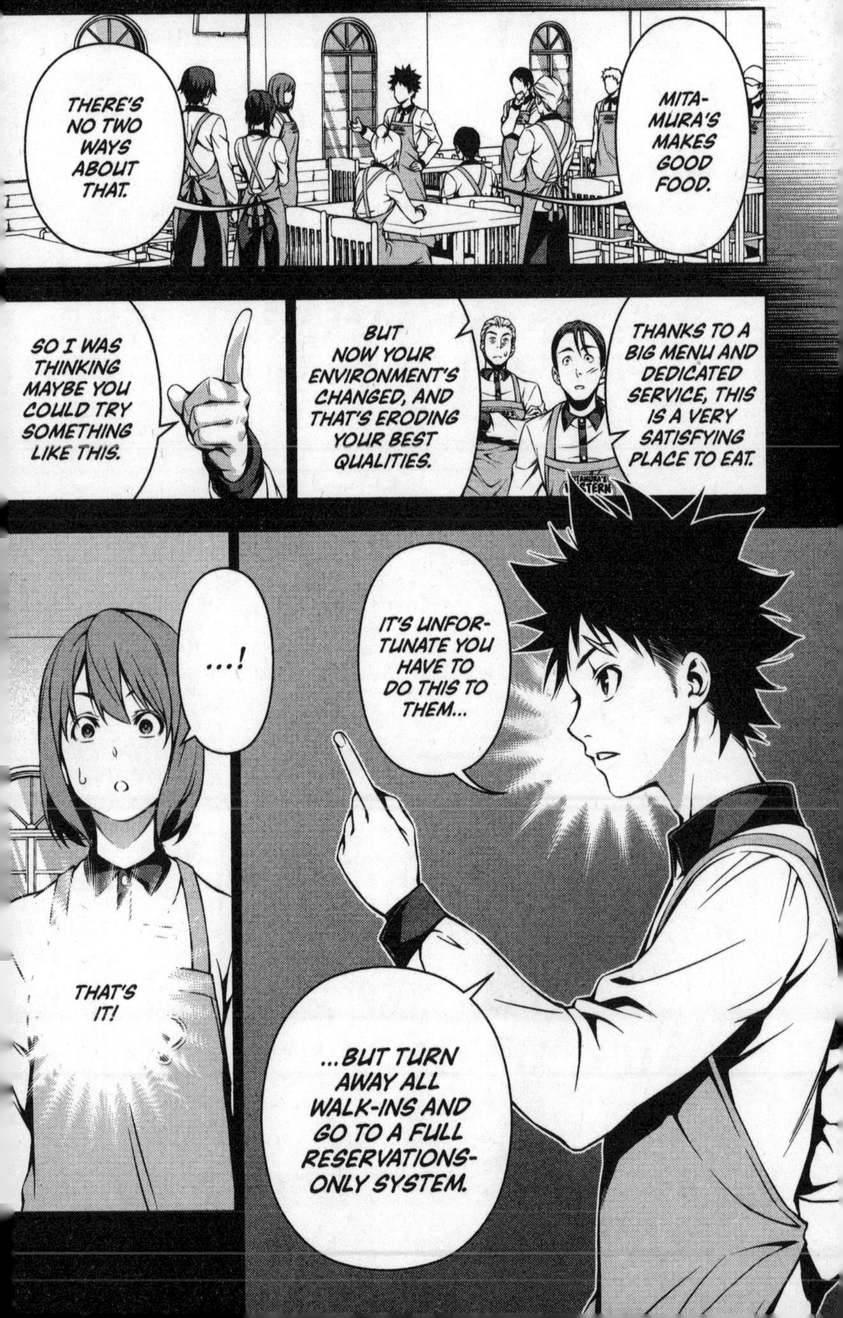
MITA-MURA'S MAKES GOOD FOOD.
THERE'S NO TWO WAYS ABOUT THAT.
THANKS TO A BIG MENU AND DEDICATED SERVICE, THIS IS A VERY SATISFYING PLACE TO EAT.
BUT NOW YOUR ENVIRONMENT'S CHANGED, AND THAT'S ERODING YOUR BEST QUALITIES.
SO I WAS THINKING MAYBE YOU COULD TRY SOMETHING LIKE THIS.
IT'S UNFOR-TUNATE YOU HAVE TO DO THIS TO THEM...
...BUT TURN AWAY ALL WALK-INS AND GO TO A FULL RESERVATIONS-ONLY SYSTEM.
...!
THAT'S IT!

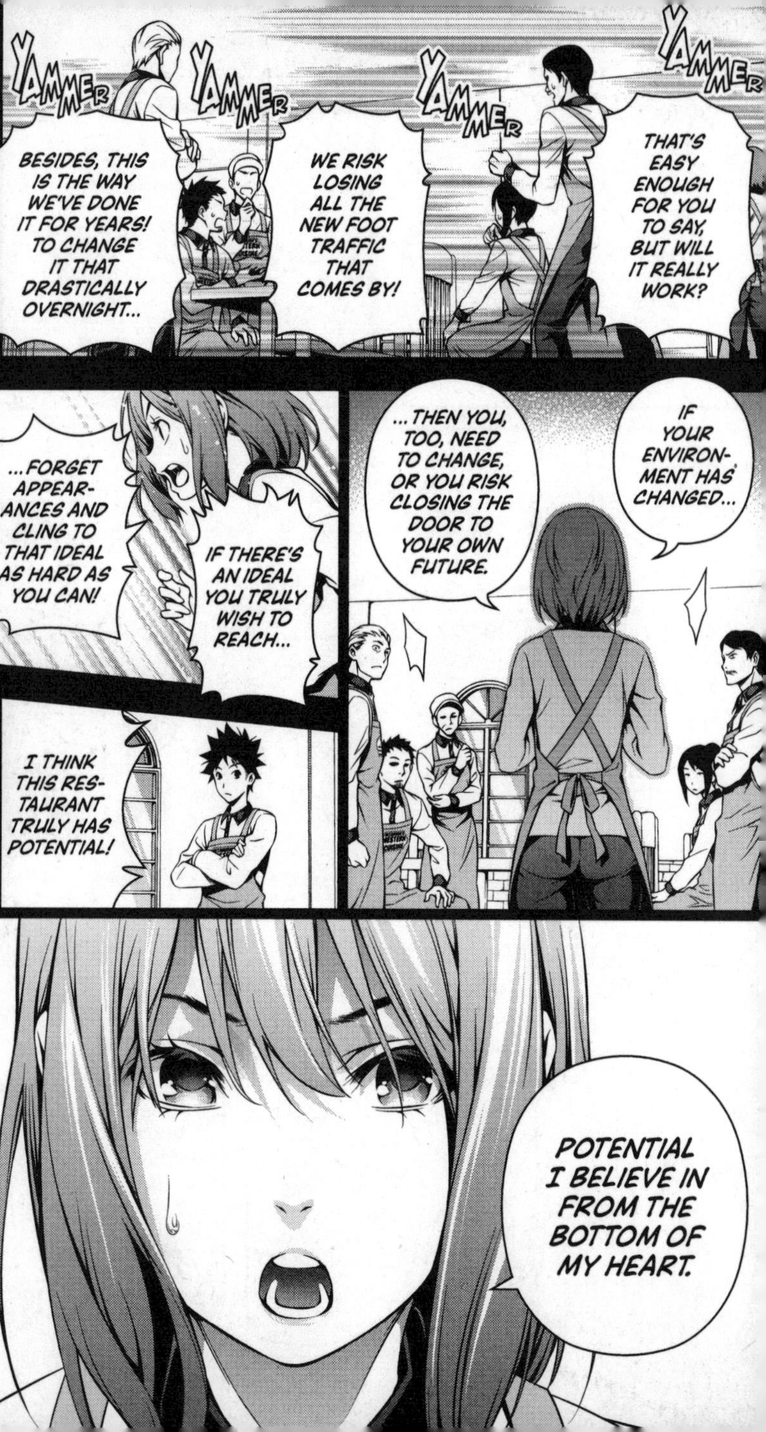
YAMMER
THAT'S EASY ENOUGH FOR YOU TO SAY, BUT WILL IT REALLY WORK?
YAMMER
WE RISK LOSING ALL THE NEW FOOT TRAFFIC THAT COMES BY!
YAMMER
BESIDES, THIS IS THE WAY WE'VE DONE IT FOR YEARS! TO CHANGE IT THAT DRASTICALLY OVERNIGHT...
YAMMER
IF YOUR ENVIRONMENT HAS CHANGED...
...THEN YOU, TOO, NEED TO CHANGE, OR YOU RISK CLOSING THE DOOR TO YOUR OWN FUTURE.
IF THERE'S AN IDEAL YOU TRULY WISH TO REACH...
...FORGET APPEARANCES AND CLING TO THAT IDEAL AS HARD AS YOU CAN!
I THINK THIS RESTAURANT TRULY HAS POTENTIAL!
POTENTIAL I BELIEVE IN FROM THE BOTTOM OF MY HEART.

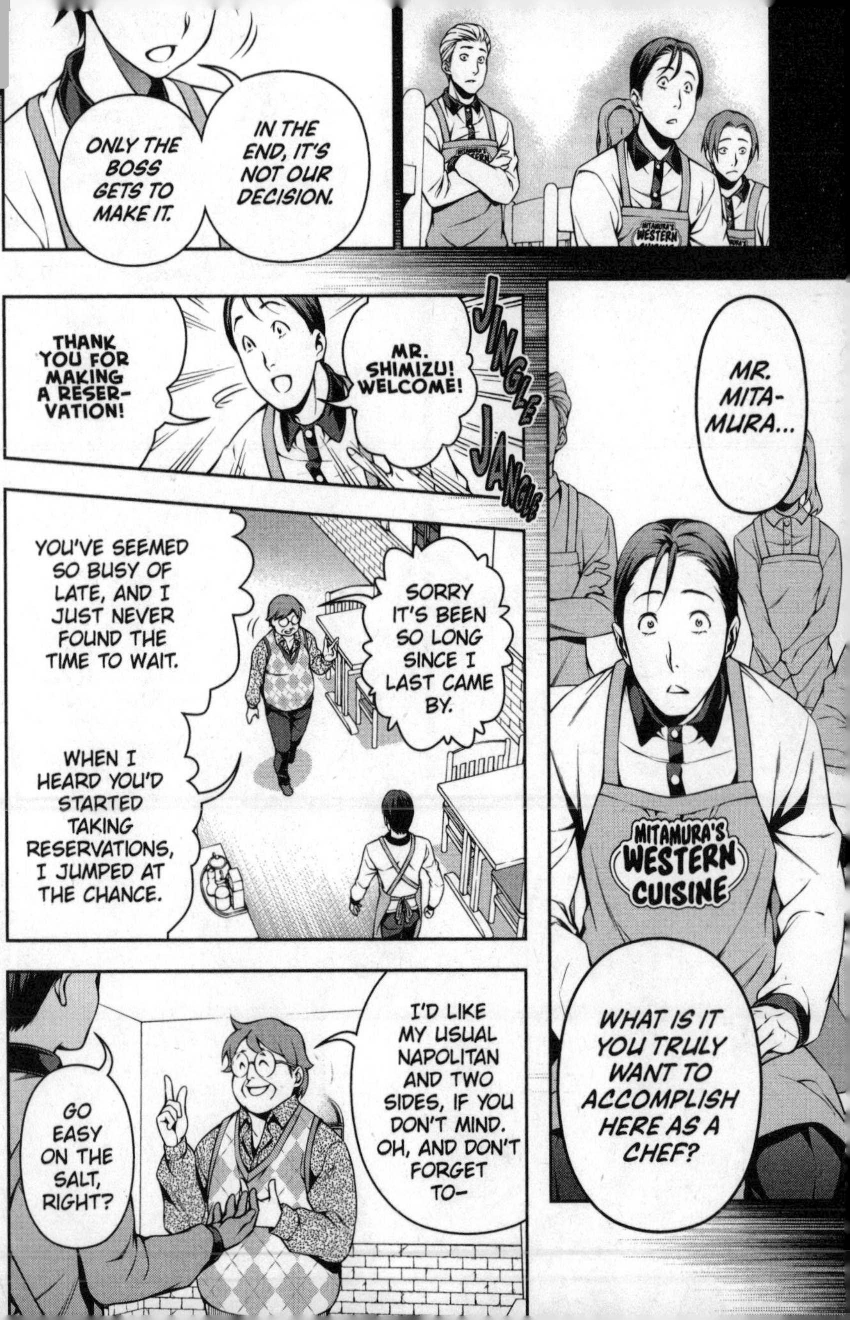
IN THE END, IT'S NOT OUR DECISION.
ONLY THE BOSS GETS TO MAKE IT.
MITAMURA'S WESTERN CUISINE
MR. MITAMURA...
MITAMURA'S WESTERN CUISINE
WHAT IS IT YOU TRULY WANT TO ACCOMPLISH HERE AS A CHEF?
JINGLE JANGLE
MR. SHIMIZU! WELCOME!
THANK YOU FOR MAKING A RESERVATION!
SORRY IT'S BEEN SO LONG SINCE I LAST CAME BY.
YOU'VE SEEMED SO BUSY OF LATE, AND I JUST NEVER FOUND THE TIME TO WAIT.
WHEN I HEARD YOU'D STARTED TAKING RESERVATIONS, I JUMPED AT THE CHANCE.
I'D LIKE MY USUAL NAPOLITAN AND TWO SIDES, IF YOU DON'T MIND. OH, AND DON'T FORGET TO—
GO EASY ON THE SALT, RIGHT?

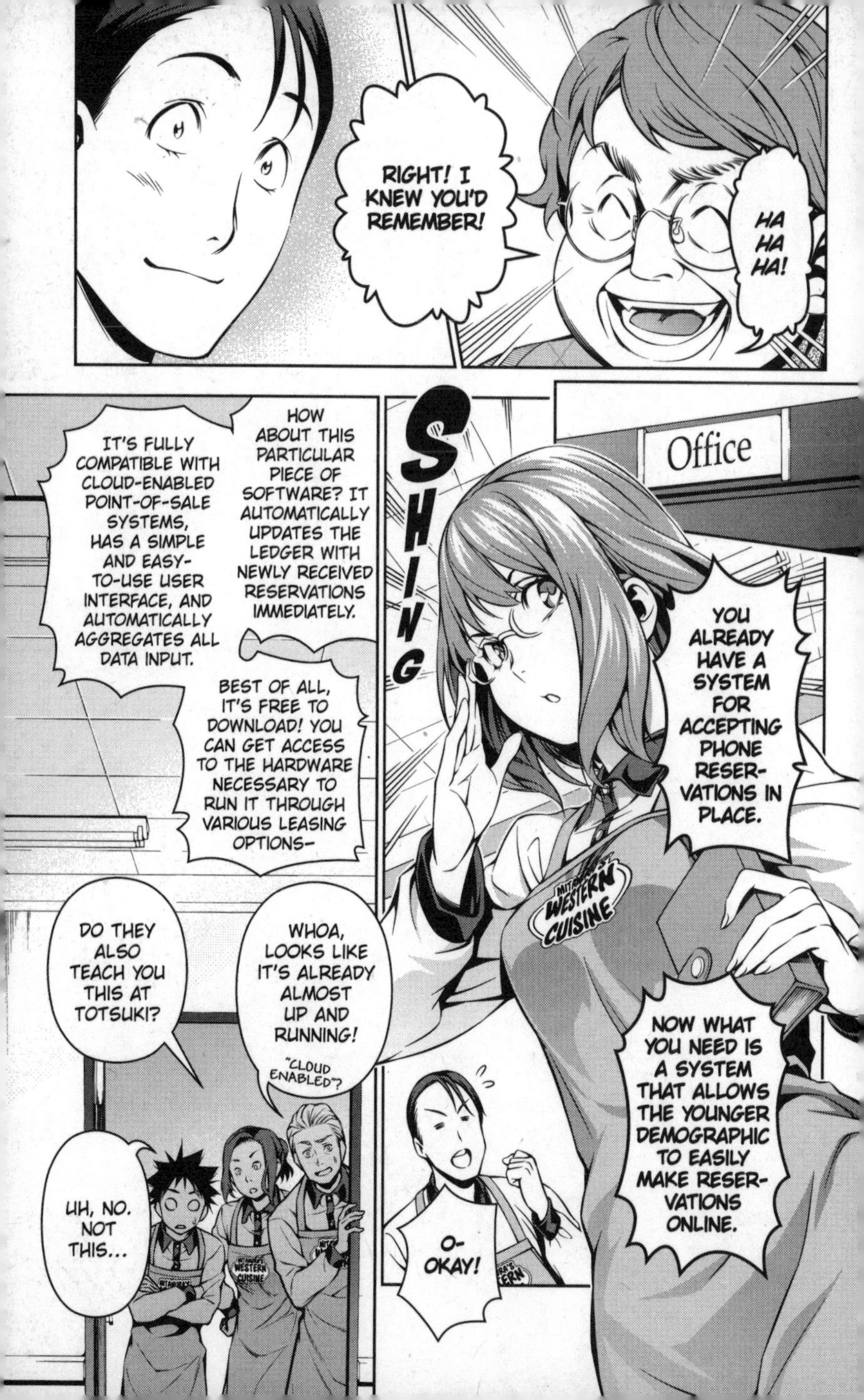
HA HA HA!
RIGHT! I KNEW YOU'D REMEMBER!
SHING
Office
YOU ALREADY HAVE A SYSTEM FOR ACCEPTING PHONE RESER-VATIONS IN PLACE.
MITAMURA'S WESTERN CUISINE
NOW WHAT YOU NEED IS A SYSTEM THAT ALLOWS THE YOUNGER DEMOGRAPHIC TO EASILY MAKE RESER-VATIONS ONLINE.
HOW ABOUT THIS PARTICULAR PIECE OF SOFTWARE? IT AUTOMATICALLY UPDATES THE LEDGER WITH NEWLY RECEIVED RESERVATIONS IMMEDIATELY.
IT'S FULLY COMPATIBLE WITH CLOUD-ENABLED POINT-OF-SALE SYSTEMS, HAS A SIMPLE AND EASY-TO-USE USER INTERFACE, AND AUTOMATICALLY AGGREGATES ALL DATA INPUT.
BEST OF ALL, IT'S FREE TO DOWNLOAD! YOU CAN GET ACCESS TO THE HARDWARE NECESSARY TO RUN IT THROUGH VARIOUS LEASING OPTIONS–
O-OKAY!
WHOA, LOOKS LIKE IT'S ALREADY ALMOST UP AND RUNNING!
"CLOUD ENABLED"?
DO THEY ALSO TEACH YOU THIS AT TOTSUKI?
UH, NO. NOT THIS...
MITAMURA'S WESTERN CUISINE

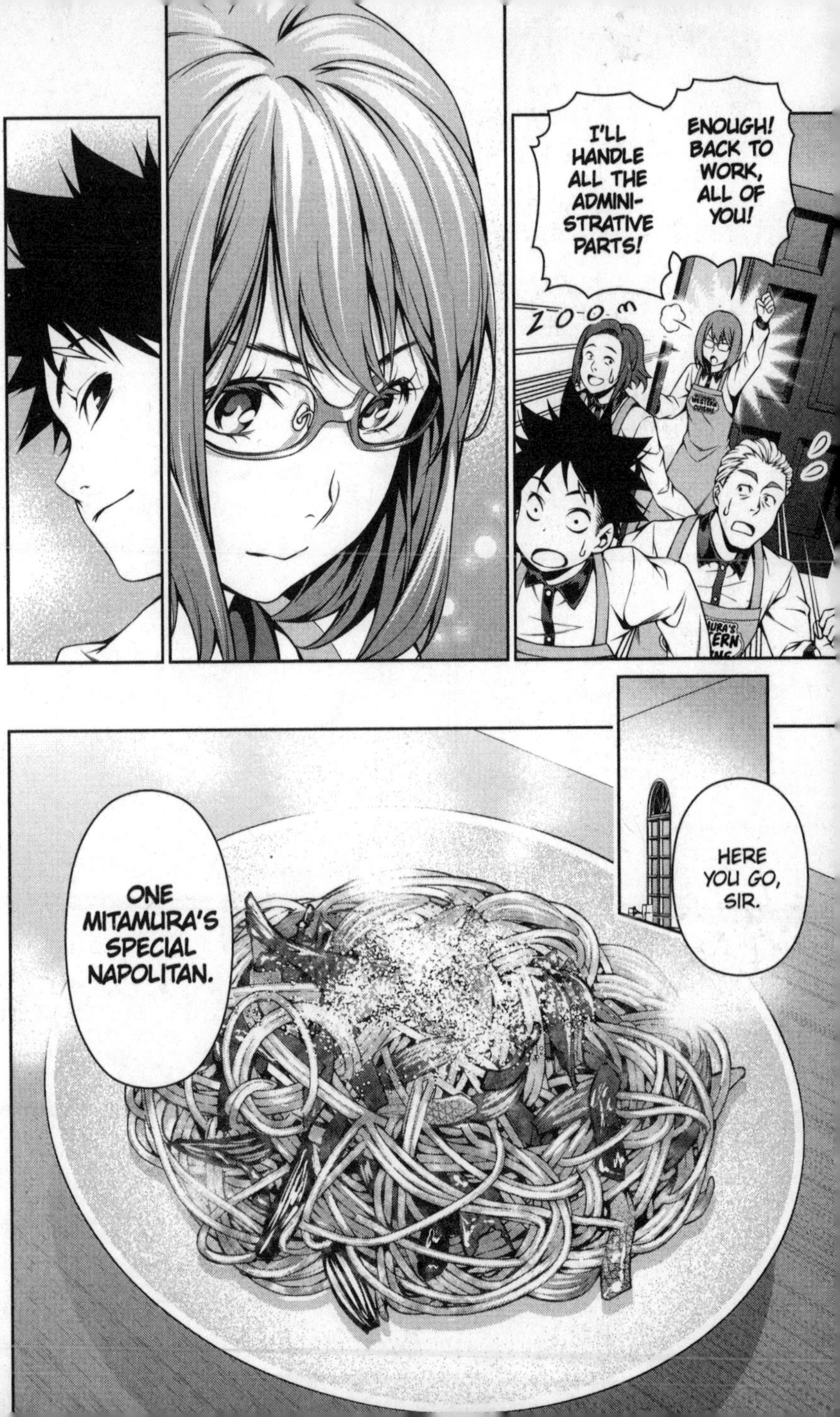
ENOUGH! BACK TO WORK, ALL OF YOU!
I'LL HANDLE ALL THE ADMINI-STRATIVE PARTS!
ZOOM
HERE YOU GO, SIR.
ONE MITAMURA'S SPECIAL NAPOLITAN.

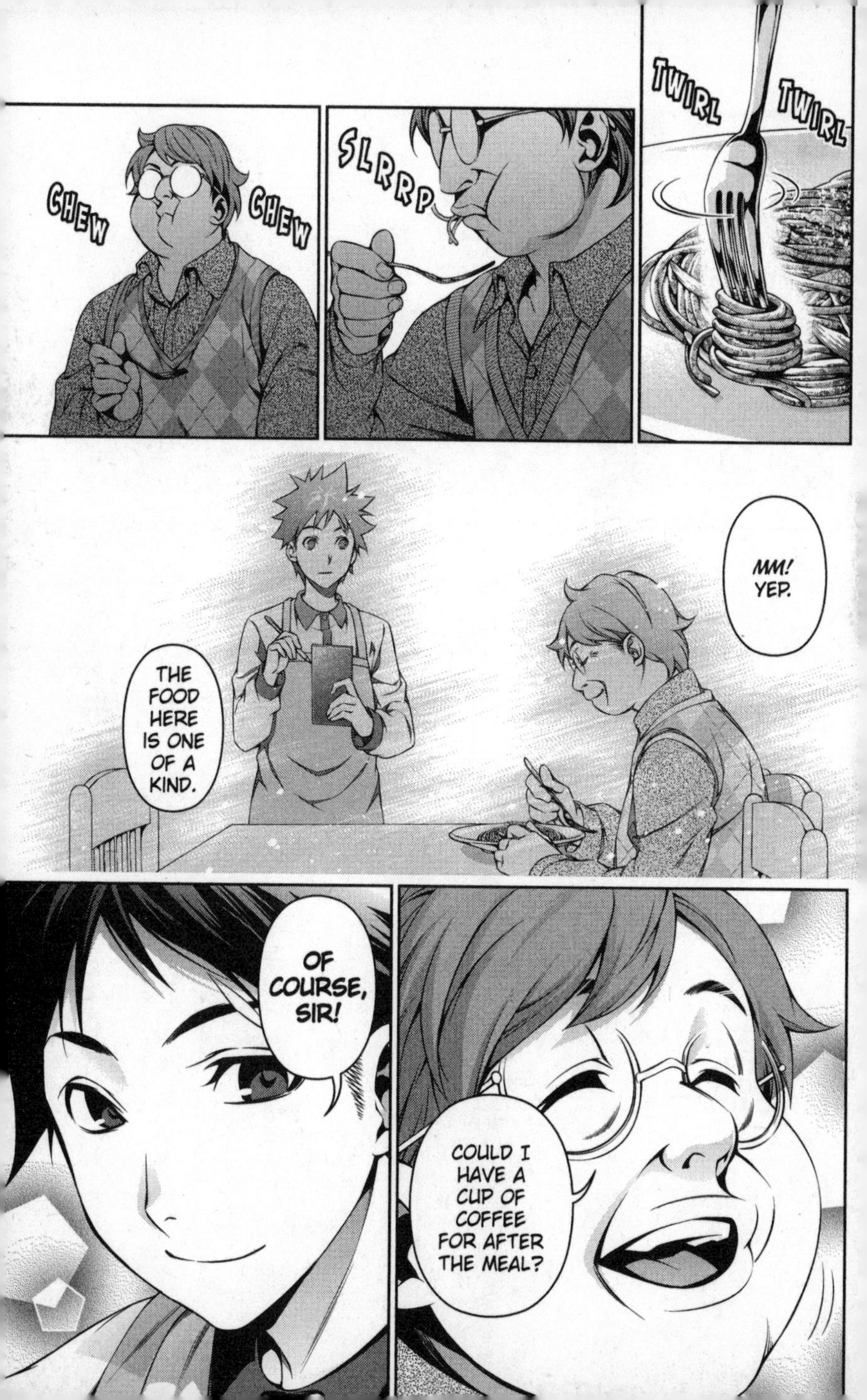
TWIRL
TWIRL
SLRRRP
CHEW
CHEW
MM! YEP.
THE FOOD HERE IS ONE OF A KIND.
COULD I HAVE A CUP OF COFFEE FOR AFTER THE MEAL?
OF COURSE, SIR!

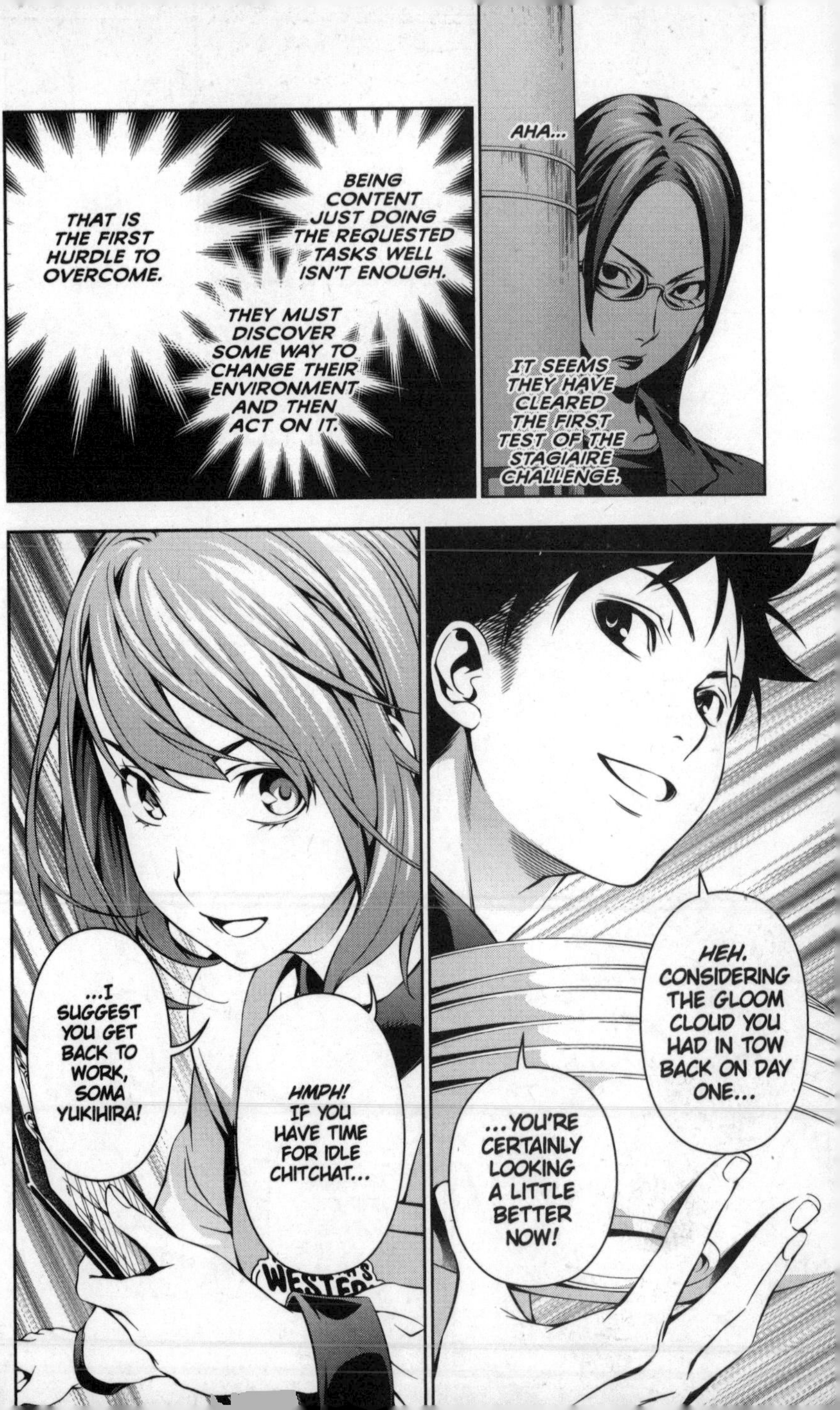
AHA...
IT SEEMS THEY HAVE CLEARED THE FIRST TEST OF THE STAGIAIRE CHALLENGE.
BEING CONTENT JUST DOING THE REQUESTED TASKS WELL ISN'T ENOUGH.
THEY MUST DISCOVER SOME WAY TO CHANGE THEIR ENVIRONMENT AND THEN ACT ON IT.
THAT IS THE FIRST HURDLE TO OVERCOME.
HEH. CONSIDERING THE GLOOM CLOUD YOU HAD IN TOW BACK ON DAY ONE...
...YOU'RE CERTAINLY LOOKING A LITTLE BETTER NOW!
HMPH! IF YOU HAVE TIME FOR IDLE CHITCHAT...
...I SUGGEST YOU GET BACK TO WORK, SOMA YUKIHIRA!

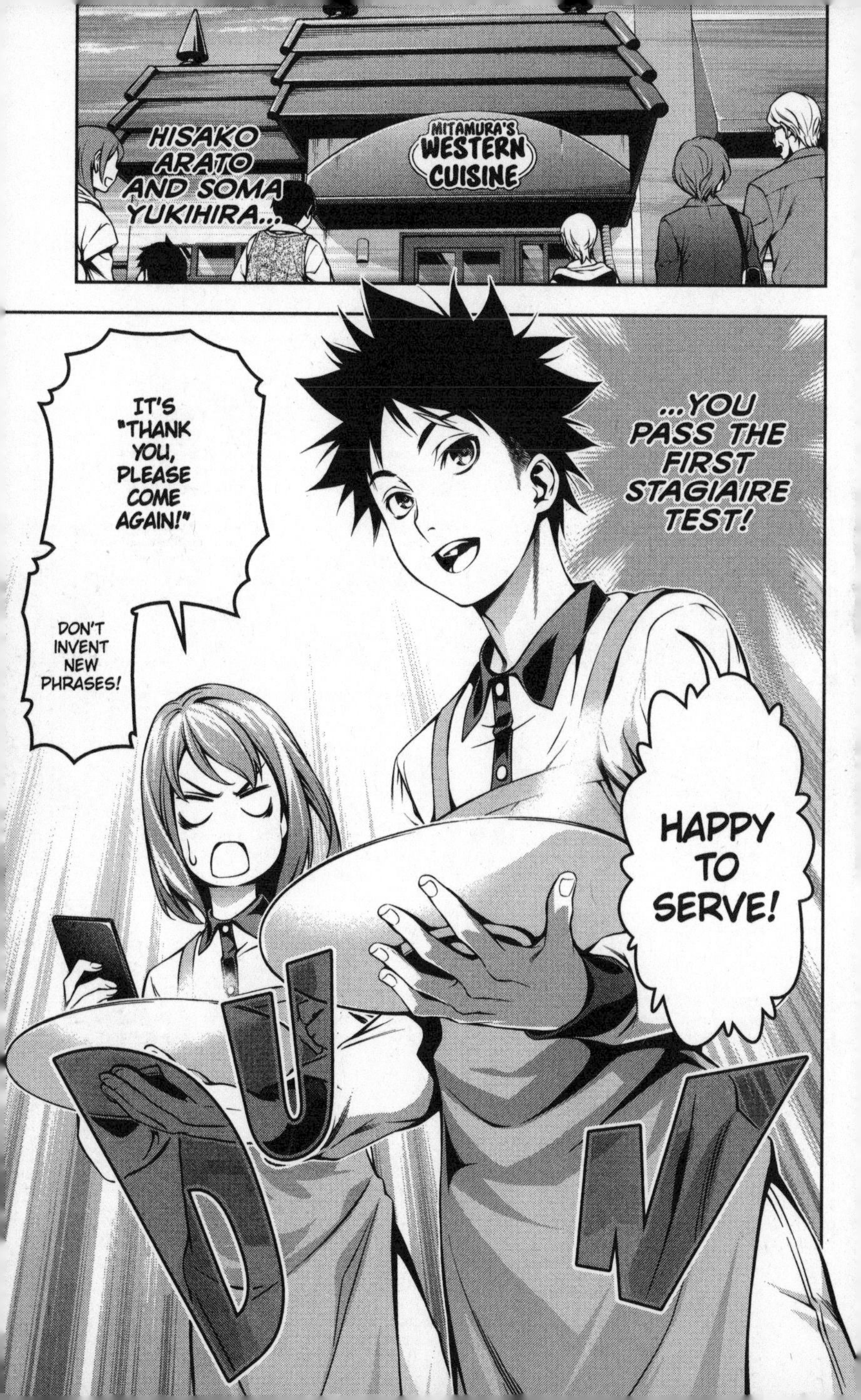
MITAMURA'S WESTERN CUISINE
HISAKO ARATO AND SOMA YUKIHIRA...
...YOU PASS THE FIRST STAGIAIRE TEST!
HAPPY TO SERVE!
IT'S "THANK YOU, PLEASE COME AGAIN!"
DON'T INVENT NEW PHRASES!
DUN

VOLUME 13
SPECIAL SUPPLEMENT!

PRACTICAL RECIPE #2

MITAMURA'S WESTERN CUISINE SPECIAL!
OLD-FASHIONED NAPOLITAN

CHIK CHIK

MITAMURA'S WESTERN CUISINE

A CLASSIC STAPLE AT YOUR LOCAL WESTERN-FOOD RESTAURANT!

● INGREDIENTS ●
(SERVES 4)

300 GRAMS SPAGHETTI NOODLES	8 TABLESPOONS TOMATO KETCHUP
6 SLICES ROAST HAM LUNCH MEAT	1 TABLESPOON SOY SAUCE
2 BELL PEPPERS	4 TABLESPOONS POWDERED PARMESAN CHEESE
1 ONION	
1 CAN SLICED MUSHROOMS	SALT, PEPPER, CHOPPED PARSLEY, PARMESAN CHEESE
2 TABLESPOONS OLIVE OIL	

A | 1 TABLESPOON EACH BUTTER, OLIVE OIL

1 CUT THE BELL PEPPERS INTO STRIPS. THINLY SLICE THE ONION. CUT THE HAM INTO STRIPS APPROXIMATELY ONE CENTIMETER WIDE. DRAIN THE CAN OF SLICED MUSHROOMS.

2 BOIL THE SPAGHETTI NOODLES FOR ABOUT ONE MINUTE LONGER THAN THE PACKAGE INSTRUCTIONS AND STRAIN. POUR THE OLIVE OIL OVER TOP AND TOSS TO COAT.

3 HEAT (A) IN A FRYING PAN AND SAUTÉ THE ONION UNTIL TENDER, THEN ADD THE HAM, BELL PEPPERS AND MUSHROOMS FROM (1) AND SAUTÉ ON HIGH HEAT.

4 ADD THE KETCHUP AND SOY SAUCE TO (3) AND SAUTÉ. REMOVE FROM HEAT AND ADD (2), MIXING UNTIL THE NOODLES ARE THOROUGHLY COATED.

5 ADD THE POWDERED PARMESAN CHEESE AND MIX THOROUGHLY. SEASON TO TASTE WITH SALT AND PEPPER. TOP WITH CHOPPED PARSLEY AND A SPRINKLE OF PARMESAN CHEESE, AND DONE!

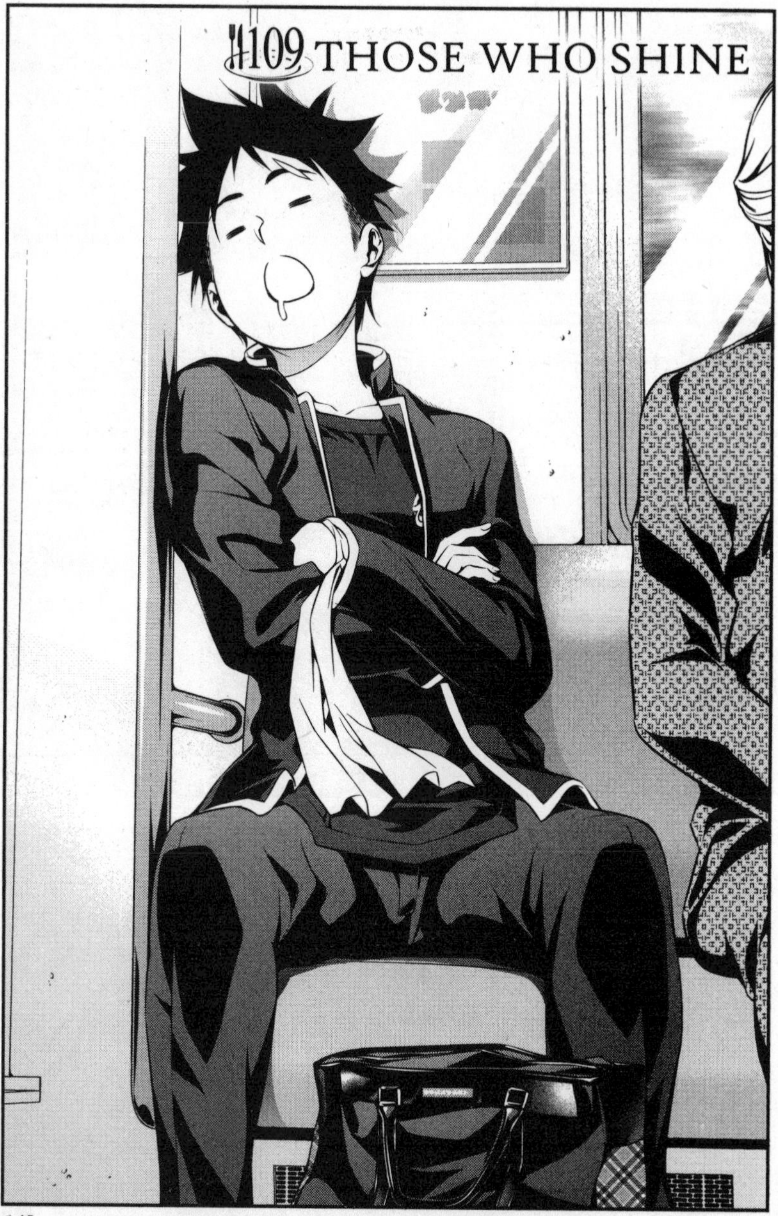
109 THOSE WHO SHINE

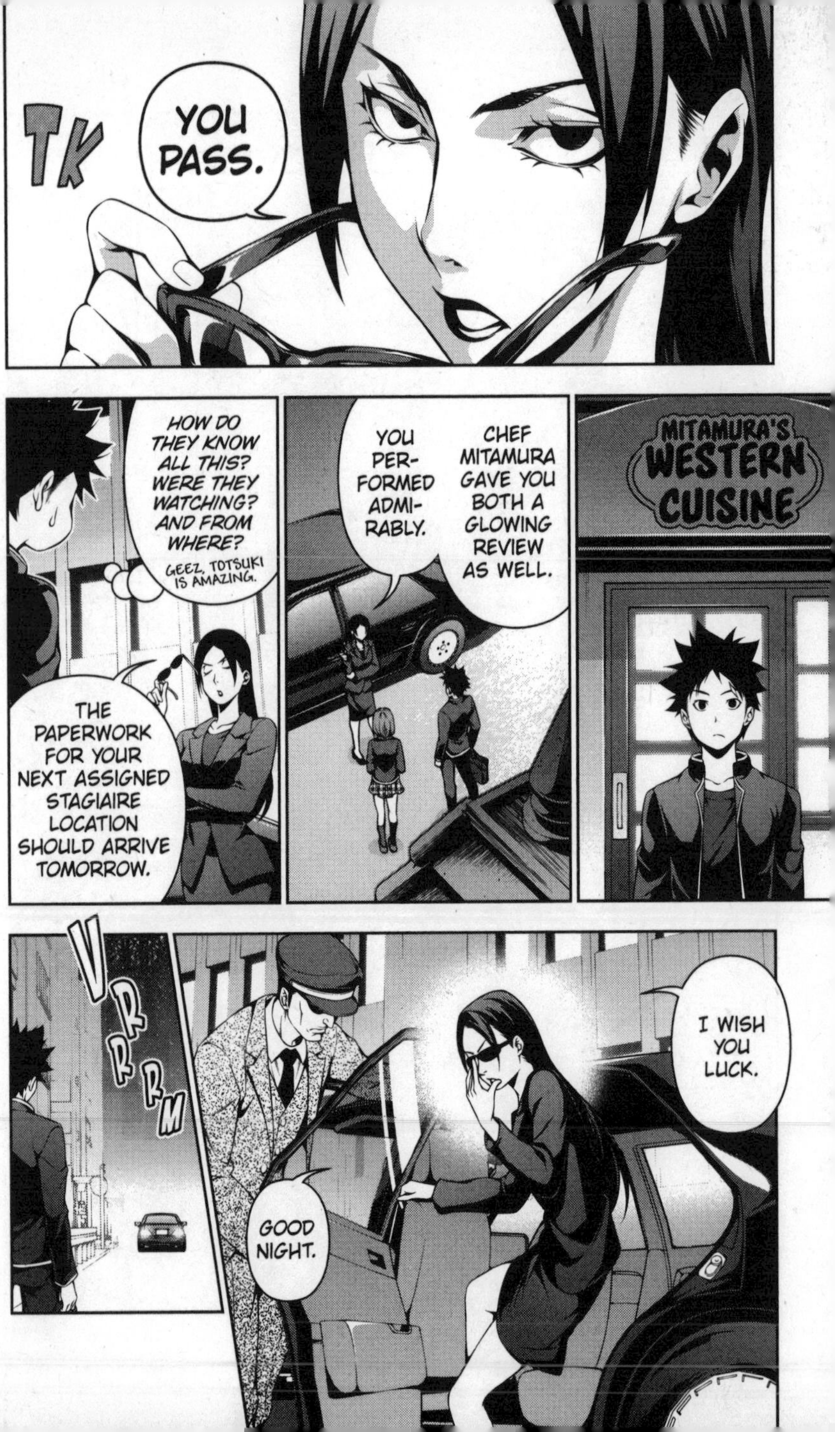
TK
YOU PASS.
MITAMURA'S WESTERN CUISINE
CHEF MITAMURA GAVE YOU BOTH A GLOWING REVIEW AS WELL.
YOU PER-FORMED ADMI-RABLY.
HOW DO THEY KNOW ALL THIS? WERE THEY WATCHING? AND FROM WHERE?
GEEZ, TOTSUKI IS AMAZING.
THE PAPERWORK FOR YOUR NEXT ASSIGNED STAGIAIRE LOCATION SHOULD ARRIVE TOMORROW.
I WISH YOU LUCK.
GOOD NIGHT.
VRRRM

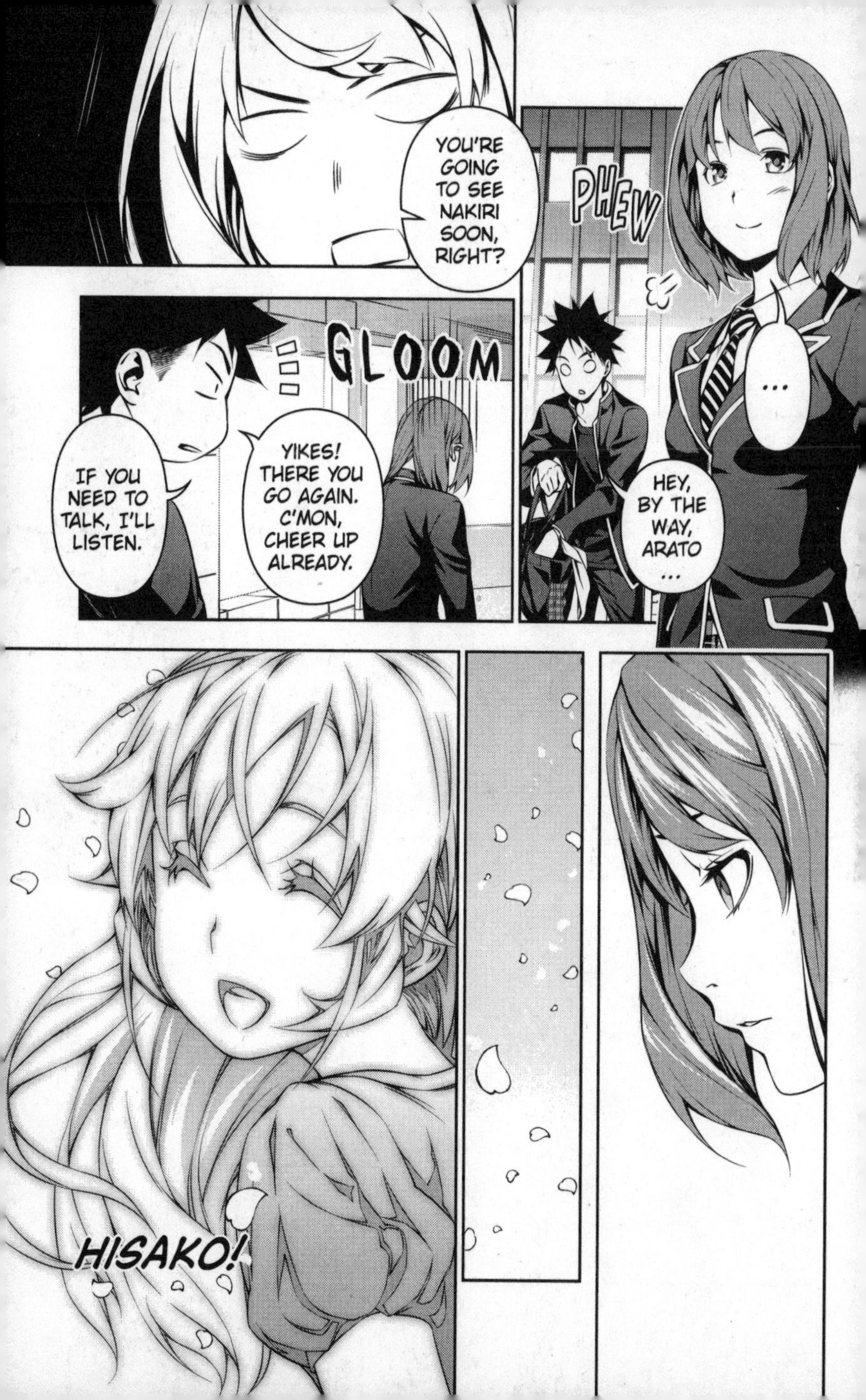
YOU'RE GOING TO SEE NAKIRI SOON, RIGHT?
PHEW
...
HEY, BY THE WAY, ARATO ...
GLOOM
YIKES! THERE YOU GO AGAIN. C'MON, CHEER UP ALREADY.
IF YOU NEED TO TALK, I'LL LISTEN.
HISAKO!

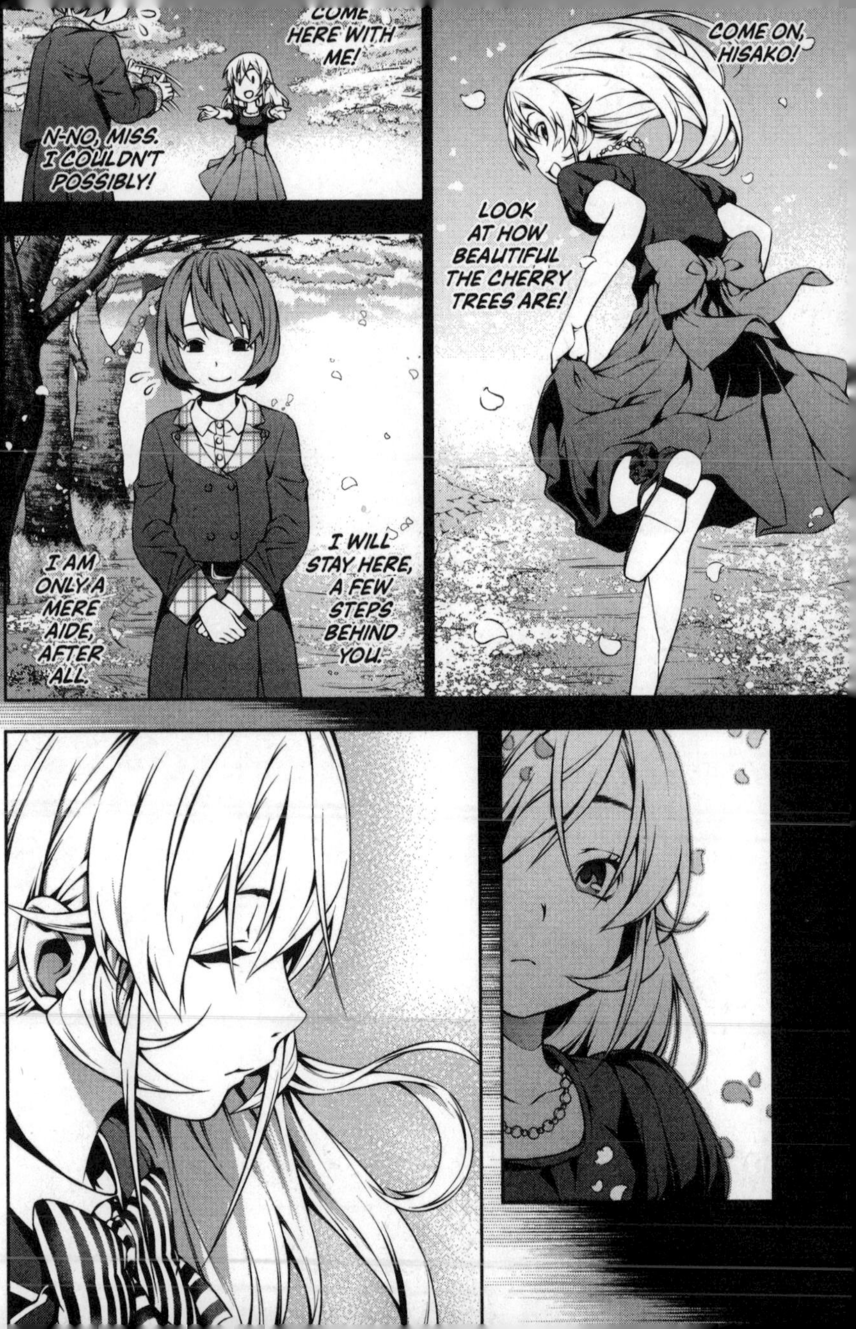
COME ON, HISAKO!
LOOK AT HOW BEAUTIFUL THE CHERRY TREES ARE!
COME HERE WITH ME!
N-NO, MISS. I COULDN'T POSSIBLY!
I WILL STAY HERE, A FEW STEPS BEHIND YOU.
I AM ONLY A MERE AIDE, AFTER ALL.

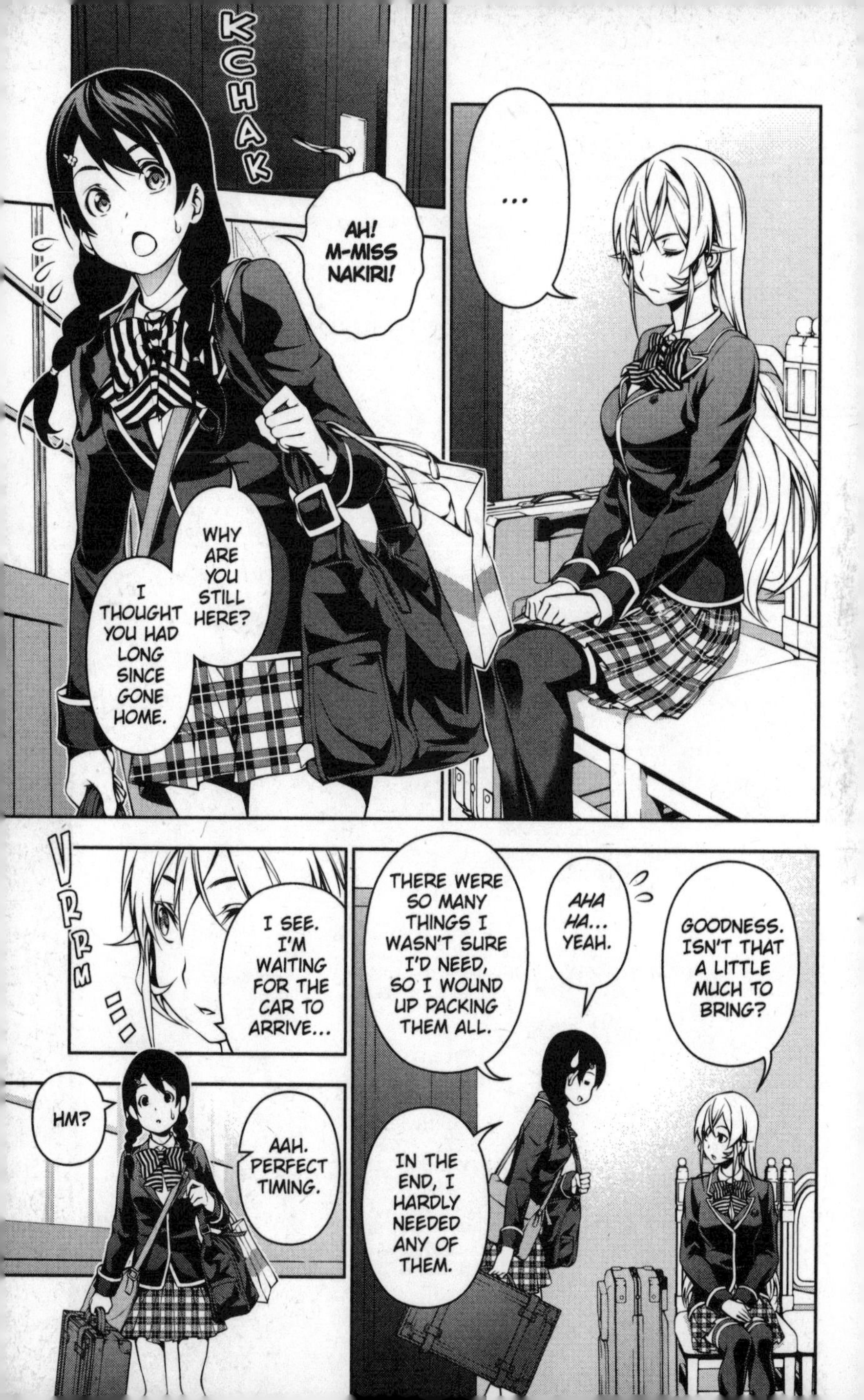
...
KCHAK
AH! M-MISS NAKIRI!
WHY ARE YOU STILL HERE?
I THOUGHT YOU HAD LONG SINCE GONE HOME.
GOODNESS. ISN'T THAT A LITTLE MUCH TO BRING?
AHA HA... YEAH.
THERE WERE SO MANY THINGS I WASN'T SURE I'D NEED, SO I WOUND UP PACKING THEM ALL.
IN THE END, I HARDLY NEEDED ANY OF THEM.
VRRM
I SEE. I'M WAITING FOR THE CAR TO ARRIVE...
AAH. PERFECT TIMING.
HM?

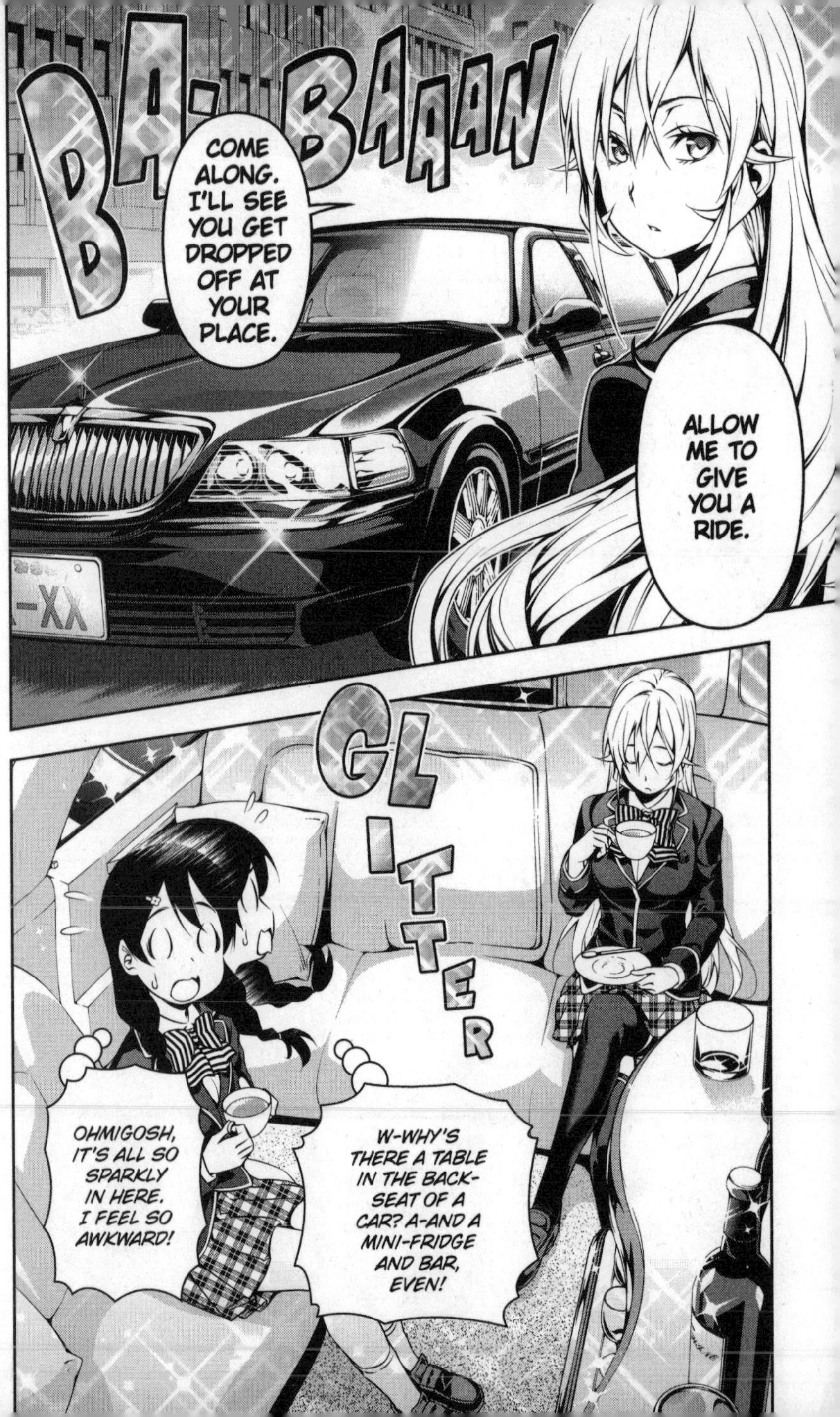
BA-BAAAN
ALLOW ME TO GIVE YOU A RIDE.
COME ALONG. I'LL SEE YOU GET DROPPED OFF AT YOUR PLACE.
GLITTER
W-WHY'S THERE A TABLE IN THE BACK-SEAT OF A CAR? A-AND A MINI-FRIDGE AND BAR, EVEN!
OHMIGOSH, IT'S ALL SO SPARKLY IN HERE. I FEEL SO AWKWARD!

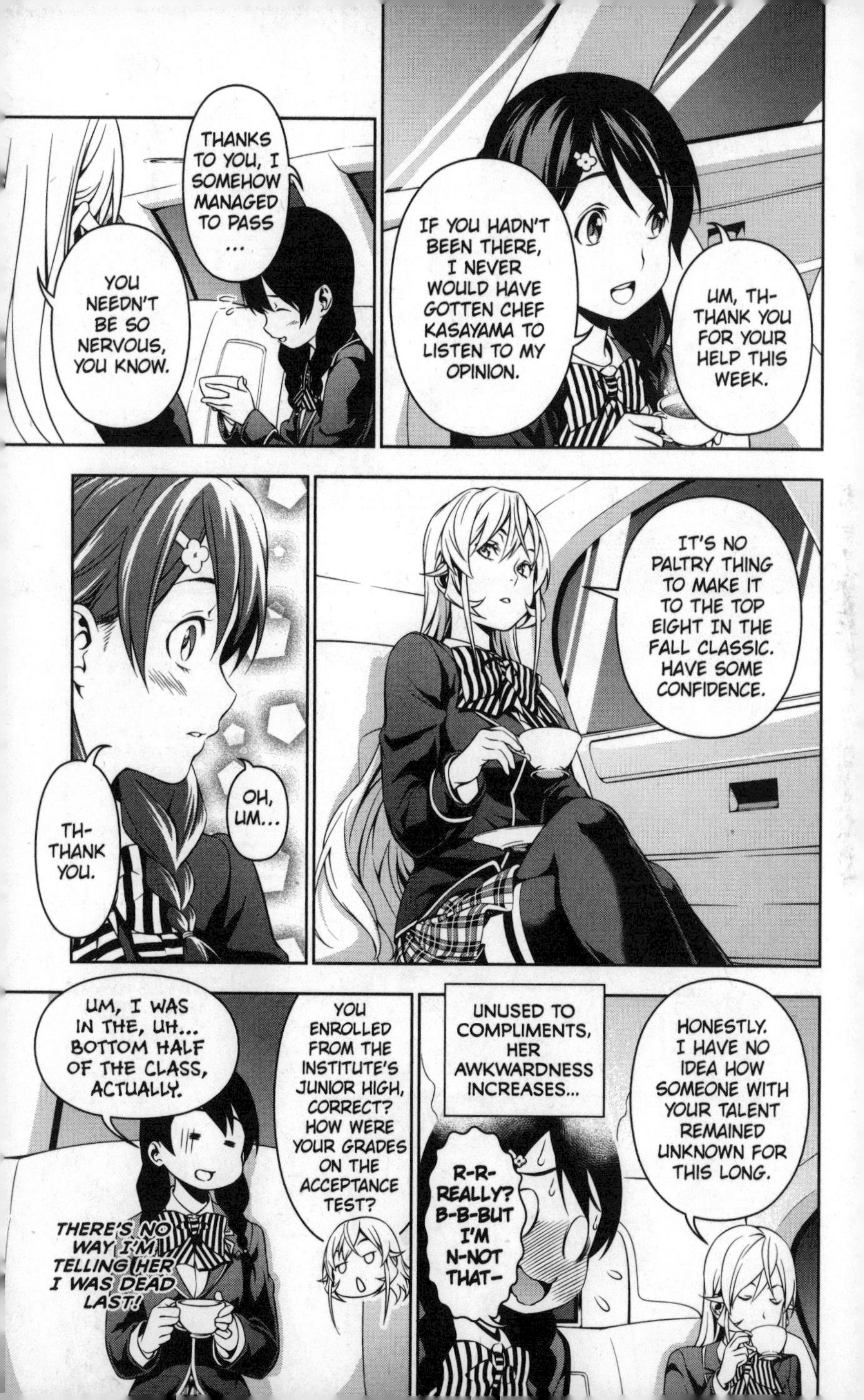
UM, TH- THANK YOU FOR YOUR HELP THIS WEEK.
IF YOU HADN'T BEEN THERE, I NEVER WOULD HAVE GOTTEN CHEF KASAYAMA TO LISTEN TO MY OPINION.
THANKS TO YOU, I SOMEHOW MANAGED TO PASS ...
YOU NEEDN'T BE SO NERVOUS, YOU KNOW.
IT'S NO PALTRY THING TO MAKE IT TO THE TOP EIGHT IN THE FALL CLASSIC. HAVE SOME CONFIDENCE.
OH, UM...
TH- THANK YOU.
HONESTLY. I HAVE NO IDEA HOW SOMEONE WITH YOUR TALENT REMAINED UNKNOWN FOR THIS LONG.
UNUSED TO COMPLIMENTS, HER AWKWARDNESS INCREASES...
R-R-REALLY? B-B-BUT I'M N-NOT THAT-
YOU ENROLLED FROM THE INSTITUTE'S JUNIOR HIGH, CORRECT? HOW WERE YOUR GRADES ON THE ACCEPTANCE TEST?
UM, I WAS IN THE, UH... BOTTOM HALF OF THE CLASS, ACTUALLY.
THERE'S NO WAY I'M TELLING HER I WAS DEAD LAST!

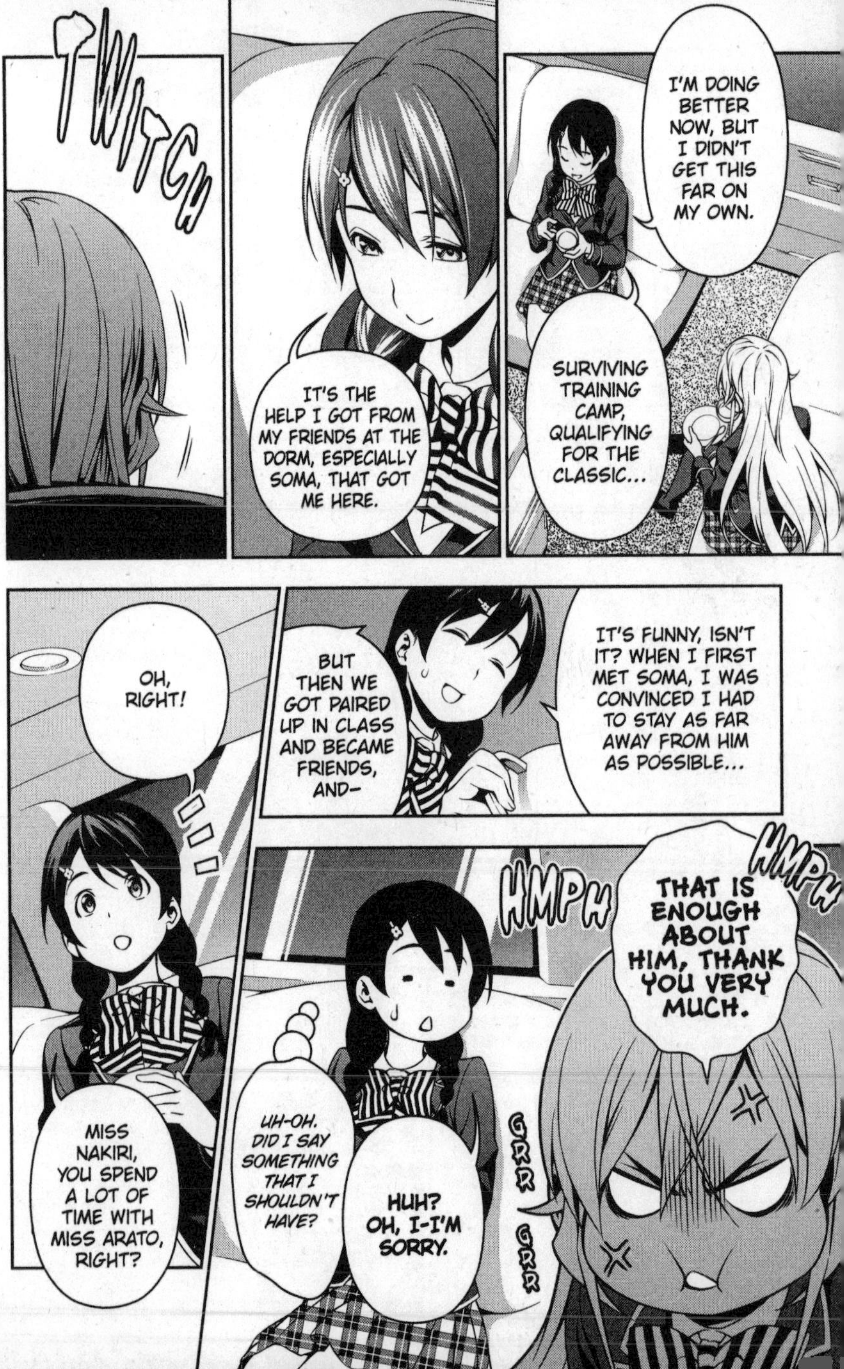
I'M DOING BETTER NOW, BUT I DIDN'T GET THIS FAR ON MY OWN.
SURVIVING TRAINING CAMP, QUALIFYING FOR THE CLASSIC...
IT'S THE HELP I GOT FROM MY FRIENDS AT THE DORM, ESPECIALLY SOMA, THAT GOT ME HERE.
TWITCH
IT'S FUNNY, ISN'T IT? WHEN I FIRST MET SOMA, I WAS CONVINCED I HAD TO STAY AS FAR AWAY FROM HIM AS POSSIBLE...
BUT THEN WE GOT PAIRED UP IN CLASS AND BECAME FRIENDS, AND–
HMPH
THAT IS ENOUGH ABOUT HIM, THANK YOU VERY MUCH.
HMPH
GRR GRR
HUH? OH, I-I'M SORRY.
UH-OH. DID I SAY SOMETHING THAT I SHOULDN'T HAVE?
OH, RIGHT!
MISS NAKIRI, YOU SPEND A LOT OF TIME WITH MISS ARATO, RIGHT?

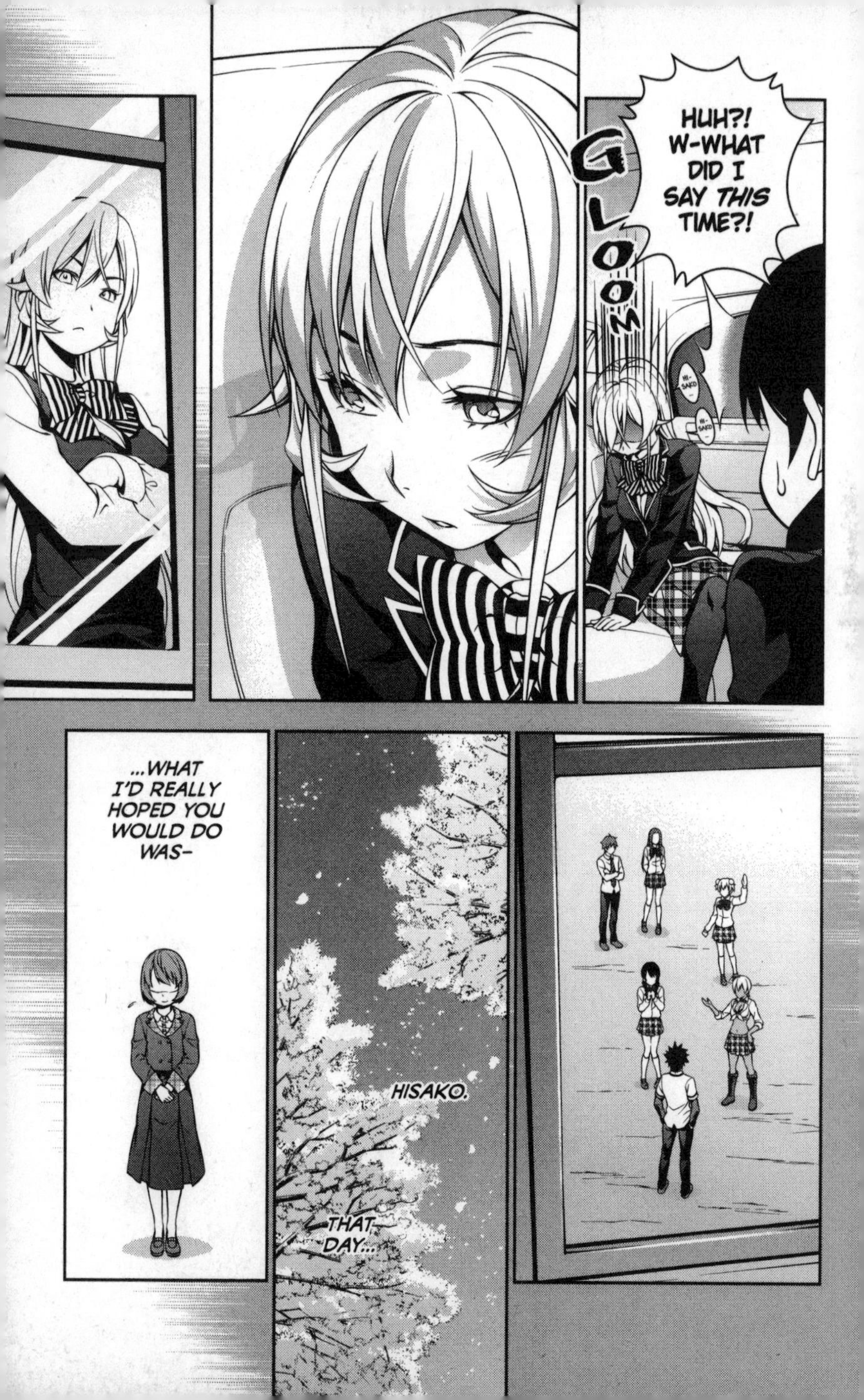
HUH?! W-WHAT DID I SAY THIS TIME?!
GLOOM
HI-SAKO...
HI-SAKO...
HISAKO.
THAT DAY...
...WHAT I'D REALLY HOPED YOU WOULD DO WAS-

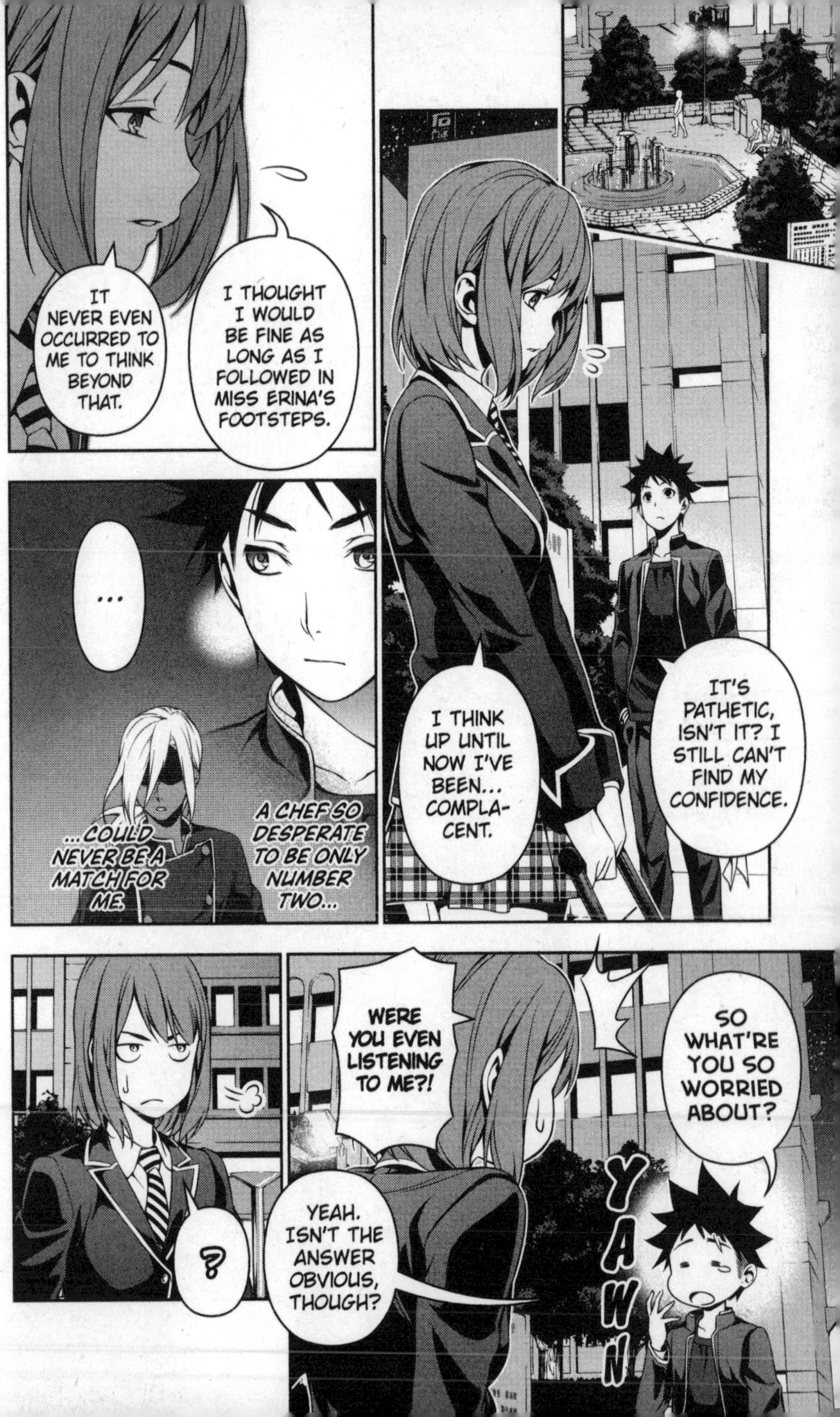
IT'S PATHETIC, ISN'T IT? I STILL CAN'T FIND MY CONFIDENCE.
I THINK UP UNTIL NOW I'VE BEEN... COMPLA-CENT.
I THOUGHT I WOULD BE FINE AS LONG AS I FOLLOWED IN MISS ERINA'S FOOTSTEPS.
IT NEVER EVEN OCCURRED TO ME TO THINK BEYOND THAT.
...
A CHEF SO DESPERATE TO BE ONLY NUMBER TWO...
...COULD NEVER BE A MATCH FOR ME.
SO WHAT'RE YOU SO WORRIED ABOUT?
YAWN
WERE YOU EVEN LISTENING TO ME?!
YEAH. ISN'T THE ANSWER OBVIOUS, THOUGH?
?

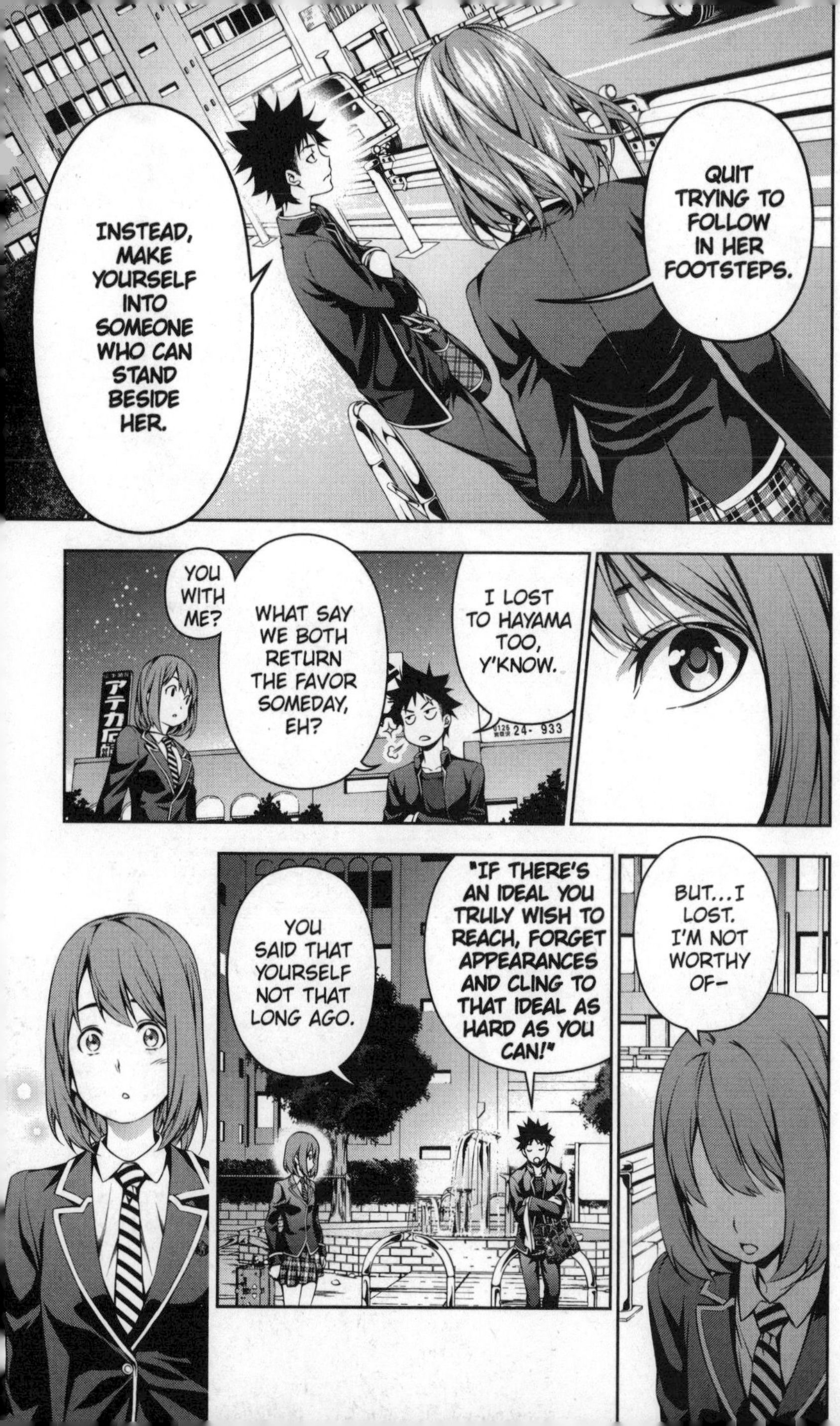
QUIT TRYING TO FOLLOW IN HER FOOTSTEPS.
INSTEAD, MAKE YOURSELF INTO SOMEONE WHO CAN STAND BESIDE HER.
I LOST TO HAYAMA TOO, Y'KNOW.
WHAT SAY WE BOTH RETURN THE FAVOR SOMEDAY, EH?
YOU WITH ME?
BUT...I LOST. I'M NOT WORTHY OF–
"IF THERE'S AN IDEAL YOU TRULY WISH TO REACH, FORGET APPEARANCES AND CLING TO THAT IDEAL AS HARD AS YOU CAN!"
YOU SAID THAT YOURSELF NOT THAT LONG AGO.

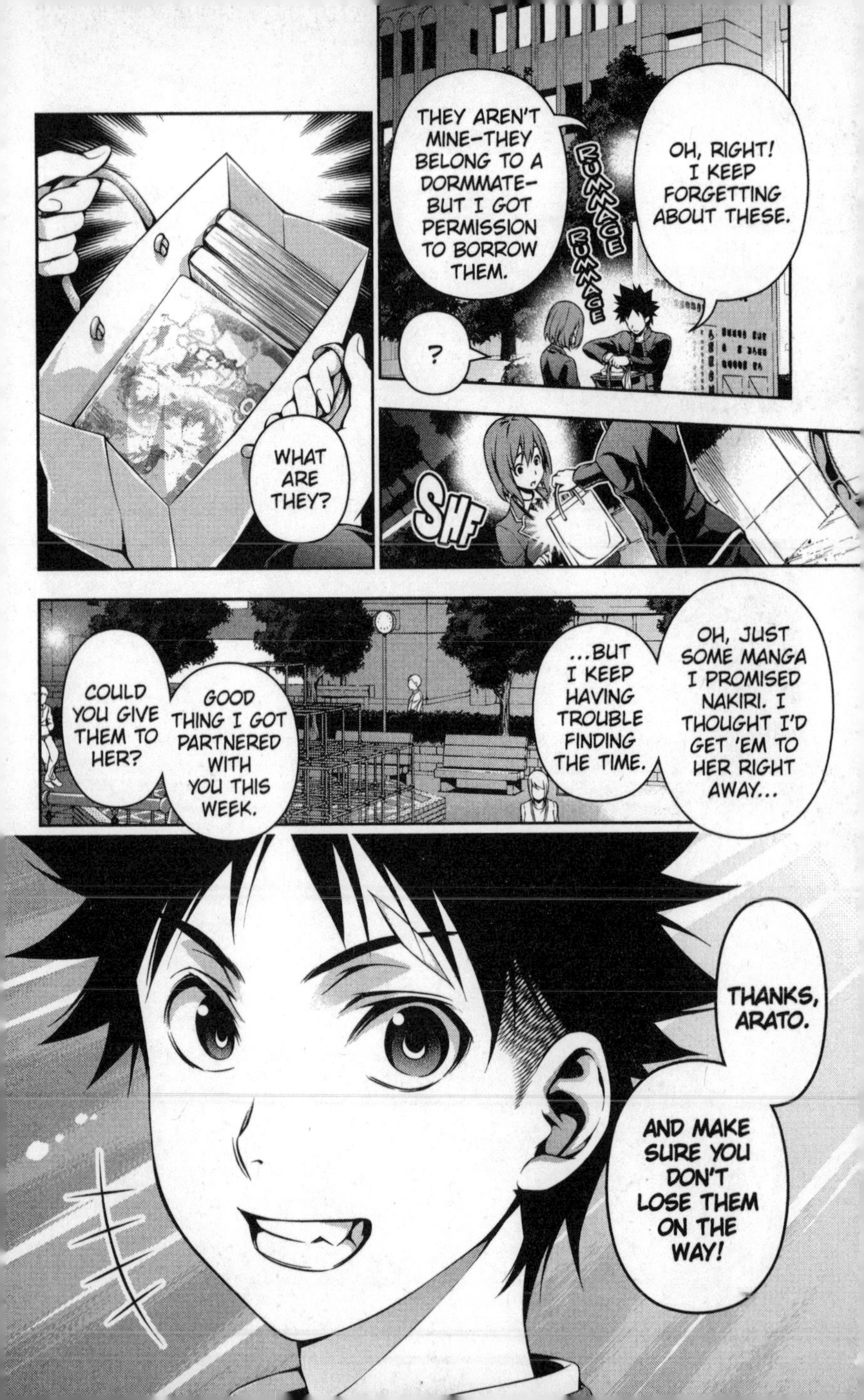
OH, RIGHT! I KEEP FORGETTING ABOUT THESE.
RUMMAGE RUMMAGE
THEY AREN'T MINE—THEY BELONG TO A DORMMATE—BUT I GOT PERMISSION TO BORROW THEM.
?
SHF
WHAT ARE THEY?
OH, JUST SOME MANGA I PROMISED NAKIRI. I THOUGHT I'D GET 'EM TO HER RIGHT AWAY...
...BUT I KEEP HAVING TROUBLE FINDING THE TIME.
GOOD THING I GOT PARTNERED WITH YOU THIS WEEK.
COULD YOU GIVE THEM TO HER?
THANKS, ARATO.
AND MAKE SURE YOU DON'T LOSE THEM ON THE WAY!

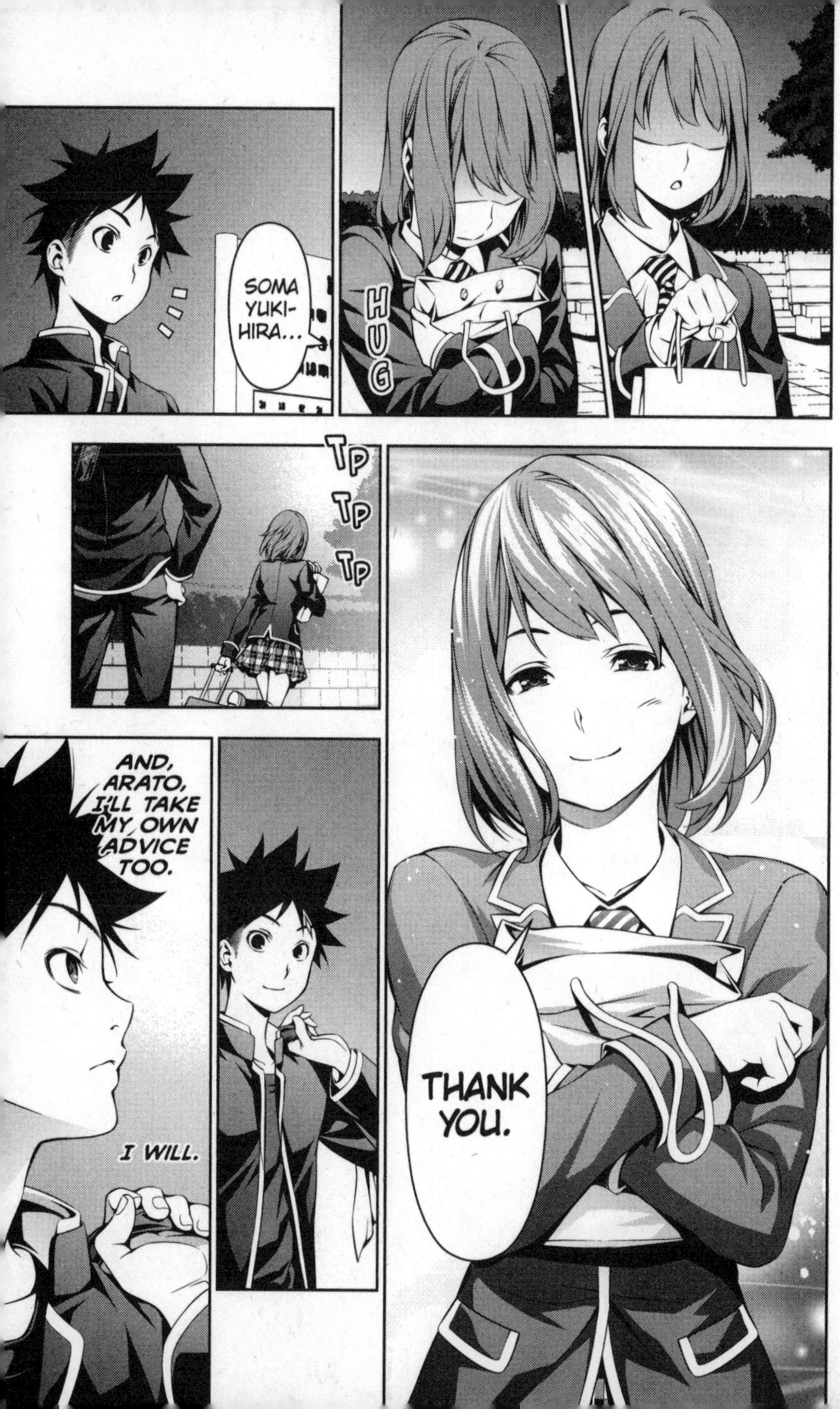
HUG
SOMA YUKI-HIRA...
THANK YOU.
Tp Tp Tp
AND, ARATO, I'LL TAKE MY OWN ADVICE TOO.
I WILL.

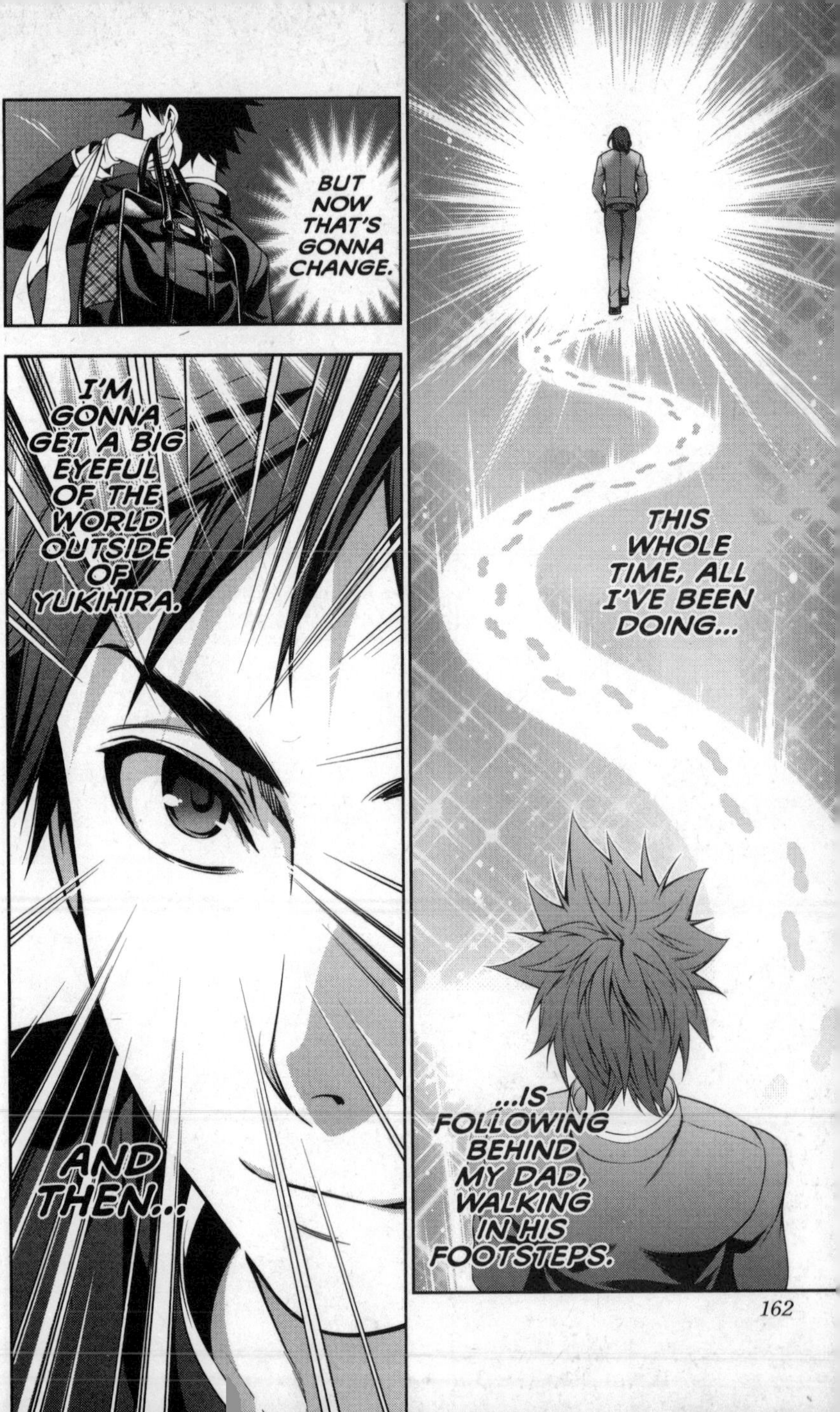
THIS WHOLE TIME, ALL I'VE BEEN DOING...
...IS FOLLOWING BEHIND MY DAD, WALKING IN HIS FOOTSTEPS.
BUT NOW THAT'S GONNA CHANGE.
I'M GONNA GET A BIG EYEFUL OF THE WORLD OUTSIDE OF YUKIHIRA.
AND THEN...

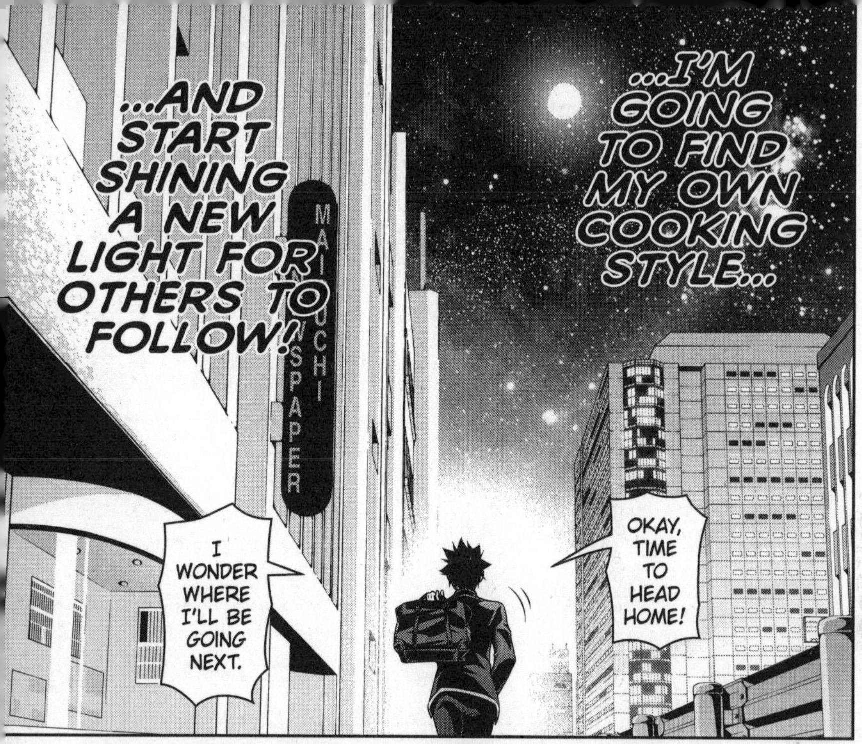
...I'M GOING TO FIND MY OWN COOKING STYLE...
...AND START SHINING A NEW LIGHT FOR OTHERS TO FOLLOW!
OKAY, TIME TO HEAD HOME!
I WONDER WHERE I'LL BE GOING NEXT.
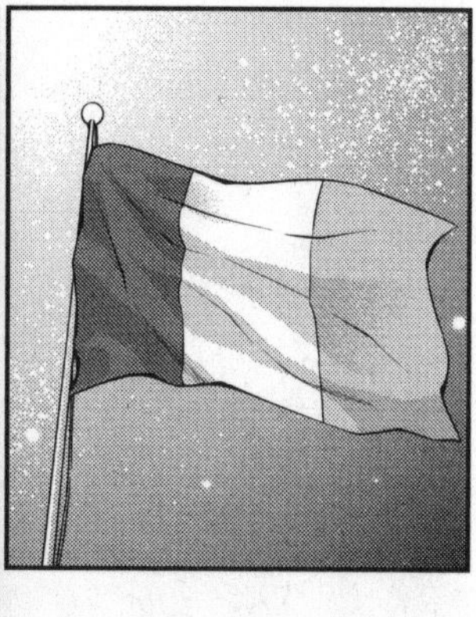
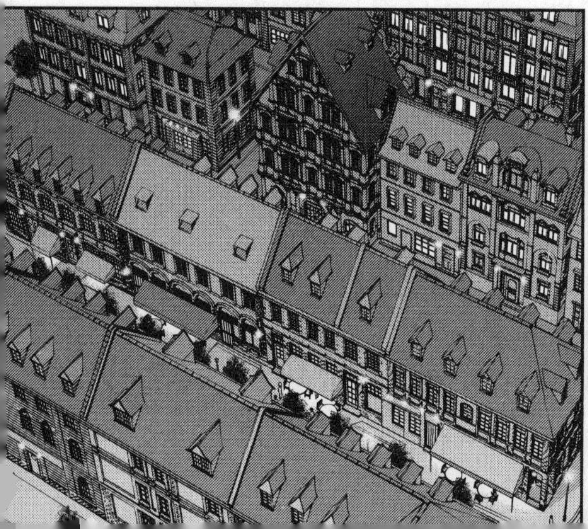

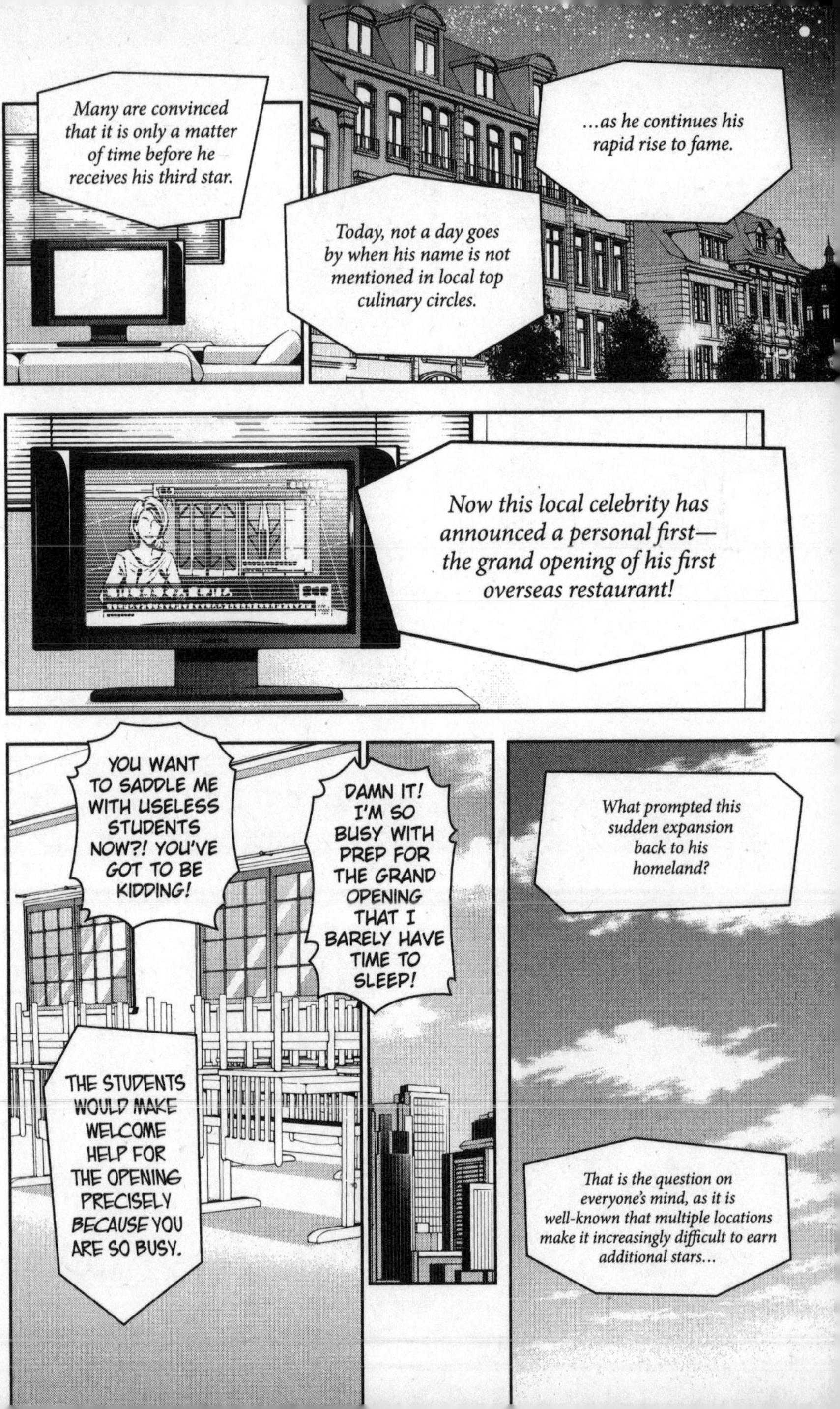
...as he continues his rapid rise to fame.
Today, not a day goes by when his name is not mentioned in local top culinary circles.
Many are convinced that it is only a matter of time before he receives his third star.
Now this local celebrity has announced a personal first—the grand opening of his first overseas restaurant!
What prompted this sudden expansion back to his homeland?
That is the question on everyone's mind, as it is well-known that multiple locations make it increasingly difficult to earn additional stars...
DAMN IT! I'M SO BUSY WITH PREP FOR THE GRAND OPENING THAT I BARELY HAVE TIME TO SLEEP!
YOU WANT TO SADDLE ME WITH USELESS STUDENTS NOW?! YOU'VE GOT TO BE KIDDING!
THE STUDENTS WOULD MAKE WELCOME HELP FOR THE OPENING PRECISELY BECAUSE YOU ARE SO BUSY.

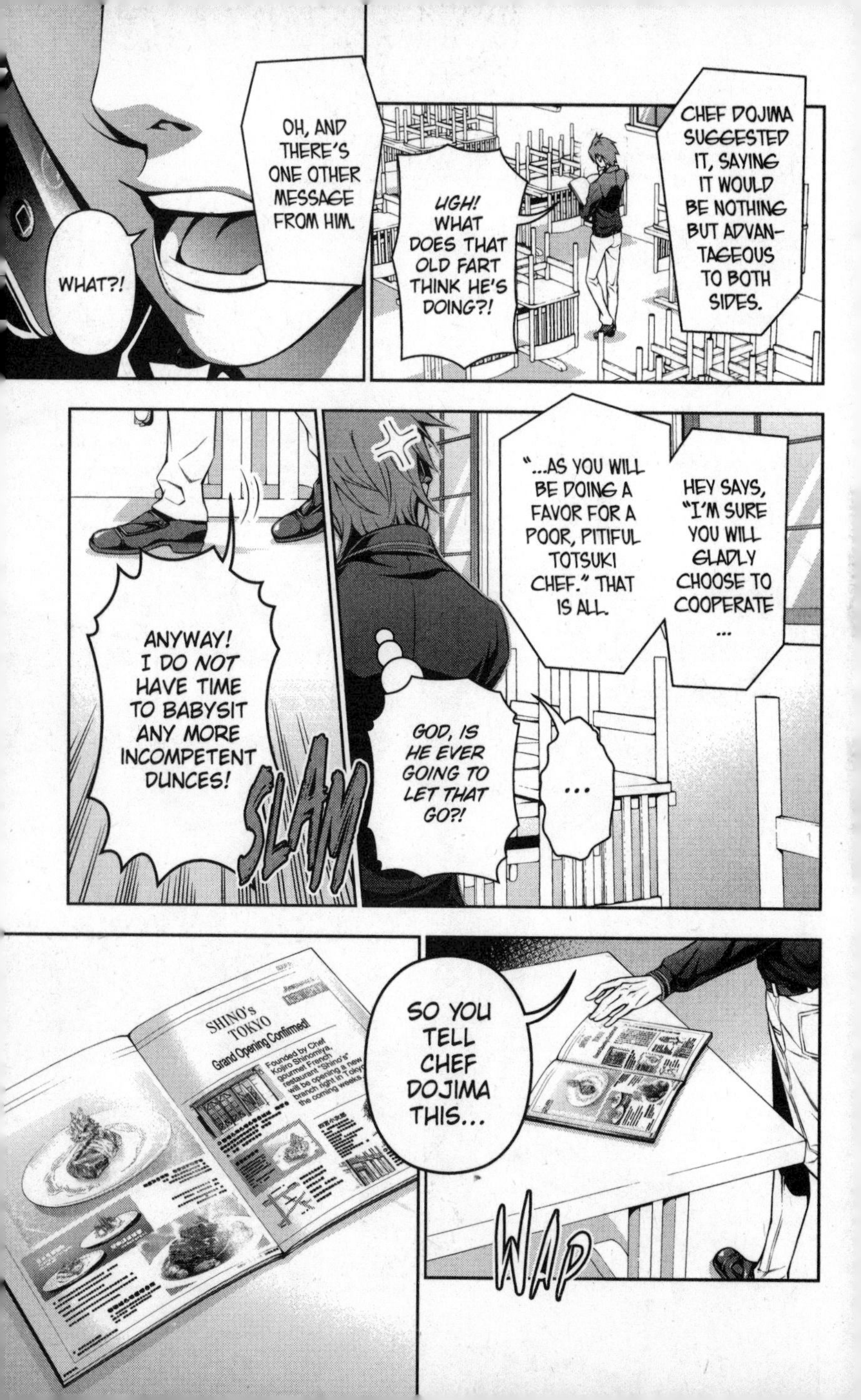
CHEF DOJIMA SUGGESTED IT, SAYING IT WOULD BE NOTHING BUT ADVANTAGEOUS TO BOTH SIDES.
UGH! WHAT DOES THAT OLD FART THINK HE'S DOING?!
OH, AND THERE'S ONE OTHER MESSAGE FROM HIM.
WHAT?!
HEY SAYS, "I'M SURE YOU WILL GLADLY CHOOSE TO COOPERATE ...
"...AS YOU WILL BE DOING A FAVOR FOR A POOR, PITIFUL TOTSUKI CHEF." THAT IS ALL.
GOD, IS HE EVER GOING TO LET THAT GO?!
...
ANYWAY! I DO NOT HAVE TIME TO BABYSIT ANY MORE INCOMPETENT DUNCES!
SLAM
SO YOU TELL CHEF DOJIMA THIS...
WAP
SHINO's TOKYO
Grand Opening Confirmed!
Founded by Chef Kojiro Shinomiya, gourmet French restaurant "Shino's" will be opening a new branch right in Tokyo in the coming weeks.

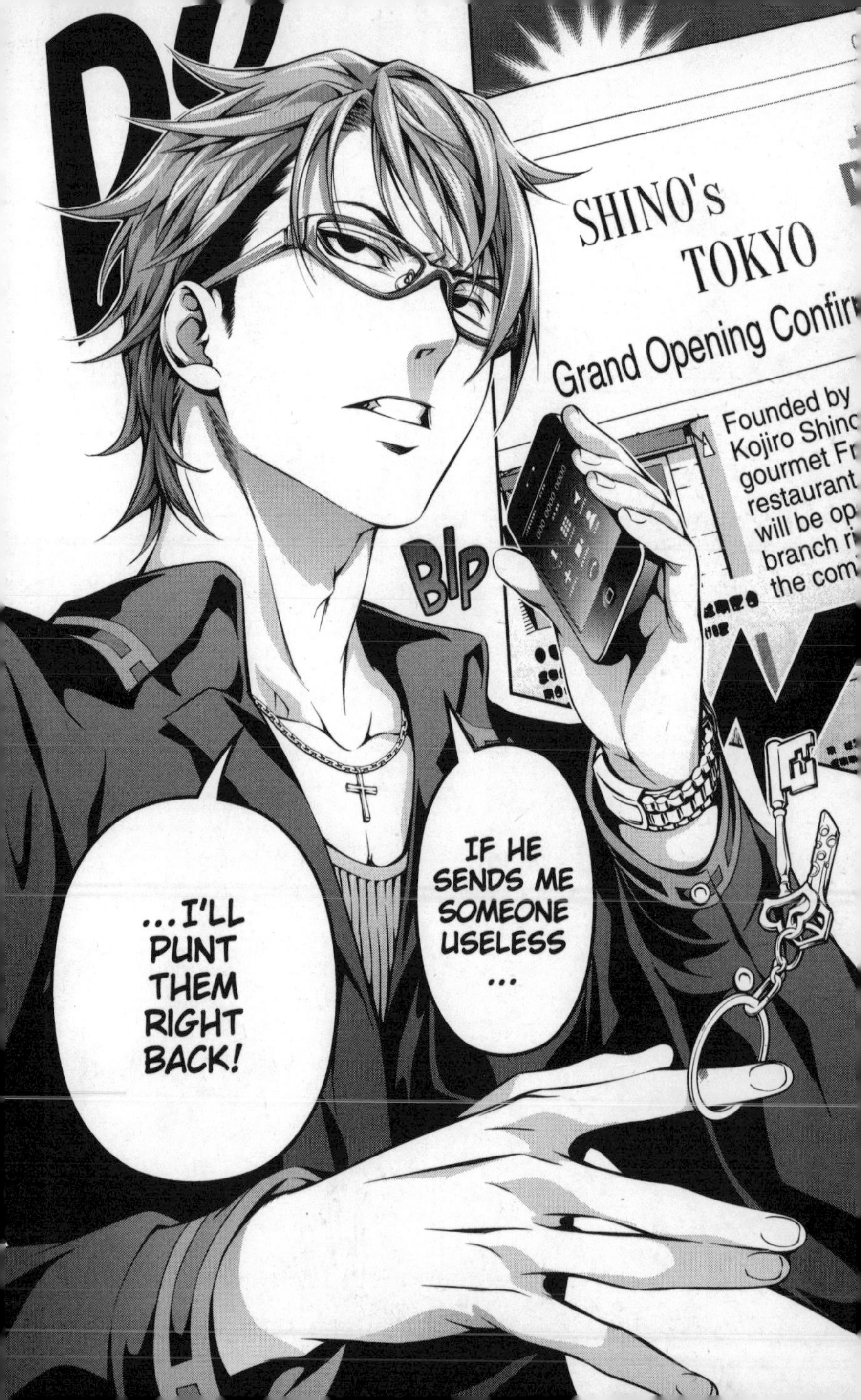
SHINO's
TOKYO
Grand Opening
Founded by
BIP
IF HE SENDS ME SOMEONE USELESS ...
...I'LL PUNT THEM RIGHT BACK!

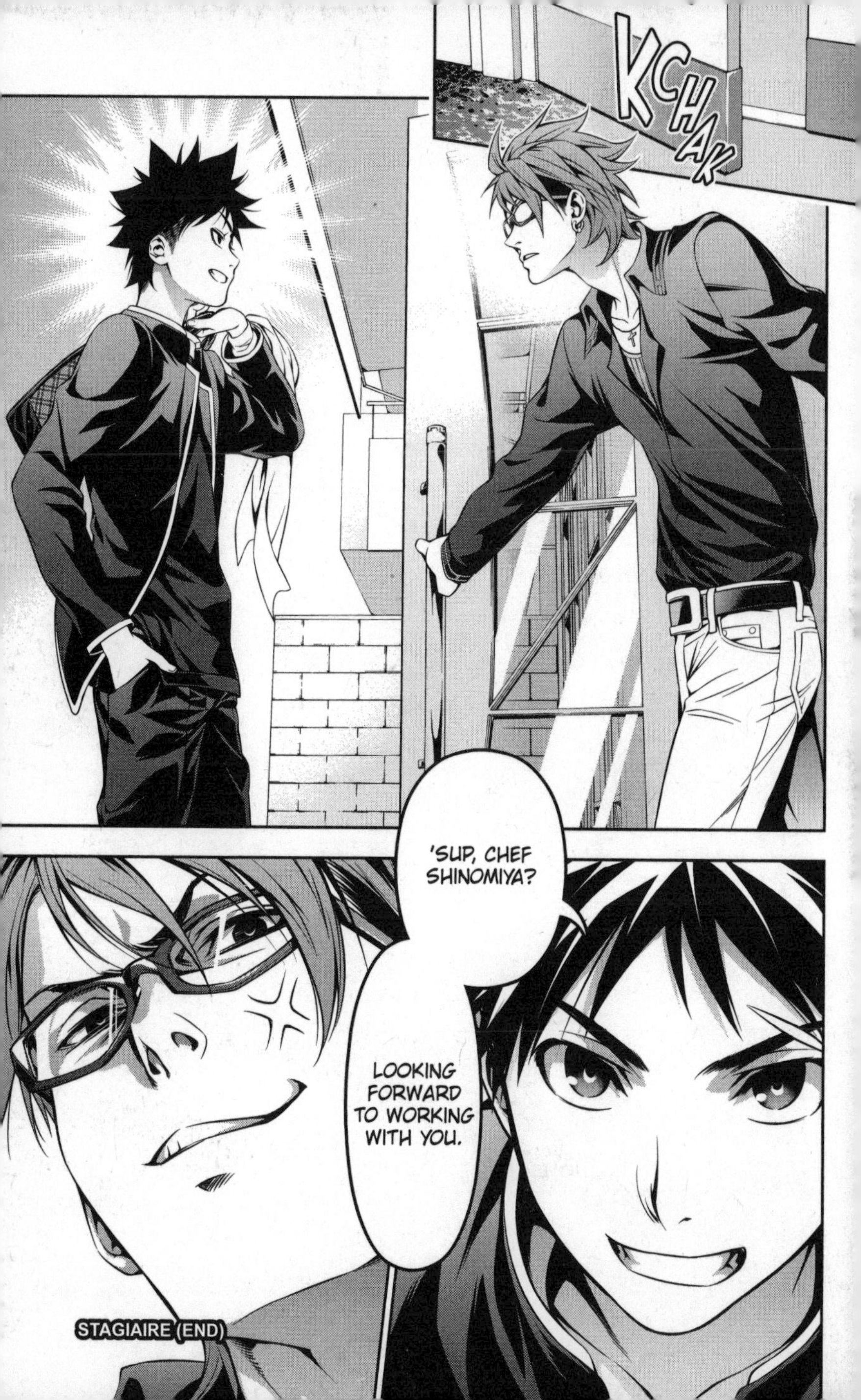
KCHAK
'SUP, CHEF SHINOMIYA?
LOOKING FORWARD TO WORKING WITH YOU.
STAGIAIRE (END)

ISOBE ISOBEE MONOGATARI
~Ukiyo wa Tsurai yo~

THANKS TO A GUEST-ARTIST SERIES RUN BY *WEEKLY SHONEN JUMP*, THE FOLLOWING PAGES CONTAIN A SHORT CHAPTER OF *FOOD WARS!* AS DRAWN BY *ISOBE ISOBEE* MANGAKA RYO NAKAMA SENSEI! WE HOPE YOU ENJOY THIS GLANCE AT A SLIGHTLY DIFFERENT *FOOD WARS!* WORLD.

THANK YOU, NAKAMA SENSEI!

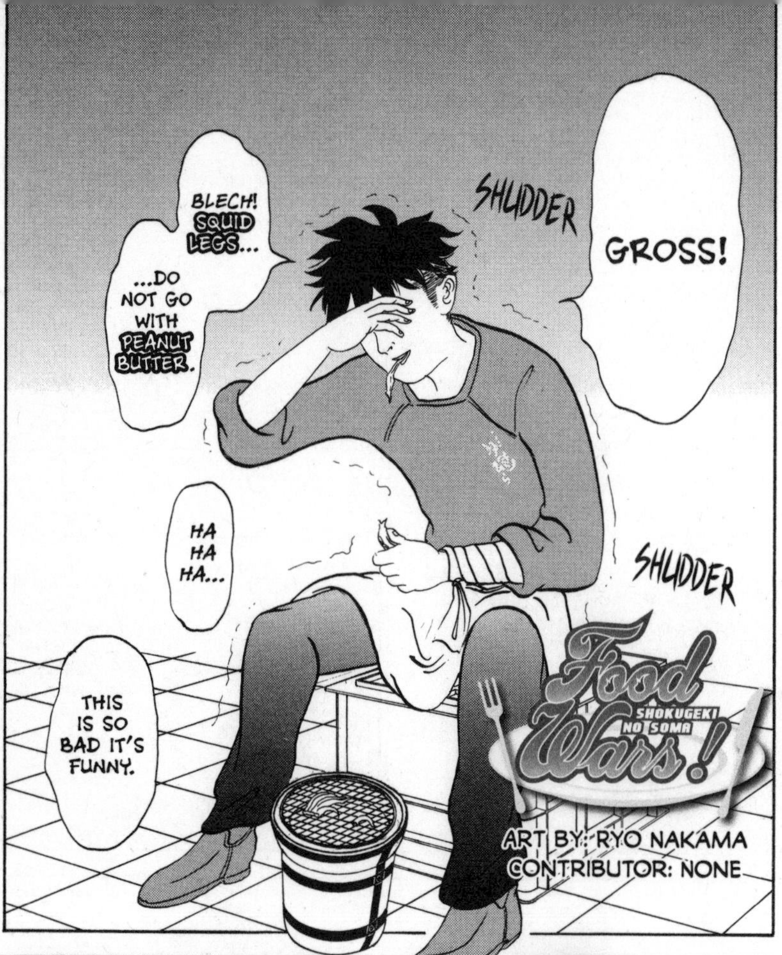
GROSS!
SHUDDER
BLECH! SQUID LEGS...
...DO NOT GO WITH PEANUT BUTTER.
SHUDDER
HA HA HA...
Food Wars! SHOKUGEKI NO SOMA
ART BY: RYO NAKAMA
CONTRIBUTOR: NONE
THIS IS SO BAD IT'S FUNNY.

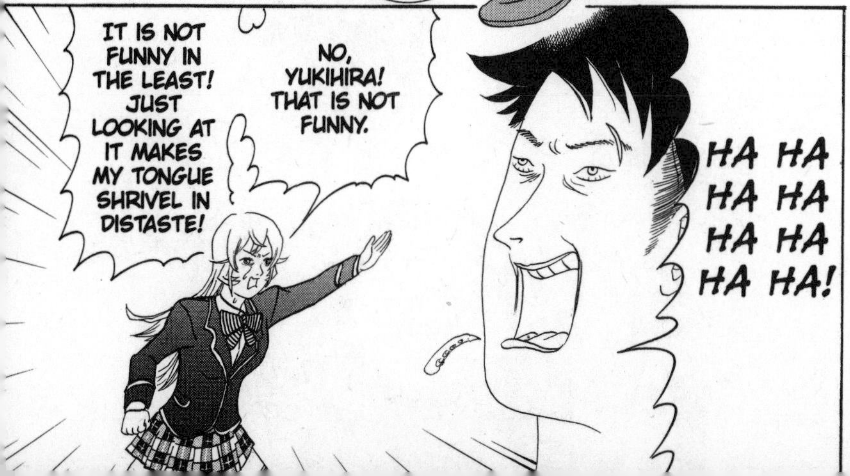
HA HA HA HA HA HA HA HA!
NO, YUKIHIRA! THAT IS NOT FUNNY.
IT IS NOT FUNNY IN THE LEAST! JUST LOOKING AT IT MAKES MY TONGUE SHRIVEL IN DISTASTE!

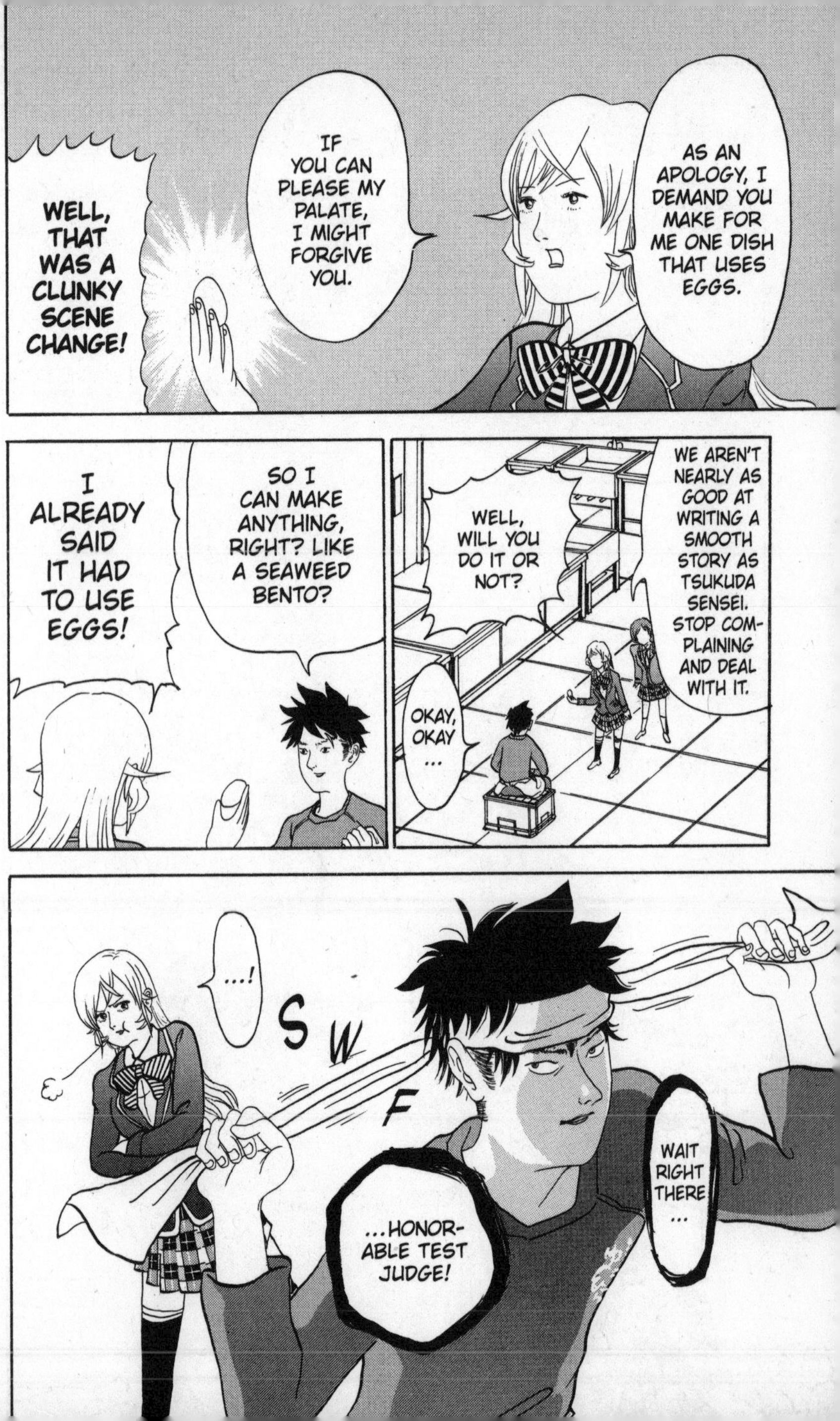
AS AN APOLOGY, I DEMAND YOU MAKE FOR ME ONE DISH THAT USES EGGS.
IF YOU CAN PLEASE MY PALATE, I MIGHT FORGIVE YOU.
WELL, THAT WAS A CLUNKY SCENE CHANGE!
WE AREN'T NEARLY AS GOOD AT WRITING A SMOOTH STORY AS TSUKUDA SENSEI. STOP COM-PLAINING AND DEAL WITH IT.
WELL, WILL YOU DO IT OR NOT?
OKAY, OKAY ...
SO I CAN MAKE ANYTHING, RIGHT? LIKE A SEAWEED BENTO?
I ALREADY SAID IT HAD TO USE EGGS!
WAIT RIGHT THERE ...
...HONOR-ABLE TEST JUDGE!
SWF
...!

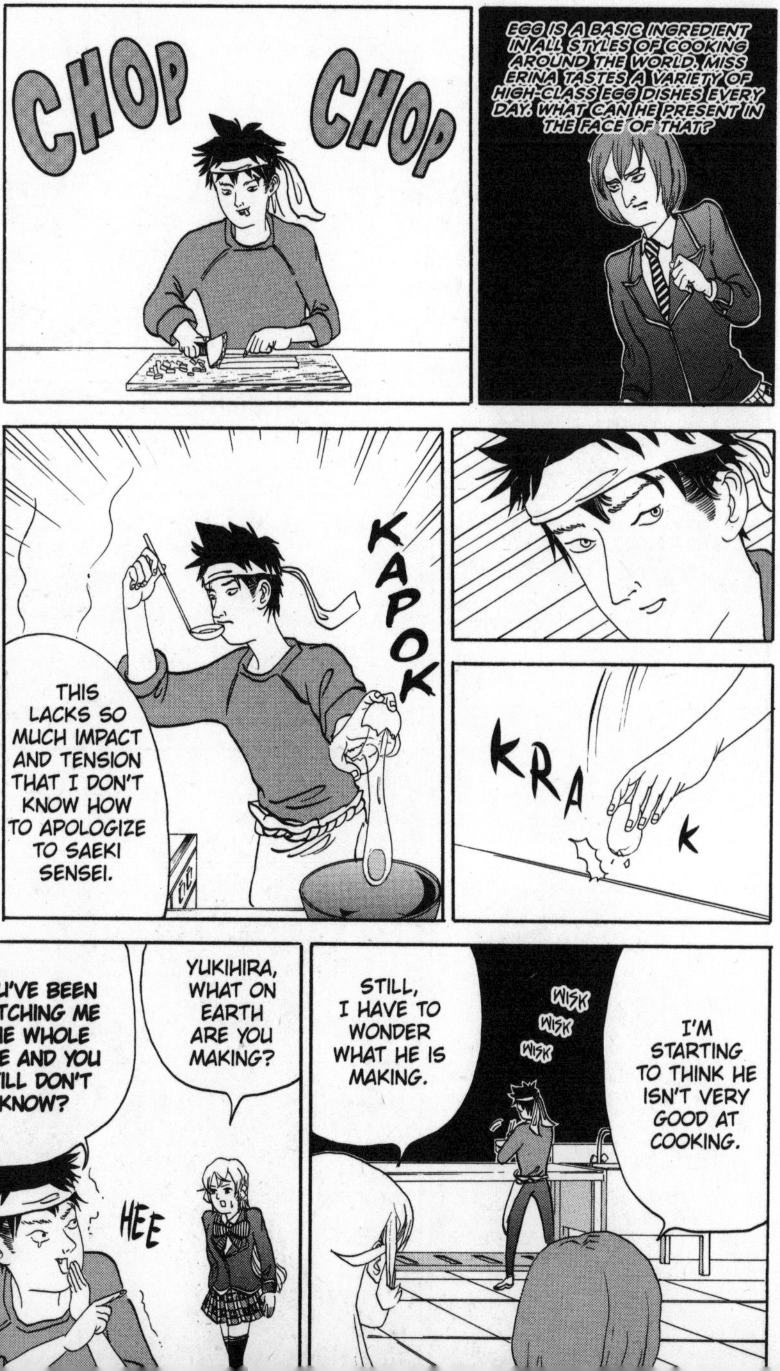
EGG IS A BASIC INGREDIENT IN ALL STYLES OF COOKING AROUND THE WORLD. MISS ERINA TASTES A VARIETY OF HIGH-CLASS EGG DISHES EVERY DAY. WHAT CAN HE PRESENT IN THE FACE OF THAT?
CHOP CHOP
KRAK
KAPOK
THIS LACKS SO MUCH IMPACT AND TENSION THAT I DON'T KNOW HOW TO APOLOGIZE TO SAEKI SENSEI.
I'M STARTING TO THINK HE ISN'T VERY GOOD AT COOKING.
WISK WISK WISK
STILL, I HAVE TO WONDER WHAT HE IS MAKING.
YUKIHIRA, WHAT ON EARTH ARE YOU MAKING?
YOU'VE BEEN WATCHING ME THE WHOLE TIME AND YOU STILL DON'T KNOW?
HEE

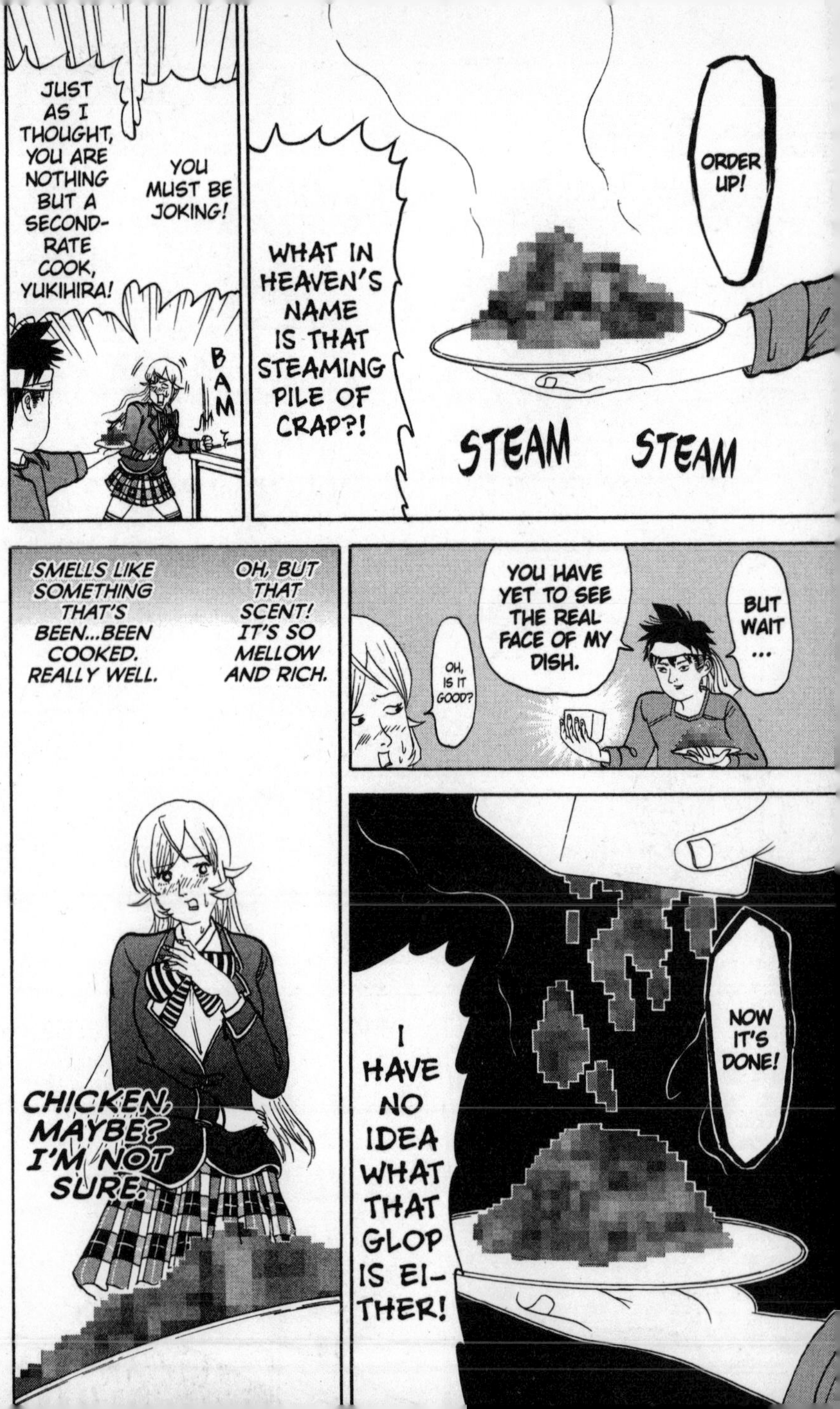
ORDER UP!
WHAT IN HEAVEN'S NAME IS THAT STEAMING PILE OF CRAP?!
STEAM STEAM
YOU MUST BE JOKING!
JUST AS I THOUGHT, YOU ARE NOTHING BUT A SECOND-RATE COOK, YUKIHIRA!
BAM
BUT WAIT...
YOU HAVE YET TO SEE THE REAL FACE OF MY DISH.
OH, IS IT GOOD?
NOW IT'S DONE!
I HAVE NO IDEA WHAT THAT GLOP IS EI-THER!
OH, BUT THAT SCENT! IT'S SO MELLOW AND RICH.
SMELLS LIKE SOMETHING THAT'S BEEN...BEEN COOKED. REALLY WELL.
CHICKEN, MAYBE? I'M NOT SURE.

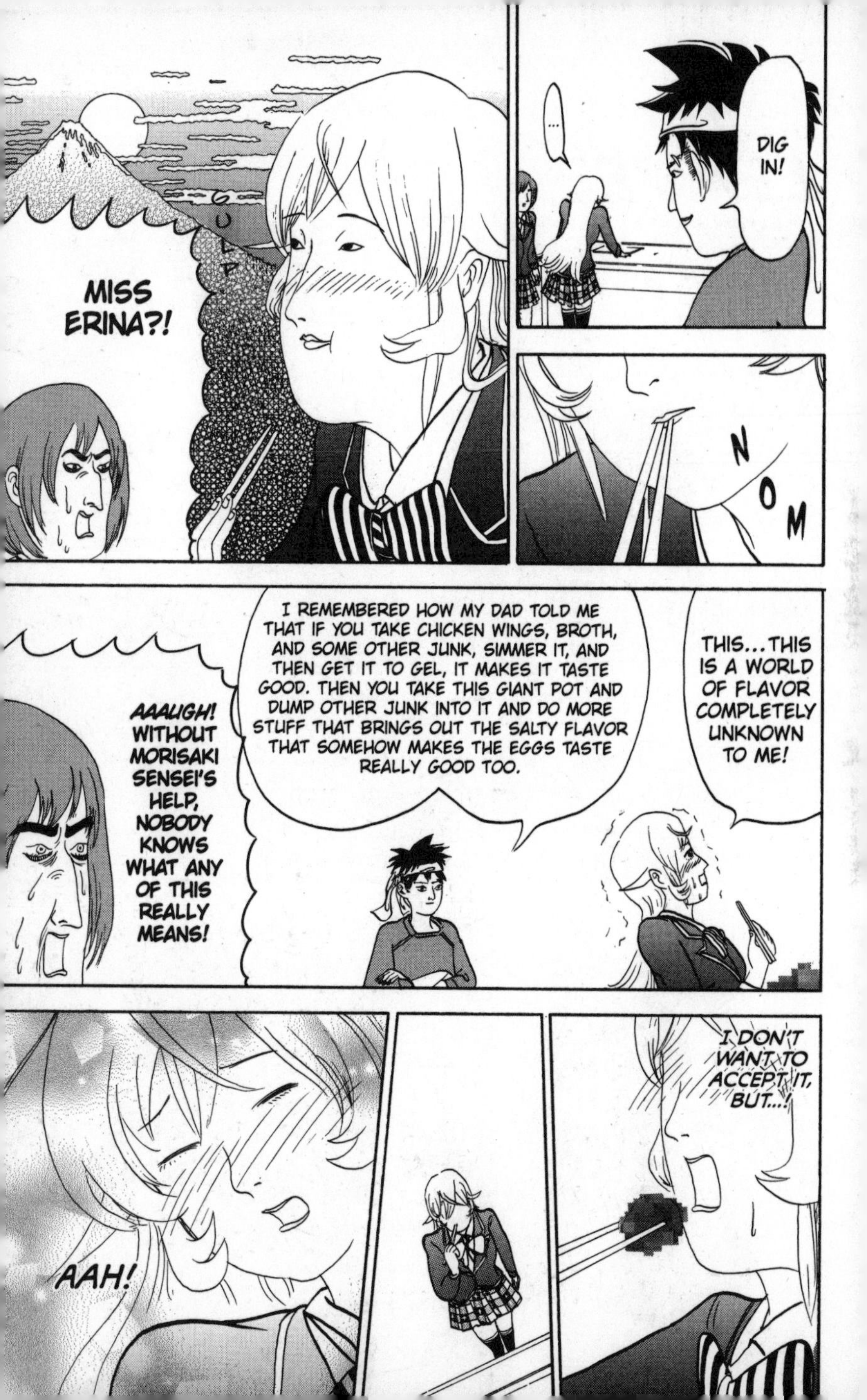
DIG IN!
...
NOM
GULP
MISS ERINA?!
THIS...THIS IS A WORLD OF FLAVOR COMPLETELY UNKNOWN TO ME!
I REMEMBERED HOW MY DAD TOLD ME THAT IF YOU TAKE CHICKEN WINGS, BROTH, AND SOME OTHER JUNK, SIMMER IT, AND THEN GET IT TO GEL, IT MAKES IT TASTE GOOD. THEN YOU TAKE THIS GIANT POT AND DUMP OTHER JUNK INTO IT AND DO MORE STUFF THAT BRINGS OUT THE SALTY FLAVOR THAT SOMEHOW MAKES THE EGGS TASTE REALLY GOOD TOO.
AAAUGH! WITHOUT MORISAKI SENSEI'S HELP, NOBODY KNOWS WHAT ANY OF THIS REALLY MEANS!
I DON'T WANT TO ACCEPT IT, BUT...!
AAH!

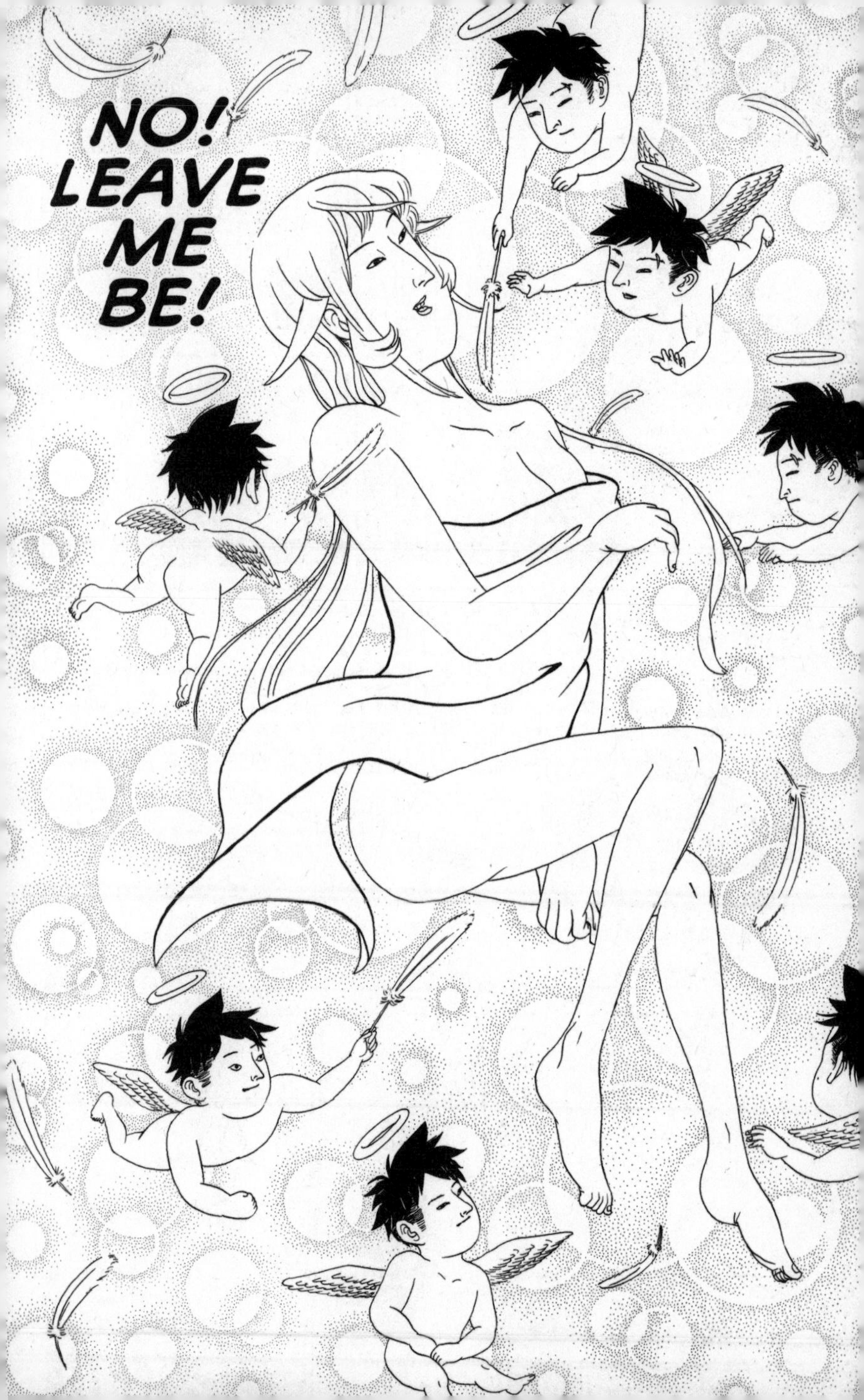
NO! LEAVE ME BE!

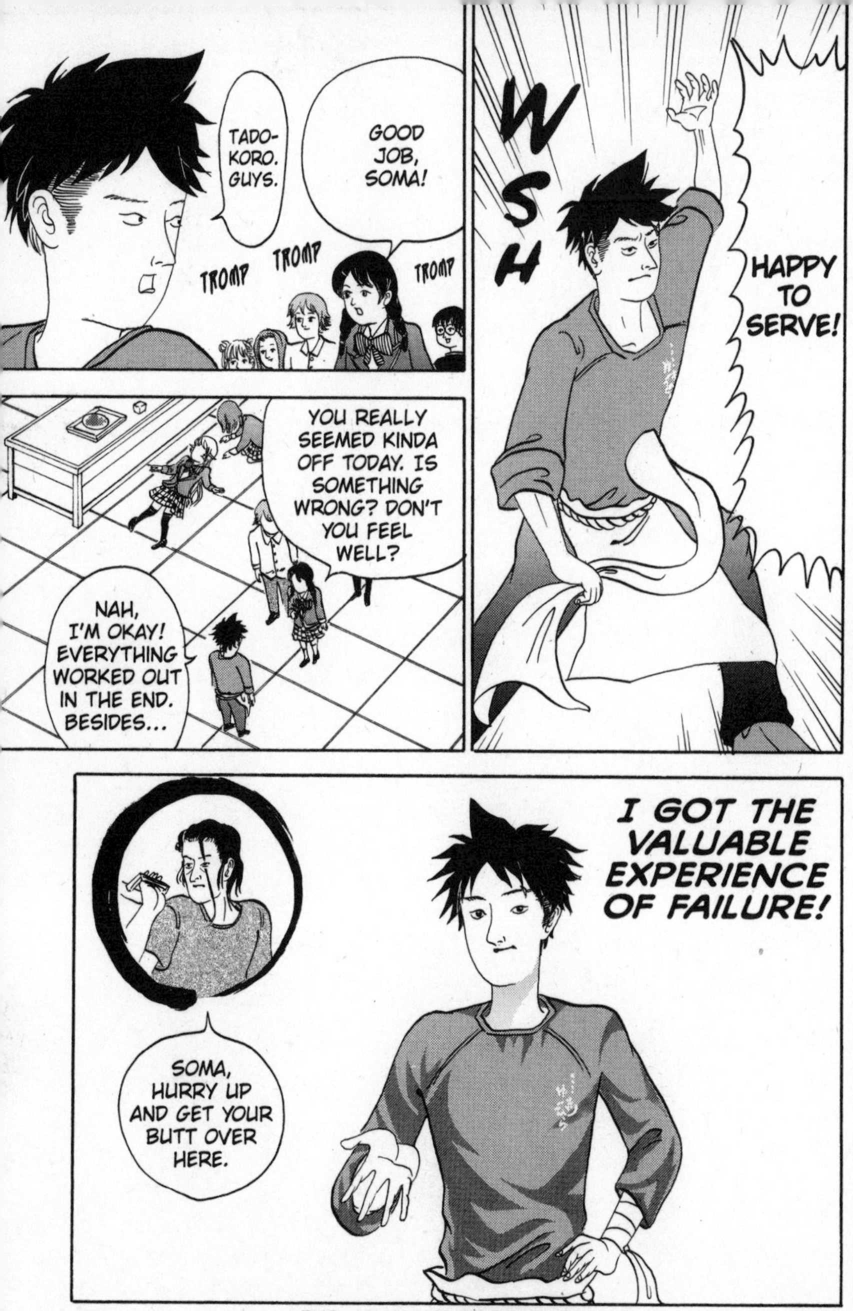
WSH
HAPPY TO SERVE!
GOOD JOB, SOMA!
TADO-KORO. GUYS.
TROMP
TROMP
TROMP
YOU REALLY SEEMED KINDA OFF TODAY. IS SOMETHING WRONG? DON'T YOU FEEL WELL?
NAH, I'M OKAY! EVERYTHING WORKED OUT IN THE END. BESIDES...
I GOT THE VALUABLE EXPERIENCE OF FAILURE!
SOMA, HURRY UP AND GET YOUR BUTT OVER HERE.

RYO NAKAMA'S *FOOD WARS!* END

IN THE
KITCHEN,
THEY WEAR
THEIR CHEF'S
UNIFORMS.
BUT WHAT DO
THEY WEAR
ON THEIR
DAYS OFF?

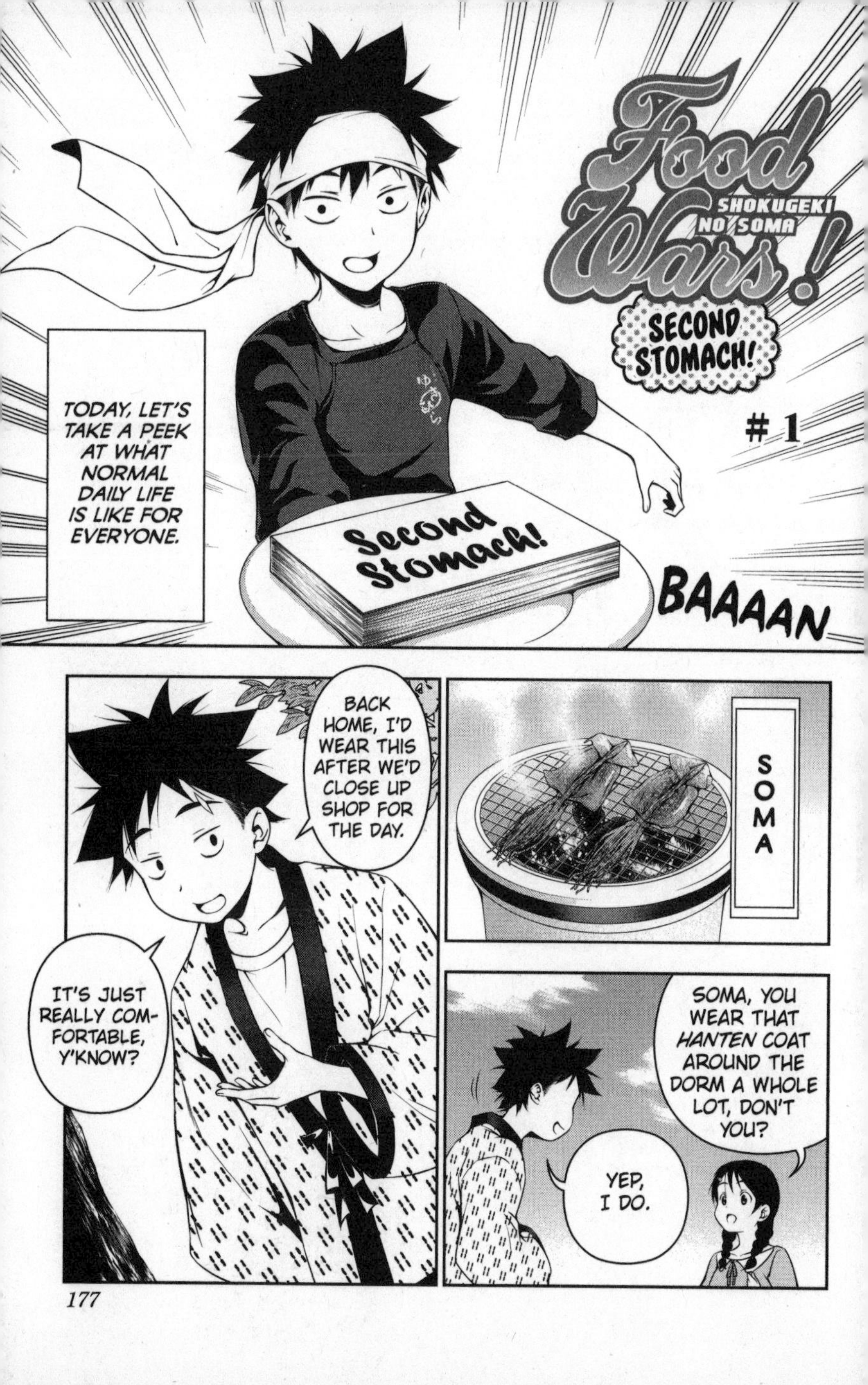
Food Wars!
SHOKUGEKI NO SOMA
SECOND STOMACH!
#1
TODAY, LET'S TAKE A PEEK AT WHAT NORMAL DAILY LIFE IS LIKE FOR EVERYONE.
Second Stomach!
BAAAAN
SOMA
SOMA, YOU WEAR THAT HANTEN COAT AROUND THE DORM A WHOLE LOT, DON'T YOU?
YEP, I DO.
BACK HOME, I'D WEAR THIS AFTER WE'D CLOSE UP SHOP FOR THE DAY.
IT'S JUST REALLY COM-FORTABLE, Y'KNOW?

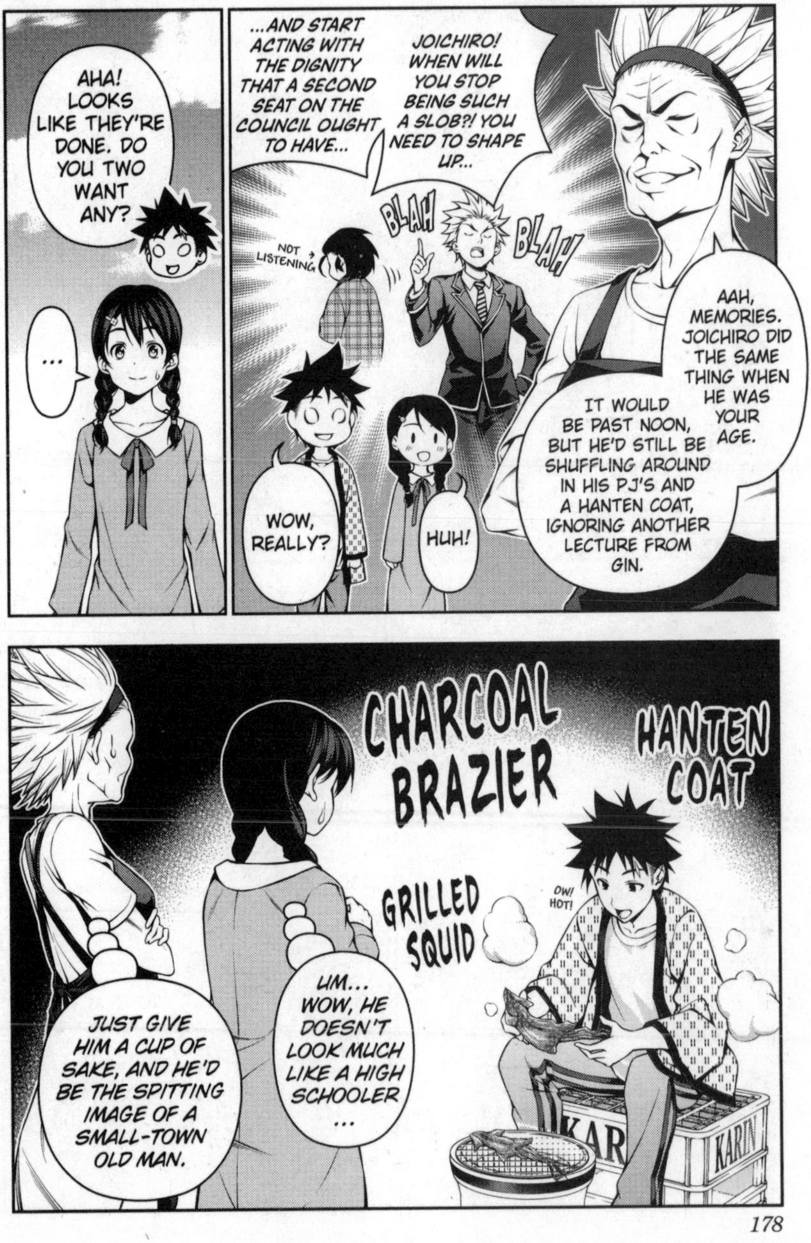

AAH, MEMORIES. JOICHIRO DID THE SAME THING WHEN HE WAS YOUR AGE.
IT WOULD BE PAST NOON, BUT HE'D STILL BE SHUFFLING AROUND IN HIS PJ'S AND A HANTEN COAT, IGNORING ANOTHER LECTURE FROM GIN.
JOICHIRO! WHEN WILL YOU STOP BEING SUCH A SLOB?! YOU NEED TO SHAPE UP...
...AND START ACTING WITH THE DIGNITY THAT A SECOND SEAT ON THE COUNCIL OUGHT TO HAVE...
BLAH
BLAH
NOT LISTENING
HUH!
WOW, REALLY?
AHA! LOOKS LIKE THEY'RE DONE. DO YOU TWO WANT ANY?
...
HANTEN COAT
CHARCOAL BRAZIER
OW! HOT!
GRILLED SQUID
KARIN
UM... WOW, HE DOESN'T LOOK MUCH LIKE A HIGH SCHOOLER ...
JUST GIVE HIM A CUP OF SAKE, AND HE'D BE THE SPITTING IMAGE OF A SMALL-TOWN OLD MAN.

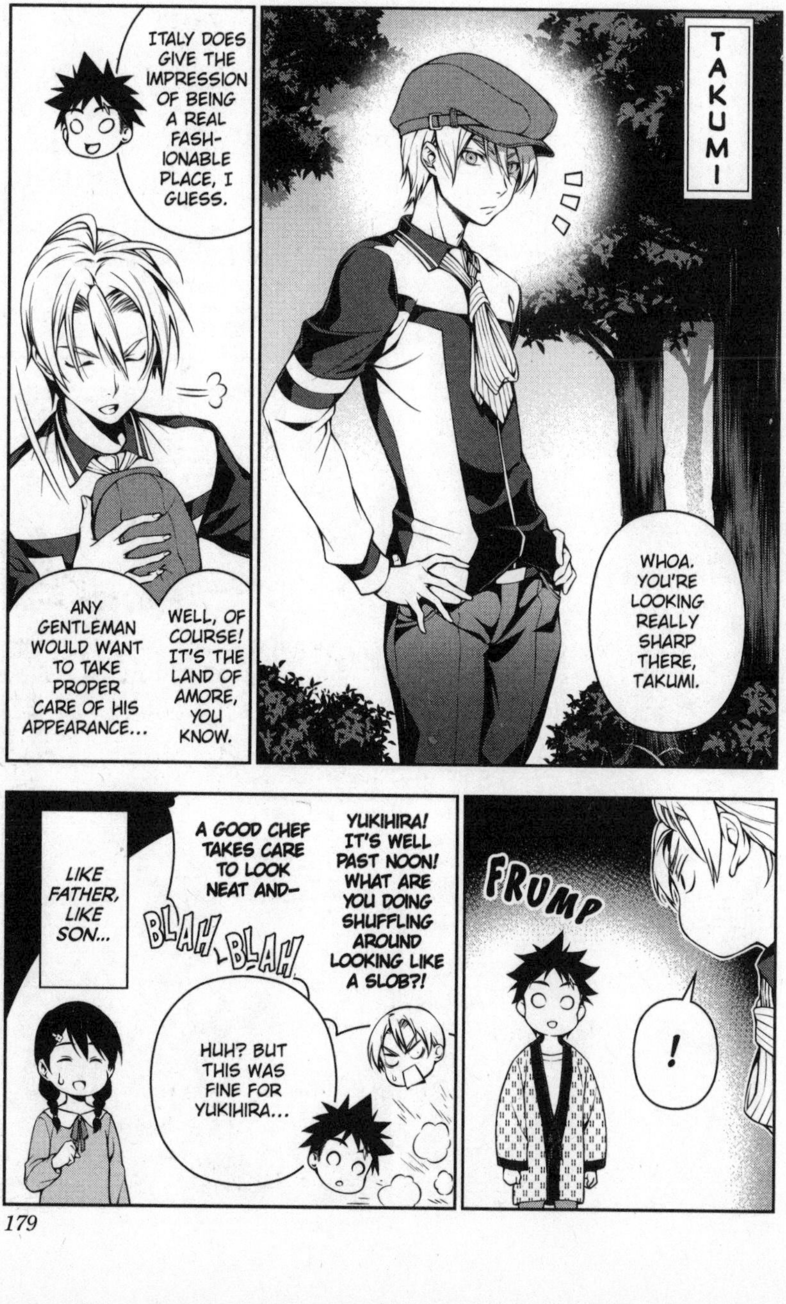
TAKUMI
WHOA. YOU'RE LOOKING REALLY SHARP THERE, TAKUMI.
ITALY DOES GIVE THE IMPRESSION OF BEING A REAL FASHIONABLE PLACE, I GUESS.
WELL, OF COURSE! IT'S THE LAND OF AMORE, YOU KNOW.
ANY GENTLEMAN WOULD WANT TO TAKE PROPER CARE OF HIS APPEARANCE...
FRUMP
!
YUKIHIRA! IT'S WELL PAST NOON! WHAT ARE YOU DOING SHUFFLING AROUND LOOKING LIKE A SLOB?!
A GOOD CHEF TAKES CARE TO LOOK NEAT AND—
BLAH BLAH
HUH? BUT THIS WAS FINE FOR YUKIHIRA...
LIKE FATHER, LIKE SON...

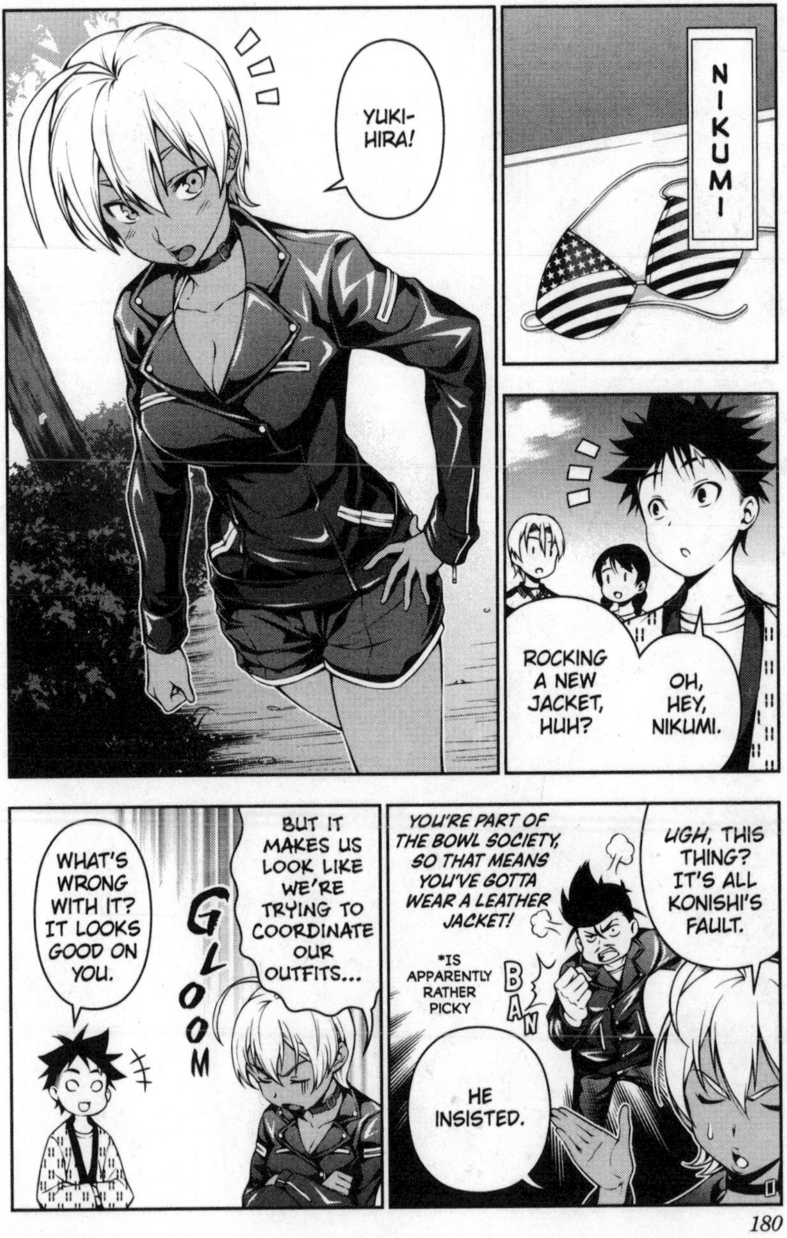
NIKUMI
OH, HEY, NIKUMI.
ROCKING A NEW JACKET, HUH?
YUKI-HIRA!
UGH, THIS THING? IT'S ALL KONISHI'S FAULT.
YOU'RE PART OF THE BOWL SOCIETY, SO THAT MEANS YOU'VE GOTTA WEAR A LEATHER JACKET!
BAN
*IS APPARENTLY RATHER PICKY
HE INSISTED.
BUT IT MAKES US LOOK LIKE WE'RE TRYING TO COORDINATE OUR OUTFITS...
GLOOM
WHAT'S WRONG WITH IT? IT LOOKS GOOD ON YOU.

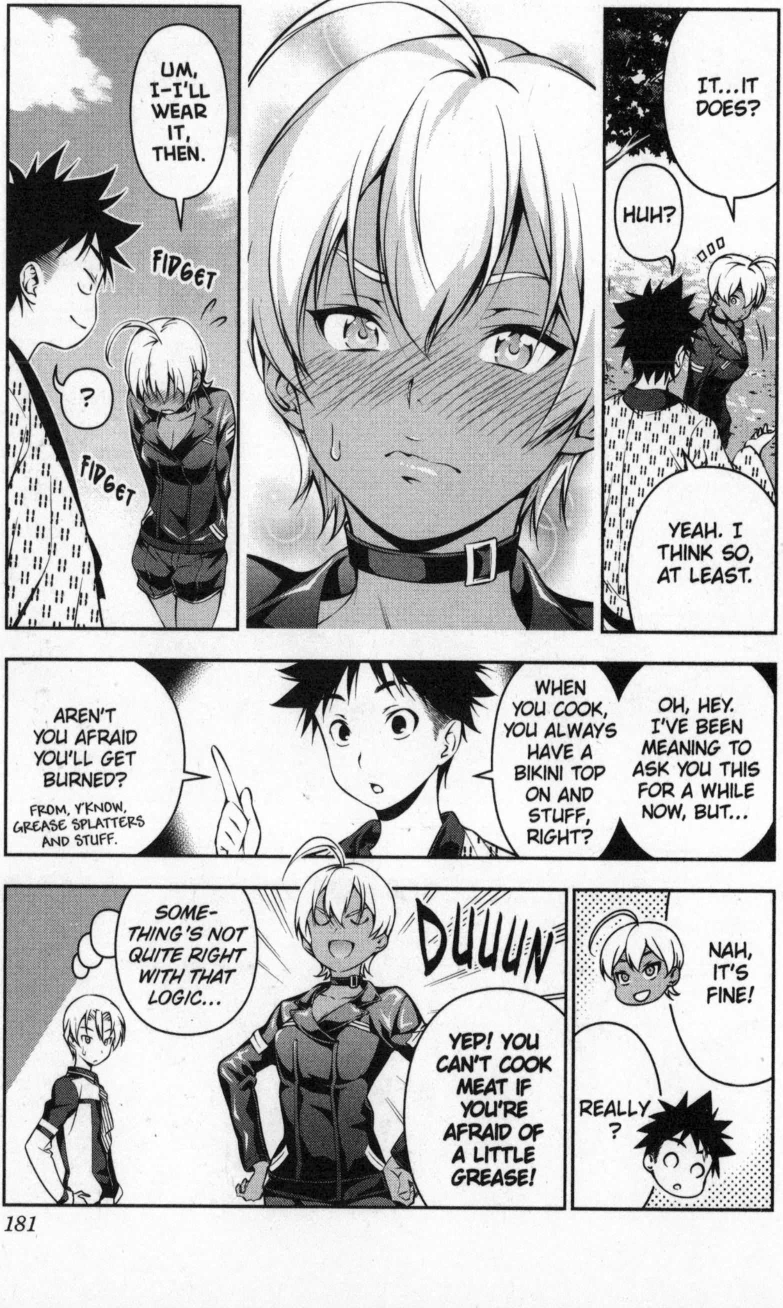
IT...IT DOES?
HUH?
YEAH. I THINK SO, AT LEAST.
UM, I-I'LL WEAR IT, THEN.
FIDGET
?
FIDGET
OH, HEY. I'VE BEEN MEANING TO ASK YOU THIS FOR A WHILE NOW, BUT...
WHEN YOU COOK, YOU ALWAYS HAVE A BIKINI TOP ON AND STUFF, RIGHT?
AREN'T YOU AFRAID YOU'LL GET BURNED?
FROM, Y'KNOW, GREASE SPLATTERS AND STUFF.
NAH, IT'S FINE!
REALLY ?
DUUUN
YEP! YOU CAN'T COOK MEAT IF YOU'RE AFRAID OF A LITTLE GREASE!
SOME-THING'S NOT QUITE RIGHT WITH THAT LOGIC...

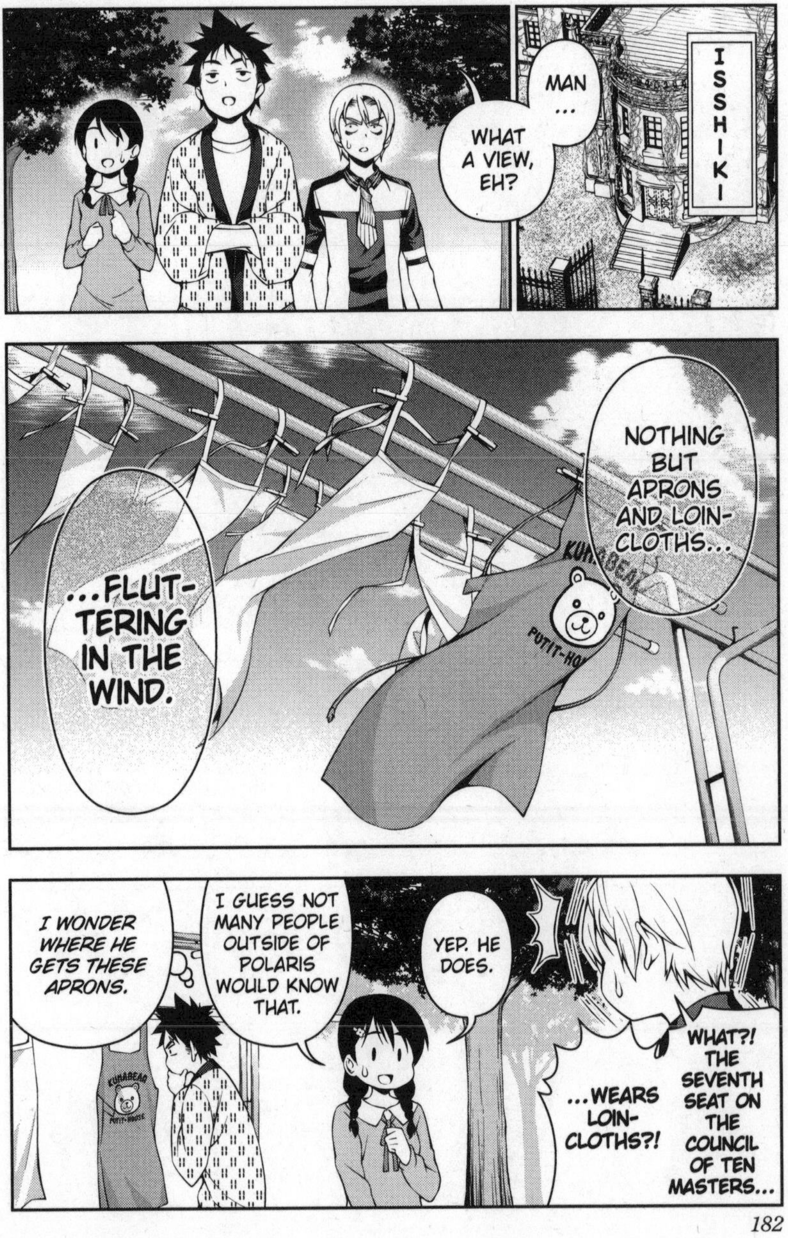
ISSHIKI
MAN ... WHAT A VIEW, EH?
NOTHING BUT APRONS AND LOIN-CLOTHS...
...FLUTTERING IN THE WIND.
WHAT?! THE SEVENTH SEAT ON THE COUNCIL OF TEN MASTERS...
...WEARS LOIN-CLOTHS?!
YEP. HE DOES.
I GUESS NOT MANY PEOPLE OUTSIDE OF POLARIS WOULD KNOW THAT.
I WONDER WHERE HE GETS THESE APRONS.
KUMABEAR
PUTIT-HOUSE

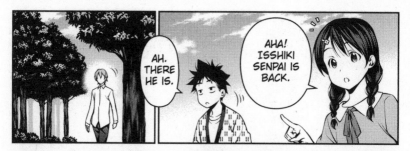

AHA! ISSHIKI SENPAI IS BACK.
AH. THERE HE IS.
TP
TP
TP
TP
TP
WHA?!
USED TO IT BY NOW
NO, HOLD ON!
NO WAY YOU CAN JUST CALL THAT A QUICK CHANGE OR EVEN AN ILLUSION!
HAPPY TO SERVE!
OH, THAT'S HIS LOINCLOTH-QUICK-CHANGE ILLUSION.
IT'S ONE OF THE SEVEN WONDERS OF POLARIS.
HEE HEE HEE HEE!

FOOD WARS! SECOND STOMACH #1 END

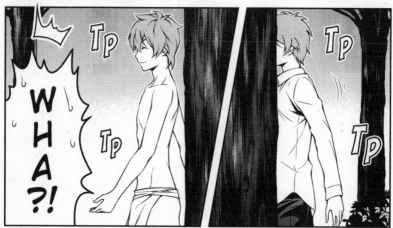

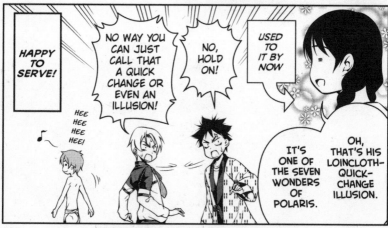

TAKE A STEP
INTO TOTSUKI
INSTITUTE'S
PAST. BACK THEN
IT LOOKED MUCH
LIKE IT DOES
TODAY...

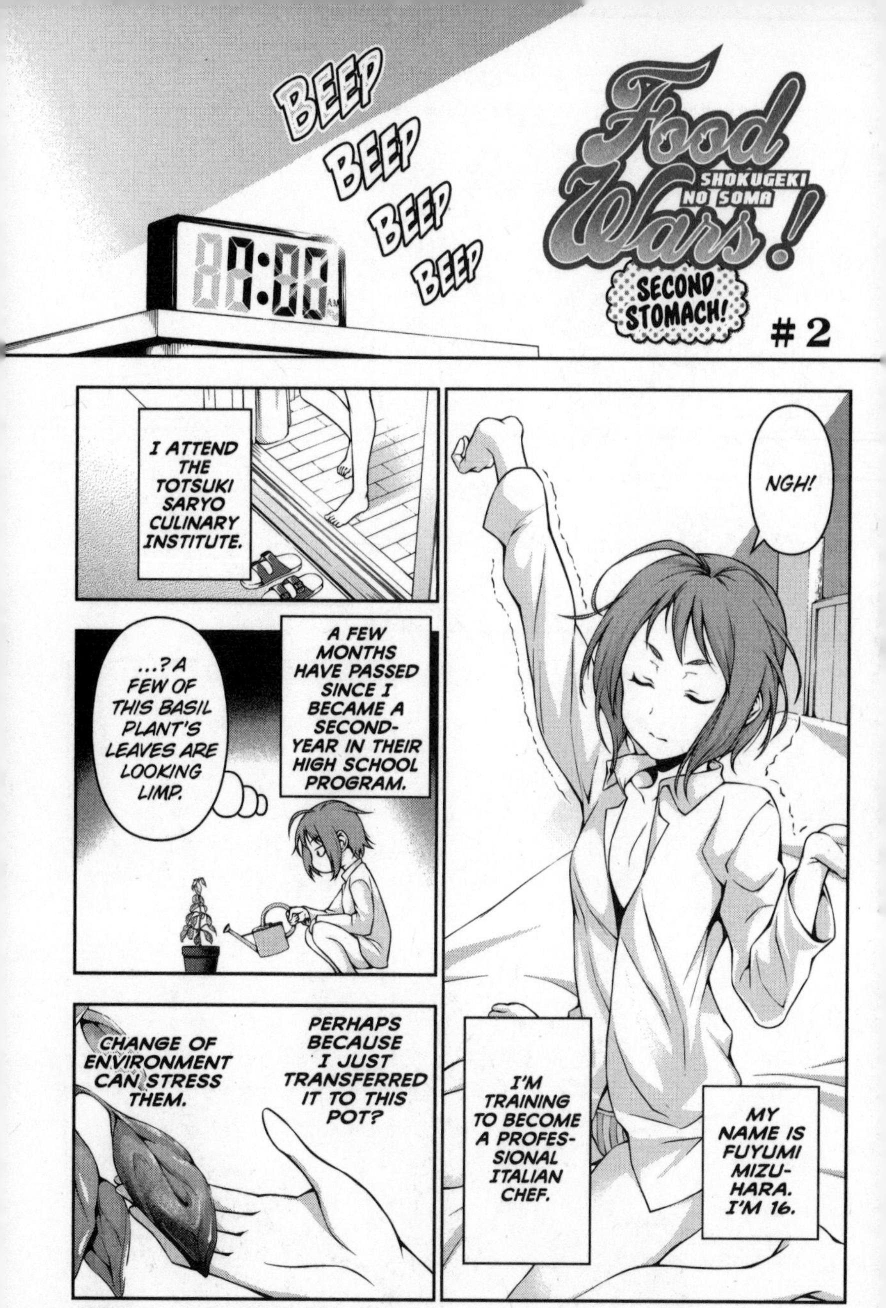
BEEP
BEEP
BEEP
BEEP
Food Wars!
SHOKUGEKI NO SOMA
SECOND STOMACH!
#2
NGH!
MY NAME IS FUYUMI MIZUHARA. I'M 16.
I'M TRAINING TO BECOME A PROFESSIONAL ITALIAN CHEF.
I ATTEND THE TOTSUKI SARYO CULINARY INSTITUTE.
A FEW MONTHS HAVE PASSED SINCE I BECAME A SECOND-YEAR IN THEIR HIGH SCHOOL PROGRAM.
...? A FEW OF THIS BASIL PLANT'S LEAVES ARE LOOKING LIMP.
PERHAPS BECAUSE I JUST TRANSFERRED IT TO THIS POT?
CHANGE OF ENVIRONMENT CAN STRESS THEM.

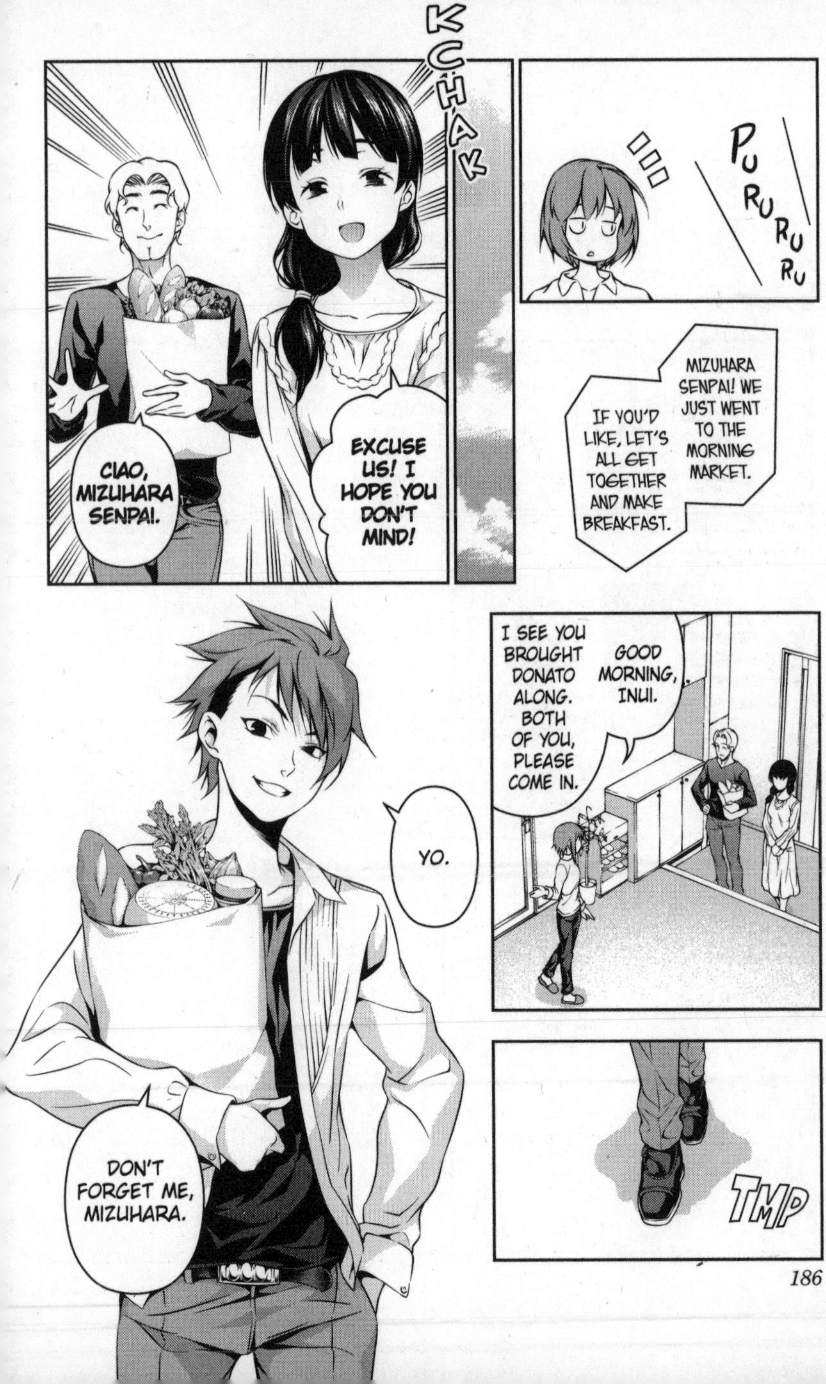
PURURURU
...
KCHAK
EXCUSE US! I HOPE YOU DON'T MIND!
CIAO, MIZUHARA SENPAI.
MIZUHARA SENPAI! WE JUST WENT TO THE MORNING MARKET.
IF YOU'D LIKE, LET'S ALL GET TOGETHER AND MAKE BREAKFAST.
GOOD MORNING, INUI.
I SEE YOU BROUGHT DONATO ALONG. BOTH OF YOU, PLEASE COME IN.
TMP
YO.
DON'T FORGET ME, MIZUHARA.

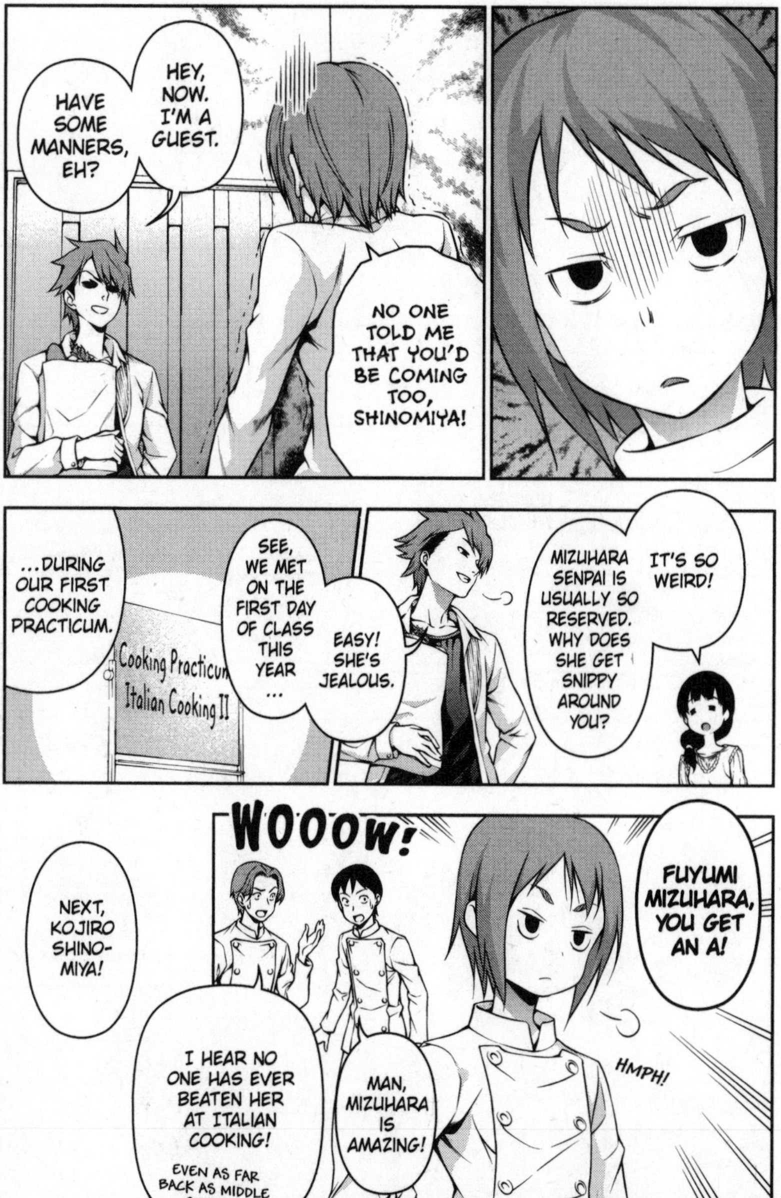
NO ONE TOLD ME THAT YOU'D BE COMING TOO, SHINOMIYA!
HEY, NOW. I'M A GUEST.
HAVE SOME MANNERS, EH?
IT'S SO WEIRD!
MIZUHARA SENPAI IS USUALLY SO RESERVED. WHY DOES SHE GET SNIPPY AROUND YOU?
EASY! SHE'S JEALOUS.
SEE, WE MET ON THE FIRST DAY OF CLASS THIS YEAR ...
...DURING OUR FIRST COOKING PRACTICUM.
Cooking Practicum
Italian Cooking II
FUYUMI MIZUHARA, YOU GET AN A!
WOOOW!
HMPH!
MAN, MIZUHARA IS AMAZING!
I HEAR NO ONE HAS EVER BEATEN HER AT ITALIAN COOKING!
EVEN AS FAR BACK AS MIDDLE SCHOOL!
NEXT, KOJIRO SHINOMIYA!

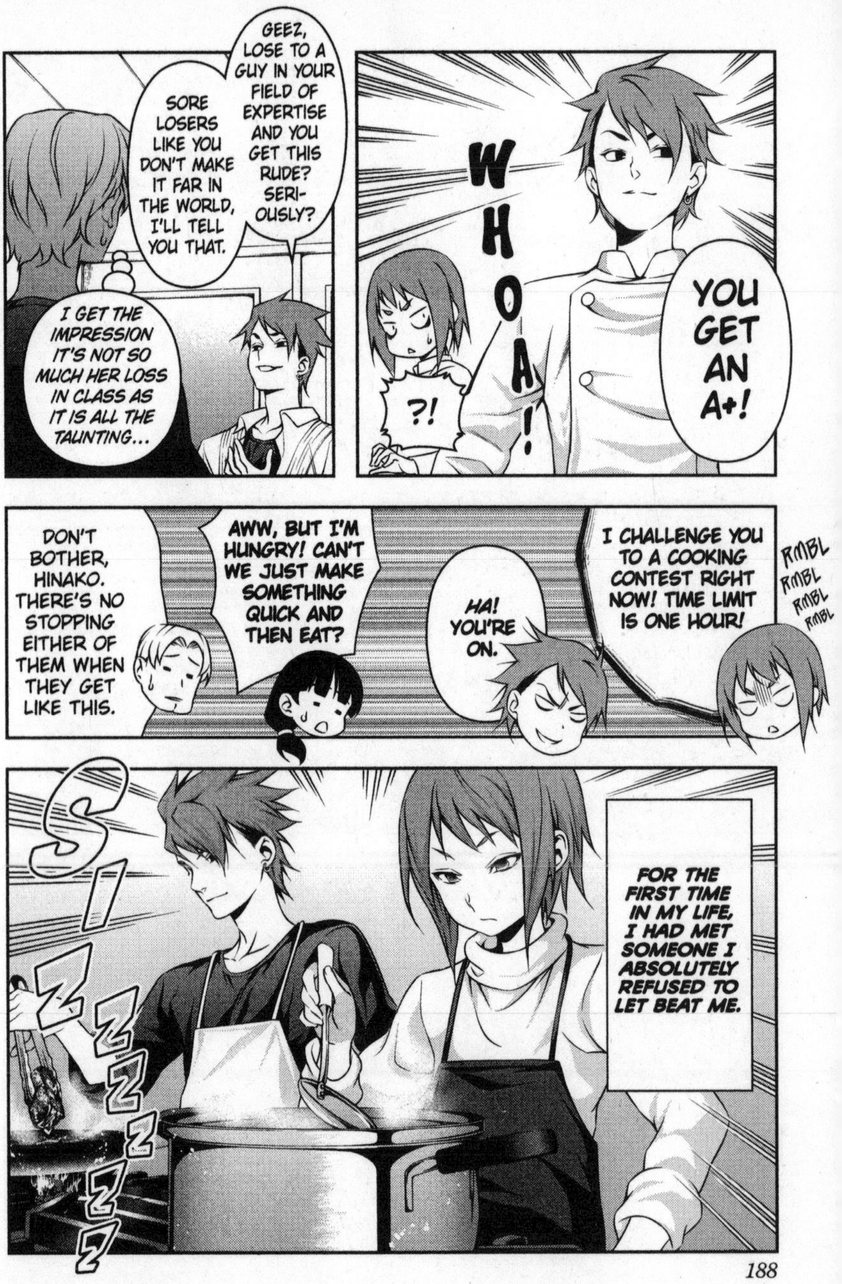
WHOA!
YOU GET AN A+!
?!
GEEZ, LOSE TO A GUY IN YOUR FIELD OF EXPERTISE AND YOU GET THIS RUDE? SERIOUSLY?
SORE LOSERS LIKE YOU DON'T MAKE IT FAR IN THE WORLD, I'LL TELL YOU THAT.
I GET THE IMPRESSION IT'S NOT SO MUCH HER LOSS IN CLASS AS IT IS ALL THE TAUNTING...
RMBL RMBL RMBL RMBL
I CHALLENGE YOU TO A COOKING CONTEST RIGHT NOW! TIME LIMIT IS ONE HOUR!
HA! YOU'RE ON.
AWW, BUT I'M HUNGRY! CAN'T WE JUST MAKE SOMETHING QUICK AND THEN EAT?
DON'T BOTHER, HINAKO. THERE'S NO STOPPING EITHER OF THEM WHEN THEY GET LIKE THIS.
FOR THE FIRST TIME IN MY LIFE, I HAD MET SOMEONE I ABSOLUTELY REFUSED TO LET BEAT ME.
SIZZZZZZ

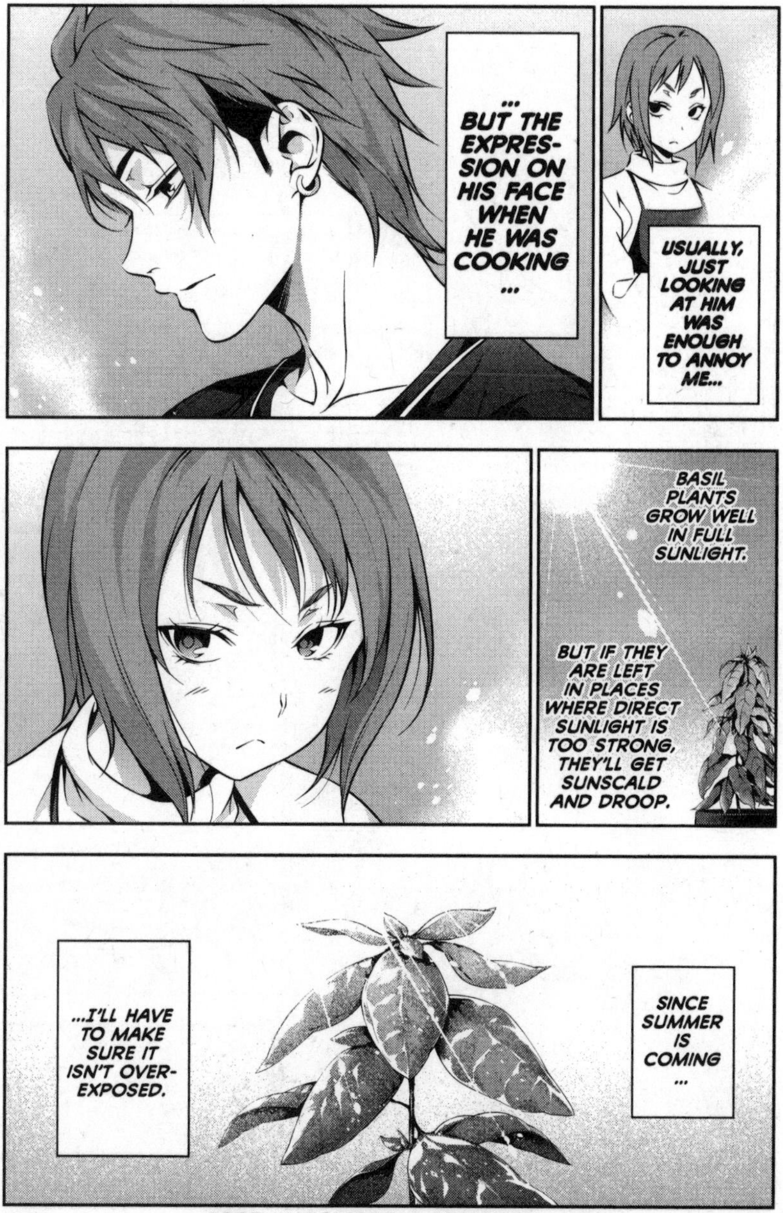
USUALLY, JUST LOOKING AT HIM WAS ENOUGH TO ANNOY ME...
... BUT THE EXPRES-SION ON HIS FACE WHEN HE WAS COOKING ...
BASIL PLANTS GROW WELL IN FULL SUNLIGHT.
BUT IF THEY ARE LEFT IN PLACES WHERE DIRECT SUNLIGHT IS TOO STRONG, THEY'LL GET SUNSCALD AND DROOP.
SINCE SUMMER IS COMING ...
...I'LL HAVE TO MAKE SURE IT ISN'T OVER-EXPOSED.

FOOD WARS! SECOND STOMACH! #2 END

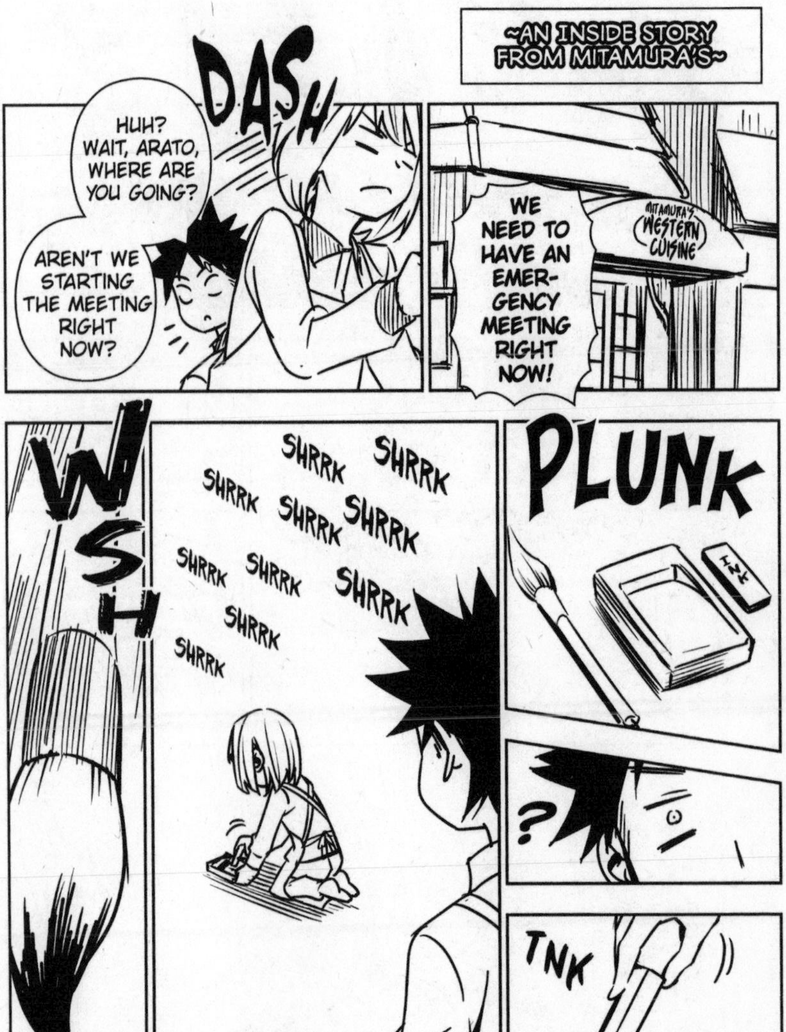
~AN INSIDE STORY FROM MITAMURA'S~
WE NEED TO HAVE AN EMERGENCY MEETING RIGHT NOW!
MITAMURA'S WESTERN CUISINE
DASH
HUH? WAIT, ARATO, WHERE ARE YOU GOING?
AREN'T WE STARTING THE MEETING RIGHT NOW?
PLUNK
INK
?
TNK
SHRRK SHRRK SHRRK SHRRK SHRRK SHRRK SHRRK SHRRK SHRRK SHRRK
WSH

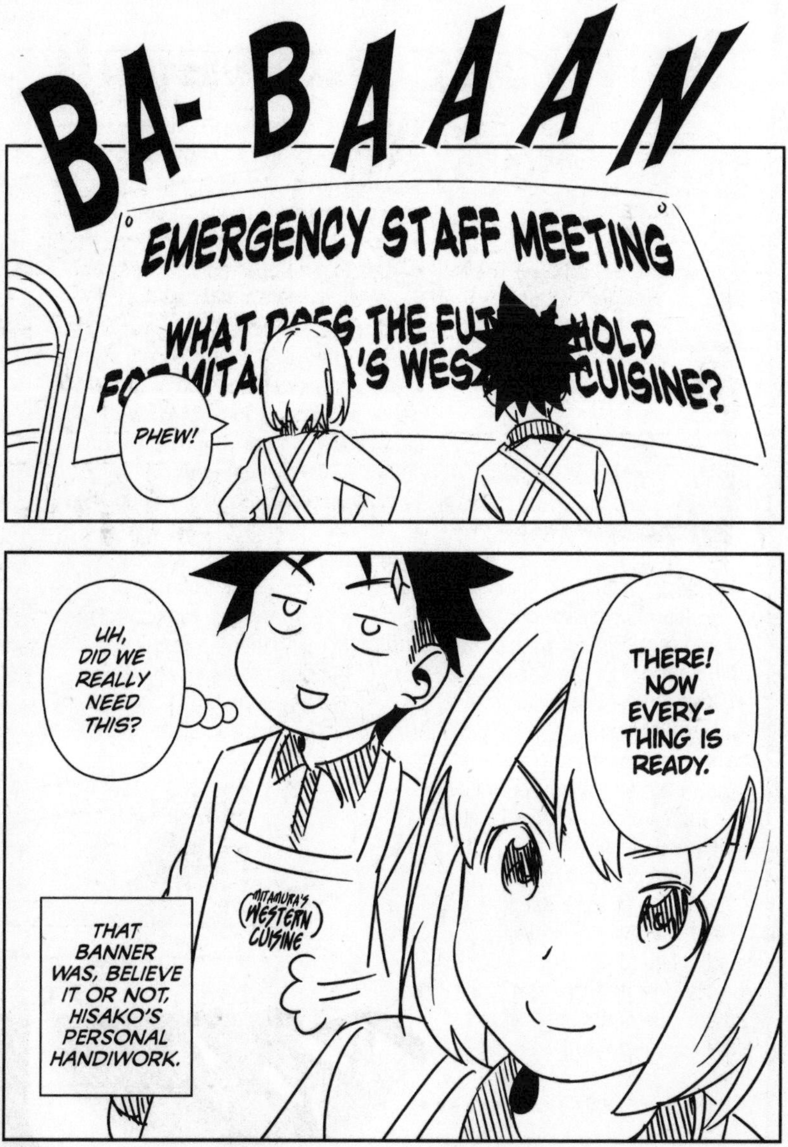
BA-BAAAN
EMERGENCY STAFF MEETING
WHAT D ES THE FU HOLD
FO MITA 'S WES CUISINE?
PHEW!
THERE! NOW EVERY-THING IS READY.
UH, DID WE REALLY NEED THIS?
MITAMURA'S WESTERN CUISINE
THAT BANNER WAS, BELIEVE IT OR NOT, HISAKO'S PERSONAL HANDIWORK.

END

You're Reading in the Wrong Direction!!

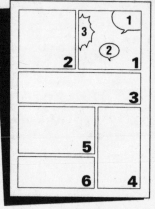

Whoops! Guess what? You're starting at the wrong end of the comic!

...It's true! In keeping with the original Japanese format, **Food Wars!** is meant to be read from right to left, starting in the upper-right corner.

Unlike English, which is read from left to right, Japanese is read from right to left, meaning that action, sound effects and word-balloon order are completely reversed... something which can make readers unfamiliar with Japanese feel pretty backwards themselves. For this reason, manga or Japanese comics published in the U.S. in English have sometimes been published "flopped"—that is, printed in exact reverse order, as though seen from the other side of a mirror.

By flopping pages, U.S. publishers can avoid confusing readers, but the compromise is not without its downside. For one thing, a character in a flopped manga series who once wore in the original Japanese version a T-shirt emblazoned with "M A Y" (as in "the merry month of") now wears one which reads "Y A M"! Additionally, many manga creators in Japan are themselves unhappy with the process, as some feel the mirror-imaging of their art skews their original intentions.

We are proud to bring you Yuto Tsukuda and Shun Saeki's **Food Wars!** in the original unflopped format.

For now, though, turn to the other side of the book and let the adventure begin...!

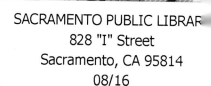

—Editor